AN APPROACH TO THE SACRED IN THE THOUGHT OF SCHOPENHAUER

Robert A. Gonzales

Mellen Research University Press
San Francisco

Library of Congress Cataloging-in-Publication Data

Gonzales, Robert A., 1952-
    An approach to the sacred in the thought of Schopenhauer / Robert A. Gonzales.
    p. cm.
    Includes bibliographical references.
    ISBN 0-7734-9818-4
    1. Schopenhauer, Arthur, 1788-1860--Religion. 2. Holy, The--History of doctrines--19th century. I. Title.
    B3149.R42G66   1992
    231--dc20   92-4106
                                                                                                          CIP

Copyright   ©1992 Robert A. Gonzales.

Editorial Inquiries:

Mellen Research University Press
534 Pacific Avenue
San Francisco
CA 94133

Order Fulfillment:

The Edwin Mellen Press
P.O. Box 450
Lewiston, NY 14092
USA

Printed in the United States of America

POR MI PADRE Y MI MADRE

TABLE OF CONTENTS

FOREWARD i

PREFACE iii

ABBREVIATIONS vii

ACKNOWLEDGEMENTS viii

INTRODUCTION ix

Chapter 1 1

The World as Representation 1
   A. Consciousness 1
      1. Its nature 1
      2. The knowing subject 2
      3. The object as representation 3
      4. The representation and Transcendental
         Idealism 5
   B. The Principle of Sufficient Reason 7
      1. Its meaning 7
      2. Its fourfold aspect 9
      3. The extent and validity of the
         principle 11
   C. Intellectual Nature of Perception 12
      1. Sensation as a given 12
      2. The role of the understanding
         (Verstand) 13
      3. Centrality of the body in perception . 16
      4. The understanding as characteristic of
         animal life 19
      5. Critique of Schopenhauer's theory of
         perception 22
   D. The Role of Reason (Vernunft) 24
      1. Preliminary remarks 24
      2. Reason and the uniqueness of man . . . 25
      3. The nature of the concept 28
   E. Time and Space 30
   F. The Subject of Willing 33
   G. Law of Causality and the phenomenon 36
      1. Causality as change 36
      2. Necessity and the law of causality . . 38

```
            3. Causality and the "Prime Mover"  . . .  40
            4. Forms of Causality . . . . . . . . . .  42
        H. Transcendental Conditions for Causality .  46
        I. Summary . . . . . . . . . . . . . . . . .  49

Chapter  2  . . . . . . . . . . . . . . . . . . . . . 51

The World as Will . . . . . . . . . . . . . . . . . . 51
        A. Schopenhauer's Understanding of Will . . . 51
            1. Rationale for knowledge from within .  51
            2. The knower as individual . . . . . . . 54
            3. The act of will and action of the
                 body . . . . . . . . . . . . . . . . 57
        B. The Will and the Noumenon . . . . . . . .  61
            1. Why the word will . . . . . . . . . .  61
            2. Characteristics of the noumenal will . 64
            3. Noumenal will's knowability . . . . .  66
        C. Will as Kernel of phenomenon . . . . . . . 70
        D. Will as Independent of Knowledge . . . . . 76
            1. Knowledge as accidental to willing . . 76
            2. Appearance of knowledge for the sake
                 of the will . . . . . . . . . . . .  79
            3. The relationship of intellect and will
                 in man . . . . . . . . . . . . . . . 80
        E. Will as Principle of Being . . . . . . . . 82
        F. The Objectification of the Will . . . . .  85
        G. The Will and Ontological Suffering . . . . 90
        H. Summary . . . . . . . . . . . . . . . . .  94

Chapter  3  . . . . . . . . . . . . . . . . . . . . . 96

The Platonic Ideas . . . . . . . . . . . . . . . . .  96
        A. The Will as Adequately Objectified . . . . 96
            1. Bridging the noumenon and the
                 phenomenon . . . . . . . . . . . . . 96
            2. The Platonic Idea as adequate
                 objectification . . . . . . . . . .  97
            3. The status of the Idea . . . . . . . .101
        B. Specific Character of the Idea . . . . . .105
            1. Ideas as opposed to concepts . . . . .105
            2. The idea as a unity ante rem . . . . .109
            3. Ideas as acts of will . . . . . . . . 111
        C. Ideas and Grades of the Will's
              Objectification . . . . . . . . . . . .111
            1. Preliminary remarks . . . . . . . . . 111
            2. Ideas in inorganic phenomena . . . . .112
            3. The status of matter . . . . . . . . .117
            4. Ideas and organic matter . . . . . . .118
            5. Ideas and the animal kingdom . . . . .120
            6. Man as a unique Idea . . . . . . . . .121
        D. Ideas and the relatedness of phenomena . .124
```

Table of Contents

  E. The Ideas as Dispersed 127
  F. The Ideas and Antecedent Rationality . . . 130
  G. Knowing the Ideas 134
    1. Knower as individual 134
    2. Scientific knowing 136
    3. The path to insight 137
  H. Knowledge of the Ideas as Genius 143
    1. Context of Schopenhauer's theory of
      genius 143
    2. Schopenhauer's theory of genius . . . 147
    3. Music and the Ideas 149
  I. The Ideas and the True Nature of Reality . 151
  J. Summary 154

Chapter 4 159

The Human Situation 159
  A. Insecurity of Man 159
  B. The Source of the Human Sickness 164
    1. Nature of willing 164
    2. Boredom 166
  C. The Affirmation of the Will-to-Live 168
    1. Clarification of the notion 168
    2. Affirmation of the body 169
    3. Sexual impulse as affirmation of the
      will 170
  D. Death and the Affirmation of the Will . . . 175
    1. Fear of death as an affirmation of
      will-to-live 175
    2. The illusion of the fear of death . . 177
    3. The significance of death 180
  E. The Egocentric Predicament of Man 182
    1. Reason for egoism 182
    2. Degrees of egoism 189
    3. Egoism and the role of the State . . . 196
    4. Epistemological basis for egoism . . . 199
  F. Summary 202

Chapter 5 204

Human Transcendence 204
  A. Contradiction of the phenomenon with
    Itself 204
    1. The co-existence of freedom and
      necessity 204
    2. Schopenhauer's concept of character . 214
    3. Character as intelligible and
      empirical 217
    4. Freedom and the feeling of
      responsibility 224
  B. Compassion as an Empirical Fact 229

Table of Contents

    C. Degrees of Denial of the Will-to-Live . . . 234
        1. Justice 234
        2. Philanthropy 239
        3. Asceticism 245
    D. Summary 258

Chapter 6 261

Religion and God 261
    A. The Role of Religion 261
        1. Introductory remarks 261
        2. Suffering as "the second way" 266
        3. Philosophy and Religion as "Systems of
           Metaphysics" 271
        4. Religion: its positive and negative
           aspects 279
    B. The Reality of God 294
        1. The untenability of the proofs for
           God's existence 294
        2. Revelation and God 300
        3. Mystery of evil and God's existence . 303
    C. The "Back Door" to the Question of God . . 307

CONCLUSION 322

BIBLIOGRAPHY 338

INDEX 354

ABBREVIATIONS

Original Works as listed in the Bibliography:

Die Welt als Wille und Vorstellung: (Vorstellung I/I)
Über die Freiheit des menschlichen Willen: (Freiheit)
Über die vierfache Wurzel des Satzes vom zureichenden Grund:
(Grund)
Über den Willen in der Natur: (Natur)
Über die Grundlage der Moral: (Grundlage)
Parerga und Paralipomena I/I: (Parerga I/I)
Über das Sehn und die Farben: eine Abhandlung: (Sehn)
Der handschriftliche Nachlaß: (Nachlaß)
Philosophische Vorlesungen: (Vorlesungen)

II. Translations as listed in the Bibliography:
On the Basis of Morality: (Basis)
On the Fourfold Root of the Principle of Sufficient Reason:
(Reason)
On the Freedom of the Will: (Freedom)
On the Will in Nature: (Nature)
Manuscript Remains: (Remains)
Parerga and Paralipomena: (Parerga)
The World as Will and Representation: (Representation)

FOREWARD

The name Schopenhauer at first evokes expectations quite different from a possible openness to the Sacred. This study, however, shows on the basis of a complete and thorough reading of Schopenhauer's works, that there is in the corpus of the great pessimist's work the possibility for a secondary way to arrive at the Holy, notwithstanding the atheism declared on Kantian and existential grounds. The author detects the importance of the Platonic Ideas, as adequate objectification of reality as will, for this secondary approach to the problem of the Sacred in the philosophy of Schopenhauer.

The outline, order and presentation of this book are excellent. For the historian some questions may still remain, however, specifically with regard to the influence of Kant's *Critique of Judgement* in Schopenhauer's thought, and the reaction of Nietzsche to his predecessor. This dissertation, with its good foundation, invites readers to further thought, and its great merit is in this invitation: Take and read.

Professor Nico Sprokel, S.J.
Pontificia Università Gregoriana
Rome, Italy
November 16, 1991

This excellent study treats a well-chosen and delimited problem in the pessimistic philosophy of Schopenhauer in a new way: God hinted at "through the back door" of aesthetic genius and mystical asceticism, which are seen in their systematic connection with Schopenhauer's philosophy.

This treatment of Schopenhauer possesses particular strength today when intellectual pessimism pervades, and when the rational optimistic argument for God's providence is looked upon with strong suspicion.

In this competent exposition of Schopenhauer's philosophy the Platonic Ideas are treated systematically as in Schopenhauer's work itself. This and the new approach to the problem of God constitutes a new and original contribution to the understanding of Schopenhauer.

Professor Carlo Huber, S.J.
Pontificia Università Gregoriana
Rome, Italy
November 21, 1991

PREFACE

Arthur Schopenhauer was born in Danzig on February 22, 1788 to Heinrich Floris Schopenhauer and his wife, Johanna Trosiener. As a child and youth, he travelled extensively with his parents who were well to do. In fact, he spent a two year period (1797-1799) in Le Havre, France with the family of a business partner of his father. The two years in Le Havre were remembered later in life by Schopenhauer as the happiest years of his childhood. They were significant in his intellectual formation inasmuch as they helped to give him a cosmopolitan outlook, and provided a springboard to his capacity for languages which he was later to manifest.

As far as early educational influences are concerned, the young Arthur was placed in the private school of Johann Christian Runge in 1799 upon returning to Hamburg, where his family had now settled. He remained there for four years, receiving an education designed specifically for future business merchants. The curriculum, however, did include pietistic religious instruction. Schopenhauer later rejected belief in a personal God, though interest in the writings of the pietists remained with him throughout his life.

On May 3, 1803 the young Arthur Schopenhauer began a tour of several European countries (Holland, England, France, Switzerland, and Austria) with his parents which lasted until August 25, 1804. His impressions of the "grand tour" are preserved in his travel diary *Reisetagebücher*. Significantly important as an influence in the later development of his religious philosophy was the negative experience he had at an English Boarding School during the summer months of 1803. Correspondence with his mother indicates that he found the "shameless bigotry" of the English to be unbearable; he resented the Sunday religious practices of the English which he Found oppressive and hypocritical. This notwithstanding, at the end of the great European trip (the late summer of 1804), he was confirmed in Danzig, the city of his birth at the Church of St. Mary, before beginning his apprenticeship in Hamburg in September of 1804 to become a merchant in accordance with his father's wishes.

After the mysterious death of his father on April 20, 1805, he began his studies at Göttingen in 1809 concentrating on the natural sciences, Plato and Kant. In the Fall of 1811 he went to the University of Berlin to hear Fichte and Schleiermacher, both of whom disappointed him. It was only after he turned to the serious study of philosophy during the years 1811-1812 that he no longer found the demands of belief in a personal God to be philosophically tenable.

In 1813 he was awarded a Doctorate from the University of Jena for his dissertation: *Über die vierfache Wurzel des Satzes vom zureichenden Grunde* (*On the Fourfold Root of the Principle of Sufficient Reason*), an essay which outlines his epistemological claims. That same year he had conversations with Goethe regarding the latter's theory of colors. In the late spring of 1814, the estranged and tense relationship that he had with his mother came to a head, with the result that he left Weimar never to see his mother again.

The years between 1814-1818 are significant inasmuch as his second philosophical work, *Über das Sehn and die Farben* (*On Vision and Color*) appeared during this time frame (1815). Moreover, his early notebooks from this same period, indicate that the main ideas and plan for his classic work, *Die Welt als Wille und Vorstellung* (*The World as Will and Representation*), were outlined and developed at this time.

With the acceptance of his manuscript by a publishing firm (Brockhaus) in March of 1818, Schopenhauer took a long trip to Italy, confident that the aforementioned work, so dear to his heart, would see the light of day with accolades. Such was not the case, however. Published in January of 1819, *Die Welt als Wille und Vorstellung* was largely ignored by the intellectual public. After successfully applying for a lectureship at the University of Berlin in the Fall of 1819, he began to deliver his *Vorlesungen* (*Lectures*) in March of 1820, but with little success. He had few students for Hegel's thought was in vogue at that time in Germany.

Discouraged and increasingly embittered, he made his second trip to Italy in May of 1822 and arrived in München a year later. Evidence indicates that this was a difficult time for him. He underwent a period of severe depression -- evoked in part by the continued cool reception of his philosophy on the part of the public, and by serious illness. He stayed for brief periods in Bad Gastein, Mannheim, and Dresden in 1824 prior to returning to Berlin in 1825 to again try his luck as a philosophy professor. His lectures once again met with no success. So he abandoned university academia, while continuing intellectual pursuits.

In 1831, he fled Berlin because of a cholera epidemic -- the same plague that killed Hegel. He then went to Frankfurt for a short period before moving to Mannheim in July 1832. He remained there until June

1833, before finally settling in Frankfurt, where he spent the rest of his life. Notwithstanding intense and continued intellectual pursuits, he did not publish anything until 1835, when *Über den Willen in der Natur (On the Will in Nature)* made its appearance. After his mother's death in 1838, Schopenhauer published two prize essays: *Über die Freiheit des menschlichen Willen (On the Freedom of the Human Will)* in 1839; *Über die Grundlage der Moral (On the Basis of Morality)* in 1840. The first was awarded first prize by the Royal Norwegian Society of the Sciences, but the second was rejected by the Royal Danish Society of Scientific Studies -- even though his was the only essay submitted. The aforementioned two works contain important aspects of Schopenhauer's moral philosophy.

In 1844 a second enlarged edition (two volumes) of *Die Welt als Wille und Vorstellung* was accepted for publication. But it too failed to catch the attention of the intellectual public. This notwithstanding, Schopenhauer continued in his fierce dedication and pursuit of truth.

He persistently pursued the solitary life of a scholar, and continued to jot down his thoughts, as his *Handschriftliche Nachlaß (Manuscript Remains)* indicate. The publication of *Parerga und Paralipomena (Parerga and Paralipomena)* in 1851 by Hayn of Berlin signaled a turning point in his fortunes which, up to this point, were met with continued disappointment. It was this work that first gained public notice with the publication of a review by John Oxenford in the *Westminster and Foreign Quarterly Review* in 1852, and a subsequent article in the same journal in 1853, entitled "Iconoclasm in German Philosophy". The article was translated into German and was published in *Vossische Zeitung* shortly thereafter,

Preface   *vii*

with the result that Schopenhauer at long last attracted the attention of the intellectual public. It was as if he had achieved fame almost overnight. In 1859 yet another enlarged two volume edition of *Die Welt als Wille und Vorstellung* appeared. By the time Schopenhauer died on September 21, 1860, he was already basking in the sunlight of belated fame. The philosophical public, which had hitherto greeted his works with silence, at long last recognized his genius.

ACKNOWLEDGEMENTS

I would like to thank Professor Carlo Huber, S.J. for his valuable advice and guidance in directing this study. Further appreciation is to be proffered to Professor Nico Sprokel, S.J. for his expertise regarding useful emendations in the manuscript. I also extend my gratitude to Professor Sister Thomas More Meehan, Ph.D, and Mr. Christopher Jagodzinski for proofreading this study; to Mr. Peter Veracka, Librarian of the A.T. Wehrle Memorial Library in Columbus, Ohio; and to Mrs. Barbara Couts and Mrs. Marianna Catalfamo for their secretarial assistance in this project. Lastly, the publication of this work would not have been possible without the encouragement of my colleagues and students at the Pontifical College Josephinum and, above all, the interest and financial assistance of Father Kenneth Grimes, Pastor of Our Lady of Peace Parish in Columbus, Ohio.

INTRODUCTION

As the title of this study indicates, I maintain that the question of God -- or to be more precise -- the question of the Sacred or Holy-- remains an open issue in Schopenhauer's philosophy. A careful analysis of his *Weltanschauung* and anthropological claims illustrates that "back door" to this question is left ajar for the student of Schopenhauer's thought. I make this claim given certain unanswerables to which Schopenhauer himself alludes in his treatment of the denial of the will-to-live, as particularly manifested in aesthetical and ethical actions -- not to mention the thorny issue of the exact status of the Platonic Ideas in his *Weltanschauung*.

Raising the question about a so-called "back door" to God, or to the Sacred in Schopenhauer's philosophy, of course, brings into focus whether a "front door" approach to the aforementioned issue has any relevance. One would justifiably presume that the question of a "back door" to the problematic at hand would not even be raised if it could be clearly ascertained that a direct approach to God were a possibility for Schopenhauer. If this were to truly be the case, the entire tenor of his philosophy would change. For a "front door" to God, from a philosophical point of view, means that it is possible to meaningfully speak about God. As this study illustrates, however, Schopenhauer maintains that any philosophical discourse about a personal Creator-God is beyond the exigence of reason in light of his acceptance of the Kantian critique which discredits the ontological, cosmological, and physico-theological proofs for God's existence. Consequently, if any access to the Holy is possible given his metaphysical claims, the issue of a so-called "back door" needs to be proposed. I contend that the unanswerables and paradoxes of Schopenhauer's philosophy constitute this "back door."

The argumentation of this study unfolds in two major parts. The first section presents Schopenhauer's metaphysical picture of reality and consists of three chapters, the purpose of which, is to ground the anthropological claims made in the second major part of this study (Chapters Four, Five, and Six).

Chapter One examines Schopenhauer's epistemological claims regarding the representational character of human cognition and distinguishes among the four types of representation possible to the human subject. The role of the faculties of understanding (*Verstand*) and reason (*Vernunft*) in representational knowing, is examined with a view to the possibility of philosophical discourse about God. The chapter concludes with a discussion of the law of causality and explains why an unmoved First Cause is an impossibility given the presuppositions made.

Chapter Two focuses on the Schopenhauer's understanding of the will as thing-in-itself. Central to this chapter is his claim that the will (as independent of knowledge) is the principle of all being, inasmuch as it grounds each phenomenon without exception. Key to the chapter are Schopenhauer's reasons for maintaining that the will is estranged, and why aseity is attributed to it. Since teleological factors are ascribed to the will, and not to God, the argumentation of the chapter maintains that there is no God in his *Weltanschauung*. The

Introduction

chapter concludes by discussing the intrinsic relationship between the estranged will and the ontological suffering which scars the face of reality. As such, a central claim in this chapter is that Schopenhauer's doctrine of the will is an attempt to explain the mystery of evil in reality.

Chapter Three focuses on the problem of the will's adequate objectification in the Platonic Ideas. The specific character of the Idea, understood as the universal form of the phenomenon, as a unity *ante re*, and as an act of will outside time, are outlined here. The problem of the Ideas and antecedent rationality, as a qualifier to Schopenhauer's pessimistic world picture, is also tentatively discussed at this point in light of the question of God, which has seemingly been excluded by Schopenhauer's metaphysics of will. The chapter continues with Schopenhauer's claim that self-transcendence is possible in the human subject via knowledge of the Ideas in aesthetic experience. A discussion regarding the exact relationship between the Ideas and the so-called "true nature" of reality, rounds out the concluding pages of the chapter, and underscores the thorny issue of relating the rational and the irrational in Schopenhauer's metaphysical system.

The second major part of this study has three sections each of which constitutes a chapter in its own right. Schopenhauer's analysis of the potentiality of the human subject to manifest two distinct and diametrically opposed types of praxis, is discussed in this section of the study. It is precisely here, once again, where the foundation is laid for the issue at hand: whether in fact the question of God remains a possibility in Schopenhauer's thought given his metaphysical and anthropological claims.

Chapter Four focuses on the human condition as scarred by the ontological nature of the diseased and estranged will which, in human beings, gains an awareness of itself. The source of the sickness in the human spirit is attributed to the nature of will-oriented cognition which gives way to a praxis of its own involving unjust and unloving actions. The specific character of affirmation of the will-to-live, and its relationship to the egocentric predicament characteristic to will-imbued consciousness, is also outlined and discussed as the chapter concludes. The question of God emerges insofar as Schopenhauer maintains that there is nothing that can be done to heal estranged willing.

Chapter Five delves into the conditions of, and possibility for, human transcendence of will-oriented cognition. As such, therefore, Schopenhauer here qualifies his pessimistic doctrine of affirmation of the will-to-live. Central to the possibility of self-transcendence is what Schopenhauer refers to as the doctrine of the denial of the will-to-live, as specifically manifested in aesthetic appreciation, justice, philanthropy, and in the ascetic's experience of "relative nothingness". The question of God, or at the very least, of the Sacred or Holy, comes to the foreground once again in that Schopenhauer is at wits end to explain these mysterious phenomena.

Chapter Six addresses the issue of religion and the question of God in a more direct fashion, given Schopenhauer's analysis of the above. As such, it ties together what has preceded in the first five chapters of this study. The chapter discusses the positive and negative aspects of religion, as a system of metaphysics, and addresses the relationship between faith and reason. With regard to the reality of God, Schopenhauer's reasons

Introduction *xiii*

for the untenability of any proofs for God's existence are given a more detailed treatment and, as such, compliment the argumentation outlined in Chapter One. As such, they aptly illustrate why a "front door" approach to God is bolted shut in his philosophical system. The last and most important section of the chapter (section C) serves as the capstone of the structure of this study. It proposes a rationale for maintaining that an approach to the Sacred paradoxically remains an open issue in Schopenhauer's thought.

What my investigation has convinced me about is that the question of the Sacred in the entire corpus of Schopenhauer's published and unpublished work (including his correspondence and recorded conversations), needs to be re-studied and re-examined. As the argumentation of this study makes clear, the dominant line of thinking has been, of course, to consider Schopenhauer's philosophy as a classic form of atheism. The works of: Safranski, Schmidt, Hasse, Hollingdale, McGill, Hübscher, Vecchiotti, et al. interpret Schopenhauer in this manner. Certainly, it cannot be denied that such an interpretation is validated by passages from his principal works, not to mention his manuscript remains, correspondence, and alleged conversations, which would likewise confirm this.

This notwithstanding, other scholars leave the issue open-ended given the essential ambiguity of the thing-in-itself coupled with the relative nature of nothingness in his system (cf. Negroni, Reconda, Penzo). Others maintain that sanctity of lifestyle perhaps provides the only clue to meaningfully speaking about the Sacred given Schopenhauer's metaphysical presuppositions (cf. Schirmacher, Hielscher). Still others suggest that Schopenhauer's early manuscripts illustrate religion, like philosophy, constitutes a manifestation of the so-called better consciousness -- a fact which shows that in the mind of the young Schopenhauer the issue of the Sacred was by no means black and white (cf. Hübscher, Mirri, Safranski, and Bridgewater). While seeing merit in the former position, I am more inclined to accept the latter stance with regard to the Sacred in Schopenhauer's thought. Accordingly, the six chapters of this study contain my argument as to why the question of the Sacred remains open for the student of Schopenhauer's thought.

With regard to the primary sources used in this study, references to the *major* works of Schopenhauer are taken from the *Zürcher Ausgabe* edition of Schopenhauer's works (Diogenes Verlag, Zürich 1977), which follows the historical-critical edition published by Arthur Hübscher (Brockhaus, Wiesbaden 1972). References to Schopenhauer's *Handscriftliche Nachlaß*, *Philosophische Vorlesungen*, *Gespräche*, *Gesammelte Briefe*, and citations from *Über das Sehn und die Farben*, are taken from other collections of Schopenhauer's works as listed in the Bibliography. In most cases, where the original German is cited, references to available English translations of Schopenhauer's principal works are also made for the reader who wishes to consult them.

Currently, I am working on two projects. The first is a textbook on metaphysics for the undergraduate student. This planned work aims, in the first place, to introduce the student to the problem of **being** as interpreted by the Aristotelian and Thomistic philosophical traditions. Secondly, its purpose is to juxtapose this analysis to classical positions taken by major modern philosophers with regard to the problem of being. The over-riding thesis of this text will be that

Introduction

a metaphysical analysis of reality remains valid for the contemporary mind.

The second project envisions a more thorough study of the problem of the Sacred in Schopenhauer's main works, the *Nachlaß* (*Manuscript Remains*), his *Gesammelte Briefe*, and *Gespräche*. The philosophical influences that shaped Schopenhauer's philosophy of religion will be part of this proposed study as well.

Robert A. Gonzales
Columbus, Ohio
May 31, 1992

PART ONE

SCHOPENHAUER'S WELTANSCHAUUNG

Chapter 1

The World as Representation

A. Consciousness

1. Its nature

Arthur Schopenhauer stands in the tradition initiated by Descartes and begins his philosophy with the human subject as a knowing being. In *Über die Freiheit des menschlichen Willens* a distinction is made between two aspects of human consciousness: consciousness of other things, which Schopenhauer also calls the cognitive faculty (*Das Erkenntnißvermögen*) and self-consciousness (*Selbstbewußtseyn*).[1] The former, as we shall see shortly, concerns the manner by which the world is given to the knowing subject and pertains to the greater portion of the whole consciousness. The latter, on the other hand, involves another type of knowing in which one knows one's own self as the subject of willing.

In *Die Welt als Wille und Vorstellung* Schopenhauer delves more thoroughly into the nature of consciousness. Here it is maintained that consciousness always presupposes an awareness of objects by the

---

[1] Arthur Schopenhauer, *Über die Freiheit des menschlichen Willens*, I., *Zürcher Ausgabe Werke in zehn Bänden*, Band VI, (Zürich: Diogenes Verlag, 1977), S. 49-50. Henceforth cited as *Freiheit*. English translation: Arthur Schopenhauer, *Essay on the Freedom of the Will*, I., trans. Konstantin Kolenda (Indianapolis: Bobbs-Merrill, 1960), pp.9-10. Henceforth cited as *Freedom*.

perceiver or knower. "A consciousness without object is no consciousness at all. A thinking subject has *concepts* for its object; a sensuously perceiving subject [referring to animal consciousness] has objects with the qualities corresponding to its organization."[2] Consciousness, therefore, is comprised of two parts, a subject and object, entailing necessarily that relationship. The following is stated in *Über die vierfache Wurzel des Satzes vom zureichenden Grunde*:

> Our knowing consciousness, appearing as outer and inner sensibility (receptivity), as understanding (*Verstand*) and as faculty of reason (*Vernunft*), is divisible into subject and object, and constitutes nothing else.[3]

2. The knowing subject

When Schopenhauer refers to man as the "knowing subject," it is important to keep in mind that the knowing subject is "that which knows all things and is known by none."[4] In other words, the "knowing subject" as such, can never be known, or become an object for anyone--not even for the knower himself--even though one

---

[2] Arthur Schopenhauer, *Die Welt als Wille und Vorstellung II*, Kap.1, *Zürcher Ausgabe in zehn Bänden*, Band III (Zürich: Diogenes Verlag, 1977), S.23. Henceforth cited as *Vorstellung*; English translation: Arthur Schopenhauer, *The World as Will and Representation*, vol.2, ch.2, trans. E.F.J. Payne (New York: Dover, 1969), p. 15. Henceforth cited as *Representation*.

[3] Arthur Schopenhauer, *Über die vierfache Wurzel des Satzes vom zureichenden Grunde*, §16, *Zürcher Ausgabe in zehn Bänden*, Band V (Zürich: Diogenes Verlag, 1977), S.41. Henceforth cited as *Grunde*. English translation: Arthur Schopenhauer, *The Fourfold Root of the Principle of Sufficient Reason*, §16, trans. E.F.J. Payne (La Salle: Open Court, 1974), p.41. Henceforth cited as *Reason*.

[4] *Vorstellung* I, §2, I, S.31; *Representation*, I, §2, p.5.

can "know" himself as a "willer".[5] Schopenhauer is categorical on this point: "...there is no *knowledge of knowing*, since this would require that the subject separated itself from knowing and yet know that knowing which is impossible."[6]

The ramifications of this will be seen shortly in Schopenhauer's understanding of the principle of sufficient reason, which involves a relationship exclusively among objects, but never one between subject and objects.[7] Accordingly, when the question about the character of objects as given in experience is treated in light of the principle of sufficient reason, the ego or knowing subject as such, is seen as transcendental and thereby outside the causal nexus of phenomena.

3. The object as representation

For Schopenhauer an object essentially is a representation of the subject: "To be object for the subject and to be our representation (*Vorstellung*) are the same thing. All our representations are objects of the subject, and all objects of the subject are our representations."[8] What does he mean exactly by the

---

[5] *Grunde*, V, §41, S.157. "Demnach erkennt das Subjekt sich nur als ein *Wollenden*, nicht aber als ein *Erkennendes*. Denn das vorstellende Ich, das Subjekt des Erkennens, kann, da es, als nothwendiges Korrelat aller Vorstellungen, Bedingung derselben ist, nie selbst Vorstellung oder Objekt werden."; *Reason*, §41, p. 208.

[6] *Ibid.*, V, S.158; *Ibid.*, p.208.

[7] *Vorstellung I*, I §5, S.41. "Man hüte sich aber vor dem grossen Mißverständiß, daß, weil die Anschauung durch die Erkenntniß der Kausalität vermittelt ist, deswegen zwischen Objekt und Subjekt das Verhältniß von Ursache und Wirkung bestehe; da vielmehr dasselbe immer nur zwischen unmittelbarem und vermittelbarem Objekt, also immer nur zwischen Objekten Statt findet...zwischen Subjekt und Objekt gar kein Verhältniß nach dem Satz vom Grunde findet..."; *Representation*, I, §5, p.13.

[8] *Grunde*, V, §16, S.41; *Reason*, §16, pp.41-42.

term "representation"? As shall be evident below, the representation is whatever comprises the content of any type of consciousness, whether it be human or animal. Hence, a representation may very well be a perception, image or concept --or anything that comes across the mind as a state of consciousness.[9]

According to Schopenhauer, there are four types of objects possible for our faculty of representation (*Vorstellungsvermögen*) which stand under the principle of sufficient reason. In the *first* place, there are "*intuitive, complete, empirical* representations (*anschauliche, vollständige, empirische Vorstellungen*)."[10] *Secondly*, there are *abstract* representations or concepts which arise because of man's faculty of reason (*Vernunft*).[11] Comprising the *third* class are representations of *space* and *time*, considered as the *formal* part of complete representations.[12]

The *fourth* class of representation is *sui generis*, and pivotal insofar as this type of representation ultimately offers one the only clue to understand the in-itselfness of reality. Hence, it is of central importance for his philosophical system. This special representation comprises but one "object", namely, "the immediate object of the inner sense, the subject of willing."[13] In other words, via the route of introspection in self-consciousness (i.e. the inner

---

[9] D.W. Hamlyn, *Schopenhauer* (London: Routledge & Kegan Paul, 1980), pp. 4-5. Cf. Patrick Gardiner, *Schopenhauer* (Baltimore: Penguin Books, 1963), p.55.

[10] *Grunde*, V, §17, S.43; *Reason*, §17, p.45.

[11] *Ibid.*, §26, S. 113; *Ibid.*, §26, p.145.

[12] *Ibid.*, §35, S.147; *Ibid.*, §35, p. 193.

[13] *Ibid.*, §40, S.157; *Ibid.*, §40, p.207.

World as Representation

sense), we know ourselves as willers, or subjects of willing.

Schopenhauer also maintains that the world (the complex which presents itself in perception) considered as representation can never take us beyond the representation itself. Concepts while related necessarily to perceptual representations, do not serve as a bridge to know what objects are in themselves. This explains in part why Schopenhauer has difficulty with any subtle philosophical jargon which would imply that a distinction might in fact be made between: a representation, an object of a representation, and a thing-in-itself.[14] He rejects this because of the impression which might arise therewith that there is more to reality than representations and the thing-in-itself. He states: "...this much is certain, that, when we reflect clearly, nothing can be found except representations and thing-in-itself."[15]

4. The representation and Transcendental Idealism

On the level of the representation "to be" means, without any exception whatsoever, "to be representation of the knowing subject". Thus, it is stated in *Die Welt als Wille und Vorstellung*: "Everything that in any way belongs and can belong to the world is inevitably associated with this being-

---

[14] Arthur Schopenhauer, "Anhang. Kritik der Kantischen Philosophie," *Vorstellung I*, II, S.544-545; Arthur Schopenhauer, "Appendix: Criticism of the Kantian Philosophy," *Representation*, I, pp.442-443.

[15] *Ibid.*, S.545; *Ibid.*, p.444.

conditioned (*Bedingtseyn*) by the subject. The world is representation."[16]

One cannot help but notice a similarity between what was outlined above and Berkeley's *esse est percipi*, a fact not denied by Schopenhauer.[17] This notwithstanding, Schopenhauer's complete philosophy is not an ontological phenomenalism as is Berkeley's. The British empiricist would maintain not only that perceived phenomena of the knowing subject are the only knowable data, but he would also assert that these 'percepts' are the *only* existents.[18] Though Schopenhauer would agree with Berkeley that "that which is," exists only for the perceiver, he would not say that nothing exists except ideas. For there is a thing-in-itself which underlies what we perceive giving it ultimate significance.[19] Besides, that of which we are always conscious in

---

[16] *Vorstellung I*, §1, I, S.29; *Representation*, I, §1, p.3.

[17] *Ibid.*, S. 30; *Ibid.* Cf. Mauice Mandelbaum, *History, Man and Reason* (Baltimore: The John Hopkins University Press, 1971), p.314.

[18] George Berkeley, *Of the Principles of Human Knowledge*, I., No.6 as found in *Principles, Dialogues, Correspondence* (Indianapolis: Bobbs-Merrill, 1965. The passage reads as follows:

> Some truths there are so near and obvious to the mind that a man need only open his eyes to see them. Such I take this important one to be, to wit, that all the choir of heaven and furniture of the earth, in a word, all those bodies which compose the mighty frame of the world, have not any subsistence without a mind -- that their *being* is to be perceived or known, that, consequently, so long as they are not actually perceived by me or do not exist in my mind or that of any other created spirit, they must either have no existence at all or else subsist in the mind of some eternal spirit -- it being perfectly unintelligible, and involving all the absurdity of abstraction, to attribute to any single part of them an existence independent of a spirit. To be convinced of which, the reader need only reflect, and try to separate in his own thoughts, the *being* of a sensible thing from its *being perceived*.

[19] John Passmore, *A Hundred Years of Philosophy* (Harmondsworth: Penguin Books, 1978), p. 96.

representational knowing, is a state of our bodily organs -- something Berkeley would never maintain.[20]

As shall be seen below, from the standpoint of the world considered as representation, Schopenhauer's epistemological notions can be regarded as a classical example of Transcendental Idealism.[21] For the world as representation presupposes its being-conditioned by the knowing subject which as "the bearer of the world, [is] the universal condition of all appearances (*Erscheinungen*), of all objects..."[22]

B. The Principle of Sufficient Reason

1. Its meaning

Schopenhauer in *Über die vierfache Wurzel des Satzes vom zureichenden Grunde* contends that all representations or "objects" stand under the principle of

---

[20] *Vorstellung I*, §1, I, S.29. "Es wird ihm dann deutlich und gewiß, daß er keine Sonne kennt und keine Erde; sondern immer nur eine Auge, das eine Sonne sieht, eine Hand, die eine Erde fühlt; daß die Welt, welche ihn umgiebt, nur als Vorstellung daist, d.h. durchweg nur in Beziehung auf ein Anderes, das Vorstellende, welches er selbst ist."; *Representation*, I, §1, p.3. See also Maurice Mandelbaum, *History, Man, & Reason* (Baltimore: The John Hopkins University Press, 1971), p.314 where the same point is underscored.

[21] Rudolf Malter, "Schopenhauer's Transzendentalismus," *International Studies in Philosophy* XIX/3 (1987), S.435. "Wenn (in Fortführung der cartesischen und kantischen Tradition) unter Transzendentalismus diejenige Konzeption des Verhältnisses von Sein und Wissen zu verstehen ist, nach welcher Sein als Sein je eröffnet ist durch Wissen und somit ein ursprünglichnotwendiger bedingend-ermöglichender Bezug des Wissens zum Sein besteht, so ist das erste Buch des Schopenhauerschen Hauptwerkes ein klassisches Stück Transzendentalphilosophie. Das erste Buch der "Welt als Wille und Vorstellung" thematisiert nämlich die ursprüngliche Eröffnung des Seins ("Welt") durch das Wissen ("Vorstellung"); es bringt also den ursprünglich-notwendigen Bezug des Seins zum Wissen und die bedingend-ermöglichende Vorgängigkeit des Wissens innerhalb der untrennbaren Wissen-Sein-Korrelation zur Sprache."

[22] *Vorstellung I*, §2, I, S.31. "Dasjenige, was Alles erkennt und von Keinem erkannt wird, ist das *Subjekt*. Es ist sonach der Träger der Welt, die durchgängige, stets vorausgesetzte Bedingung alles Erscheinungen, aller Objekts: denn nur für das Subjekt ist, was nur immer daist."; *Representation*, I, §2, p.5.

sufficient reason which, in its simplest form, states that everything has a ground for its existence.[23] Moreover, it is underscored: *"Now it is found that all our representations stand one with another in a lawful connection that in form is determinable a priori by virtue of which, nothing existing by itself and independent, [and] also nothing single and detached, can become object for us."* [24]

This, of course, means that all knowing on the phenomenological plane fits into patterns. Objects of knowledge are necessarily inter-related. Hence, if one knows a given object X or a set of facts about it, there is always something in relation to that X that enables one to understand it. Necessity, for Schopenhauer, is the hallmark of every appearance, great or small.

> ...no truth is more certain than this, that all that happens, be it small or great, transpires with complete *necessity*. Consequently, at every given moment of time, the entire condition of all things is firm and exactly determined by the state that just preceded it; and so it is with the stream of time upwards to infinity and backwards into infinity.[25]

---

[23] *Grund*, §5, V, S.17. "Weiterhin soll gezeigt werden, daß der Satz vom zureichenden Grunde ein gemeinschaftlicher Ausdruck mehrerer a *priori* gegebener Erkenntnisse ist. Vorläufig muß er indessen in irgend einer Formel aufgestellt werden. Ich wähle die Wolfische als die allgemeinste: *Nihil est sine ratione cur potius sit, quam not sit.* [Nichts ist ohne Grund, warum es eher ist, als dass es nicht ist: *Ontologia*, §70.] Nichts ist ohne Grund warum es sei."; *Reason*, §5, p.6.

[24] *Ibid*, §16, S.41. "Nun aber findet sich, daß alle unsere Vorstellungen unter einander in einer gesetzmäßigen und der Form nach a priori bestimmbaren Verbindung stehn, vermöge welcher nichts für sich Bestehendes und Unabhängiges, auch nichts Einzelnes und Abgerissenes, Objekt für uns werden kann."; *Ibid.*, §16, p.42.

[25] *Vorstellung II*, Kap.25, III, S.373; *Representation*, II, ch.25, p.319.

2. Its fourfold aspect

The principle of sufficient reason has a fourfold dimension corresponding to the relations that can exist among the four types of representations possible in experience. "Their number can be reduced to *four*, since it agrees with *four classes* into which everything is divided that can for us become an object, thus all our representations."[26] In each of the relations among the various representations the principle of sufficient reason appears in a different form, but it is always the same principle which springs from the same root.[27]

As was stated above, all representations are necessarily linked. In the case of the *first* class (the "intuitive, complete and empirical representations"), the principle of sufficient reason appears as the law of causality, which Schopenhauer calls "*the principle of sufficient reason of becoming (Werdens), principium rationis sufficientis fiendi.*"[28] Schopenhauer contends that the law of causality pertains to changes that take place in phenomena, which explains his rationale for calling the principle of sufficient reason "the principle of becoming". Any change that takes place is always grounded by a change in another given phenomenon.

With regard to abstract representations which comprise the *second* class of objects, the principle is called "*the principle of sufficient reason of knowing*

---

[26] *Grunde*, §16, V, S.41; *Reason*, §16, p.42.

[27] *Ibid.*, S. 41-42. "In jeder derselben werden wir den Satz vom zureichenden Grund in einer andern Gestalt auftreten, sich aber überall dadurch, daß er den oben angegebenen Ausdruck zuläßt, als den selben und als aus der hier angegebenen Wurzel entsprossen zu erkennen geben sehn."; *Ibid.*

[28] *Ibid.*, §20, S.49; *Ibid.*, §20, pp.52-53.

(*Erkennens*), *principium rationis sufficientis cognoscendi*."[29] Here the principle deals with judgements, "the combining or separating of two or more concepts under various restrictions and modifications..."[30] In order for a judgement to express a piece of knowledge, it must have a ground or reason.

The *third* class of representations pertains to space and time as pure forms of intuition. Schopenhauer states that space and time are so constituted that all their parts stand in mutual relation to each other, which means that every part is determined and conditioned by another.[31] The relation in space is called "position" (*Lage*) whereas in time it is called "succession" (*Folge*).[32] These relations are made intelligible solely by means of pure intuition *a priori*. The law whereby these relations are grasped is called by Schopenhauer "*the principle of sufficient reason of being (Seyns), principium rationis sufficientis essendi*."[33]

The *fourth* class of representation pertains to the subject of willing which becomes object of the inner sense, or self-consciousness. Here the principle of sufficient reason has a special form that corresponds to the uniqueness of this type of representation. Schopenhauer says that the principle in this case "appears as *the principle of sufficient reason of acting (Handelns), principium rationis sufficientis agendi*, or

---

[29] *Ibid.*, §29, S.121; *Ibid.* §29, p.156.

[30] *Ibid.*; *Ibid.*

[31] *Ibid.*, §36, S. 148. "Raum und Zeit haben die Beschaffenheit, daß alle ihre Theile in einem Verhältniß zu einander stehn, in Hinsicht auf welches jeder derselben durch einen andern bestimmt und bedingt ist."; *Ibid.*, §36, p.194.

[32] *Ibid.*; *Ibid.*

[33] *Ibid.*; *Ibid.*

World as Representation

more briefly, *the law of motivation.*"[34] Here the problematic involves what exactly it is that evokes action in human beings, but also in animals. Accordingly, the principle of sufficient reason under the form of the law of motivation pertains to ethics.

3. The extent and validity of the principle

It was already mentioned above that the knowing subject stands apart from the causal nexus and that the *ego* as knower is transcendental. Accordingly, the knowing subject does not stand under the aforementioned principle of sufficient reason, which exclusively combines only representations with one another.[35] Schopenhauer underscores its limitation:

> The principle of sufficient reason is not...a *veritas aeterna*, that is, it does not have unconditioned validity (*unbedingte Gültigkeit*) before, outside, and above the world, but only a relative and conditioned one, applying only in the appearance (*Erscheinung*); it may appear as the necessary nexus of space or time, or as causality, or as the law of the ground of knowledge.[36]

Knowledge mediated by the principle of sufficient reason can never give us metaphysical insight which, as such, lies beyond the appearance or phenomenon. Though every science has for its guidance one or another of the forms of the principle of sufficient reason,[37] comprehension of the inner nature of things cannot be obtained via this route.

---

[34] *Ibid.*, §43, S.162; *Ibid.*, §43, p.214.

[35] *Vorstellung I* §5, I, S.43; *Representation*, I, §5, p.15.

[36] *Ibid.*, §7, S.63; *Ibid.*, §7, p.32.

[37] *Grunde*, §51, V, S.174; *Reason*, §51, p.230-231.

Phenomenological 'knowing' scratches but the surface of things. Schopenhauer is convinced of this fact and he states: "...to grasp the *essence in itself* (*das Wesen an sich*) of things is absolutely impossible on the path of mere *knowledge* and *representation*, since this knowledge always comes to things *from without* (*von außen*), and must therefore remain eternally *outside* (*draußen*) them."[38] Hence, via the representation, all that can be known, in the final analysis, are images and names.[39]

C. Intellectual Nature of Perception

1. Sensation as a given

An important notion in Schopenhauer's epistemology is the intellectual nature of perception. The adjective "intellectual" is applied to perception because the understanding (*Verstand*), by means of the *a priori* law of causality, creates and produces the objective world out of the raw data of sensations felt by the body. In the paragraphs which follow I will, first of all, highlight passages that illustrate why Schopenhauer considers perception to be the work of the understanding. Secondly, I will discuss the nature of the understanding as such.

In the first place, Schopenhauer tries to distinguish between sensation (*Empfindung*) and objective perception (*objektive Anschauung*) by underscoring that the former is completely subjective. Sensation even in

---

[38] *Vorstellung II*, Kap.1, III, S.19-21; *Representation*, II, ch.1, p.12.

[39] *Vorstellung I*, §17, I, S.142. "Wir sehn schon hier, daß *von außen* dem Wesen der Dinge nimmermehr beizukommen ist; wie immer man auch forschen mag, so gewinnt man nichts, als Bilder und Namen."; *Representation*, I, §17, p.99.

the noblest organs of sense is nothing more than a local specific feeling (*Gefühl*) containing nothing objective.[40] Accordingly, sensation of every kind "remains an event (*Vorgang*) in the organism itself; but as such, it is restricted to the region beneath the skin; for this reason, in itself, [sensation] can never contain anything which may lie beyond this skin, and hence outside ourselves."[41]

It is this 'private' aspect of sensation, in which changes reach one's consciousness via the inner sense, where the form of time alone applies, that gives sensation its completely subjective character.[42] Moreover, because sensation pertains only to "sentient" essents, it goes without saying that an organic body plays a central role. The body is a given which, as it were, supplies the raw material for sensations which the understanding (*der Verstand*) of each sentient essent uses to construct the perceptual world which appears as a *Vorstellung*.

2. The role of the understanding (*Verstand*)

Schopenhauer contends that objective perception arises because of the work of the understanding. He is categorical on that point: "the understanding itself has first to create the objective world: for this cannot merely walk (*hineinspazieren*) into our heads, finished already in advance (*schon vorher fertig*), through the

---

[40] *Grunde*, §21, V, S.67; *Reason*, §21, p.76.

[41] *Ibid*. "Denn die Empfindung jeder Art ist und bleibt ein Vorgang im Organismus selbst, als solcher aber auf das Gebiet unterhalb der Haut beschränkt, kann daher, an sich selbst, nie etwas enthalten, das jenseits dieser Haut, also außer uns läge."; *Ibid*.

[42] *Ibid.*; *Ibid*.

senses and openings of their organs."⁴³ What happens is that the cognitive faculty (i.e. the faculty of understanding) applies its sole form (the law of causality) to the raw data of the senses, with the end result being, that objective perception arises.⁴⁴ Schopenhauer has been criticized for his treatise on how the entire process of perception exactly happens.⁴⁵ Let us quote, however, Schopenhauer's words directly in order to first see what he means by the intellectual nature of perception:

> ...by virtue of its own particular form and so *a priori*, that is, prior to all experience (because up to that time it is not yet possible), the understanding grasps the given sensation of the body as an effect (a word which only the understanding grasps), that as such must necessarily have a *cause*. Simultaneously the understanding receives for its assistance space, the form of the *outer* sense, which likewise lies predisposed in the intellect, i.e.,in the brain, in order to place that cause *outside* the organism; because in that way, first of all, there arises for it an outside whose possibility is simply space, so that pure intuition (*reine Anschauung*) *a priori* must supply the foundation for empirical intuition.⁴⁶

---

⁴³ *Ibid.*, S. 68; *Ibid.*, p.78.

⁴⁴ *Ibid.*, S.67. "Erst wenn der *Verstand*, --eine Funktion, nicht einzelner zarter Nervenenden, sondern des so künstlich und räthselhaft gebauten, drei, ausnahmsweise aber bis fünf Pfund wiegenden Gehirns, --in Thätigkeit geräth und seine einzige und alleinige Form, *das Gesetz der Kausalität*, in Anwendung bringt, geht eine mächtige Verwandlung vor, indem aus der subjektiven Empfindung die objektive Anschauung wird."; *Ibid.* p.77.

⁴⁵ Patrick Gardiner, *Schopenhauer* (Baltimore: Penguin Books, 1963), pp. 105-109; Alfred Schaefer, *Probleme Schopenhauers* (Berlin: Berlin Verlag,1984), S. 23-24; Hamlyn, pp. 19-21; Mandelbaum, p.314.

⁴⁶ *Grunde*, §21, V, S. 67-68. "Er nämlich faßt, vermöge seiner selbsteigenen Form, also *a priori*, d.i. *vor* aller Erfahrung (denn diese ist bis dahin noch nicht möglich), die gegebene Empfindung des Leibes als eine *Wirkung* auf (ein Wort, welches er allein versteht), die als solche nothwendig eine *Ursache* haben muß. Zugleich nimmt er die ebenfalls im Intellekt, d.i. im Gehirn, prädisponirt liegende Form des *äußern* Sinnes zu Hülfe, den *Raum*, um jene Ursache *außerhalb* des

From what has just been quoted above, sensations of the body are taken as a given for the faculty of the understanding. Characteristic to that faculty is the ability to grasp any given sensation as an effect that must have a cause. Sensations are the starting point for intellectual perception of the world, inasmuch as their modifications are given prior to all intuitive perception of the empirical world. This claim is also asserted in *Über das Sehn und die Farben: eine Abhandlung*.[47]

With the senses of taste, hearing and smell, the presence of objects is merely 'announced' to the perceiver. Schopenhauer maintains that their data alone do not supply the raw material necessary to result in an intuitive and objective perception, i.e. the representation which the perceiver creates from sensory data. Thus, a representation of a rose, for example, cannot be constructed in the perceiver on the basis of its smell alone. Nor can a blind man obtain representations of musicians and instruments from the mere hearing of music.[48] Properly speaking, "two senses, touch and sight, are useful for objective intuition (*objektiven Anschauung*)...[in that] they alone

---

Organizmus zu verlegen: denn dadurch erst entsteht ihm das Außerhalb, dessen Möglichkeit eben der Raum ist; so daß die reine Anschauung *a priori* die Grundlage der empirischen abgeben muß."; *Reason*, §21, pp. 77-78. See also *Vorstellung II*, Kap.4, III, S.48-49; *Representation*, II, ch.4, p. 37-38.

[47] Arthur Schopenhauer, *Über das Sehn und die Farben: eine Abhandlung*, Kap.1, *Sämmtliche Werke*, Band III, (Leipzig: Inselverlag, 1905-1910), S.700. Henceforth cited as *Sehn*. "Die Sinne sind bloß die Ausgangspunkte dieser Anschauung der Welt. Ihre Modifikationen sind daher vor aller Anschauung gegeben, als bloße Empfindungen, sind die Data, aus denen erst im Verstande die erkennende Anschauung wird."; *On Vision*, as found in "Appendix," *Reason*, p. 254. Henceforth cited as *Vision*.

[48] *Grunde*, §21, V, S.69; *Reason*, §21, p.79.

supply the data from whose basis the understanding allows the objective world to come about..."⁴⁹

Schopenhauer then outlines *four* essential tasks the understanding does fulfill on the basis of the aforementioned sensory data. In the *first* place, the understanding sets aright the impression of the object which appears reversed and upside down on the retina of the eye.⁵⁰ *Secondly*, it converts the sensations of both sight and touch into a single perception of what is a double impression in the case of sight and manifold impressions in the case of touch.⁵¹ *Thirdly*, the understanding constructs bodies from mere surfaces previously obtained which entails the addition of a third dimension.⁵² In the *fourth* place, the understanding recognizes the distance of objects in front of the perceiver. Thus, while vision may give us the direction in which objects lie, it does not give their distance and place, which can only be supplied by the understanding.⁵³

3. Centrality of the body in perception

From the above discussion, it is clear that the sensations one has of one's own body give the body a position of primacy among the hierarchy of empirical representations. While considering the body as an "immediate object" has some validity, Schopenhauer

---

⁴⁹ *Ibid.*, S. 68-69; *Ibid.*

⁵⁰ *Ibid.*, S.73-74; *Ibid.*, pp. 86-87.

⁵¹ *Ibid.*, S.74,76; *Ibid.*, pp. 87,90.

⁵² *Ibid.*, S.78-79; *Ibid.*, p.93.

⁵³ *Ibid.*, S.80; *Ibid.*, p.95.

maintains that in the strict sense it is not accurate to do so. This notwithstanding, the expression "immediate object" may be used, but only in a figurative sense.[54] Why so? Because strictly speaking, perception (*Wahrnehmung*) of the body's sensations *(Empfindungen)* alone constitutes what is immediate. The body itself is not yet given as an object.[55]

In the true sense of the term, the body is known as object indirectly (*mittelbar*) because "like all other objects it presents itself in the understanding or brain (which is the same) as the known cause of a subjectively given effect and precisely in that way, presents itself *objectively*."[56] This happens only given each of the body's parts acting on each of its senses, for example the eye seeing the body or the hand touching the body, which allows the understanding (based on the data it has) to spatially construct the body.[57] In this respect one's own body is akin to other objects given in experience because it too is a creation of the understanding. But Schopenhauer states that "the existence of my person or of my body *as an extended and acting thing (als eines Ausgedehnten und Wirkenden)*

---

[54] *Ibid.*, §22, S.100; *Ibid.*, §22, p.121.

[55] *Ibid.* "Denn, obwohl die Wahrnehmung seiner Empfindungen eine schlechthin unmittelbare ist; so stellt doch er selbst sich dadurch noch gar nicht als Objekt dar; sondern soweit bleibt Alles noch subjektiv, nämlich Empfindung." *Ibid.*

[56] *Ibid.*, S. 101; *Ibid.*

[57] *Ibid.*; *Ibid.* See also *Vorstellung II*, Kap.1, III, S.13: "Nämlich als *Objekt*, d.h. als ausgedehnt, raumerfüllend und wirkend, erkenne ich meinen Leib nur in der Anschauung meines Gehirns: diese ist vermittelt durch die Sinne, auf deren Data der anschauende Verstand seine Funktion, von der Wirkung auf die Ursache zu gehn, vollzieht und dadurch, indem das Auge den Leib sieht, oder die Hände ihn betasten, die räumliche Figur konstruirt, die im Raume als mein Leib sich darstellt. Keineswegs aber ist mir unmittelbar, etwan im Gemeingefühl des Leibes, oder im innern Selbstbewußtseyn, irgend eine Ausdehnung, Gestalt und Wirksamkeit gegeben, welche dann zusammenfallen würde mit einem Wesen selbst, das demnach, um so dazuseyn, keines Andern, in dessen Erkenntniß es sich darstellte, bedürfte." *Representation*, II, ch.1, p. 6.

always presupposes a *knowing being* different from it since it is an existence in the apprehension, in the representation, and hence an existence *for another being*."[58] This means in effect that the body is a phenomenon of the brain (*Gehirnphänomen*) regardless as to whether it is one's own or that of another.[59] The body, therefore, is an object among other objects. As such, it is subordinated to the principle of sufficient reason which governs phenomena.

This notwithstanding, one's own body has a character that other objects can never have. The body is not only a phenomenon of the brain (as is the case with other empirically-given representations or objects), but it anchors the sensations that are the springboard from which perception of the world arises. Via the inner sense we are immediately aware of our own sensations, in addition to the pictures received from the outer sense. But of other objects, we have merely the knowledge that is gained by the images in our mind.[60] Only in this respect, can the body indeed be regarded as an "immediate" object since it is characterized by a sensibility that indirect objects outside the skin cannot have. In fact, Schopenhauer attributes to the body a certain primacy and directness which other objects, as given in perception, always lack.

---

[58] *Vorstellung II*, Kap.1, III, S.13; *Representation*, II, ch.1, p.6.

[59] *Ibid*. "In der That ist es ein Gehirnphänomen, gleichviel ob das Gehirn, in welchem es sich darstellt, der eigenen, oder einer fremden Person angehört."; *Ibid*.

[60] *Ibid*., S.18. "Das Subjektive und das Objektive bilden kein Kontinuum: das unmittelbar Bewußte ist abgegränzt durch die Haut, oder vielmehr durch die äußersten Enden der vom Cerebralsystem [Hirnnervensystem] ausgehenden Nerven. Darüber hinaus liegt eine Welt, von der wir keine andere Kunde haben, als durch Bilder in unserm Kopfe."; *Ibid*., p.10.

World as Representation 19

The body's centrality in Schopenhauer's conception of the world as representation is indicated clearly by the opening sentences of *Die Welt als Wille und Vorstellung*. Immediately after asserting that "the world is my representation" ("*Die Welt ist meine Vorstellung*"), Schopenhauer adds that it becomes clear and certain to the knowing subject that he "does not know a sun and an earth; but always only an eye that sees a sun, a hand that feels an earth; that the world which surrounds him is only there as representation, that is, always only in relation to another thing, that which represents (*das Vorstellende*)..."[61] It is apparent, then, that consciousness entails an awareness of the state of our own bodily organs.

4. The understanding as characteristic of animal life

It goes without saying that Schopenhauer's notion of the understanding differs radically from Kant's.[62] In no way is it discursive or abstract. It has nothing to do with subsuming the data given in intuition under pure concepts or categories so as to give rise to experience.[63] Schopenhauer reduces the faculty of the understanding to the mere grasping of the causal

---

[61] *Vorstellung I*, §1, I, S.29; *Representation*, I, §1, p.3.

[62] Immanuel Kant, *Critique of Pure Reason*, trans. Norman Kemp Smith (London: Macmillan Education, 1987), A68/B93, p.105. The passage reads as follows:

> The understanding has thus far been explained merely negatively, as a non-sensible faculty of knowledge. Now since without sensibility we cannot have any intuition, understanding cannot be a faculty of intuition. But besides intuition there is no other mode of knowledge except by means of concepts. The knowledge yielded by understanding, must therefore be by means of concepts, and so is not intuitive, but discursive.

[63] Kant, *The Critique of Pure Reason*, B143, p.160.

nexus. It is succinctly stated that "the law of causality is the real, but also the only function of the understanding, and the remaining eleven categories are only blind windows."[64]

This means in effect that the first class of intuitive, complete and empirical representations is the work of a cognitive faculty that has nothing to do with conceptualization. He states that "our thinking is not useful to impart reality to perceptions (Anschauungen); this they have insofar as they are capable of it (empirical reality) through themselves."[65] Given the above discussion, the empirical reality that appears as perceptual representation is the work of a cognitive faculty that is not exclusive to man alone:

> Now, therefore, as there is no intuition without understanding, all animals undoubtedly have this mental faculty. In fact understanding distinguishes animals from plants as reason does human beings from animals. For really the distinguishing *character of animality is knowledge*, and this necessitates, by all means, understanding.[66]

Über den Willen in der Natur explicitly alludes to the cognitive faculty (*das Erkenntnißvermögen*) that animals have which distinguishes them from plants.[67] Because of

---

[64] "Kritik der Kantischen Philosophie," *Vorstellung I*, II, S.548.; "Criticism of the Kantian Philosophy," *Representation*, I, p.446.

[65] *Ibid.*, S.543-544; *Ibid.* p.443.

[66] *Sehn*, Kap.1, *Sämmtliche Werke*, III, S.698.; *Vision*, in *Reason*, p.251.

[67] Arthur Schopenhauer, *Über den Willen in der Natur*, "Pflanzen-Physiologie," *Zürcher Ausgabe Werke in zehn Bänden*, V (Zürich: Diogenes, 1977), S.265. Henceforth cited as *Natur*. English translation: *On the Will in Nature*, trans. Mme. K. Hillebrand (London: George Bell & Sons, 1889), p.292. The German text (S.265) runs as follows:

> Erinnern wir uns aus dem vorhergehenden Abschnitte, daß bei den Thieren das Erkenntnißvermögen, wie jedes andere Organ, nur zum Behuf ihrer Erhaltung eingetreten ist und daher in genauem und unzählige Stufen zulassendem Verhältniß zu den Bedürfnissen jeder

that faculty, animals can have perceptual representations. Accordingly, it is not at all surprising that Schopenhauer also states that "the capacity to have representations (*Fähigkeit zu Vorstellungen*) and therefore consciousness (*Bewußtseyn*) may have infinite gradations in the series of animals."[68]

Herein lies the reason for Schopenhauer's asserting that understanding characterizes all animal life. All animals, accordingly, may be said to perceive. Since "intellectual" perception is necessarily mediated by the law of causality in the intellect or brain, all animals (even the most primitive) because they perceive, "must have understanding, that is to say, knowledge of the law of causality, although in a very different degree of keenness and clearness."[69] In short, for the animals their world is also representation.

Thierart steht; dann werden wir begreifen, daß die Pflanze, da sie so sehr viel weniger Bedürfnisse hat, als das Thier, endlich gar keiner Erkenntniß mehr bedarf. Dieserhalb eben ist, wie ich oft gesagt habe, das Erkennen, wegen der dadurch bedingten Bewegung auf Motive, der wahre und wesentliche Gränze bezeichende Charakter der Thierheit.

[68] *Freiheit*, III., VI, S.71; *Freedom*, III., p.33.

[69] *Grunde*, §21, V, S.92; *Reason*, §21, p.110. See also *Vorstellung I*, §6, I, S. 50. "Aus dem Gesagten ergiebt sich, daß alle Thiere Verstand haben, selbst die unvollkommensten: denn sie alle erkennen Objekte, und diese Erkenntniß bestimmt als Motiv ihre Bewegungen. - Der Verstand ist in allen Thieren und allen Menschen der nämliche, hat überall die selbe einfache Form: Erkenntniß der Kausalität, Uebergang von Wirkung auf Ursache und von Ursache auf Wirkung, und nichts außerdem. Aber die Grade seiner Schärfe und die Ausdehnung seiner Erkenntnißsphäre sind höchst verschieden, mannigfaltig und vielfach abgestuft, vom niedrigsten Grad, welcher nur das Kausalitätsverhältniß zwischen dem unmittelbaren Objekt und den mittelbaren erkennt, also eben hinreicht, durch den Uebergang von der Einwirkung, welche der Leib erleidet, auf deren Ursache, diese als Objekt im Raum anzuschauen, bis zu den höheren Graden der Erkenntniß des kausalen Zusammenhanges der bloß unmittelbaren Objekte unter einander, welche bis zum Verstehn der zusammengesetztesten Verkettungen von Ursachen und Wirkungen in der Natur geht. Denn auch dieses Letztere gehört immer noch dem Verstande an, nicht der Vernunft..."; *Representation*, I, §6, p.21.

5. Critique of Schopenhauer's theory of perception

Before considering what Schopenhauer means by reason (*Vernunft*), at this juncture, some critical observations can be made so as to place what is to follow in context. Distinguishing sensation from perception in itself is not problematic, nor is the assertion that perception has an intellectual character. But the explanation as to how exactly this takes place is riddled with difficulties. True, a distinction is made between the merely formal part of empirical perception and its application to empirical data. But this qualifier does not remove the evident problems that arise in Schopenhauer's theory of perception. In the first place, he states that the understanding (which is nothing more than a brain function) not only has the a *priori* capability of grasping the principle of cause and effect before experience as such arises, but he also suggests that the understanding can even distinguish one cause from another.

Thus, sensations of the body are grasped as being effects of a cause by a faculty (*Verstand*) which, as we just saw, is not in any way discursive or exclusive to man.[70] Grasping them as effects, the understanding knows that they must necessarily have their causes outside the organism. Since there is no "outside" as of yet, space is summoned from the wings to create that object or objects that are said to be causing the sensation which the understanding already has grasped as an effect.

---

[70] *Grunde*, §21, V, S.68. "Diese...Verstandesoperation ist jedoch keine diskursive, reflektive, *in abstracto*, mittelst Begriffen und Worten, vor sich gehende; sondern eine intuitive und ganz unmittelbare."; *Reason*, §21, p.78.

This, however, is problematic because what Schopenhauer is asserting is that a yet-to-be-given object (which still cannot be an object of experience since experience has not yet arisen) is causing an effect in the immediate object (the body), which also as such is not yet an object of experience. Both this yet-to-be-given object understood as cause, and the to-be-given object which is home to the sensations grasped as effects, become objects of experience only after the understanding effects the transformation and thus creates perception as such.

Moreover, since the intellect is equated with the brain as Schopenhauer states, it would appear that it would thereby be a phenomenon.[71] This, of course, becomes problematic against the backdrop of his contention that the knowing subject can know everything, but is knowable by no one. The knowing subject that represents is not a phenomenon. It therefore stands isolated and independent of the principle of sufficient reason. But how can one reconcile Schopenhauer's relating the cognitive faculty closely with the brain which would consequently make it a phenomenon? This would in theory, at least, make it knowable in human beings who are capable of abstract reflection.

What we have here, in short, is a classic case of putting the cart before the horse. To say that sensations are effects of something that is not yet an object of experience is one thing that already gives way to problems. But when it is asserted that the body which is home to the sensations also has to be created as an

---

[71] Cf. Schaefer, S.26. "Obwohl Schopenhauer sich als erkenntniskritischer Idealist versteht, geht er in seinem Anti-Idealismus bis zur Identification von Intellekt und Gehirn, woraus folgt: »Der Intellekt ist wie seine Objekte bloße Erscheinung.«...Dann aber wäre der Intellekt nicht nur Erkennendes, sondern Erkanntes -- aber vom wem erkannt?"

object of experience, this makes Schopenhauer's explanation even more unacceptable. For the sensations grasped as effects cannot properly be sensations if there is no body that is already given as an object. Against this backdrop, Schopenhauer's four tasks of the understanding, introduced so as to give a fuller picture of the to-be-given-object, are suspect if not untenable.

D. The Role of Reason (Vernunft)

1. Preliminary remarks

In the preceding section Schopenhauer's notion of perception was discussed and critiqued. His contention that empirical representations are the work of the cognitive faculty or understanding was outlined so as to underscore the intellectuality of perception not only in man, but in all animal life. It was also stated that *thought* which is proper to man, adds nothing to empirical representations already given by the understanding. In fact, as shall be seen below, thinking which always involves conceptualization, is necessarily limited even when it comes to describing what is given as an "intuitive, complete and empirical" representation.[72]

In this section three main points shall be raised. In the first place, the nature of reason and its significance will be briefly outlined. Secondly, the specific character of the abstract representation or concept will be treated, so as to delineate the secondary

---

[72] These representations are intuitive (*anschauliche*) insofar as they are opposed to concepts that are merely thought. They are complete (*vollständige*) insofar as they contain not merely what is formal but what is material in appearances (*Erscheinungen*). They are empirical (*empirische*) insofar as they have their origin in the sensation (*Empfindung*) of sensitive bodies to which they refer as evidence for their reality. See *Grunde*, §17, V, S.43; *Reason*, §17, p.45.

World as Representation 25

nature of the concept as such. The third point examines Schopenhauer's contention that concepts must be based on perceptual, complete, and empirical representation. In light of the discussion to follow, it will be seen why the concept as such is inadequate to describe reality.

2. Reason and the uniqueness of man

For Schopenhauer human consciousness consists not only of sensibility and understanding, but also reason.[73] Even though the three aspects are distinguishable, in reality they form a continuum in man's case. Accordingly, in human beings perception of the world is linked with conceptualization. Unlike the animal where nothing stands between it and the empirical representations it receives through its cognitive faculty, man is a step removed from the given-ness of the empirical world. "Between the animal and the external world there stands nothing; but between us and that world there are always our thoughts about it, and these often make us inaccessible to it, and it to us."[74]

Now the fundamental essence of our reasoning as human beings is the ability to form concepts. In light of this, Schopenhauer calls reason "the faculty of thought" (*Denkvermögen*) or "faculty of abstraction" (*Abstraktionsvermögen*) which entails "the capacity to form concepts" (*Fähigkeit, Begriffe zu bilden*).[75]

---

[73] *Grunde*, §16, V, S.41. "*Unser erkennendes Bewußtseyn, als äußere Sinnlichkeit (Receptivität), Verstand und Vernunft auftretend, zerfällt in Subjekt und Objekt, und enthält nichts außerdem.*"; *Reason*, §16, p. 41.

[74] *Vorstellung II*, Kap.5, III, S.74; *Representation*, II, ch.5, p.61.

[75] *Grunde*, §27, V, S.116. "*Unsere Vernunft, oder das Denkvermögen, hat, wie in Obigem gezeigt worden, zu ihrem Grundwesen das Abstraktionsvermögen, oder die Fähigkeit, Begriffe zu bilden.*"; *Reason* §27, p.150.

Reason is also described as "the *faculty of concepts*" (*Vermögen der Begriffe*) which comprises a "quite special class of general, non-perceptible (*allgemeiner, nicht anschaulicher*) representations, symbolized and fixed only by words...which differentiates man from animals and gives him dominion over the earth."[76]

Because of the presence of abstract representations or concepts, consciousness in man's case takes on a new dimension which Schopenhauer calls "reflection" (*Reflexion*) which distinguishes him completely from the animals.[77] Because of reason, human beings are liberated from the present moment; future and past now form part of his consciousness.[78] Since the concept frees human beings from the slavery of the present moment, they may be said to have elective choice (*Wahlentscheidung*) which enables them to balance mutually exclusive motives against each other.[79] A human being, moreover, can speak and laugh which again attests to the presence of the faculty of reason which animals do not have.[80] Besides this, it can be said that reflective deliberation is the root of man's technical and practical

---

[76] "Kritik der Kantischen Philosophie," *Vorstellung I*, II, S.631; "Criticism of the Kantian Philosophy," *Representation*, I, p.518.

[77] *Vorstellung I*, §8, I, S.68; *Representation*, I, §8, p. 36.

[78] *Ibid.*; *Ibid.*

[79] *Grunde*, §20, V, S.63. "Beim Thier, dessen Intellekt ein einfacher, daher nur die Erkenntniß der Gegenwart liefernder ist, fällt jene Nothwendigkeit leicht in die Augen. Der Intellekt des Menschen ist doppelt: er hat, zur anschaulichen, auch noch die abstrakte Erkenntniß, welche nicht an die Gegenwart gebunden ist: d.h. er hat Vernunft. Daher hat er eine Wahlentscheidung, mit deutlichem Bewußtseyn: nämlich er kann die einander ausschließenden Motive als solche gegen einander abwägen..."; *Reason*, §20, p.72.

[80] *Ibid.*, §26, S.113; *Ibid.*, §26, p.145.

World as Representation 27

achievements.[81] All these phenomena, so familiar to all of us, stem from the faculty of reason peculiar to human beings.

It is interesting to underscore once again how different Schopenhauer's notion of reason is from that of Kant.[82] As the above indicates, for Schopenhauer the essential nature of reason consists only in the formation of concepts. The Kantian system, on the other hand, gives reason the task of seeking the unconditioned.[83] Underscoring that the essential nature of reason "by no means consists in the demand for an unconditioned",

---

[81] *Ibid.*, §27, S.117. "Diese Besonnenheit nun wieder, also die Fähigkeit sich zu *besinnen*, zu sich zu kommen, is eigentlich die Wurzel aller seiner theoretischen und praktischen Leistungen, durch welche der Mensch das Thier so sehr übertrefft."; *Ibid.*, §27, p. 151.

[82] Recall that in Kant's philosophy the categories create a unity of the manifold that is in space and time and that this activity is that of the understanding. Reason, on the other hand, seeks to create a unity by bringing as many concepts and judgements under a general rule. It seeks the conditions of the conditions. The following passage from the *Critique of Pure Reason* speaks for itself:

> ...reason, in its logical employment, seeks to discover the universal condition of its judgement (the conclusion), and the syllogism of its condition under a universal rule (the major premise). Now since this rule is itself subject to the same requirement of reason, and the condition of the condition must therefore be sought (by means of a prosyllogism) whenever practicable, obviously the principle peculiar to reason in general, in its logical employment, is:--to find for the conditioned knowledge obtained through the understanding the unconditioned whereby its unity is brought to completion (B364), p.306.

[83] Kant states in the *Critique of Pure Reason*:

> As is easily seen, what pure reason alone has in view is the absolute totality of the synthesis *on the side of the conditions* (whether of inherence, of dependence, or of concurrence); it is not concerned with absolute completeness *on the side of the conditioned*. For the former alone is required in order to presuppose the whole series of the conditions, and to present it *a priori* to the understanding. Once we are given a complete (and unconditioned) condition, no concept of reason is required for the continuation of the series; for every step in the forward direction from the condition to the *conditioned* is carried through the understanding itself. The transcendental ideas thus serve only for *ascending*, in the series of conditions, to the unconditioned, that is, to principles (B393, pp.324-325).

Schopenhauer continues as follows: "Reason, as a faculty of knowledge, can always be concerned only with objects; every object for the subject, however, is necessarily and irrevocably subordinated and given over to the principle of sufficient reason, *a parte ante* as well as *a parte post*."[84] In this respect, it is clear that the transcendental pure Ideas of "world", "soul", and "God", which promote a reduction of our knowledge into a systematic ensemble in the Kantian system, do not have this function in the Schopenhauerian *Weltanschauung*.

3. The nature of the concept

As was already stated above, concepts constitute the second class of representations possible to man. In *Über die vierfache Wurzel des Satzes vom zureichenden Grunde* Schopenhauer calls concepts "representations from representations" (*Vorstellungen aus Vorstellungen*) as opposed to intuitive representations (*anschauliche Vorstellungen*) which only animals can have.[85] In *Die Welt als Wille und Vorstellung* Schopenhauer says essentially the same thing, but with a slight nuance. Underscoring that because reflection is "necessarily the copy (*Nachbildung*) or repetition of the original perceptual world," he adds that "concepts are quite appropriately called representations of representations (*Vorstellungen von Vorstellungen*)."[86]

Accordingly, all concepts are essentially abstractions. Schopenhauer says as much: "One has

---

[84] "Kritik der Kantischen Philosophie," *Vorstellung I*, II, S. 591; "Criticism of the Kantian Philosophy," *Representation*, I, p.483.

[85] *Grunde*, §26, V, S.114; *Reason*, §26, p.146.

[86] *Vorstellung I*, §9, I, S.72-73; *Representation*, I, §9, p.40.

called such abstract representations *concepts* (*Begriffe*), since each of them contains (*begreift*) in (or rather under) itself many innumerable individual things, and hence is an *aggregate* (*Inbegriff*) thereof."[87] Because a concept is a unity produced from a plurality of particulars by means of abstraction it may be called an *unitas post rem*.[88]

Although concepts are fundamentally different from representations of perception, they stand in a necessary relation to them -- a claim that Hume makes about the relation between impressions and ideas, which are faint copies of the former.[89] An abstract representation or concept has "all value and meaning only through its relation to the perceptual representation (*anschauliche Vorstellung*), without which it would be worthless and empty (*werth- und inhaltlos*)."[90] In fact, without this relation abstract representations would be "nothing" precisely because this relation "constitutes their whole nature and existence."[91] In this sense, therefore, the higher one climbs the ladder of abstraction the more difficult it is for a concept to be related to a given intuitive, complete and empirical perception. Accordingly, the most general concepts such as being, essence and the like are the "emptiest and

---

[87] *Ibid.*; *Ibid.*

[88] *Ibid.*, §49, S. 297; *Ibid.*, §49, p.234-235.

[89] David Hume, *A Treatise of Human Nature* (Harmondsworth: Penguin Books, 1969), Book One, Part One, Section One, p.49.

[90] *Vorstellung I*, §17, I, S. 137; *Representation*, I, §17, p.95.

[91] *Ibid.*, §9, S.72-73. "Obgleich nun also die Begriffe von den anschaulichen Vorstellungen von Grund aus verschieden sind, so stehn sie doch in einer nothwendigen Beziehung zu diesen, ohne welche sie nichts wären, welche Beziehung folglich ihr ganzes Wesen und Daseyn ausmacht."; *Ibid.*, §9, p.40

poorest" and in the final analysis "mere husks."[92] Concepts are such, that were it not for the fixing and retention of representations by arbitrary signs (words), they would slip away from our consciousness.[93]

In short, because abstract representations necessarily must have as their basis some empirical representation, this explains why the most abstract concepts are the most difficult to grasp. But this also highlights the basic poverty of the concept to describe the real. True, concepts give man great advantages. Because of reason which mediates them, human beings have lordship over the world. Yet given the fact that concepts always are abstractions, they fall short of adequately capturing the empirical world given in perception. Language, therefore, is limited in all respects, especially when it tries to describe what transcends empirical experience.

E. Time and Space

Time and space constitute for Schopenhauer the purely formal part of intuitive, complete and empirical representations and comprise the *third* class of

---

[92] *Grunde*, §26, V, S. 114-115. "Je höher man nun in der Abstraktion aufsteigt, desto mehr läßt man fallen, also desto weniger denkt man noch. Die höchsten, d.i. die allgemeinsten Begriffe sind die ausgeleertesten und ärmsten, zuletzt nur noch leichte Hülsen, wie z.B. Seyn, Wesen, Ding, Werden u. dgl.m.-"; *Reason*, §26, p.147.

[93] *Ibid.*, S.115. "Da nun, wie gesagt, die, zu abstrakten Begriffen sublimirten und dabei zersetzten Vorstellungen alle Anschaulichkeit eingebüßt haben; so würden sie dem Bewußtseyn ganz entschlüpfen und ihm zu den damit beabsichtigten Denkoperationen gar nicht Stand halten; wenn sie nicht durch willkürliche Zeichen sinnlich fixirt und festgehalten würden: diese sind die Worte."; *Ibid.*, p.148.

representations.⁹⁴ They are called "pure intuitions" (*reine Anschauungen*) insofar as "they are objects of the faculty of representation (*Vorstellungsvermögen*) by themselves, separated from complete representations and from the determination of being full or empty..."⁹⁵

Thus, "pure" lines and points cannot be represented, but only intuited *a priori*. The same is true with infinite extension (*unendliche Ausdehnung*) and the infinite divisibility (*unendliche Theilbarkeit*) of space and time. They are objects of pure intuition and consequently completely foreign to empirical perception.⁹⁶

Perceptual and complete representations always involve sensuous perception insofar as the senses are the starting point that gives way to the world we perceive. Time and space, on the other hand, are totally different. Schopenhauer states categorically in *Die Welt als Wille und Vorstellung*: "Time and space...each by itself, are...intuitively representable (*anschaulich vorstellbar*) without matter; matter, on the other hand, not without them."⁹⁷ Accordingly, matter (Materie) is what distinguishes empirical representations from the pure representations of space and time. Seen from a different angle, matter is the perceptibility (*Wahrnehmbarkeit*) of

---

⁹⁴ *Ibid.*, §35, S.147. "Die dritte Klasse der Gegenstände für das Vorstellungsvermögen bildet der formale Theil der vollständigen Vorstellungen, nämlich die *a priori* gegebenen Anschauungen der Formen des äußern und innern Sinnes, des Raums und der Zeit."; *Ibid,*, §35, p.193.

⁹⁵ *Ibid.*; *Ibid.*

⁹⁶ *Ibid.*; *Ibid.*

⁹⁷ *Vorstellung I*, §4, I, S.36; *Representation*, I, §4, p.9.

space and time on the one hand, and causality which has become objective (*objektiv gewordene*) on the other.[98]

Since space and time are the formal components of every object given in experience, they can be said to comprise the skeleton of each perceptual and complete representation without exception. This being the case, space and time can never be thought away even though one might theoretically in a moment of playful fancy think away everything in them.[99] Schopenhauer states this truth from another angle which brings into focus both the transcendental ideality of the world on the one hand and its empirical reality on the other: "Indeed space is only in my head; but empirically my head is in space."[100]

Before moving on to consider the *fourth* class of representation, one more distinction has to be raised. Up until this point two kinds of representations have been discussed. It was stated with regard to the first that they are the work of the understanding. With regard to the second it was underscored that concepts are the work of the faculty of reason. Thus, both *understanding* and *reason* can be seen as the *subjective correlatives* of the representations proper to each. The same is also true of *space* and *time*. Their subjective correlative is called *pure sensibility* (*reine Sinnlichkeit*).[101]

---

[98] *Grunde*, §35, V, 147.; *Reason*, §35, p.193.

[99] *Vorstellung II*, Kap.4, III, S.61. "Die Zeit läßt sich nicht wegdenken, jedoch Alles aus ihr./ "Der Raum läßt sich nicht wegdenken, jedoch Alles aus ihm."; *Representation*, II, ch.4, p.48.

[100] *Ibid.*, Kap.2, S.28; *Ibid.*, ch.2, p.19.

[101] *Grunde*, §42, V, S.160; *Reason*, §42, p.212. See also *Vorstellung I*, §4, I, S.38. "Das subjektive Korrelat von Zeit und Raum für sich, als leere Formen, hat Kant reine Sinnlichkeit genannt, welcher Ausdruck, weil Kant hier die Bahn brach, beibehalten werden mag; obgleich er nicht recht paßt, da Sinnlichkeit schon Materie voraussetzt."; *Representation*, I, §4, p.11.

F. The Subject of Willing

The *fourth* type of representation constitutes for every human being but *one* object: the immediate object (*unmittelbare Objekt*) of the inner sense, the subject of willing.[102] At the outset let it be underscored that the subjective correlative in this case is the inner sense, or generally speaking, the self-consciousness (*Selbstbewußtseyn*).[103]

Schopenhauer underscores the special character of this type of representation. It differs from empirically-given intuitive representations in that, as an object of the inner sense, it appears only in successive states in time.[104] Unlike empirical representations, whose complex is possible given the nexus of time, space and causality; this particular object is not given to the cognitive faculty (*Erkenntnißvermögen*) whose representations comprise the greater portion of the whole consciousness.[105] One does not see this "object" with the eyes of the body as one would, for example, see the foliage of trees. Since all knowing presupposes the subject/object relationship, if there is to be knowledge in the case of this *fourth* class of representation, something has to be the subject, and

---

[102] *Grunde*, §40, V, S. 157; *Reason*, §40, p.207.

[103] *Ibid.*, §§40,41, S.157; §42, S.160; *Ibid.*, §§40,41, p.207; §42, p.212.

[104] *Ibid.*, §40, S. 157. "...sie begreift für Jeden nur ein Objekt, nämlich das unmittelbare Objekt des innern Sinnes, *das Subjekt des Wollens*, welches für das erkennende Subjekt Objekt ist und zwar nur dem innern Sinn gegeben, daher es allein in der Zeit, nicht im Raum, erscheint, und auch da noch, wie wir sehn werden, mit einer bedeutenden Einschränkung."; *Ibid.*, §40, p.207.

[105] *Freiheit*, I., VI, S.50. "Aus dem Gesagten erhellt, daß von unserm gesammten Bewußtseyn überhaupt der bei weitem größte Theil nicht das *Selbstbewußtseyn*, sondern das *Bewußtseyn anderer Dinge*, oder das Erkenntnißvermögen, ist."; *Freedom*, I., p.10.

something has to be the object. However, because the ego can never be known, the object in this case is referred to as "the subject of willing". Schopenhauer states that "the Ego which represents (*das vorstellende Ich*), the subject of knowing, can itself never become representation or object, since as necessary correlative of all representations, it is their condition."[106] Here lies the reason for Schopenhauer maintaining that the object of the inner sense cannot be the transcendental ego, but the subject of willing.

By introducing this distinction, two types of knowing are juxtaposed: normal cognitive knowing which pertains to perceptual representations; and inner knowledge which comes to a person via the path of introspection. Schopenhauer states: "When we look into our inner self (*in unser Inneres blicken*), we always find ourselves as *willing* (*wollend*)."[107] Accordingly, one's own willing is the object of self-consciousness.[108]

Now willing, the object of the inner sense, "has many degrees from the mildest wish to passion."[109] Thus, willing is disguised under various modifications and degrees. The essential element is difficult to discern, but among all manifestations of willing are "all desiring, striving, wishing, demanding, longing, hoping, loving, rejoicing, exalting, and the like, no less than

---

[106] *Grunde*, §41, V, S.157; *Reason*, §41, p.208.

[107] *Ibid.*, §42, S.160; *Ibid.*, §42, p.211.

[108] *Freiheit*, I., VI, S.50-51. "Wie dem auch sei, so ist unsere nächste Frage: was enthält nun das Selbstbewußtseyn? oder: wie wird der Mensch sich seines eigenes Selbsts unmittelbar bewußt? Antwort: durchaus als eines *Wollenden*. Jeder wird, bei Beobachtung des eigenen Selbstbewußtseyns bald gewahr werden, daß sein Gegenstand allezeit das eigene Wollen ist."; *Freedom*, I., pp.10-11.

[109] *Grunde*, §42, V, S. 160; *Reason*, §42, p.211.

not willing or resisting, abhorring, fleeing, fearing, being angry, hating, lamenting, suffering pains--in short, all emotional states and passions."[110] Consequently, according to Schopenhauer, "willing" includes not only all emotional states (*Affekte*) but even movements of our inner nature (*Bewegungen unsers Innern*), subsumed under the wide concept of feeling (*Gefühl*).[111]

Feelings of pleasure (*Lust*) and displeasure (*Unlust*) in their various degrees are likewise subsumed under the aforementioned concept. Schopenhauer underscores that they can be traced back to the affections of desiring or abhorring, thus "to the will itself becoming conscious of itself as satisfied, or unsatisfied, restrained or unleashed."[112] Pleasant and unpleasant sensations (*Empfindungen*) enter directly into the self-consciousness as "something which is in conformity with the will (*ein dem Willen Gemäßes*) or as something disagreeable to it (*ihm Widerwärtiges*)."[113]

What the above entails is that there be some type of a fusion between the subject of willing and the subject of knowing because otherwise it cannot be said that it is I who am experiencing the various affectations of the will. Schopenhauer notes, therefore, that there is a mysterious identity between the subject of willing and the subject of knowing so much so, in fact, that the word "I" includes both.[114] He describes this as "the

---

[110] *Freiheit*, I., VI, S.51; *Freedom*, I., p. 11.

[111] *Grunde*, §42, V, S.160; *Reason*, §42, p.211.

[112] *Freiheit*, I., VI, S.51; *Freedom*, I., pp.11-12.

[113] *Ibid.*, S.51-52; *Ibid.*, p.12.

[114] *Grunde*, §42, V, S.160; *Reason*, §42, p.211.

miracle *par excellence*" noting that this inexplicable identity is the "knot of the world" (*Weltknoten*).[115]

As shall been seen below as the argumentation of this study proceeds, Schopenhauer maintains that the clue to the in-itselfness of the world lies here. But for our immediate purposes, this identification illustrates why actions of animals and human beings are evoked by perceptual representations which affect the inner core that they are as subjects of willing. Accordingly, Schopenhauer states that "all those movements of the will, that alternating wanting and not wanting -- which in its continual ebbing and flowing constitutes the sole object of self-consciousness or, if one prefers, of the inner sense -- stand in a universal and generally acknowledged relation to that which is perceived (*Wahrgenommenen*) and known (*Erkannten*) in the external world.[116]

G. Law of Causality and the phenomenon

1. Causality as change

When Schopenhauer alludes to "real" objects, he means representations of the *first* class. He is categorically clear in this regard as the following passage from *Über die vierfache Wurzel des Satzes vom zureichenden Grunde* indicates: "...when I in the course of the essay make use of the expression *real objects* (*reale Objekte*) for the sake of brevity and easier comprehensibility, nothing other is to be understood than just the reality of perceptual, empirical

---

[115] *Ibid.*; *Ibid.*

[116] *Freiheit*, I., VI, S.52; *Freedom*, I., p.12.

representations, in themselves always remaining ideal, which are connected together as a complex."[117]

The law of causality, therefore, applies to all real objects of the external world without exception.[118] It appears as 'the principle of sufficient reason of becoming' in that it concerns the appearance and disappearance of states of objects as given in experience.[119] Though it may be applied to every single empirical perception without exception, it cannot be applied to the world as a whole.[120]

The law of causality, accordingly, in Schopenhauer's *Weltanschauung* is reduced to efficient causality as operative in material objects. So as to avoid confusion, Schopenhauer states: "...it is of the highest importance that one have perfectly clear and fixed ideas about the true and real meaning of the law of causality, about the range of its value, and therefore clearly realize above all things, that it solely and

---

[117] *Grunde*, §19, V, S.48-49. "Anmerk. Ich bemerke bei Gelegenheit der Haupterörterung dieses Paragraphen, daß, wenn ich, im Fortgange der Abhandlung, mich, der Kürze und leichtern Faßlichkeit halber, des Ausdrucks *reale Objekte* bedienen werde, darunter nichts Anderes zu verstehen ist, als eben die anschaulichen, zum Komplex der an sich selbst stets ideal bleibenden empirischen Realität verknüpften Vorstellungen."; *Reason*, §19, p.52.

[118] *Freiheit*, III., VI, S.66. "Das Gesetz der Kausalität steht a *priori* fest, als die allgemeine Regel, welcher alle reale Objekte der Aussenwelt ohne Ausnahme unterworfen sind. Diese Ausnahmslosigkeit verdankt es eben seiner Apriorität."; *Freedom*, III., p.28.

[119] *Grunde*, §20, V, S.49. "In der nunmehr dargestellten Klasse der Objekte für das Subjekt, tritt der Satz vom zureichenden Grunde auf als *Gesetz der Kausalität*, und ich nenne ihn als solches den *Satz vom zureichenden Grunde des Werdens*, *principium rationis sufficientis fiendi*. Alle in der Gesammtverstellung, welche den Komplex der erfahrungsmässigen Realität ausmacht, sich darstellenden Objekte sind, hinsichtlich des Laufes der Zeit, durch ihn mit einander verknüpft."; *Reason*, §20, pp.52-53.

[120] *Vorstellung II*, Kap.4, III, S.56. "Ueberhaupt also findet das Gesetz der Kausalität auf alle Dinge in der Welt Anwendung, jedoch nicht auf die Welt selbst: denn es ist der Welt *immanent*, nicht transscendent: *mit ihr* ist es gesetzt und *mit ihr* aufgehoben. Dies liegt zuletzt daran, dass es zur blossen Form unsers Verstandes gehört und, mit sammt der objektiven Welt, die deshalb bloße Erscheinung ist, durch ihn bedingt ist"; *Representation*, II, ch.4, p.43.

exclusively refers to *changes* (*Veränderungen*) of material states and absolutely to nothing else whatsoever."[121] The very same law applies, for example, to the actions of human beings as it does for the impact of stones, but always only in relation to events or changes.[122]

Regarding causality in this manner illustrates why Schopenhauer believes that all objects which "present themselves in the complete representation (*Gesammtvorstellung*) which constitutes the complex of empirical reality, as regards the appearance and disappearance of their states and hence in the direction of the current of time, are connected with each other through the law of causality."[123] Thus, if a new state of one or several objects appears, another state will have necessarily preceded it from which the new state follows in a regular, ordered relationship.

2. Necessity and the law of causality

In *Über die Freiheit des menschlichen Willens* Schopenhauer distinguishes among three types of necessity: physical, logical, and mathematical.[124] Moral necessity is also mentioned in *Über die vierfache*

---

[121] *Grunde*, §20, V, S.51; *Reason*, §20, pp. 55-56.

[122] *Vorstellung II*, Kap.4, III, S.56. "...es gilt vom Thun des Menschen, wie vom Stoße des Steines; jedoch...immer nur in Bezug auf Vorgänge, auf Veränderungen."; *Representation*, II, ch.4, p.43.

[123] *Grunde*, §20, V, S.49; *Reason*, §20, p.53.

[124] *Freiheit*, I., VI, S. 47. "Je nachdem nun dieser zureichende Grund ein logischer, oder ein mathematischer, oder ein physischer, genannt Ursache, ist, word die *Nothwendigkeit* eine logische (wie die der Konklusion, wenn die Prämissen gegeben sind), eine mathematische (z.B. die Gleichheit der Seiten des Dreiecks, wenn die Winkel gleich sind), oder eine physische, reale (wie der Eintritt der Wirkung, sobald die Ursache daist) seyn: immer aber hängt sie, mit gleicher Strenge, der Folge an, wenn der Grund gegeben ist."; *Freedom*, I., p.7.

Wurzel des Satzes vom zureichenden Satzes.[125] Since Schopenhauer maintains that there is a mysterious fusion between the subject of knowing and that of willing, moral necessity can really be considered as a category that fits under physical necessity. For all existents that are governed by motivation are likewise given in space and time as empirical representations.

The "necessary" is "that which follows from a given sufficient ground."[126] Accordingly, an absence of necessity would be identical with the absence of a determining sufficient ground. Since all real objects are bound together in their relations by causality understood as change in the state of objects, they too are bound by necessity without exception. There is nothing accidental in Schopenhauer's world picture.

The "accidental" (*das Zufällige*) as the opposite of that which is necessary (*das Nothwendige*), "is only relatively so (*nur relativ ein solches*)."[127] Schopenhauer states this because "in the real world where the accidental is encountered, every occurence (*Begebenheit*) is necessary in relation to its cause."[128] This can be said even though in relation to other events which are contemporaneous and spatially contiguous with it, an event may be said to be accidental.[129]

An event or occurence with no ground or reason is an impossibility in Schopenhauer's *Weltanschauung*. If

---

[125] *Grunde*, §49, V, S. 171; *Reason*, §49, p.49. Moral necessity asserts that once a motive presents itself, one necessarily does an action in accordance with the character that is inborn and immutable.

[126] *Freiheit*, I., VI, S.47; *Freedom*, I., p.7.

[127] *Ibid.*, S. 48; *Ibid.*, pp.7-8.

[128] *Ibid.*; *Ibid.*, p.8.

[129] *Ibid.*; *Ibid.*

it could be conjectured that freedom (considered as the absence of necessity per se) existed, then it could be referred to as the "absolutely accidental" -- an admittedly problematic concept for him.[130] Applied to the thorny issue of the freedom of the will, this would mean that in the case of a "free act", there would not be a determining ground. Given Schopenhauer's earlier claims, however, this would contradict his notion of a universe in which phenomena are bound by strict necessity. For in this case, at least, there would be something (i.e. a "free act") that seemingly would not have a determining or sufficient ground.

The necessity that binds all phenomena together guarantees that a certain order or teleology manifest itself at all times. For Schopenhauer observes: "What would happen to this world if necessity did not penetrate and hold all things together, but especially govern the procreation of individuals? -- A monster, a rubbish heap (*Schutthaufen*), a caricature (*Fratze*) without sense or meaning, that is to say, the work of true and real chance."[131] In short, a rationality permeates every phenomenon that presents itself as representation to the knower.

3. Causality and the "Prime Mover"

It goes without saying that in such a conception of causality, the notion of a First Cause or

---

[130] *Ibid.* "Nun müßte aber das Freie, da Abwesenheit der Nothwendigkeit sein Merkmal ist, das schlechthin von gar keiner Ursache Abhängige seyn, mithin definirt werden als das *absolut Zufällige*: ein höchst problematischer Begriff, dessen Denkbarkeit ich nicht verbürge, der jedoch sonderbarer Weise mit dem der *Freiheit* zusammentrifft."; *Ibid.*

[131] *Ibid.*, III., S.100.; *Ibid.*, III., p.63.

Prime Mover is impossible. For, strictly speaking, no given object can ever be regarded as a cause of another.[132] Causes do not concern the bringing of something else into existence. Rather, they pertain to changes in the form of indestructible matter.[133]

For Schopenhauer the law of causality is *a priori* and transcendental in that it is known independently of experience, but applies universally to each object of experience. It states that given a "relatively" first state of matter, a second equally definite state must follow. Accordingly, because every cause is a change, we are necessarily bound to ask about the change that preceded it ad infinitum:

> The law of causality is...not so obliging as to allow itself to be used like a cab which we dismiss after we arrive at our destination. On the contrary, it is like the broom that is brought to life by Goethe's apprentice magician which, once set in motion, neither stops running nor fetching water, so that only the old wizard himself can bring it to rest.[134]

Looking at causality in this manner has, of course, serious implications in the thorny issue as to whether or not one can prove God's existence. In the immediately preceding section the inherent poverty of the concept to describe even representations of perception was underscored. This of course highlights the inadequacy of

---

[132] *Grunde*, §20, V, S. 51. "Es hat aber gar keinen Sinn zu sagen, ein Objekt sei Ursache eines andern; zunächst, weil die Objekte nicht bloß die Form und Qualität, sondern auch die *Materie* enthalten, diese aber weder entsteht, noch vergeht; und sodann, weil das Gesetz der Kausalität sich ausschließlich auf *Veränderungen*, d.h. auf den Ein- und Austritt der Zustände in der Zeit bezieht..."; *Reason*, §20, p.55.

[133] *Ibid.*, S.51-52. "...während doch, bei der Kausalität, es sich offenbar nur um Formveränderungen der unentstandenen und unzerstörbaren Materie handelt und ein eigentliches Entstehn, eine Ins-Daseyn-treten des vorher gar nicht Gewesenen, eine Unmöglichkeit ist."; *Ibid.*, p. 56.

[134] *Ibid.*, S.53; *Ibid.*, pp. 58-59.

the concept to describe God who is not an empirical representation. Given Schopenhauer's understanding of causality, the God question does not pertain in anyway whatsoever to the world of perceptual representations. But this issue will be treated subsequently in Chapter Six which pertains specifically to religion and the problem of Sacred or Holy.

4. Forms of Causality

Schopenhauer divides all empirical representations into three classes: inorganic phenomena, unconscious organic phenomena and conscious phenomena (where the representation as such arises). In each of these types of phenomena, the law of causality takes on a specific form marked with equal necessity. I now turn to each level respectively. This distinction made by Schopenhauer is important because it corresponds to basic levels of the will's objectification, which shall be considered in the next two chapters of this study.

4a. Cause in its most narrow sense (*Ursache*)

A cause in its narrowest sense can be defined as "that by virtue of which all mechanical, physical and chemical changes in objects of experience take place."[135] In *Die Welt als Wille und Vorstellung* Schopenhauer states: "I call *cause* in the narrowest sense of the word that state of matter which, while it brings about another state with necessity, itself suffers a change just as great as that which it causes."[136]

---

[135] *Freiheit*, III., VI, S.68; *Freedom*, III., p.30.

[136] *Vorstellung I*, §23, I, S.160; *Representation*, I, §23, p.115.

Schopenhauer underscores that two of Newton's laws are involved in changes that transpire in inorganic phenomena. In the first place, Newton's third law ('action and reaction are equal to each other') holds true because the antecedent state (the cause) undergoes the same change as the state which follows which is called the effect.[137] Secondly, in light of Newton's second law (the degree of the effect corresponds exactly to the degree of the cause), effects increase in exact proportion to the cause.[138] Thus, when the type of effect is known, the degree of the effect can be immediately known from the intensity of the degree of the cause.

4b. Cause as stimulus (Reiz)

The stimulus is the type of cause which determines all changes of organic life. Thus, the changes and developments of plants and the vegetative, unconscious part of animal life involve this type of causality.[139] The stimulus is unlike the cause as narrowly understood in that the distinctive signs that mark causality in inorganic phenomena are absent.

With the stimulus there is no proportionality between the cause and the effect. That is to say, action and reaction are in the case of the stimulus not equal to each other and there is no uniformity between its

---

[137] *Freiheit*, III., VI, S.68; *Freedom*, III., p.30. See also *Vorstellung I*, §23, I, S.160 (*Representation*, I, §23, p.115); *Grunde*, §20, V, S.62 (*Reason*, §20, p.70).

[138] *Ibid*.

[139] *Grunde*, §20, V, S.62; *Reason*, §20, p.70.

intensity and the intensity of its effect.[140] Schopenhauer gives two examples to illustrate what he means. He notes that the growth of plants can be hastened by heat, but too much heat may very well kill the plant. Similarly, he observes that wine and opium can enhance mental capacity, but too much of one or both has the exact opposite result.[141]

4c. Cause as motive (*Motiv*)

The third type of causality is proper to all animal life as such, including man and thereby warrants closer attention and a lengthier treatment. The "motive" is the type of causality which "directs true animal life, hence *action* (*Thun*), that is to say, the external actions of all animals which happen with consciousness."[142] Because the medium of motives is knowledge (*Erkenntniß*), susceptibility (*Empfänglichkeit*) to motives requires an intellect.[143] Knowledge broadly understood, as was seen above in the section on the understanding, is equated with the capacity to have empirically-given representations -- something which Schopenhauer maintains is characteristic of all animal life regardless as to whether it may be endowed with reason or not.

Specifically speaking, what happens with motives is that once they enter the consciousness (given the susceptibility of that which perceives), an action ensues as a result of the representation that has just

---

[140] *Freiheit*, III., VI, S.69; *Freedom*, III., p.31.

[141] *Ibid.*, S.69-70; *Ibid.*, p.31.

[142] *Grunde*, §20, V, S.62; *Reason*, §20, p.70.

[143] *Ibid.*; *Ibid.*, p.70-71.

flashed across the screen of the brain. Consequently, a 'motive' needs only to be perceived in order to operate, an important fact which differentiates it completely from the 'stimulus' which requires contact.[144]

Schopenhauer maintains that the difference between cause, stimulus and motive "is obviously merely the consequence of the level of susceptibility (*Empfänglichkeit*) of beings..."[145] This difference in susceptibility is most evident in the fact that often human beings do actions as a result of a mere glance, whereas inanimate stones have to be kicked. This notwithstanding, in both cases, sufficient causes prompt movement and do so with necessity.[146]

In short, motives operate with necessity in both animals and man. This necessity might indeed be easier to observe in animals whose brain is capable only of perceptual representations. With man it is more difficult because of his more specialized double intellect (*Verstand/Vernunft*) which renders him independent of his perceptual surroundings and enables him to balance motive against counter-motive.[147] But

---

[144] *Ibid.*, S.62-63. "Die Wirkungsart eines Motivs aber ist von der eines Reizes augenfällig verschieden: die Einwirkung desselben nämlich kann sehr kurz, ja sie braucht nur momentan zu seyn: denn ihre Wirksamkeit hat nicht, wie die des Reizes, irgend ein Verhältniß zu ihrer Dauer, zur Nähe des Gegenstandes und dergleichen mehr; sondern das Motiv braucht nur wahrgenommen zu seyn, um zu wirken..."; *Ibid.*,p.71.

[145] *Ibid.*, S.63. "Der Unterschied zwischen Ursache, Reiz und Motiv ist offenbar bloß die Folge des Grades der *Empfänglichkeit* der Wesen: je größer diese, desto leichterer Art kann die Einwirkung seyn..."; *Ibid.*

[146] *Ibid.*; *Ibid.*

[147] *Ibid.* "Der Intellekt des Menschen ist doppelt: er hat, zur anschaulichen, auch noch die abstrakte Erkenntniß, welche nicht an die Gegenwart gebunden ist: d.h. er hat Vernunft. Daher hat er eine Wahlentscheidung, mit deutlichem Bewußtseyn: nämlich er kann die einander ausschließenden Motive als solche gegen einander abwägen..." ; *Ibid.* See also *Natur*, "Pflanzen-Physiologie," V, S.274: "...beim Menschen, wo sich die Vorstellung sogar zum Begriffe gesteigert hat und nun eine ganze unsichtbare Gedankenwelt, die er im

Schopenhauer contends that notwithstanding the relative elective choice that man has, in the end, "the stronger motive decides (*bestimmt*) him and his action ensues with necessity just as the rolling of a ball which has been struck."[148]

H. Transcendental Conditions for Causality

Before completing this chapter, there remains one more matter that needs to be examined so as to complete this analysis of the world as representation and set the stage for a treatment of the world as will. Since no cause operates in a vacuum, Schopenhauer asserts that some presupposed givens exist which can be referred to as the transcendental conditions of causality as such. Early in his treatment of causality in *Über die vierfache Wurzel des Satzes vom zureichenden Grunde* Schopenhauer states that matter (*Materie*) and the original forces of nature (*Naturkräfte*) stand outside the causal nexus. Matter remains untouched because it is the "*bearer* of all changes, or that by which such changes happen."[149] The forces of nature are likewise excluded from all change in that it is by virtue of their being presupposed that all causes work (*vermöge welcher alle Ursachen wirken*).[150] In light of this fact, for Schopenhauer the natural forces "are outside all time and precisely for that reason... exist always and everywhere, omnipresent and

---

Kopf herumträgt, Motive und Gegenmotive für sein Thun liefert und ihn von der Gegenwart und anschaulichen Umgebung unabhängig macht, da ist jener Zusammenhang für die Beobachtung von außen gar nicht mehr, und selbst für die innere nur durch abstraktes und reifes Nachdenken erkennbar."

[148] *Grunde*, §20, V, S.63; *Reason*, §20, p.72.

[149] *Ibid.*, S.60; *Ibid.*, p.67.

[150] *Ibid.*; *Ibid.*, p.68.

eternal, always ready to manifest themselves as soon as the opportunity to do so occurs at the guidance of causality (*am Leitfaden der Kausalität*)."[151] Accordingly, both matter and the natural forces may be considered to be givens.

Schopenhauer nuances the above in *Über die Freiheit des menschlichen Willens*. He contends that every cause in the world that brings about its effect never occurs in a vacuum. So something is always presupposed. Thus, there is a correspondence between the cause as such and the nature of the particular being which has within itself the power that makes it susceptible for the evoking of an effect.[152] Consequently, all effects originate from two factors, an inner one as the above implies and an outer one. In this regard, Schopenhauer states that "every causality and every explanation from it presupposes original force (*ursprüngliche Kraft*); for this reason precisely, the explanation never explains everything, but there always remains something inexplicable (*ein Unerklärliches übrig läßt*)."[153]

With regard to inorganic phenomena, all explanations presuppose natural forces which manifest themselves in phenomena.[154] The natural force, as was

---

[151] *Ibid.*; *Ibid.*

[152] *Freiheit*, III., VI, S.85. "Jetzt aber wollen wir uns auch daran erinnern, was überhaupt eine *Ursache* ist: die vorhergehende Veränderung, welche die nachfolgende nothwendig macht. Keineswegs bringt irgend eine Ursache in der Welt ihre Wirkung ganz und gar hervor, oder macht sie aus nichts. Vielmehr ist allemal etwas da, worauf sie wirkt, und sie veranlaßt bloß zu dieser Zeit, an diesem Ort und an diesem bestimmten Wesen eine Veränderung, welche stets der Natur des Wesens gemäß ist, zu der also die *Kraft* bereits in diesem Wesen liegen mußte."; *Freedom*, III., p.47

[153] *Ibid.*; *Ibid.*, p.48.

[154] *Ibid.*; *Ibid.*

stated initially, is beyond explanation in that it stands beyond the causal nexus. This notwithstanding, it serves as the principle of explanation in inorganic phenomena, and is referred to as the "common substratum" (*gemeinsame Unterlage*) that is present in every effect that takes place within the inorganic sphere of the phenomenon.[155] As such, the natural force is that which endows causes with efficacy regardless as to how often the times of its appearance may be.[156]

Thus, Schopenhauer mentions that phenomena of magnetism are traced back to the original force of electricity. Heavenly bodies presuppose gravitation as a force by virtue of which particular causes operate so as to determine the course of bodies. Chemistry likewise presupposes the secret forces which manifest themselves when reactions between chemicals take place. Mechanics, concerned as it is with thrust and pressure, presupposes its natural forces. The same is true with regard to explanations of physiology which presuppose the life force (*Lebenskraft*) which reacts in a definite way to inner and outer stimuli.[157]

Moving on to the special causality that motivation is, the same consistent pattern holds true. "Here too the cause calls forth only the manifestation of a force which cannot be traced back to further causes, and consequently cannot be further explained."[158] In this case, the force is called "will" (*Wille*). Unlike

---

[155] *Ibid.*; *Ibid.*

[156] *Vorstellung I*, §26, I, S.179. "Denn Das eben, was einer Ursache, so unzählige Male sie eintreten mag, immer die Wirksamkeit verleiht, ist eine Naturkraft..."; *Representation*, I, §26, p.131.

[157] *Freiheit*, III., VI, S.86; *Freedom*, III., pp.48-49.

[158] *Ibid.*; *Ibid.*, p.49.

the natural forces which are known merely from "the outside", the will is immediately known from "within" by virtue of the self-consciousness.[159] Only given the presupposition that such a will exists and that it is of a determined nature, do causes (motives) which are directed to it work.[160]

The special and individually determined nature of the will that is presupposed in actions of conscious beings having an animal body is called the "character" by Schopenhauer. Since it is not known *a priori*, but manifests itself only in experience, it is more properly referred to as the "empirical character". Because the same motives affect people differently, with human beings the character is individual whereas in animals the preponderance of the species character abounds.[161] Like the natural forces it too is groundless and inexplicable.[162]

I. Summary

Having discussed the transcendental conditions that unlock the wheels of causality in Schopenhauer's

---

[159] *Ibid.*; *Ibid.*

[160] *Ibid.* "Nur unter der Voraussetzung, daß ein solcher Wille vorhanden und, im einzelnen Fall, daß er von bestimmter Beschaffenheit sei, wirken die auf ihn gerichteten Ursachen, hier Motive gennant."; *Ibid.*

[161] *Ibid.*; *Ibid.*

[162] *Vorstellung I*, §24, I, S.171. "Denn in jedem Ding in der Natur ist etwas, davon kein Grund je angegeben werden kann, keine Erklärung möglich, keine Ursache weiter zu suchen ist: es ist die specifische Art seines Wirkens, d.h. eben die Art seines Daseyns, sein Wesen...Was dem Menschen sein unergründlicher, bei aller Erklärung seiner Thaten aus Motiven vorausgesetzter Charakter ist; eben das ist jedem unorganischen Körper seine wesentliche Qualität, die Art seines Wirkens, deren Aeußerungen hervorgerufen werden durch Einwirkung von außen, während hingegen sie selbst durch nichts außer ihr bestimmt, also auch nicht erklärlich ist: ihre einzelnen Erscheinungen, durch welche allein sie sichtbar wird, sind dem Satz vom Grund unterworfen: sie selbst ist grundlos."; *Representation*, I, §24, p.124.

Weltanschauung, the central components that comprise the representational character of the world have been given an overview sufficient for the purposes of this study. The stage is now set for an analysis of what Schopenhauer means by the world as will. As shall be seen subsequently, the inner content of the empirically-given perceptions of our consciousness cannot be gleaned by representational knowing mediated by the principle of sufficient reason. Given the limitations of representational knowledge, it can only glean the surface of reality and never pierce the very essence of things. Schopenhauer contends that the inner content of any empirically-given representation comes from another unique and distinct knowledge which comes from within. The following chapter is an analysis of this highly important claim.

Chapter 2

The World as Will

A. Schopenhauer's Understanding of Will

1. Rationale for knowledge from within

Kant, in his emphasizing the phenomena-noumena distinction, had denied the possibility of knowing things-in-themselves.[163] Only phenomena can be known: that is, objects as they *appear* to the subject. Schopenhauer, however, opened up the possibility for another type of knowledge which comes from within, a knowledge which manifests itself in all acts of volition whatever form they might take. I ask the reader to recall the *fourth* type of representation as discussed in chapter one of this study before proceeding further.

It was noted above that the whole consciousness is comprised of two parts: consciousness of other things in which the cognitive faculty (*das Erkenntnißvermögen*) is involved [in man consisting of sensibility, understanding, and reason]; and the Self-consciousness or

---

[163] Immanuel Kant, *Critique of Pure Reason*, A258=B314: "When...we say that the senses represent objects *as they appear*, and the understanding objects *as they are*, the latter statement is to be taken, not in the transcendental, but in the purely empirical meaning of the terms, namely as meaning that the objects must be represented as objects of experience, that is, as appearances in thoroughgoing interconnection with one another, and not as they may be apart from their relation to possible experience (and consequently to any of the senses), as objects of the pure understanding. Such objects of the pure understanding will always remain unknown to us; we can never even know whether such a transcendental or exceptional knowledge is possible under any conditions--at least not if it is to be the same kind of knowledge as that which stands under our ordinary categories."

inner sense, which may be said to have but one object, the subject of willing. It was also underscored that because the subject of willing is known only by the inner sense, solely the form of time applies here. In this respect, we know ourselves as willers through successive states of time via the path of interiorization or introspection. This knowledge, which is direct and immediate, is totally unlike external knowing which involves the "seeing" of perceptual objects in both space and time. The self-consciousness, accordingly, is that other portion of the whole consciousness that places one in contact with the unique representation that the subject of willing is. Schopenhauer also states that the concept of *will* is *sui generis* in that it is the only one whose origin is not in the phenomenon (*Erscheinung*):

> ...the concept of *will* is of all possible concepts the only one that has its origin *not* in the phenomenon (*Erscheinung*), not in the mere perceptual (*anschaulicher*) representation, but rather comes from within (*aus dem Innern*); it proceeds from the most immediate consciousness of everyone in which each one knows his own individuality, according to its essence, immediately, without any form, even without that of subject and object; for here that which knows and that which is known coincide (*zusammenfallen*).[164]

It is important to underscore once again that "willing" for Schopenhauer includes all emotional states and all movements of our inner nature -- anything that can be subsumed under the very wide concept of feeling. Willing can have many degrees, therefore, from the mildest wish to most passionate desire. It refers to any desire or striving, to rejoicing, to lamenting, to loving and hating, etc. It is obvious, therefore, that by willing Schopenhauer is not merely referring to deliberate acts

---

[164] *Vorstellung I*, §22, I, S.157; *Representation*, I, §22, p.112.

of will and formal decisions that are immediately put into effect as a result thereof.[165] He makes a distinction between a voluntary act (*Willkür*) and will (*Wille*) in order to underscore that the will can exist independently of knowledge.[166] The significance of this claim is to be explained later when his equating will with the noumenon is discussed.

However, his rationale for distinguishing between ordinary representational knowing (whereby perceptions in space and time are given) and the aforementioned more immediate knowledge, is to highlight the limitation of the former when it comes to knowing the underlying significance of reality. Is the world more than a mere conglomerate of perceptual representations that flashes across the mental screen of consciousness, which would in that case make it seem like an "empty dream or a ghostlike vision"?[167] What can it be then? Schopenhauer is convinced that its fundamental nature must be fundamentally different from that of the mere empirically-given representation:

> This is just as much certain, that this about which we are enquiring must be something completely and in its whole essence fundamentally different (*nach Grundverschiedenes*) from the representation; for this reason, the forms and laws of the

---

[165] *Freiheit*, I., VI, S.51. "Jeder wird, bei Beobachtung des eigenen Selbstbewußtseyn bald gewahr werden, daß sein Gegenstand allezeit das eigene Wollen ist. Hierunter hat man aber freilich nicht bloß die entschiedenen, sofort zur That werdenden Willensakte und die förmlichen Entschlüsse, nebst den aus ihnen hervorgehenden Handlungen zu verstehn."; *Freedom*, I., p.11.

[166] *Natur*, "Physiologie und Pathologie," V, S.221. "Vor allen Dingen aber muß man Wille von Willkür zu unterscheiden wissen und einsehn, daß jener ohne diese bestehn kann; was freilich meine ganze Philosphie voraussetzt. Willkür heißt der Wille da, wo ihn Erkenntniß beleuchtet, und daher Motive, also Vorstellungen, die ihn bewegenden Ursachen sind: Dies heißt, objektiv ausgedrückt, wo die Einwirkung von außen, welche den Akt verursacht, durch ein *Gehirn*, vermittelt ist."; *Nature*, "Physiology and Pathology," p.238.

[167] *Vorstellung I*, §17, I, S.141; *Representation*, I, §17, pp.98-99.

> representation must be wholly foreign to it. One cannot, therefore, reach it from the representation under the guidance of those laws that merely combine objects, representations, with one another, which are the forms of the principle of sufficient reason.[168]

Accordingly, the inner nature or content of perceptual representations cannot be had "from without" (*von außen*). However splendid the panorama of those representations might be, all efforts to glean the essence of the real from a thorough investigation of them using knowledge mediated by the principle of sufficient reason are doomed to frustration. The external route of normal day-to-day knowing leads only to "images and names (*Bilder und Namen*)."[169] Thus, Schopenhauer lays the ground for an investigation of that inner nature via a different path: from the self-consciousness whose object is the subject of willing. Since the form of time only applies in this case, such "knowledge" differs from normal representational knowing concerned with objects in space and time.

2. The knower as individual

There seems to be something within the spirit of man that orients him towards that which he perceives. The question at the very outset (as was implied directly above) is whether something that is merely a representation, or a series of images and names, can engross or captivate the human being who beholds it. In this respect, Schopenhauer is correct in focusing his attention on the "perceptual representation"

---

[168] *Ibid.*, S. 141-142; *Ibid.*

[169] *Ibid.*, S.142; *Ibid.*

(*anschauliche Vorstellung*), and endeavoring to arrive at a knowledge of its "content" (*Inhalt*) and its "more precise determinations" (*näheren Bestimmungen*) and "forms" (*Gestalten*), so as to see whether the merely "felt significance" (*gefühlte Bedeutung*) of the images that so captive us, might not indeed be more than just that.[170]

Schopenhauer then goes on to say that the clue to these questions is linked to man's corporeality: "...the meaning of the world...that stands before me simply as my representation, or the transition from it as the mere representation of the knowing subject to whatever it may yet be besides this, could never be found if the investigator himself were nothing more than the purely knowing subject (a winged cherub without a body)."[171] One finds, or discovers, soon enough that one's own body is unlike other bodies given in cognitive perception. Schopenhauer surmises that if it could hypothetically be imagined that one were simply a "pure knowing subject", then one's particular body could be considered akin to other representations and known in the same way.[172]

But such is not the case. One's own body has an entirely different character, an immediacy as it were, that other "bodies" given in space and time do not have. In this respect, Schopenhauer believes that the clue to the inner significance of the external perception that

---

[170] *Ibid.*, S. 137; *Ibid.*, p.95.

[171] *Ibid.*, S.142; *Ibid.*, p.99.

[172] *Ibid.* "Dieser Leib ist dem rein erkennenden Subjekt als solchem eine Vorstellung wie die andere, ein Objekt unter Objekten: die Bewegungen, die Aktionen desselben sind ihm insoweit nicht anders, als wie die Veränderungen aller andern anschaulichen Objekte bekannt, und wären ihm eben so fremd und unverständlich, wenn die Bedeutung derselben ihm nicht etwan auf eine ganz andere Art enträthselt wäre."; *Ibid.*

the body is, as representation of the cognitive faculty, can be gleaned. This is due to the knower's condition of being flesh and bone. Thus, he "finds himself rooted in this world as *individual*", which is to say simply, that his knowing is nevertheless mediated through a body whose affections are the very point of departure for the perception (*Anschauung*) of this world.[173]

Once again, since knowing from without is disqualified as being inherently incapable of revealing the inner content and significance of perceptual representations in general and one's own self in particular, the only other path possible to man that might successfully offer him a clue is from within, the avenue whereby human beings know themselves individually as no one else can. Thus, Schopenhauer categorically states that at least as far as one's own corporeality is concerned, its inner significance and content can be attained from within:

> ...the answer to the riddle is given to the subject of knowledge appearing as individual, and this answer is *Will*. This and this alone gives him the key to his own phenomenon; it reveals to him the significance, shows him the inner mechanism (*Getriebe*) of his own being, his actions, [and] his movements.[174]

What the above, therefore, asserts is that in the case of the individuality particular to each of us, the inner content of the complex of representations that we are to our external cognitive faculties, can be known. We are willers through and through; everyone of us without exception.

---

[173] *Ibid.*; *Ibid.*

[174] *Ibid.*; *Ibid.*

3. The act of will and action of the body

Having asserted that willing is the inner nature of the phenomenon that each of us is, and that willing constitutes a different type of knowledge, Schopenhauer next addresses the implications of this insight. As was the case in chapter one with regard to how perceptions are given, the body once again plays a central role. In intelligent perception the body is given as an empirical representation. In self-consciousness the body is given in what is immediately known to everyone: the affections of the will.

What Schopenhauer does next is collapse any real distinction between an act of the will and a movement of the body: "Every true act of [man's] will is also at once and inevitably a movement of his body; he cannot actually will the act without at the same time perceiving that it appears as a movement of the body."[175] He goes on to assert that the act of the will and the action of the body are not two different states connected by the law of causality. Rather, they are one and the same thing given in two different ways. On the one hand, the body is given in perception; on the other, it is given directly in the self-consciousness in states of willing. Given this identity, an action of the body is "nothing but the act of will objectified, i.e. which has become visible in perception."[176]

---

[175] *Ibid.*, §18, S.143; *Ibid.*, §18, p.101.

[176] *Ibid.* "Der Willensakt und die Aktion des Leibes sind nicht zwei objektiv erkannte verschiedene Zustände, die das Band der Kausalität verknüpft, stehn nicht im Verhältniß der Ursache und Wirkung; sondern sie sind Eines und das Selbe, nur auf zwei gänzlich verschiedene Weisen gegeben: ein Mal ganz unmittelbar und ein Mal in der Anschauung für den Verstand. Die Aktion des Leibes ist nichts Anderes, als der objektivirte, d.h. in die Anschauung getretene Akt des Willens."; *Ibid.*

The aforementioned identity is such that all impressions on the body are impressions on the will. Schopenhauer calls an impression that is contrary to the will, pain (*Schmerz*); one that is in accord with it is called gratification (*Wohlbehagen*) or pleasure (*Wollust*).[177] Pain and pleasure are not to be considered as representations. Rather, as "immediate affections of the will in its appearance" which the body is, they can be described as "a forced momentary willing or non-willing of the impression which the body undergoes (*erleidet*)."[178] Schopenhauer would also maintain that the aforementioned identity between an act of willing and an action of the body is approachable via an analysis of the will itself. What he means by this is that agitations of the will always have ramifications on the state of the body. Referring to that very same identity, he writes that "every vehement and excessive movement of the will, that is, every emotion, agitates the body and its inner workings directly and immediately, and disturbs the body and its vital functions."[179] He lists some examples in *Über den Willen in der Natur* that illustrate this well. He states that "the acceleration of the heart in joy and fear, blushing in shame, turning pale in terror and in concealed anger, weeping in affliction, erection with voluptuous representations, difficult breathing and accelerated intestinal activity in great fear, saliva in the mouth at excessive sumptuousity, nausea at the sight of disgusting things" are all

---

[177] *Ibid.*, S.144; *Ibid.*, p.101.

[178] *Ibid.*; *Ibid.*

[179] *Ibid.*, S.144-145; *Ibid.*

indicative of a certain "sympathy" (*Mitleidenschaft*) between the will and body."[180]

Along the same lines, presupposing that identification, the knowledge one has of his or her willing via the path of interiorization, cannot be separated from that of the body. In fact, for Schopenhauer the body is the very condition for the representation of the will known to the inner sense. He states as follows:

> I know my will not as a whole (*im Ganzem*), not as a unity, not perfectly according to its essence, but rather, I know it only in particular acts, thus in time, which is the form of the phenomenon of my body, as [it is] of each body. For this reason, the body is the condition of the knowledge of my will. Accordingly, without my body I cannot, in reality, represent (*vorstellen*) my will.[181]

Schopenhauer goes to the extent of identifying the action of the body with that of the will in order to underscore what it is that underlies or underpins the phenomenal manifestations that each of us are as *individuals*, that is, as persons of flesh and bone who *will*. But he notes that this identification, which is known from within, is not a demonstrable truth -- or something that can be deduced or inferred from the principle of sufficient reason. Why? Because what is involved is the referring of what appears as a representation (the body) to what is not a representation given in both space and time, namely the will.[182]

---

[180] *Natur*, "Physiologie und Pathologie," V, S.227-228; *Nature*, "Physiology and Pathology," pp.246-247.

[181] *Vorstellung I*, §18, I, S.145; *Representation*, 1, §18, pp.101-102.

[182] *Ibid.*, S.145-146. "Die nun vorläufig dargestellte Identität des Willens und des Leibes kann nur...aus dem unmittelbaren Bewußtseyn, aus der Erkenntniß *in concreto*, zum Wissen der Vernunft erhoben, oder in die Erkenntniß *in abstracto* übertragen werden: hingegen kann sie ihrer Natur nach niemals bewiesen, d.h. als

But this notwithstanding, Schopenhauer is convinced of its truth which can be expressed in different ways: "My body and my will are one; or, that which as perceptual representation I call my body, I call my will insofar as I am conscious of it in an entirely different way comparable with no other; or, my body is the *objectivity* of my will; or, irrespective of the fact that my body is my representation, it is still only my will; and so on."[183] In other words, simply said, the will is the being-in-itself (*Wesen an sich*) of each of our own bodies--that which our bodies may be besides being objects of perception or representations.[184]

To sum up, then, our bodies can be seen from a double perspective. As representations appearing in space and time, they manifest themselves to the cognitive faculties as would other perceptual representations. They do have a certain primacy, however, given their more direct character. Though one's body may be a mere representation, nonetheless, it is still one's uniquely

---

mittelbare Erkenntniß aus einer andern unmittelbaren abgeleitet werden, eben weil sie selbst die unmittelbarste ist, und wenn wir sie nicht als solche auffassen und festhalten, werden wir vergebens erwarten, sie irgend mittelbar, als abgeleitete Erkenntniss wiederzuerhalten. Sie ist eine Erkenntniß ganz eigener Art, deren Wahrheit eben deshalb nicht ein Mal eigentlich unter eine der vier Rubriken gebracht werden kann, in welche ich in der Abhandlung über den Satz vom Grund, § 29 ff., alle Warheit getheilt habe, nämlich in logische, empirische, transcendentale und metalogische: denn sie ist nicht, wie alle jene, die Beziehung einer abstrakten Vorstellung auf eine andere Vorstellung, oder auf die nothwendige Form des intuitiven, oder des abstrakten Vorstellung, oder auf das Verhältniß, welches eine anschauliche Vorstellung, der Leib, zu dem hat, was gar nicht Vorstellung ist, sondern ein von *toto genere* Verschiedenes: Wille."; *Ibid.*, p.102.

[183] *Ibid.* S.146; *Ibid.*, pp.102-103.

[184] *Ibid.*, §20, S.150. "Als des eigenen Leibes Wesen an sich, als dasjenige, was dieser Leib ist, außerdem daß er Objekt der Anschauung, Vorstellung ist, giebt, wie gesagt, der *Wille* zunächst sich kund in den willkürlichen Bewegungen dieses Leibes, sofern diese nämlich nichts Anderes sind, als die Sichtbarkeit der einzelnen Willensakte, mit welchen sie unmittelbar und völlig zugleich eintreten, als Ein und das Selbe mit ihnen, nur durch die Form der Erkennenbarkeit, in die sie übergegangen, d.h. Vorstellung geworden sind, von ihnen unterschieden."; *Ibid.*, §20, p.106.

personal representation -- a quality other more indirect representations not only do not have, but cannot have.

On the other hand, we are conscious of our bodies in the acts of willing that are even more so uniquely our own. Taking the path of introspection results in the discovery that we are willing beings through and through. This willing comprises for Schopenhauer the essence in itself of the body -- so much so in fact, that the body is but the representation of the will which is object of the inner sense.

The above being the case, at least as far as one's own personal body is concerned, the inner content of this so-called privileged representation is what the inner sense discovers, namely, willing. This having been said, the stage has been set for an examination of Schopenhauer's contention that the noumenon, hitherto unknowable by the Kantian critique, is in fact the **will**.

B. The Will and the Noumenon

1. Why the word will

By juxtaposing the two types of knowledge possible to man, Schopenhauer not only indicates the limitation of normal cognitive knowing whereby the world appears as a complex of perceptions, but points out the path whereby one might know what the inner content of perceptions comprises, or what things-in-themselves are. Since the way "from without" takes us only so far in this quest, the way "from within" promises better success.

In the section which immediately preceded, it was proposed that the inner content of at least one perception could be known: namely, that of ourselves as corporeal beings endowed with consciousness, as "individuals". Introspection gives us a different perspective of ourselves. We discover that the object of self-consciousness is one of **willing**. Schopenhauer even goes so far as to assert that the representation that our body is to cognitive knowing "from without", is in reality, one of **willing** "from within". It is this willing which Schopenhauer identifies with the thing-in-itself. He states:

> ...I have emphasized that other truth that we are not merely the *knowing subject*, but rather on the other side, *we ourselves* are part of the known thing; *we ourselves are the thing-in-itself*. Consequently, a way *from within* stands open to us to that very specific and inner nature of things to which we cannot penetrate *from* without...The *thing-in-itself* can, precisely as such, come into consciousness only quite directly, namely by this means: that *it itself become conscious of itself*...[185]

The route of introspection, therefore, ushers the knowing subject through a subterranean passage at the very core of the human consciousness in which the in-itselfness or inner content of our reality as corporeal beings endowed with consciousness is discovered: namely, the *will*. In fact, Schopenhauer surmises that where "a knowing consciousness" (*ein erkennenden Bewußtseyn*) is added to that essence (*Wesen*) that lies at the basis of all phenomena, which in its direction inward becomes *self-consciousness*, then that essence exhibits itself to this consciousness as that which is so familiar and mysterious, which is denoted by the word *will*."[186]

Schopenhauer believes that the concept of the *will* alone suffices for the thing-in-itself because of

---

[185] *Vorstellung II*, Kap.18, III, S.228; *Representation*, II, ch.18, p.195.

[186] *Ibid.*, Kap.25, S.372; *Ibid.*, ch.25, p.318.

World as Will

all possible concepts, it is the only one whose origin does not arise from the mere representation of perception, but which comes from within, from the depths of the consciousness of everyone.[187] Thus, the word *will* in Schopenhauer's thought does not represent an unknown quantity, or something arrived at by inferences or syllogisms.[188] Schopenhauer categorically states: "by the word *will* we denote anything but an unknown X; rather, on the contrary, we denote that which, at least from *one* side, is infinitely better known and more intimate than anything else."[189] Accordingly, since the thing-in-itself is not a reality that is merely inferred, or something that is known indirectly and merely in the abstract, an arbitrarily chosen word to stand as a symbol for an unknown quantity will not do.[190] Herein the rationale for the word *will* can be seen.

---

[187] *Vorstellung I*, §22, I, S.157. "...der Begriff *Wille* ist der einzige, unter allen möglichen, welcher seinen Ursprung *nicht* in der Erscheinung, *nicht* in bloßer anschaulicher Vorstellung hat, sondern aus dem Innern kommt, aus dem unmittelbarsten Bewußtseyn eines Jeden hervorgeht, in welchem dieser sein eigenes Individuum, seinem Wesen nach, unmittelbar, ohne alle Form, selbst ohne die von Subjekt und Objekt, erkennt und zugleich selbst ist, da hier das Erkennende und das Erkannte zusammenfallen."; *Representation*, I, §22, p.112.

[188] *Ibid.*, S.156. "Nun aber bezeichnet das Wort *Wille*, welches uns, wie ein Zauberwort, das innerste Wesen jedes Dinges in der Natur aufschließen soll, keineswegs eine unbekannte Größe, ein durch Schlüsse erreichtes Etwas; sondern ein durchaus unmittelbar Erkanntes und so sehr Bekanntes, daß wir, was Wille sei, viel besser wissen und verstehn, als sonst irgend etwas, was immer auch sei.-"; *Ibid.*, p.111.

[189] *Vorstellung II*, Kap.25, III, S.372; *Representation*, I, ch.25, p.318.

[190] *Vorstellung I*, §22, I, S.156. "-Auf die entgegengesetzte Weise würde mich aber der mißverstehn, der etwan meinte, es sei zuletzt einerlei, ob man jenes Wesen an sich aller Erscheinung durch das Wort Wille, oder durch irgend ein anderes bezeichnete. Dies würde der Fall seyn, wenn jenes Ding an sich etwas wäre, auf dessen Existenz wir bloß *in abstracto* erkennten: dann könnte man es allerdings nennen wie man wollte: der Name stände als bloßes Zeichen einer unbekannten Größe da."; *Representation*, I, §22, p.111.

2. Characteristics of the noumenal will

The clue to what Schopenhauer means by the will as noumenon was already given in Chapter One of this study when the question of the *fourth* class of representation was raised. It was stated that the unique character of this particular representation consists in the fact that it is only known via the inner sense in successive states in time. This representation, therefore, does not involve a "seeing" with the eyes of the body since it does not appear in space as do other perceptual representations.

It goes without saying that for Schopenhauer the will as thing-in-itself is not a phenomenon. Accordingly, he states that it "is completely different and entirely free from all forms of the phenomenon into which it first enters when it appears, and which therefore concern only its *objectivity (Objektität)*, and are foreign to the will itself."[191] Along the same lines, what Schopenhauer calls "the most universal form of the phenomenon", that of being object for subject, cannot be predicated of the noumenal will.[192] Anything which has to do with the principle of sufficient reason does not in the least pertain to the noumenal will.

Schopenhauer goes on to introduce a favorite notion of his when speaking of the phenomenal order of things as opposed to that of the noumenal: space and time as "the *principium individuationis*".[193] Because

---

[191] *Ibid.*, §23, S.157; *Ibid.*, §23, p.112.

[192] *Ibid.*; *Ibid.*

[193] *Ibid.* "Schon die allgemeinste Form aller Vorstellung, die des Objekts für ein Subjekt, trifft ihn nicht; noch weniger die dieser untergeordneten, welche insgesammt ihren gemeinschaftlichen Ausdruck im Satz vom Grunde haben, wohin bekanntlich auch Zeit und Raum gehören, und folglich auch die durch diese

the principle of individuation pertains to the perceptual world of plurality in which space, time and causality hold true, the noumenal will presents a stark contrast. Schopenhauer juxtaposes the world of phenomenal particulars where necessity binds all appearances together to the groundlessness of the will. It is succinctly stated that "the will as thing-in-itself...lies outside the sphere of the principle of sufficient reason in all its forms, and is consequently absolutely groundless, although its phenomena in space and time are innumerable."[194]

What the above means in effect is that there is only *one* noumenal will. Notwithstanding a multiplicity of particulars, it is the same will that objectifies itself in each phenomenon. "By virtue of the simplicity which pertains to the will as the thing-in-itself, as the metaphysical in the phenomenon, its *essence* admits of no degree, but it is always entirely itself."[195] There is as much of the will present in any given person as in a small insect, for example.[196]

But it is important to underscore that the will's oneness is not akin to the unity of a concept which originates through its abstraction from a multiplicity of particulars. Nor is it like the oneness of an object whose unity is known in contrast to possible

---

allein bestehende und möglich gewordene Vielheit. In dieser letztern Hinsicht werde ich, mit einem aus der alten eigentlichen Scholastik entlehnten Ausdruck, Zeit und Raum das *principium individuationis* [den Existenzgrund der Einzelwesen] nennen, welches ich ein für alle Mal zu merken bitte."; *Ibid.*

[194] *Ibid.*, S.158; *Ibid.*, p.113.

[195] *Vorstellung II*, Kap.19, III, S.240; *Representation*, II, ch.19, p.206.

[196] *Ibid.* "Selbst im kleinsten Insekt ist der Wille vollkommen und ganz vorhanden: es will was es will, so entschieden und vollkommen wie der Mensch. Der Unterschied liegt bloß in dem was es will, d.h. in den Motiven, welche aber Sache des Intellekts sind."; *Ibid.*

plurality. In a word the will is one simply "as that which lies outside time and space, the *principium individuationis*, i.e. the possibility of plurality."[197]

3. Noumenal will's knowability

Schopenhauer is in agreement with Kant with regard to the limitations of cognitive knowing in that he too admits that mere phenomena as seen "from the outside" can never propel one to the heights of knowing things-in-themselves.[198] In this regard Schopenhauer is interested in ascertaining what the limits of normal cognitive patterns are so that the way might be paved for determining exactly where knowledge attained by introspection can lead. The rationale for the first book of *Die Welt als Wille und Vorstellung* as well as for *Über die vierfache Wurzel des Satzes vom zureichenden Grunde* is precisely to delineate the limits of normal cognitive knowing, but in light of a further end.[199] For the route of introspection ultimately leads to what Schopenhauer in his handwritten notes sometimes calls "the better consciousness" which "raises [him] into a

---

[197] *Vorstellung I*, §23, I, S.158; *Representation*, I, §23, p.113.

[198] *Vorstellung II*, Kap.18, III, S.229. "*Kants* Hauptresultat läßt sich im Wesentlichen so resumiren: »Alle Begriffe, denen nicht eine Anschauung in Raum und Zeit (sinnliche Anschauung) zum Grunde liegt, d.h. also die nicht aus einer solchen Anschauung geschöpt worden, sind schlechterdings leer, d.h. geben keine Erkenntniß. Da nun aber die Anschauung nur *Erscheinungen*, nicht Dinge an sich, liefern kann; so haben wir auch von Dingen an sich gar keine Erkenntniß« -- Ich gebe dies von Allem zu..."; *Representation*, II, ch.18, p.196.

[199] Cf.Rüdiger Safranski, *Schopenhauer und die wilden Jahre der Philosophie* (München: Carl Hanser Verlag, 1987), S.230.

world where neither personality and causality, nor subject and object are given."[200]

While Schopenhauer admits with Kant that phenomenal knowing can only take us so far, he parts with him insofar as he contends that there can indeed be a type of knowledge about the thing-in-itself which is the will. For him, however, the willing that each of us is privy to via the path of introspection, is not a "perception" (*Anschauung*) because all perception is spatial. But in like fashion, "willing" cannot be called "empty". For inasmuch as it comprises what is most intimate in the consciousness of every person, it is "more real" than any other knowledge; this notwithstanding its not being an object as given in space.[201]

Furthermore, since willing is known only via successive acts of time, it cannot be known *a priori*. Strictly *a posteriori*, willing can therefore never be anticipated in the particular case.[202] One's own will is revealed via successive acts of time that take place in experience. Experience, in other words, reveals to

---

[200] Arthur Schopenhauer, *Der handschriftliche Nachlaß*, Band I (*Frühe Manuskripte*), herausgegeben von Arthur Hübscher (München: Deutscher Taschenbuch Verlag), #81, S.42. Henceforth cited as *Nachlaß*. "Ich aber sage: in dieser Zeitlichen, Sinnlichen, Verständlichen Welt...giebt es wohl Persönlichkeit und Kausalität, ja sie sind sogar nothwendig. -- Aber das bessre Bewußtseyn in mir erhebt mich in eine Welt wo es weder Persönlichkeit und Kausalität noch Subjekt und Objekt mehr giebt. Meine Hoffnung und mein Glaube ist daß dieses bessre (übersinnliche außerzeitliche) Bewußtseyn mein einziges werden wird: darum hoffe ich es ist kein Gott."

English translation: Arthur Schopenhauer, *Manuscript Remains*, vol.I (*Early Manuscripts*), edited by Arthur Hübscher and translated by E.F.J. Payne (Oxford: Berg, 1988), #81, p.44. Henceforth cited as *Remains*.

[201] *Vorstellung II*, Kap.18, III, S.229. "...diese [die Erkenntniss des Wollens] ist weder eine Anschauung (denn alle Anschauung ist räumlich) noch ist sie leer; vielmehr ist sie realer, als irgend eine andere."; *Representation*, ch.18, II, p.196.

[202] *Ibid.*; *Ibid.*

the knower who he or she is as a willer. This notwithstanding, "*willing* is the sole opportunity we have to understand from within (*Innern*) any event which manifests itself externally."²⁰³ Willing comprises an "immediate known" (*unmittelbare Bekannte*) which accordingly distinguishes it from all remaining things (*alles Übrige*) that are given as mere representations.²⁰⁴

Though our willing is known to us "immediately", even this claim needs to be qualified. As was stated, willing is manifested *a posteriori* via successive states of time. This means, therefore, that the noumenon which is object of the inner sense can never appear in its pristine form. It is as if man's corporeality and temporality, while paradoxically revealing what the noumenon is, at the same time, irremediably conceal it.

The inner knowledge in question is free from two of the forms belonging to the outer knowledge (space and causality which are involved in sense perception), but is shackled as it were, by time as well as "that of being known (*Erkanntwerdens*) and knowing in general (*Erkennens überhaupt*)."²⁰⁵ This entails that the will can never be known "as a whole" (*im Ganzen*) or "in and for itself" (*an und für sich*).²⁰⁶ Accordingly, notwithstanding all that can actually be attained by inner knowledge, it too is limited. Not even the inner

---

²⁰³ *Ibid.*; *Ibid.*

²⁰⁴ *Ibid.*; *Ibid.*

²⁰⁵ *Ibid.*, S.230; *Ibid.*, p.197.

²⁰⁶ *Ibid.*; *Ibid.*

World as Will

eye can behold the noumenon in its quintessential and pure form.[207]

In light of the thick shroud of mystery that covers the noumenon that the will is, some questions arise at this point. Is it really the noumenon that is being known given the stubborn attachment of the form of time in all cases of inner knowledge?[208] Can it be that knowledge of willing itself is a form of representational knowing since the form of time remains? Is there a proportionality of some type between the willing that manifests itself via successive acts in time and the will itself as outside of time? Schopenhauer was aware of these difficulties as the following indicates:

> ...the question can still be raised what that will, which presents itself in the world and as the world, is ultimately and absolutely in itself; in other words, what it is, quite apart from the fact that it presents itself as *will*, or in general *appears* (*erscheint*) that is to say, *is known* in general. This question can *never* be answered because as was said, being-known (*Erkannt-werden*) itself contradicts being-in-itself (*Ansich-seyn*), and each known (*Erkannte*) is, as such, only phenomenon (*Erscheinung*).[209]

Here again, therefore, but this time from the perspective of the inner sense, the limitation of knowledge is underscored by Schopenhauer. True, he is convinced that willing is the inner content of the phenomenon that each one of us is. But he will not go so far as to assert

---

[207] *Ibid*. "Demnach hat in dieser innern Erkenntniß das Ding an sich seine Schleier zwar großen Theils abgeworfen, tritt aber doch nicht ganz nackt auf."; *Ibid*.

[208] Cf.Harald Höffding, A *History of Modern Philosophy*, vol.2, trans. B.E. Meyer (New York: Dover, 1955), p.226. "How...can the will, which is itself phenomenon, and which we know by the help of ideas, be identical with the thing-in-itself?"

[209] *Vorstellung II*, Kap.18, III, S.231; *Representation*, II, ch.18, p.198.

that the willing that is known by introspection reveals the mysterious noumenon in its naked and pristine form for the eye of the inner sense to behold from within. Quite the contrary, interior reflection even for Schopenhauer can only bring one to the very threshold of a peculiar mystery -- to questions for which there simply are no answers.

C. Will as Kernel of phenomenon

Keep in mind that the noumenal will is one and outside the forms of space and time, and hence outside the causal nexus. The conscious choice to trek the path of introspection makes one privy to the noumenal reality one is as willing through and through. Schopenhauer is convinced that the choice to follow the road of introspection, not only holds the promise of offering one the key to solve the riddle of one's own being, but likewise gives one a clue to what comprises the inner content of the world that presents itself as a complex of perceptual representations. Thus, he states: "...we must learn to understand nature from ourselves, not ourselves from nature."[210] What this in effect entails is an extension of the concept of *will* to all phenomena.[211]

This endeavor of Schopenhauer to comprehend the significance of all phenomena that appear before the knowing consciousness will prove to be highly significant

---

[210] *Ibid.*, S.229; *Ibid.*, p.196.

[211] *Vorstellung I*, §22, I, S.156. "Das uns unmittelbar bekannte innerste Wesen eben dieser Erscheinung müssen wir nun in Gedanken rein aussondern, es dann auf alle schwächeren, undeutlicheren Erscheinungen des selben Wesens übertragen, wodurch wir die verlangte Erweiterung des Begriffs Wille vollziehn."; *Representation*, §22, I, p.111.

for his *Weltanschauung*. For ultimately it explains why an ontological pessimism scars the inner essence of what comprises our real world.[212] Knowledge of the will, therefore, becomes a guiding principle whereby all other phenomenal particulars are understood. Convinced as he is about this kind of knowledge, Schopenhauer writes the following: "it will become the key to the knowledge of the innermost being of the whole of nature inasmuch as he [the reader] now transfers it [referring to the knowledge of the will] to all those phenomena that are given to him... merely in a one-sided way, as *representation* alone."[213]

Schopenhauer continues by underscoring that to the person who has followed the path of introspection and is thus able to perceive the tapestry of the real from the standpoint of the inner eye, the very same will that is encountered as object of the inner sense, can be recognized in phenomena similar to oneself, namely, in other human beings and animals. Further reflection leads to an even more startling conclusion: that the noumenal

---

[212] Cf. Safranski, S.14. "Die 'wilden Jahre der Philosophie' ignorierten diesen Philosophen des 'Heulens und Zähneklapperns' und der uralten Kunst des kontemplativen Lebens, das zur Ruhe kommen will. Sie ignorierten einen Philosophen, der, seiner Zeit weit voraus, die drei großen Kränkungen des menschlichen Größenwahns zusammen- und zu Ende gedacht hat. Die kosmologische Kränkung: Unsere Welt ist eine der zahllosen Kugeln im unendlichen Raum, auf der ein »Schimmelüberzug lebender und erkennender Wesen« existiert. Die biologische Kränkung: Der Mensch ist ein Tier, bei dem die Intelligenz lediglich den Mangel an Instinkten und die mangelhafte organische Einpassung in die Lebenswelt kompensieren muß. Die psychologische Kränkung: Unser bewußtes Ich ist nicht Herr im eigenen Hause."

Cf.Volker Spierling, "Die Drehwende der Moderne. Schopenhauer zwischen Skeptizismus und Dogmatismus," *Materialien zu Schopenhauers »Die Welt als Wille und Vorstellung«*, herausgegeben, kommentiert und eingeleitet von Volker Spierling (Frankfurt am Main: Suhrkamp, 1984), S.14f. for a more detailed treatment of how Schopenhauer reflected about the "three sicknesses" mentioned later by Freud.

[213] *Vorstellung I*, §21, I, S.154; *Representation*, I, §21, p.109.

will permeates everything that presents itself as an object of experience.[214]

Schopenhauer, therefore, appears to make an illicit logical jump in that the supposed knowledge one has of himself or herself as a willing and striving being is transferable to the whole of reality. The forces of nature as they appear in inorganic and organic phenomena are thereby identical with the will in ourselves.[215] Thus, the word *will* describes that dynamic force within ourselves and everything in the world which is "the sole kernel of every phenomenon (*der alleinige Kern jeder Erscheinung*)."[216] The will is, as it were, hypostatized so as to permeate every object given in experience.

---

[214] *Ibid.* "Nicht allein in denjenigen Erscheinungen, welche seiner eigenen ganz ähnlich sind, in Menschen und Thieren, wird er als ihr innerstes Wesen jenen nämlichen Willen anerkennen; sondern die fortgesetzte Reflexion wird ihn dahin leiten, auch die Kraft, welche in der Pflanze treibt und vegetirt, ja, die Kraft, durch welche der Krystall anschießt, die, welche den Magnet zum Nordpol wendet, die, deren Schlag ihm aus der Berührung heterogener Metalle entgegenfährt, die, welche in den Wahlverwandtschaften der Stoffe als Fliehn und Suchen, Trennen und Vereinen erscheint, ja, zuletzt sogar die Schwere, welche in aller Materie so gewaltig strebt, den Stein zur Erde und die Erde zur Sonne zieht,- diese Alle nur in der Erscheinung für verschieden, ihrem innern Wesen nach aber als das Selbe zu erkennen, als jenes ihm unmittelbar so intim und besser als alles Andere Bekannte, was da, wo es am deutlichsten hervortritt, *Wille* heißt."; *Ibid.*, pp.109-110.

[215] *Natur*, "Einleitung," V, S.202. "...sage ich, dieses *Ding an sich*, dieses Substrat aller Erscheinungen, mithin der ganzen Natur, nichts Anderes ist, als jenes uns unmittelbar Bekannte und sehr Vertraute, was wir im Innern unsers eigenen Selbst als *Willen* finden...; ja, daß dieser Wille, als das alleinige Ding an sich, das allein wahrhaft Reale, allein Ursprüngliche und Metaphysische, in einer Welt, wo alles Uebrige nur Erscheinung, d.h. bloße Vorstellung, ist, jedem Dinge, was immer es auch seyn mag, die Kraft verleiht, vermöge deren es daseyn und wirken kann; daß demnach nicht allein die willkürlichen Aktionen thierischer Wesen, sondern auch das organische Getriebe ihres belebten Leibes, sogar die Gestalt und Beschaffenheit desselben, ferner auch die Vegetation der Pflanzen, und endlich selbst im unorganischen Reiche die Krystallisation und überhaupt jede ursprüngliche Kraft, die sich in physischen und chemischen Erscheinungen manifestirt, ja, die Schwere selbst, - an sich und außer der Erscheinung, welches bloß heißt außer unserm Kopf und seiner Vorstellung, geradezu identisch sind mit Dem, was wir in uns selbst als *Willen* finden, von welchem *Willen* wir die unmittelbarste und intimste Kenntniß haben, die überhaupt möglich ist."; *Nature*, "Introduction," pp.216-217.

[216] *Vorstellung I*, §23, I, S.164; *Representation*, I, §23, p.118.

Unlike Kant's thing-in-itself, the will is no longer an unknown X beyond rational analysis. But Schopenhauer characterizes it as an irrational force. The will considered in-itself "is lacking in knowledge (*erkenntnißlos*) and is only a blind, irresistible urge (*ein blinder, aufhaltsamer Drang*) as we still see it appear in inorganic and vegetative nature and their laws and also in the vegetative part of our lives."[217] It is a frustrated will because it has no ultimate aim; its nature is to forever strive without the hope of final satisfaction.[218]

There is some conjecture that Schopenhauer's extension of the concept *will* to the whole of phenomena was inspired in part by his study of Buddhism and Brahmanism during the intense period of intellectual reflection prior to the appearance of *Die Welt als Wille und Vorstellung* in January of 1819.[219] Relevant to the discussion at hand is the exact relationship between Brahman and Atman.[220] At a specific period in the history of Hindu thought, the unity between the two was grasped. Atman and Brahman, as the supports of Being,

---

[217] *Ibid.*, §54, II, S.347; *Ibid.*, §54, p.275.

[218] *Ibid.*, §56, S.386. "Zuvörderst wünsche ich, daß man hier sich diejenige Betrachtung zurückrufe, mit welcher wir das zweite Buch beschlossen, veranlaßt durch die dort aufgeworfene Frage, nach dem Ziel und Zweck des Willens; statt deren Beantwortung sich uns vor Augen stellte, wie der Wille, auf allen Stufen seiner Erscheinung, von der niedrigsten bis zur höchsten, eines letzen Zieles und Zweckes ganz entbehrt, immer strebt, weil Streben sein alleiniges Wesen ist, dem kein erreichtes Ziel ein Ende macht, das daher keiner endlichen Befriedigung fähig ist, sondern nur durch Hemmung aufgehalten werden kann, an sich aber ins Unendliche geht."; *Ibid.*, §56, p.308.

[219] Dorothea W. Dauer, *Schopenhauer as Transmitter of Buddhist Ideas* (Berne: Herbert Lang & Co., 1969), pp.8-9.

[220] *Ibid.*, pp.12-13. "The traditional Brahmanic view was to assume the *brahman* as the ultimate reality which is 'All-One', and to consider individualized existence an emanation of this *brahman* made tangible by the illusory veil of maya. The individual 'soul' was in its substance identical with the *brahman*."

both came to represent the supreme reality as experienced respectively in the subjective and objective orders. Stated simply, the difference between the two worlds for all practical purposes collapsed. For Atman was identified with Brahman.[221]

In Schopenhauer's thought it is underscored that the same subjectively recognized will can be gleaned in the whole of the real. As such, it even appears that it is not the individual *per se* who wills -- who is the conglomeration of concrete willing and needing -- that is foremost in the scenario Schopenhauer paints. For it is stated in *Parerga und Paralipomena*: "What craves so vehemently for existence is merely *indirectly* the individual; directly and strictly speaking, it is the will-to-live (*der Wille zum Leben*) in general, which is one and the same for all (*welcher in Allen Einer und derselbe ist*)."[222]

As the above clearly suggests, the will is equated with an insatiable hunger or craving for life in all its manifestations. "Everything presses and pushes towards *existence* (*Daseyn*), where possible to *organic* existence, that is, towards *life*; consequently, to the

---

[221] Cf. Thomas Berry, *Religions of India: Hinduism, Yoga, Buddhism* (New York: The Bruce Publishing Co.,1971), p.12. "Both Atman and Brahman designate the final reality, the inner support of all beings, the one behind all multiplicity. Each has its own origin, however, in a different aspect of man's experience of reality. Atman indicates one absolute of being, experienced subjectively as the support of a person's own existence. Brahman came to designate the absolute reality as this is experienced objectively as the support of the visible world. It was a great moment when the identity of these two was perceived: 'Thou are that', meaning that the deepest subjective reality is identical with the absolute manifested in the world without."

[222] Arthur Schopenhauer, *Parerga und Paralipomena II*, §141, *Zürcher Ausgabe Werke in zehn Bänden*, Band IX (Zürich: Diogenes Verlag, 1977), S.305. Henceforth to be cited as *Parerga*. English translation: Arthur Schopenhauer, *Parerga and Paralipomena*, vol.2, §141, trans. E.F.J. Payne (Oxford: Clarendon Press, 1974), p.281. Henceforth to be cited as *Parerga*.

gradation (*Steigerung*) most possible thereof."[223] In animal nature the will-to-live can especially be seen as comprising the very "keynote" (*Grundton*) or quintessence of its being.[224] What is most striking, however, is that this universal craving for life which characterizes the will, compels it to seize every opportunity to grasp for itself any material capable of life, and shirk in horror when in any given particular phenomenon, imminent death or destruction signals its passage once again into nothingness.[225]

This strange way of speaking almost seems to attribute a degree of consciousness to the so-called "blind" will. But this is not exactly what Schopenhauer means. While stating that the will is certainly a universal craving for life, that same noumenal will is not linked in any way to knowledge as shall be seen in the section that immediately follows.

This notwithstanding, Schopenhauer does state that parts of the body "must correspond completely to the chief desires (*Hauptbegehrungen*) by which the will manifests itself; they must be the visible expression of the same (*derselben*)."[226] Accordingly, teeth, throat, and intestinal canal together comprise what Schopenhauer calls "objectified hunger" (*objektivirte Hunger*); the

---

[223] *Vorstellung II*, Kap.28, III, S.410; *Representation*, II, ch.28, p.350.

[224] *Ibid.*; *Ibid.*

[225] *Ibid.* "Man betrachte diesen universellen Lebensdrang, man sehe die unendliche Bereitwilligkeit, Leichtigkeit und Ueppigkeit, mit welcher der Wille zum Leben, unter Millionen Formen, überall und jeden Augenblick, mittelst Befruchtungen und Keimen, ja, wo diese mangeln, mittelst *generatio aequivoca*, sich ungestüm ins Daseyn drängt, jede Gelegenheit ergreifend, jeden lebensfähigen Stoff begierig an sich reißend: und dann wieder werfe man einen Blick auf den entsetzlichen Allarm und wilden Aufruhr desselben, wann er in irgend einer einzelnen Erscheinung aus dem Daseyn weichen soll."; *Ibid.*

[226] *Vorstellung I*, §20, I, S.153; *Representation*, I, §20, p.108.

genitals "objectified sexual drive" (*objektivirte Geschlechtstrieb*); grasping hands and nimble feet correspond to the "more indirect strivings of the will they represent."[227]

    All this, of course, acts like a boomerang and in reality says more about the character of the noumenal will as such. It is as if at the very core of the real that the noumenon supposedly is, there can be said to be (in an analogical and loose sense) an "awareness" sufficient enough not only for a craving of life in its multiform dimensions, but also for a striving after a highest possible objectification. Such an observation can be validly made even though Schopenhauer does not state this categorically.

D. Will as Independent of Knowledge

1. Knowledge as accidental to willing

    The above discussion notwithstanding, it is to be recalled that the concept of *will* is extended so as to embrace the entire spectrum of the complex of representations that the world as given in perception is. Accordingly, for Schopenhauer in the strict sense, willing cannot be linked with knowledge inasmuch as the far greater portion of phenomenal reality lacks any type of consciousness. In fact, he likes to remind his readers that the complete separation of willing from

---

[227] *Ibid.*; *Ibid.*

World as Will 77

knowledge is a feature in his teaching that sets him apart from other philosophers.[228]

Knowledge, which appears in beings that occupy the higher places on the ladder of being, is of a secondary and later origin than the will which is not only "fundamentally different" from knowledge, but completely independent from it; so much so in fact, that the will can exist and manifest itself without it, as is actually the case, from the animal downward.[229] Along the same lines, the very fact that the intellect or brain is a phenomenon means for Schopenhauer that the will (as the sole thing-in-itself) is what not only is most truly real, but what is original and metaphysical (insofar as it transcends the phenomenon).[230]

This will have implications in Schopenhauer's ethics, as shall be seen in part two of this study, insofar as for him ethics is not grounded in reason as such, but arises from a metaphysical basis, namely the noumenal will and its relation to knowledge.[231] Recall

---

[228] *Natur*, "Physiologie und Pathologie," V, S.219. "Der Grundzug meiner Lehre, welcher sie zu allen je dagewesen in Gegensatz stellt, ist die gänzliche Sonderung des Willens von der Erkenntniß, welche beide alle mir vorhergegangenen Philosophen als unzertrennlich, ja, den Willen als durch die Erkenntniß, die der Grundstoff unsers geistigen Wesens sei, bedingt und sogar meistens als eine bloße Funktion derselben angesehn haben."; *Nature*, "Physiology and Pathology," p.236.

[229] *Ibid.*, "Einleitung," S.202. "...dieser *Wille*, weit davon entfernt, wie alle bisherigen Philosophen annahmen, von der *Erkenntniß* unzertrennlich und sogar ein bloßes Resultat derselben zu seyn, von dieser, die ganz sekundär und spätern Ursprungs ist, grundverschieden und völlig unabhängig ist, folglich auch ohne sie bestehn und sich äußern kann, welches in der gesammten Natur, von der thierischen abwärts, wirklich der Fall ist."; *Nature*, "Introduction," p.216.

[230] *Ibid.* "...ja, daß dieser Wille, als das alleinige Ding an sich, das allein wahrhaft Reale, allein Ursprüngliche und Metaphysische, in einer Welt, wo alles Uebrige nur Erscheinung, d.h. bloße Vorstellung, ist, jedem Dinge, was immer es auch seyn mag, die Kraft verleiht, vermöge deren es daseyn und wirken kann..."; *Ibid.*, pp.216-217.

[231] *Vorstellung I*, §12, I, S.95. "Endlich geht auch Tugend und Heiligkeit nicht aus Reflexion hervor, sondern aus der innern Tiefe des Willens und deren Verhältniß zum Erkennen. Diese Erörterung gehört an eine ganz andere Stelle dieser Schrift: nur so viel mag ich hier bemerken, daß die auf das Ethische sich

Schopenhauer's contention that reason's essential nature consists primarily in abstraction and thus with the formation of concepts. In no way is its nature necessarily linked with the search for an unconditioned or the grounding of a morality. But let us forego discussion of matters related to this for the present so as to concentrate on the issue at hand.

What is essentially being said is that knowledge is accidental to willing. "Unconsciousness (*Bewußtlosigkeit*) is the original and natural condition of all things, consequently also the basis from which, in particular species of beings, consciousness arises as their highest efflorescence; on account of which, also then unconsciousness still always predominates (*verwaltet*)."[232] Schopenhauer immediately goes on to add that though most beings lack consciousness, "they act nevertheless according to the laws of their nature, i.e. of their will."[233] Thus, for example, in *Über den Willen in der Natur* he predicates will to plants insofar

---

beziehenden Dogmen in der Vernunft ganzer Nationen die selben seyn können, aber das Handeln in jedem Individuo ein anderes, und so auch umgekehrt: das Handeln geschieht, wie man spricht, nach *Gefühlen*: d.h. eben nur nicht nach Begriffen, nämlich dem ethischen Gehalte nach. Die Dogmen beschäftigen die müßige Vernunft: das Handeln geht zuletzt unabhängig von ihnen seinen Gang, meistens nicht nach abstrakten, sondern nach unausgesprochenen Maximen, deren Ausdruck eben der ganze Mensch selbst ist. Daher, wie verschieden auch die religiosen Dogmen der Völker sind, so ist doch bei allen die gute That von unaussprechlicher Zufriedenheit, die böse von unendlichem Grausen begleitet: erstere erschüttert kein Spott: von letzterem befreit keine Absolution des Beichtvaters. Jedoch soll hiedurch nicht geleugnet werden, daß bei der Durchführung eines tugendhaften Wandelns Anwendung der Vernunft nöthig sei: nur ist sie nicht die Quelle desselben; sondern ihre Funktion ist eine untergeordnete, nämlich die Bewahrung gefaßter Entschlüsse, das Vorhalten der Maximen, zum Widerstand gegen die Schwäche des Augenblicks und zur Konsequenz des Handelns."; *Representation*, I, §12, p.58.

[232] *Vorstellung II*, Kap.15, II, S.165; *Representation*, II, ch.15, p.142.

[233] *Ibid*.; *Ibid*.

as the noumenal will is the substratum of their being as it is of each and every existent.[234]

2. Appearance of knowledge for the sake of the will

What transpires with the appearance of knowledge is that an up-to-this-point perceptionless will suddenly becomes conscious of itself. Schopenhauer contends that knowledge then becomes at the same time "the sounding board (*Resonanzboden*) of the will and in that way the tone which ensues (*entstehenden Ton*) is the consciousness."[235] Why this happens is explained by Schopenhauer simply in light of the needs of the will, something which he feels attests to the essential imperfection of the intellect. "The defective nature of the intellect...will not surprise us...if we look back at its origin and destiny...Nature has brought it forth for the service of an individual will; therefore, it is only destined to know things insofar as they furnish the motives of such a will, not to fathom them or to comprehend their essence in itself."[236] In *Über den Willen in der Natur* it is likewise asserted that "the will furnished each kind of animal (*Thiergestalt*) with an

---

[234] *Natur*, "Pflanzen-Physiologie," V, S.264. "Von der Erkenntniß, oder Vorstellung, haben die Pflanzen bloß ein Analogon, ein Surrogat; aber den Willen haben sie wirklich und ganz unmittelbar selbst: denn er, als Ding an sich, ist das Substrat ihrer Erscheinung, wie jeder."; *Nature*, "Physiology of Plants," p.290.

[235] *Ibid*. "Wie die Welt trotz der Sonne finster bliebe, wenn keine Körper dawären, das Licht derselben zurückzuwerfen, oder wie die Vibration einer Saite der Luft und selbst irgend eines Resonanzbodens bedarf, um zum Klange zu werden; so wird der Wille erst durch den Zutritt der Erkenntniß sich seiner selbst bewußt: die Erkenntniß ist gleichsam der Resonanzboden des Willens und der dadurch entstehende Ton das Bewußtseyn."; *Ibid*., p.291.

[236] *Vorstellung II*, Kap.15, III, S.165; *Representation*, II, ch.15, p.142.

intellect as a medium for the preservation (*Erhaltung*) of the individual and the species."[237]

3. The relationship of intellect and will in man

This accidental character of knowledge has ramifications for the relationship between intellect and will in the case of man himself. It goes without saying that the will as thing-in-itself constitutes "the inner, true, and indestructible nature of man..."[238] As with other organic phenomena the will manifests itself in human beings primarily by showing its same identical nature as a great attachment to life, care for the individual and the species, egoism, and a lack of consideration for others.[239]

Schopenhauer uses some colorful images to describe the relationship between the intellect and the will: that of the former striking the tune and the latter dancing to it; or that of the intellect as a lame sighted man carried by a strong blind man, representing the will.[240] This he does so as to underscore the role the intellect plays in the presentation of perceptions

---

[237] *Natur*, "Vergleichende Anatomie," V, S.246; *Nature*, "Comparative Anatomy," p.269.

[238] *Vorstellung II*, Kap.19, III, S.234; *Representation*, II, ch.19, p.201.

[239] *Ibid.*, S.240. "Wenn wir die Stufenreihe der Thiere abwärts durchlaufen, sehn wir den Intellekt immer schwächer und unvollkommener werden: aber keineswegs bemerken wir eine entsprechende Degradation des Willens. Vielmehr behält dieser überall sein identisches Wesen und zeigt sich als große Anhänglichkeit am Leben, Sorge für das Individuum und Gattung, Egoismus und Rücksichtslosigkeit gegen alle Andern, nebst den hieraus entspringenden Affekten. Selbst im kleinsten Insekt ist der Wille vollkommen und ganz vorhanden: es will was es will, so eintschieden und vollkommen wie der Mensch."; *Ibid.*, p.206.

[240] *Ibid.*, S.242: "Man sieht, der Intellekt spielt auf und der Wille muß dazu tanzen."; S.243: "In Wahrheit aber ist das treffendeste Gleichniß für das Verhältniß Beider der starke Blinde, der den sehenden Gelähmten auf den Schultern trägt."; *Ibid.*, pp. 208,209.

which act as motives to excite the will. But even here the will's primacy is affirmed. The will so permeates consciousness that it holds and underpins representations that are given in the perceptual world.

> What gives consciousness its unity and connectedness (*Zusammenhang*) by pervading all its representations, is its substratum (*Unterlage*) and its permanent supporter [which] cannot be conditioned by the consciousness. Consequently, it can be no representation. On the contrary, it must be the *prius* of consciousness and the root of the tree of which consciousness is the fruit. This, I say, is the *will*; it alone is unchangeable and absolutely identical and has brought forth consciousness for its own purposes.[241]

Accordingly, for Schopenhauer, the intellect has a certain impotence given its accidental nature to transform or alter basic willing which comprises the core of our consciousness. The will is always in command since it constitutes the core of man.[242] Wild and impetuous, the relentless and egoistic will pushes the intellect hither and thither by its desires -- an intellect essentially in bondage to its whims.[243] No system of ethics can mold or improve the will. "Over willing itself...over its main tendency or fundamental maxim, the intellect has no power."[244] Though intellect

---

[241] *Ibid.*, Kap.15, S.162; *Ibid.*, ch.15, pp.139-140.

[242] *Ibid.*, Kap.19, S.243. "Man nennt dies »Herr über sich seyn«: offenbar ist hier der Herr der Wille, der Diener der Intellekt; da jener in letzter Instanz stets das Regiment behält, mithin den eigentlichen Kern, das Wesen an sich des Menschen, ausmacht."; *Ibid.*, ch.19, p.208.

[243] *Ibid.*, S.247. "...der Intellekt...als...ein bloßer Sklave und Leibeigener des Willens, nicht aber, wie dieser...noch aus eigener Kraft und eigenem Drange thätig ist; daher er vom Willen leicht bei Seite geschoben und durch einen Wink desselben zur Ruhe gebracht wird; während er seinerseits, mit der äußersten Anstrengung, kaum vermag, den Willen auch nur zu einer kurzen Pause zu bringen, um zum Worte zu kommen."; *Ibid.*, p.212.

[244] *Ibid.*, S.260; *Ibid.*, p.223.

and will separate themselves very distinctly in man, in the final analysis, for Schopenhauer "the will shows itself as that which is the stronger, the invincible, the unalterable, the primitive, and, at the same time, also as the essential, that upon which everything depends."[245]

E. Will as Principle of Being

It has now been asserted that the will constitutes the inner core of every phenomenon without exception that appears in space and time. Accordingly, it is inconceivable to think of any given phenomenon without at the same time calling to mind the noumenal will which presents itself in it. Given that Schopenhauer asserts that the will's intrinsic nature consists not in its being attached to an intellect (as we know it anyway), the world of phenomenal particulars is not the work of a mind. Schopenhauer is clear on this important claim:

> We can say to begin with, therefore: the world is not made with the help of knowledge and consequently not from without, but rather from within...For the intellect is recognized by us solely from animal nature and consequently as a thoroughly secondary and subordinated principle in the world, a product of latest origin. It can for this reason never have been the condition for [the world's] existence. Neither can a *mundus intelligibilis*...precede the *mundus sensibilis*; for it receives its matter (*Stoff*) from this alone. An intellect has not brought forth nature; rather, nature the intellect.[246]

---

[245] *Ibid.*; *Ibid.*

[246] *Natur*, "Vergleichende Anatomie," V, S.237-238; *Nature*, "Comparative Anatomy," pp.257-258.

Since the will is absolutely independent of the principle of sufficient reason, unlike the phenomenon, it knows no necessity. Therefore, it is absolutely free and groundless since the concept of freedom merely is the absence of necessity. Accordingly, one of the noumenal will's predicates is aseity as is clear in the following words of Schopenhauer: "...aseity must then also belong to the will, for as free, i.e., as thing-in-itself and therefore not subjected to the principle of sufficient reason, it can be no more dependent on another thing in its being and essence than it can in its doing and acting."[247] What scholastics named the "aseity of God" he attributes to the noumenal will in its groundlessness.[248] He states further: *"My teaching explains the existence of the world (which they maintain to be a work of God) from the omnipotence (Allmacht) of the Will."*[249]

These claims which Schopenhauer makes, however, become very problematic against the backdrop of a teleological facticity that is so evident in the world. Since the will not only fills everything and gives itself immediately in everything as that which is original, it is in effect the principle of all being. In fact, Schopenhauer goes so far as to state that "all

---

[247] *Vorstellung II*, Kap.25, III, S.374; *Representation*, II, ch.25, p.320.

[248] *Nachlaß*, IV.I (*Die Manuskriptbücher der Jahre 1832-1852*), S.102. "Was die Scholastiker die Aseität Gottes nannten, ist im Grunde eben das was ich dem Willen beilege und seine Grundlosigkeit genannt habe."; *Remains (The Manuscript Books of 1830-1852 and Last Manuscripts)*, p.124.

[249] *Ibid.*, S.170. "*Meine Lehre* erklärt das Daseyn der Welt, welche man für ein *Werk Gottes* hielt, aus der Allmacht des *Willens*."; *Ibid.*, p.196.

teleological facts can be explained from the will of the being in which they are founded."[250]

The question, however, that arises is precisely this: how can a blind, aimless and universally striving will (which as noumenon grounds the phenomenon) possibly explain the order visible in the world as given in perception? Later in this study, it will be seen that this same will that so impetuously craves life has the same capacity to turn on itself, an occurrence which Schopenhauer calls the denial of the will-to-live. Moreover, the same will that is present as a dull and blind urge in lifeless inorganic matter, has the capacity to objectify itself in human beings who are gifted with reason. It would seem though that a completely irrational will would bring forth complete chaos instead of the ordered and purposeful world we see, a factor that implies that the will must have some structurability of its own.[251]

Was not Schopenhauer aware of the above difficulties? It is difficult to say, but it is not altogether far-fetched to conjecture with Alfred Schmidt that Schopenhauer's occasional lapses into Hegelian-like phrases like "world-spirit" or "spirit of nature" themselves suggest that the German pessimist was indeed

---

[250] *Natur*, "Vergleichende Anatomie," V, S.238. "Wohl aber tritt der Wille, als welcher Alles erfüllt und in Jeglichem sich unmittelbar kund giebt, es dadurch bezeichnend als seine Erscheinung, überall als das Ursprüngliche auf. Daher eben lassen alle teleologischen Thatsachen sich aus dem Willen des Wesens selbst, an dem sie befunden werden, erklären."; *Nature*, "Comparative Anatomy," p.258.

[251] Cf.Alfred Schmidt, *Die Wahrheit im Gewande der Lüge* (München: Serie Piper, 1986), S.67. "Ein völlig vernunftloser Wille brächte ein Chaos, keine geordnete, zielstrebige Welt hervor...Ohne die Annahme einer Strukturiertheit auch der Welt als Wille ist es unmöglich, den Sprung vom dunklen Drang bloßer Naturkräfte zum Genie und Heiligen zu erklären."

aware of the objections mentioned above.[252] Along these lines, as was stated above, it is almost inconceivable not to predicate some kind of an awareness to a noumenal will that can do all the things Schopenhauer says it can do. Seen from this angle, therefore, the will would have to be "streaked" by some type of rationality so as to explain the reasonableness that the phenomenon nevertheless shows.

F. The Objectification of the Will

Given the discussion in the preceding sections, it can be said that the will as thing-in-itself, is free from all forms of knowledge that would entail a subject-object relationship. Because it lies outside time and space, plurality is not one of its predicates. In a word, it is one and completely independent of the principle of sufficient reason. Yet, the fact of the matter is that, according to Schopenhauer, the monistic will objectifies itself in a plurality of inanimate, organic, animal and human phenomena.

In the first level of inanimate matter where gravity, impenetrability, rigidity, fluidity, elasticity, magnetism, chemical properties, and the like are said to manifest themselves, the metaphysical will reveals itself first as a "blind craving, an obscure, dull urge (*einen blinden Drang, ein finsteres, dumpfes Treiben*) remote from all direct knowableness (*Erkennbarkeit*)."[253]

---

[252] As a case in point, refer to *Parerga II*, Kap.14, §172, IX, S.349 (English translation: *Parerga*, II, ch.14, §172, p.321). Cf. Schmidt, S.193. "-- Daß Schopenhauer selbst der Unmöglichkeit innegeworden ist, den Willen als schlechthin irrational zu interpretieren, geht unter anderem daraus hervor, daß er bisweilen in die Terminologie seines Todfeindes Hegel verfällt, wenn er den Willen als »Weltgeist« oder »Naturgeist« bezeichnet."

[253] *Vorstellung I*, §27, I, S.201; *Representation*, I, §27, p.149.

Inorganic matter, therefore, comprises the simplest and weakest form of the will's objectification.²⁵⁴

Accordingly, Schopenhauer underscores that the noumenal will as a "blind craving" and "knowledge-less striving" underpins the whole of inorganic nature as well as the "original forces" (*ursprünglichen Kräften*) which are givens for the law of causality to work.²⁵⁵ He adds, moreover, that in the case of inorganic phenomena all trace of individual character is lost in that the original forces manifest themselves in countless exactly similar and regular phenomena as multiplied in time and space.²⁵⁶

The passage from inanimate matter to organic matter is highly significant. Here nature makes a significant jump indeed. Plant life is more specialized and individualized both as regards internal organization and in terms of response to stimuli. Writes Schopenhauer: "Objectifying itself more clearly from grade to grade (*von Stufe zu Stufe*), the will still also works in the plant kingdom where proper causes are no longer the band of its phenomena but rather stimuli."²⁵⁷
Underscoring that the will in this level also acts in the vegetative part of the animal phenomenon in the production, formation, and maintenance of its inner

---

²⁵⁴ *Ibid.*; *Ibid.*

²⁵⁵ *Ibid.*; *Ibid.*

²⁵⁶ *Ibid.* "Als solcher blinder Drang und erkenntnißloses Streben erscheint er aber noch in der ganzen unorganischen Natur, in allen den ursprünglichen Kräften, welche aufzusuchen und ihre Gesetze kennen zu lernen, Physik und Chemie beschäftigt sind, und jede von welchen sich uns in Millionen ganz gleichartiger und gesetzmäßiger, keine Spur von individuellem Charakter ankündigender Erscheinungen darstellt, sondern bloß vervielfältigt durch Zeit und Raum, d.i. durch das *principium individuationis*, wie ein Bild durch die Facetten eines Glases vervielfältigt wird."; *Ibid.*

²⁵⁷ *Ibid.*; *Ibid.*, pp.149-150.

economy, nonetheless, even here the will still completely acts without knowledge as an "obscure driving force" (*finstere treibende Kraft*).[258]

Quite logically, with the appearance of animal life, more specialization and individualization take place. Sexual reproduction, for example, is more pronounced. Instinctual behavior patterns become manifest. The central nervous system and brain reach a higher plateau of organization. But most significantly, perception and purposeful movements come to the foreground which entails that knowledge makes an appearance already in their case which in turn entails that a "world as representation" has arisen. Underscoring that movement in animals depends on the perception of motives, Schopenhauer continues:

> ...because of this, knowledge here becomes necessary which therefore enters as an expedient (*Hülfsmittel*), μηχανή, needed at this stage (*Stufe*) of the will's objectification for the preservation of the individual and the reproduction of the species. It steps forth represented by the brain or a larger ganglion, just as every effort or determination of the self-objectifying will is represented by an organ, i.e. is manifested for the representation itself as an organ. Only with this expedient, μηχανή, the *world as representation* now stands out at one stroke with all its forms, object and subject, time, space, plurality, and causality. The world now shows its second side; hitherto mere *will*, it is now at the same time *representation*, object of the knowing subject.[259]

Schopenhauer goes on to assert that animals can be exposed to illusion and deception. Though they have representational capacities based on their perceptual

---

[258] *Ibid.*; *Ibid.*, p.150.

[259] *Ibid.*, S.201-202; *Ibid.*, p.150.

faculties, they can neither conceptualize nor reflect; they are thereby bound to the present.[260] Though bound to the eternal present, animals manifest the will even more clearly. Futility and fruitlessness characterize their phenomenon notwithstanding the teleological facticity that animal life manifests. The nature of the will blatantly shows itself in them where gratification is momentary, where struggle is constant, where everything is a hunter and hunted.[261]

On the highest level of the pyramid stands man. A complex, highly-specialized and individualized being, with him the faculty of reason and self-consciousness arise. Illuminated as such by a two-fold knowledge (*Verstand* and *Vernunft*), he towers above the other grades of the will's objectification. Yet even in man's case, the addition of *Vernunft* is only a means which the will uses to preserve the individual and the species. The following illustrates this well:

> Knowledge in general, rational (*vernünftige*) as well as perceptual (*anschauliche*), proceeds originally from the will itself. It belongs to higher grades of its objectification as a mere μηχανή, a means (*Mittel*) for the preservation of the individual and the species, just as every organ of the body. Destined originally, therefore, for the

---

[260] *Ibid.*, S.202. "Die Thiere sind schon dem Schein, der Täuschung ausgesetz. Sie haben indessen bloß anschauliche Vorstellungen, keine Begriffe, keine Reflexion, sind daher an die Gegenwart gebunden, können nicht die Zukunft berücksichtigen."; *Ibid.*, p.151.

[261] *Vorstellung II*, Kap.28, III, S.414-415. "Jedoch wird am einfachen, leicht übersehbaren Leben der Thiere die Nichtigkeit und Vergeblichkeit des Strebens der ganzen Erscheinung leichter faßlich. Die Mannigfaltigkeit der Organisationen, die Künstlichkeit der Mittel, wodurch jede ihrem Element und ihrem Raube angepaßt ist, kontrastirt hier deutlich mit dem Mangel irgend eines haltbaren Endzweckes; statt dessen sich nur augenblickliches Behagen, flüchtiger, durch Mangel bedingter Genuß, vieles und langes Leiden, beständiger Kampf, *bellum omnium* [Krieg aller], Jedes ein Jäger und Jedes gejagt, Gedränge, Mangel, Noth und Angst, Geschrei und Geheul darstellt: und das geht so fort, *in secula seculorum* [in alle Ewigkeit], bis ein Mal wieder die Rinde des Planeten bricht."; *Representation*, II, ch.28, p.354.

service of the will, for the accomplishment of its aims, knowledge remains almost universally completely subservient to it. Such is the case with all animals and with almost all men.[262]

As was stated early in this study when the matter of abstract representations was considered, concepts empower man to liberate himself from the shackles of the present which bind animals. But the gift to conceptualize is a two-edged sword. While it confers lordship over creation, it makes both the past and future serve as motives for the will and thereby magnifies the futility and suffering already so visible in the animal kingdom.[263] "Man, as the most complete (*vollkommenste*) objectification of that will, is accordingly also the most necessitous among all beings: he is concrete willing and needing through and through; he is a concretion (*Konkrement*) of a thousand needs."[264]

This notwithstanding, the unique character of man who comprises the will's highest objectification, lies in the fact that via this secondary capacity of knowledge that reason is, enslavement to knowing patterns under the principle of sufficient reason can be transcended. Freed from the aims of the will, knowledge in man can not only exist for itself "as the clear mirror

---

[262] *Vorstellung I*, §27, I, S.204; *Representation*, I, §27, p.152.

[263] *Vorstellung II*, Kap.28, III, S.419. "Aus der dargelegten Ursprünglichkeit und Unbedingtheit des Willens ist es erklärlich, daß der Mensch ein Daseyn voll Noth, Plage, Schmerz, Angst, und dann wieder voll Langerweile, welches, rein objektiv betrachtet und erwogen, von ihm verabscheut werden müßte, über Alles liebt und dessen Ende, welches jedoch das einzige Gewisse für ihn ist, über Alles fürchtet."; *Representation*, II, ch.28, p.359.

[264] *Vorstellung I*, §57, II, S.390-391; *Representation*, I, §57, p.312.

of the world", but can also turn on the will and point for him the path of salvation.[265]

G. The Will and Ontological Suffering

It was shown above why Schopenhauer grounds the teleological facticity of the world in the very will itself. Notwithstanding this important claim, he clearly insists that the visible order which the phenomenal world manifests, ought not blind one to the inherent suffering that scars the very face and core of the reality we perceive. He is categorical on this important point as the following indicates:

> We see in nature everywhere strife, conflict and the alteration of victory, and we shall from now on precisely recognize more clearly therein that variance (*Entzweiung*) with itself essential to the will. Every grade of the will's objectification fights (*streitig...macht*) for the matter, the space, and the time of another.[266]

Why the suffering? Why the horror? Why the estrangement? Schopenhauer gives us the clue in his analysis of human willing itself in that all willing presupposes as its very core, an antecedent condition of needing, lacking, and suffering which can never be healed. Nothing can possibly satisfy an ontological will scarred as it is by an inexplicable estrangement. Schopenhauer is strongly convinced of this:

---

[265] *Ibid.*, §27, I, S.204. "Jedoch werden wir im dritten Buche sehn, wie in einzelnen Menschen die Erkenntniß sich dieser Dienstbarkeit entziehn, ihr Joch abwerfen und frei von allen Zwecken des Wollens rein für sich bestehn kann, als bloßer Spiegel der Welt, woraus die Kunst hervorgeht; endlich im vierten Buch, wie durch diese Art der Erkenntniß, wenn sie auf den Willen zurückwirkt, die Selbstaufhebung desselben eintreten kann, d.i. die Resignation, welche das letzte Ziel, ja, das innerste Wesen aller Tugend und Heiligkeit, und die Erlösung von der Welt ist."; *Ibid.*, §27, p.152.

[266] *Ibid.*, S.197; *Ibid.*, pp.147-148.

> Willing and striving is the will's whole essence, [which can be] fully compared to an unquenchable thirst. The basis of all willing is need (*Bedürftigkeit*), lack (*Mangel*), therefore pain (*Schmerz*), which is already original to it and falls to it (*anheimfällt*) by its nature (*Wesen*)."[267]

It makes little sense to speak about a *Summum Bonum* in this respect. For "good" is a relative concept related only to the desiring will -- a claim already made by Thomas Hobbes in his classic work, the *Leviathan*.[268] A *Summum Bonum*, whatever that might be, would be that which ultimately halts the frustrated striving of the will. Given Schopenhauer's presuppositions, such a reality is an impossibility as the following passage indicates:

> ...every good is essentially *relative*; for it has its essence only in relation to a desiring will. Accordingly, *absolute good* is a contradiction; highest good, *summum bonum*, signifies the same thing, that is, in reality a final satisfaction of the will, after which no fresh willing would take place; a last motive, the attainment of which would yield an imperishable satisfaction of the will. According to our discussion up to now..., such a thing is unthinkable. The will can just as little through some satisfaction cease to will always again and anew, as time can end or begin; for the will there is no lasting

---

[267] *Ibid.*, §57, II, S.390; *Ibid.*, p.312.

[268] Thomas Hobbes, *Leviathan*, Part I, Chapter 6, as found in *The English Works of Thomas Hobbes of Malmesbury*, edited by Sir William Molesworth, Bart. Vol. III (London: John Bohn, 1966), p.41. The text reads as follows:

> But whatsoever is the object of any man's appetite or desire, that is it which he for his part calleth *good*: and the object of his hate and aversion *evil*; and of his contempt, *vile* and *inconsiderable*. For these words of good, evil, and contemptible, are ever used with relation to the person that useth them: there being nothing simply and absolutely so; nor any common rule of good and evil, to be taken from the nature of the objects themselves; but from the person of the man, where there is no commonwealth; or, in a commonwealth, from the person that representeth it; or from an arbitrator or judge, whom men disagreeing shall by consent set up, and make his sentence the rule thereof.

fulfillment which completely and forever satisfies its striving.[269]
Accordingly, it is this given brokenness and scarredness that characterizes the whole of the real without exception. In this sense, for Schopenhauer it is evil which is positive; good is negative. "All satisfaction (*Befriedigung*), or what one usually calls happiness (*Glück*), is really and essentially always *negative* only, and never positive."[270] The "good" which is defined only in reference to the desiring will, is at best illusory; for the will can never be satisfied. Will-filled consciousness can never have happiness as its fruit.[271] Herein lies Schopenhauer's rationale for underscoring the mysterious frustration which not only permeates, but also scars the very essence of what comprises the core of each and every phenomenon without exception.

Nevertheless, Schopenhauer thinks he has solved an important philosophical question: What is it that propels reality despite the tension and strife everywhere

---

[269] *Vorstellung I*, §65, II, S.450; *Representation*. I, §65, p.362.

[270] *Ibid.*, §58, S.399; *Ibid.*, §58, p.319.

[271] *Vorstellung I*, §38, I, S.252. "Alles *Wollen* entspringt aus Bedürfniß, also aus Mangel, also aus Leiden. Diesem macht die Erfüllung ein Ende; jedoch gegen einen Wunsch, der erfüllt wird, bleiben wenigstens zehn versagt: ferner, das Begehren dauert lange, die Forderungen gehn ins Unendliche; die Erfüllung ist kurz und kärglich bemessen. Sogar aber ist die endliche Befriedigung selbst nur scheinbar: der erfüllte Wunsch macht gleich einem neuen Platz: jener ist ein erkannter, dieser ein noch unerkannter Irrthum. Dauernde, nicht mehr weichende Befriedigung kann kein erlangtes Objekt des Wollens geben: sondern es gleicht immer nur dem Almosen, das dem Bettler zugeworfen, sein Leben heute fristet, um seine Quaal auf Morgen zu verlängern. - Darum nun, solange unser Bewußtseyn von unserm Willen erfüllt ist, solange wir mit dem Drange der Wünsche, mit seinem steten Hoffen und Fürchten, hingegeben sind, solange wir Subjekt des Wollens sind, wird uns nimmermehr dauerndes Glück, noch Ruhe. Ob wir jagen, oder fliehn, Unheil fürchten, oder nach Genuß streben, ist im Wesentlichen einerlei: die Sorge für den stets fordernden Willen, gleichviel in welcher Gestalt, erfüllt und bewegt fortdauernd das Bewußtseyn; ohne Ruhe aber ist durchaus kein wahres Wohlseyn möglich. So liegt das Subjekt des Wollens beständig auf dem drehenden Rade des Ixion, schöpft immer im Siebe der Danaiden, ist der ewig schmachtende Tantalus."; *Ibid.*, §38, p.196.

present -- an ontological turmoil which seemingly should be self-destructive? For the fundamental character of existents as given in perception seems to be their contingency and transitoriness. Death's foreboding shadow looms with dreadful certainty over each organic phenomenon. Inorganic matter is subject to change. Rocks crumble and metals corrode before the endless stream of time. Schopenhauer's answer is unequivocally clear: it is the metaphysical will whose kernel is "timeless" and "indestructible" that explains ultimately why the above is so.[272]

This brings us to a full circle once again to Schopenhauer's initial intention to discover what the inner content of perceptual representations might be. He is convinced that his teaching has not only determined what the thing-in-itself is, but that the will which we find within ourselves comprises in like fashion the very core of the real as represented in perception.[273] Given

---

[272] *Parerga II*, §66, IX, S.107. "Der Grundcharakter aller Dinge ist Vergänglichkeit: wir sehn in der Natur Alles, vom Metall bis zum Organismus, theils durch sein Daseyn selbst, theils durch den Konflikt mit Anderm, sich aufreiben und verzehren. Wie könnte dabei die Natur das Erhalten der Formen und Erneuern der Individuen, die zahllose Wiederholung des Lebensprocesses, eine unendliche Zeit hindurch, aushalten, ohne zu ermüden; wenn nicht ihr eigener Kern ein Zeitloses und dadurch völlig Unverwüstliches wäre, ein Ding an sich, ganz anderer Art, als seine Erscheinungen, ein allem Physischen heterogenes Metaphysisches? - Dieses ist der *Wille* in uns und in Allem."; *Parerga*, II, §66, p.95.

[273] "An Julius Frauenstädt," Frankfurt a.M., den 6. Aug.1852, Brief 279, *Arthur Schopenhauer Gesammelte Briefe*, herausgegeben von Arthur Hübscher (Bonn: Bouvier Verlag Herbert Grundmann, 1987), S.288. Schopenhauer underscores the pivotal importance of the will being the thing-in-itself for his philosophical system as a whole. Cf. the following: "Sie haben die Warheit gerade auf den Kopf gestellt und gelangen daher zu dem Satz, daß ich hätte, wie Kant, unbestimmt lassen sollen was das Ding an sich sei: -- *quae, qualis, quanta!* Da möchte man sich dem Teufel ergeben! -- Da könnte ich ja gleich meine ganze Philosophie zum Fenster hinauswerfen. Das ist ja eben meine große Entdeckung, daß Kants Ding an sich. Das ist, was wir im Selbstbewußtseyn als den *Willen* finden, und daß dieser vom Intellekt ganz verschieden und unabhängig ist, daher auch ohne diesen vorhanden, in allen Wesen. Aber dieser Wille ist Ding an sich bloß in Bezug auf die *Erscheinung*: er ist das was diese ist, unabhängig von unserer Wahrnehmung und Vorstellung: das eben heißt *an sich*: daher ist er das Erscheinende in jeder Erscheinung, der Kern des Wesens. Als solches ist er Wille, Wille zum Leben."

this already lengthy discussion on the will as noumenon however, it seems clear enough that what interests Schopenhauer most of all (when all is said and done), is the mystery of suffering and evil that scars the whole of the real, and human beings in particular. He thinks that the clue to this universally visible scarredness lies within man himself whose striving and restless willing comprises indeed what is most immediate to the consciousness, a true "ens realissimum."[274] Seen from this perspective, Schopenhauer's decision as a young man to philosophize about reality's dark side from the sickness within the human spirit, makes more sense.[275]

H. Summary

Having examined what Schopenhauer means by the world as will, the ground has been sufficiently tilled to move into one more area before concluding part one of this study. The central point to keep in mind is that the noumenal will (to the extent that we can know it) comprises the inner content and kernel of each and every phenomenon which entails that the whole of the real is

---

[274] *Natur*, "Hinweisung auf die Ethik," V, S.340. ""Wenn ich also sage »Wille, Wille zum Leben«; so ist das kein *ens rationis* [Gedankending], keine von mir selbst gemachte Hypostase, auch kein Wort von ungewisser, schwankender Bedeutung: sondern wer mich frägt, was es sei, den weise ich an sein eigenes Inneres, wo er es vollständig, ja, in kolossaler Größe vorfindet, als ein wahres *ens realissimum* [allerrealstes Wesen]. Ich habe demnach nicht die Welt aus dem Unbekannten erklärt; vielmehr aus dem Bekanntesten, das es giebt, und welches uns auf eine ganz andere Art bekannt ist, als alles Uebrige."; *Nature*, "Reference to Ethics," p.376.

[275] *Arthur Schopenhauers Gespräche*, herausgeben von Arthur Hübscher (Stuttgart-Bad Cannstatt: Friedrich Fromman Verlag, 1971), S.22. Cf. "Christoph Martin Wieland," [April 1811], 21: "Schopenhauer hatte Wieland besucht, als dieser 78 Jahre alt war. Wieland hatte ihm abgeraten, lediglich Philosophie zu studieren, was doch kein solides Fach wäre. *Antwort*: »Das Leben ist eine mißliche Sache, ich habe mir vorgesetzt, es damit hinzubringen, über dasselbe nachzudenken.« -- Zuletzt habe Wieland gesagt: »Ja es scheint mir jetzt, Sie haben recht getan (daß Sie richtig gewählt haben), junger Mann, ich verstehe jetzt Ihre Natur; bleiben Sie bei der Philosophie.«

scarred and disordered in its very essence. The multiplicity of particulars in the phenomenal order is but a facade given to the eyes of perception, too often blind to an underlying monism and unity.

From time to time the teleological facticity of the world was underscored despite Schopenhauer's contention that the will in its essence comprises something that is irrational and without any final aim. Though the noumenal will is estranged within itself and purposeless, phenomena tend to stubbornly present themselves arrayed with the vestiture of a teleology that attracts the eye of the beholder. Granted, Schopenhauer says that this very facticity stems from the will itself. But if this is so, the noumenon would then also have an added dimension not clearly emphasized by Schopenhauer: that of an inherent rationality.

The above paradox comes to a head when Schopenhauer suddenly introduces the Platonic Ideas into his *Weltanschauung*. Because of their importance for this study, a detailed analysis of what Schopenhauer means by them is warranted. The following chapter, therefore, represents an effort to attain the above end.

Chapter 3

The Platonic Ideas

A. The Will as Adequately Objectified

1. Bridging the *noumenon* and the *phenomenon*

A close look at the world of real individuals and entities illustrates that at each level of the will's objectification contest and struggle can be seen. The underlying reason for the disorder visible on the phenomenal sphere is the estrangement intrinsic to the will itself. Thus, Schopenhauer underscores that every level of the will's objectification fights for the matter, the time and the space of another. At all levels of phenomena (inorganic and organic as well) "the will-to-live generally feasts on itself (*an sich selber zehrt*), and is in different forms its own nourishment."[276] All things that comprise the world are, therefore, the objectification of one and the same will which makes them identical according to their inner nature as will.[277]

For Schopenhauer plurality in general is conditioned by space and time, which he calls the *principium individuationis*. All our knowing on the phenomenal sphere (the domain of plurality) is governed

---

[276] *Vorstellung I*, §27, I, S.197; *Representation*, I, §27, p.147.

[277] *Ibid.*, S.194. "Ja, weil eben alle Dinge der Welt die Objektität einen und selben Willens, folglich dem innern Wesen nach identisch sind."; *Ibid.*, p.144.

World as Idea 97

by the principle of sufficient reason. The thing-in-itself, namely the noumenal will, transcends representational knowledge in that it is free from all forms of normal cognitive knowing under the principle of sufficient reason. It was likewise emphasized that the will as noumenon is free even from the most universal form of the phenomenon, i.e. that of being object for the subject. As thing-in-itself, the will lies outside of time, space and causality. Succinctly said, "the plurality (*Vielheit*) of things in space and time that together are the objectivity (*Objektität*) of the will, accordingly, does not affect it, and notwithstanding such plurality, the will remains indivisible."[278]

Schopenhauer's position is clear for all to see. On the one hand, there is the noumenal will which, as an aimless striving, in some manner subsists outside the world of phenomenal particulars. But on the other hand, there exist phenomena which are revelatory of the diseased will. What is it that can bridge the noumenal oneness of the will (which, as such, is outside of space, time, and causality) and phenomena which are governed by the principle of sufficient reason? Schopenhauer appears to be between a rock and a hard place. For since the two orders of being are radically different, it would appear that a thick wall divides both despite Schopenhauer's insistence that phenomena all reveal what the will is.

2. The Platonic Idea as adequate objectification

So as to address the problem that the above suggests, Schopenhauer introduces a novel doctrine when he speaks about the will's objectification in phenomenal

---

[278] *Ibid.*, §25, S.175; *Ibid.*, §25, p.128.

reality as given in perception.[279] At the very outset of this discussion two thirds into the second book of the first volume of *Die Welt als Wille und Vorstellung*, he states that the "[will's] coming forward *(Hervortreten)* into visibility, its objectification, has gradations *(Abstufungen)* which are as endless as those between the feeblest twilight and the brightest sunlight, the strongest tone and softest echo."[280] But what is interesting to note, is both the place he assigns to the gradations in question, and what he calls them. As the following indicates, Schopenhauer distinguishes *gradations* from *particulars* or *individuals*. The gradations are identified with the *Platonic Ideas*:

> ...those different grades *(Stufen)* of the will's objectification, which are expressed in countless individuals, exist as the unattained patterns *(unerreichten Musterbilder)* of these, or as the eternal forms of things, not themselves entering into time and space, the medium of individuals. On the contrary, they remain fixed, subject to no change *(keinem Wechsel unterworfen)*, always being *(immer seiend)*, never having become. Those [particular things], however, arise and pass away; they always become and never are...I say that these *grades of the objectification of the will* are nothing other than Plato's *Ideas (Ideen)*.[281]

---

[279] Cf. Heinrich Hasse, *Schopenhauer* (München: Verlag Ernst Reinhardt, 1926), S.225-226. "Steht der ur-eine Wille als das zeitlose, raumlose, grundlose Ding an sich einer unbegrenzten Vielheit und Mannigfaltigkeit empirischer Erscheinungen gegenüber, so erhebt sich die Frage, in welchem Verhältniß dieser jenseits aller Gesetze der Vorstellung waltende Urwille zu dem unermeßlichen Reich der Erscheinungen steht, in welche er ausstrahlt und in welchen er sich objektiviert. Es ist ein Verhältniß eigentümlicher Art, welches nicht nach dem Satz vom zureichenden Grunde begreifbar ist, inbesondere nicht als ein ursächliches gefaßt werden darf. Wenn Schopenhauer lehrt: Der Wille als Ding an sich objektiviert sich in seinen Erscheinungen, so bedeutet das: Er stellt sich im Rahmen der allgemeinen Vorstellungsgesetzte irgendwie als objektive Gegebenheit in der anschauliche Körperwelt dar."

[280] *Vorstellung I*, §25, I, S.176; *Representation*, I, §25, p.128.

[281] *Ibid.*, S.177; *Ibid.*, p.129.

These grades, therefore, are clearly distinct from "individuals" or "particulars" and serve as their *eternal forms* or *prototypes*. So as to avoid all ambiguity, Schopenhauer states: "by *Idea* I understand every definite and fixed *grade of the will's* objectification, in so far as it is thing-in-itself and is therefore foreign to plurality, whose grades indeed have a certain relation to particular things as their eternal Forms (*ewigen Formen*), or prototypes (*Musterbilder*)."[282] But lest one prematurely conclude that these gradations of the will's objectification have an ontological status of their own in a world apart, Schopenhauer's own words ought to be kept in mind: "Aristotle's *forma substantialis* denotes exactly what I call the degree of the will's objectification in a thing."[283] Accordingly, a renowned scholar the likes of Arthur Hübscher, writes in *Denker gegen den Strom*:

> The Ideas are...the enduring timeless forms of ephemeral beings of nature which, multiplied through time and space, become visible in an imperfect way in the innumerable individual, ephemeral objects. They converge with that which Aristotle and the Scholastics had called *formae substantiales*.[284]

Notwithstanding Schopenhauer's appeal to the Aristotelian notion of the "substantial form" to clarify what exactly is meant by the Idea in his *Weltanschauung*, he is clearly attempting to reconcile Kant's doctrine of the thing-in-itself with the Platonic Ideas. Just as the thing-in-itself is beyond the realm of phenomena as given to human cognitive faculties, so too do the Platonic Ideas

---

[282] *Ibid.*; *Ibid.*, p.130.

[283] *Ibid.*, §27, S.193; *Ibid.*, §27, p.143.

[284] Arthur Hübscher, *Denker gegen den Strom* (4.Aufl., Bonn: Bouvier Verlag, 1988), S.119.

completely transcend the world of sensible things.²⁸⁵ Accordingly, Schopenhauer asserts that the "inner meaning of both teachings is the same in that both declare the visible world to be an appearance (*Erscheinung*) which in itself is empty (*nichtig*), and has meaning and borrowed reality only through that thing which expresses itself in it (in one case the thing-in-itself, in the other the Ideas)."²⁸⁶

Nevertheless, Schopenhauer's manuscript notes indicate that his thinking with regard to the relationship between the noumenal will and the Idea underwent an evolution or development in the years prior to the publication of *Die Welt als Wille und Vorstellung* in January of 1819. At least one early fragment in the *Nachlaß* dating from the year 1814 illustrates that Schopenhauer initially identified the thing-in-itself with the Platonic Idea:

> ...now the Platonic Idea is Kant's thing-in-itself, in other words, is free from time and space, and therefore from plurality, change, beginning and end. It alone is the οντως ον, or the thing-in-itself.²⁸⁷

But by the beginning of 1815 indications are that Schopenhauer had identified the will, perceived in internal experience and felt in the body, with the thing-in-itself -- a will devoid of rationality.²⁸⁸ As a case in point, another fragment written in 1814 reads as follows: "The *world as thing-in-itself* is a great will which does not know what it wills; for it does not *know* but merely wills just because it is a will and nothing

---

²⁸⁵ *Ibid.*, §31, S.222-223; *Ibid.*, §31, pp.170-171.

²⁸⁶ *Ibid.*, S.224; *Ibid.*, p.172.

²⁸⁷ *Nachlaß*, I, #250, S.150; *Remains*, I, #250, p.163.

²⁸⁸ Cf. Safranski, S.299.

else."²⁸⁹ Accordingly, even by this time, Idea and thing-in-itself are not to be identified. With the publication of *Die Welt als Wille und Vorstellung* there is a complete bifurcation between the thing-in-itself as *will* and the *Idea*. Succinctly stated: "Idea and thing-in-itself are not absolutely one and the same: rather, the Idea for us is only the immediate (*unmittelbare*), and therefore adequate objectivity (*adäquate Objektität*) of the thing-in-itself, which itself, however, is the *will* -- the will in so far as it has still not been objectified, has not yet become representation."²⁹⁰ The particular thing (*Das einzelne*) that appears before consciousness in accordance with the principle of sufficient reason, is only an "indirect objectification of the thing-in-itself (which is the will)..."²⁹¹ It cannot be considered an entirely "adequate objectification of the will" because in any given particular thing, the noumenon is obscured by those forms whose common expression is the aforementioned principle of sufficient reason.²⁹²

3. The status of the Idea

It would appear that the Ideas in Schopenhauer's view of reality constitute a separate sphere of being consisting of ideal entities. Certainly the language he uses gives rise to this impression insofar as he calls them prototypes or exemplars in

---

[289] *Nachlaß*, I, #278, S.169; *Remains*, I, #278, pp.184-185.

[290] *Vorstellung I*, §32, I, S.227; *Representation*, I, §32, p.174.

[291] *Ibid.*, S.228; *Ibid.*, p.175.

[292] *Ibid.* "Die einzelnen Dinge aber sind keine ganz adäquate Objektität des Willens, sondern diese ist hier schon getrübt durch jene Formen, deren gemeinschaftlicher Ausdruck der Satz vom Grunde ist, welche aber Bedingung der Erkenntniß sind, wie sie dem Individuo als solchem möglich ist."; *Ibid.*

relation to particulars given in experience.[293] In this respect, given the problematic of the exact status of the Ideas in Schopenhauer's *Weltanschauung*, his view of reality appears to be three-tiered consisting of the noumenal will, representations and Ideas.[294] But the difficulty involved in adopting this view of Schopenhauer's thinking, is that he himself would reject any attempt to interpret his thought in this manner: "... the world is on the one side, entirely *representation*, just as, on the other it is entirely *will*."[295] Moreover, he has already stated that the Idea, while being an exemplar or prototype, is also very much akin to the Aristotelian notion of the "substantial form" in a thing -- which, of course, suggests that the Idea in Schopenhauer's *Weltanschauung* is not being given an ontological status of its own. An Idea is a representation, but one that enjoys a special status; it

---

[293] Cf.Hamlyn, pp.103-104. "Did he, for example, really think that there was a separate world of ideal entities, distinct from the world of the senses, as Plato seems to have done? Such a conception fits rather badly with a point of view that is, in origin at least, Kantian (although he does try to argue (WR I 31, pp.170ff...) for a kind of reconciliation between Kant and Plato). Did he, on the other hand, think of the Ideas as Kantian 'ideas of reason', as some later, Kantian interpreters of Plato were inclined to do? What Schopenhauer himself says on the matter does not suggest so, since he speaks of the Kantian misuse of the word, and he quotes with approval a summary of Plato's views by Diogenes Laertius, which says that in Plato's view the Ideas exist in nature as exemplars and that other things are like them and exist as likenesses of them (WR I 25, p.130...). Hence he appears to regard them as prototypes or ideal patterns, and these he identifies with what he calls grades of objectification of the will."

[294] Cf.Bryan Magee, *The Philosophy of Schopenhauer* (Oxford: Clarendon Press, 1983), p.239. Magee's contention is that the Ideas comprise a "third constituent of total reality" as the following indicates: "...whereas Schopenhauer's philosophy makes so much of presenting itself to us as an account of reality in terms of two irreducible categories -- the noumenon and the phenomena -- it actually makes use of three; what he shows us is not a two-decker reality consisting of will and representations but a three-decker reality consisting of will, Platonic Ideas and representations."

[295] *Vorstellung I*, §1, I, S.31; *Representation*, I, p.4. Cf. *Vorstellung I*, I, S.215. "...diese Welt, in der wir leben und sind, ihrem ganzen Wesen nach, durch und durch *Wille* und zugleich durch und durch *Vorstellung* ist."; *Representation*, §1, I, p.162.

World as Idea

transcends the principle of sufficient reason. Schopenhauer clarifies what he means by this:

> The Platonic Idea is...necessarily object, something known, a representation, and precisely through this, but only through this, is it different from the thing-in-itself. It has laid aside merely the subordinate forms of the phenomenon (*Erscheinung*), which we include under the principle of sufficient reason; or rather it has still not entered into them. However, it has retained the first and most universal form, that of the representation in general, that of being object for a subject.[296]

The language Schopenhauer uses above nevertheless does not clarify the issue at hand: whether the Platonic Ideas have an ontological status of their own. Even though reality may not be three-tiered, Arthur Hübscher is correct when he underscores that "the realm of the ideas pushes itself (*schiebt sich*) between the universal primal will as thing-in-itself and the abundance of its appearances."[297] In yet another paragraph the renowned Schopenhauer scholar states that the Ideas "appear in the total world of appearances as intermediate stages (*Mittelstufen*) between the unity of the thing-in-itself, the primal will and the plurality of its appearances."[298]

Schopenhauer, however, redeems himself by insisting that the Idea is itself a special type of representation: one that has cast off the subordinate forms of the phenomenon which are bound to a will-oriented intellect. In this respect, via the Ideas, "the *world as representation*...stands out whole and pure, the

---

[296] *Ibid.*, §32, S.228; *Ibid.*, §32, p.175.

[297] Hübscher, S.119.

[298] *Ibid.*, S.120.

complete objectification of the will takes place, for only the Idea is the adequate objectivity of the will."[299] Accordingly, it would be short-sighted and indeed inaccurate to consider the doctrine of the Platonic Ideas as a type of useless appendage to Schopenhauer's metaphysical system, as some scholars seem to imply.[300] Far from being an obex to the coherent structure of his system, they are key for understanding his metaphysical picture of reality and his theory of genius. Moreover, their introduction illustrates why Schopenhauer would reject any type of reductive materialism, as shall be evident once the course of the argumentation proceeds.[301]

---

[299] *Vorstellung I*, §34, I, S.233; *Representation*, I, §34, p.179.

[300] Cf. James D. Chanksy, "Schopenhauer and Platonic Ideas: A Groundwork for an Aesthetic Metaphysics," as found in Eric von der Luft, ed., *Schopenhauer: New Essays in Honor of His 200th Birthday* (Lewiston: The Edwin Mellen Press, 1988), pp.67-68. As a case in point, refer to the following works: Bryan MaGee, *The Philosophy of Schopenhauer* (Oxford: Clarendon Press, 1983), p.239; D.W. Hamlyn, *Schopenhauer* (London: Routledge & Kegan Paul, 1980), p.103; and Hilde Hein, "Schopenhauer and Platonic Ideas," *Journal of the History of Philosophy* 4 (1966):144.

[301] Cf. Terri Graves Taylor, "Platonic Ideas, Aesthetic Experience, and the Resolution of Schopenhauer's 'Great Contradiction'," *International Studies in Philosophy* 19 (1987), p.45:
   The phenomenal status of individual wills will become clearer once we understand the role the Platonic forms play in the noumenal Will's manifestation. In fact, although the standard interpretations seem to treat the Platonic forms as an embarrassing addition to Schopenhauer's system, they seem to be the key to understanding his metaphysics.

   Part of the impetus for introducing them seems to have been not only to explain aesthetic experience but to block reductive materialism. Writing slightly earlier than Schopenhauer, Lamark had suggested that life was 'merely the effect of warmth and electricity.' Schopenhauer countered him by claiming that each natural kind was a representation of a Platonic form. Unfortunately, his only justification is the explanatory adequacy of his metaphysical scheme.

B. Specific Character of the Idea

1. Ideas as opposed to concepts

Schopenhauer underscores that an *Idea* is similar to a *concept* in that it also is a unity which represents a plurality of actual things.[302] However, he does distinguish between the two which is important to keep in mind. The following are his definitions of the *concept* and *Idea* respectively:

> The *concept* is abstract, discursive, completely undetermined within its sphere, determined only by its limits, attainable and comprehensible only to each person who has the faculty of reason, communicable by words without further mediation, entirely exhausted by its definition.[303]

> The *Idea*, on the other hand, to be defined perhaps as the adequate representative of the concept, is completely perceptive, and although representing an infinite number of individual things, is nevertheless thoroughly definite.[304]

a. Normal intuitions and the Ideas

Up until now the Ideas have been defined as definite grades of the will's objectification which have a relation to particular things as their eternal Forms or

---

[302] *Vorstellung I*, §49, I, S.295-296. "Obgleich Idee und Begriff etwas Gemeinsames haben, darin, daß Beiden als Einheiten eine Vielheit wirklicher Dinge vertreten."; *Representation*, I, §49, p.233.

[303] *Ibid.*, S.296. "Der *Begriff* ist abstrakt, diskursiv, innerhalb seiner Sphäre völlig unbestimmt, nur ihrer Gränze nach bestimmt, Jedem der nur Vernunft hat erreichbar und faßlich, durch Worte ohne weitere Vermittlung mittheilbar, durch seine Definition ganz zu erschöpfen."; *Ibid.*, p.234.

[304] *Ibid.* "Die *Idee* dagegen, allenfalls als adäquater Repräsentant des Begriffs zu definiren, ist durchaus anschaulich und, obwohl eine unendliche Menge einzelner Dinge vertretend, dennoch durchgängig bestimmt."; *Ibid.*

prototypes. The immediately preceding distinction between concepts and Ideas casts further light on the significance and role of the Platonic Idea in his *Weltanschauung*. An important notion to keep in mind is what was just underscored above: that the Idea's universality is akin to that of a concept in that it applies to many particulars, but yet has a "perceptibility" and "definiteness" that a concept can never have, since the latter always involves the act of abstraction.

Further insight into what Schopenhauer means by the notion of the Idea is found in his epistemological treatise, *Über die vierfache Wurzel des Satzes vom zureichenden Grunde*, when in dealing with mathematics, he refers to "normal intuitions" distinguishing them from concepts as well. He underscores, first of all, that the concept pertains to the sciences as such, whereas "*normal intuitions*" (*Normalenanschauungen*), that is, figures and numbers, concern mathematics.[305] But then he notes that the latter are "legislative" (*gesetzgebend*) for all experience and thereby combine the comprehensiveness (*das Vielumfassende*) of the concept with the thorough definiteness (*durchgängigen Bestimmtheit*) of individual representations."[306]

What this means in effect, however, is that the normal intuition has a certain uniqueness. Each number, for example, would constitute a unique universal insofar

---

[305] *Grunde*, §39, V, S.151. "Nur die zwölf Axiome Euklids läßt man auf bloßer Anschauung beruhen, und sogar beruhen von diesen eigentlich nur das neunte, elfte, und zwölfte auf einzelnen verschiedenen Anschauungen, alle die andern aber auf der Einsicht, daß man in der Wissenschaft nicht, wie in der Erfahrung, es mit realen Dingen, die für sich neben einander bestehn und ins Unendliche verschieden seyn können, zu thun habe; sondern mit Begriffen, und in der Mathematik mit Normalanschauungen, d.h. Figuren und Zahlen..."; *Reason*, §39, p.198.

[306] *Ibid.*; *Ibid.*

as there would be no place for exactly similar two's, threes or fours, etc., but only identities.[307] Schopenhauer continues by underscoring that unlike the concept, the normal intuition is precisely determined throughout, and in this manner "leaves no room for universality (*Allgemeinheit*) through that which is left undetermined (das *Unbestimmtgelassene*)."[308] Hence, the rationale for it being an intuition. This notwithstanding, Schopenhauer states that these normal intuitions are nevertheless "universal" in that they are "the mere forms of all appearances and as such apply to all real objects to which such a form belongs."[309] Therefore, the normal intuition combines the universality of a concept with the definiteness of a given intuition, something a concept can never do in that its formation always involves leaving behind a residue.

For our purposes, the above discussion is significant insofar as Schopenhauer notes that what holds good for these intuitions "would apply to what Plato says about his Ideas."[310] What holds true in the case of numbers is also the case with the Ideas in his philosophy. In a footnote to the above discussion Schopenhauer is even more specific:

> The *Platonic Ideas* may possibly be described as normal intuitions which would be valid like the mathematical, not only for the formal, but also for the material [part] of complete representations. Thus they may be described as complete representations (*vollständige Vorstellungen*) which, as such, would be

---

[307] Hamlyn, pp.32-33; 104.

[308] *Grunde*, §39, V, S.151; *Reason*, §39, p.198.

[309] *Ibid.*; *Ibid.*

[310] *Ibid.*; *Ibid.*

thoroughly determined, and still, at the same time, like concepts concern many things.[311]

b. The Idea as universal form of the phenomenon

This juxtaposition between normal intuitions and Ideas, as far as their being merely universal forms of phenomena, needs to be underscored. In a subsequent essay ("*Von der Erkenntniß der Ideen*") found in the supplements of volume two of *Die Welt als Wille und Vorstellung*, Schopenhauer states that contemplation of the Ideas allows one to grasp the purely objective nature of a phenomenon and entails that the human intellect has, to a degree at least, transcended will-oriented cognition.[312] Such contemplation enables one to grasp only what is essential in a particular thing, that which comprises its peculiar character and which is, accordingly, "the complete expression of the essence that presents itself to perception (*Anschauung*) as an object comprehended (*aufgefasst*) not in relationship to an individual will..."[313] This is, therefore, in accord with what Schopenhauer says about the Ideas being representations of a special class inasmuch as they retain solely the most universal form of the phenomenon -- that of being object for the subject. Moreover, it is in keeping with his likening the Idea to the substantial form of a thing.

---

[311] *Ibid.*; *Ibid.*, p.206.

[312] *Vorstellung II*, Kap.29, IV, S.432. "Hat der Intellekt Kraft genug, das Uebergewicht zu erlangen und die Beziehungen der Dinge auf den Willen ganz fahren zu lassen, um statt ihrer das alle Relationen hindurch sich aussprechende, rein objektive Wesen einer Erscheinung aufzufassen; so verläßt er, mit dem Dienste des Willens zugleich, auch die Auffassung bloßer Relationen und damit eigentlich auch die des einzelnen Dinges als solchen."; *Representation*, II, ch.29, pp.363-364.

[313] *Ibid.*; *Ibid.*

2. The idea as a unity *ante rem*

This essential and intelligible core (the Idea as such) constitutes a unity that is universal in that it applies to many particulars. It is definite in that the Idea comprises an intuitional or perceptual unity as well. Schopenhauer further distinguishes Ideas from concepts by asserting that the former can be regarded as *universalia ante rem*, whereas the latter can be *universalia post rem*. The following illustrates what he means:

> The Idea is the unity (*Einheit*) that has fallen into plurality (*Vielheit*) by virtue of the temporal and spatial form (*Zeit-und Raumform*) of our intuitive apprehension. The *concept*, on the other hand, is the unity which has again been established (*wieder hergestellte*) by means of abstraction through our faculty of reason (*Vernunft*); the latter can be described as *unitas post rem*, and the former *unitas ante rem*.[314]

Schopenhauer, in later supplements to *Die Welt als Wille und Vorstellung* notes that the original unity of an Idea is dispersed into the plurality of existing particulars by our sensual, perceptive faculties. The unity is restored, as it were, through the reflection of reason but only *in abstracto*, as a concept or universal which equals the Idea in extension, but nevertheless has a different form. This entails, however, that the Idea loses its perceptibility and distinctness in the

---

[314] *Vorstellung I*, §49, I, S.297; *Representation*, I, §49, pp.234-235.

process.³¹⁵ Schopenhauer then adds, so as to clarify matters:

> In this sense (but in no other) one could, in the language of the scholastics, characterize the Ideas as *universalia ante rem*, and the concepts as *universalia post rem*. Individual things stand between both, the knowledge of which, even the animal has.³¹⁶

Given the above nuance ("In this sense [but in no other]"), Schopenhauer again appears to deny that Ideas have an ontological status of their own in the strict sense of the word, which would be in keeping with the Transcendental Idealism in which he stands.³¹⁷ But as the discussion already indicates, it will be increasingly difficult to see how the Ideas are not in someway antecedent to perceiving beings gifted with reason; for the Ideas already constitute an adequate representation of will. As such, they comprise the essential crust (but not the core) of the knowable that presents itself to human consciousness on the representational level: namely, the purely objective nature of the phenomenon.

---

³¹⁵ *Vorstellung II*, Kap.29, IV, S.434. "Den *Unterschied* zwischen der Idee und dem Begriff habe ich § 49 des ersten Bandes genugsam hervorgehoben. Ihre *Aehnlichkeit* hingegen beruht auf Folgendem. Die ursprüngliche und wesentliche Einheit einer Idee wird, durch die sinnlich und cerebral bedingte Anschauung des erkennenden Individuums, in die Vielheit der einzelnen Dinge zersplittert. Dann aber wird, durch die Reflexion der Vernunft, jene Einheit wieder hergestellt, jedoch nur *in abstracto*, als Begriff, *universale*, welcher zwar an *Umfang* der Idee gleichkommt, jedoch eine ganz andere *Form* angenommen, dadurch aber die Anschaulichkeit, und mit ihr die durchgängige Bestimmtheit, eingebüßt hat."; *Representation*, II, ch.29, pp. 365-366.

³¹⁶ *Ibid*. "In diesem Sinne (jedoch in keinem andern) könnte man, in der Sprache der Scholastiker, die Ideen als *universalia ante rem*, die Begriffe als *universalia post rem* bezeichnen: zwischen Beiden stehn die einzelnen Dinge, deren Erkenntniß auch das Thier hat."; *Ibid*.

³¹⁷ Cf. Hamlyn, *Schopenhauer*, p.104. "...Schopenhauer is less concerned with the ontological status of the Ideas than with their logical character as representations. Hence, when he says that the grades of the objectification of the will are Ideas in Plato's sense, we are not meant to ask whether in that case they exist in another world or whatever. The real question at issue is their logical status as representations (or, as we might put it, the logical status of their content).

World as Idea

This notwithstanding, it has to be kept in mind that these Ideas, or grades of the will's objectification, also serve as prototypes or exemplars to which individual particulars in space and time approximate.

3. Ideas as acts of will

Schopenhauer also says that the different Ideas as specific grades of the will's objectification, can be considered as "individual, and in themselves simple acts of will, in which its inner being expresses itself more or less."[318] Individuals or particulars would thereby be phenomena of those acts in time, space and plurality.[319] So as to approach further the question of the exact status of the Ideas, let us use Schopenhauer's explanation of the Idea as a given act of will and apply it to phenomena which are revelatory of not only the Ideas, but also in final analysis, the will.

C. Ideas and Grades of the Will's Objectification

1. Preliminary remarks

Let us recall that Schopenhauer underscores that the will's gradations can indeed be countless, which would thereby seem to entail that the number of Ideas is countless. Nevertheless, Schopenhauer contends that the noumenal will objectifies itself in three basic strata of phenomenological being: in *inorganic* entities, in *organic* substances, and in the various degrees of

---

[318] *Vorstellung I*, §28, I, S.207; *Representation*, I, §28, p.155.

[319] *Ibid.* "...die Individuen...sind wieder Erscheinungen der Ideen, als jener Akte, in Zeit und Raum und Vielheit."; *Ibid.*

intelligent life. These are distinctions purposely selected by Schopenhauer because they correspond to the three forms of causality that govern each and every phenomenon given in experience: causality respectively understood in its most narrow sense as *action/reaction*, but also as *stimulus*, and *motive*.

2. Ideas in inorganic phenomena

In inorganic phenomena, natural forces constitute the immediate objectification of the will at its lowest level and, as such, may be called Ideas.[320] Schopenhauer mentions gravity and impenetrability as examples of natural forces that appear in all matter without exception. But he also adds that other forces of nature such as electricity, rigidity, fluidity, magnetism, chemical properties and the like rule over respective pieces of matter. All can be regarded as "immediate phenomena of the will" (*unmittelbare Erscheinungen des Willens*), which means that they are groundless and not subject to the principle of sufficient reason, even though their individual phenomena are.[321]

---

[320] *Vorstellung I*, §26, I, S.182-183. "Jede allgemeine ursprüngliche Naturkraft ist also in ihrem innern Wesen nichts Anderes, als die Objektification des Willens auf einer niedrigen Stufen: wir nennen eine jede solche Stufe eine ewige *Idee*, in Plato's Sinn."; *Representation*, I, §26, p.134.

[321] *Ibid.*, S.178. "Als die niedrigste Stufe der Objektivation des Willens stellen sich die allgemeinsten Kräfte der Natur dar, welche theils in jeder Materie ohne Ausnahme erscheinen, wie Schwere, Undurchdringlichkeit, theils sich unter einander in die überhaupt vorhandene Materie getheilt haben, so daß einige über diese, andere über jene, eben dadurch specifisch verschiedene Materie herrschen, wie Starrheit, Flüssigkeit, Elasticität, Elektricität, Magnetismus, chemische Eigenschaften und Qualitäten jeder Art. Sie sind an sich unmittelbare Erscheinungen des Willens, so gut wie das Thun des Menschen, sind als solche grundlos, wie der Charakter des Menschen, nur ihre einzelnen Erscheinungen sind dem Satz vom Grund unterworfen, wie die Handlungen des Menschen..."; *Ibid.*, p.130.

World as Idea

His essential point concerns the groundlessness of the so-called natural forces as immediate appearances, or phenomena, of the noumenal will. While inorganic phenomena are all subject to the principle of sufficient reason, the same cannot be said of the intangible natural forces. Thus, for Schopenhauer, the natural forces "can be called neither effect (*Wirkung*) nor cause (*Ursache*), but rather are the preceding and presupposed conditions of all causes and effects through which their own inner being is unfolded and revealed."[322]

This is not to say that there is not some type of interplay between causes and effects on the phenomenal sphere. The very opposite is true, but in a qualified sense insofar as natural forces manifest themselves when the conditions are right in inorganic phenomena. Though independent of the cause/effect relationship, a force of nature can be considered as that which endows a cause with efficacy no matter how often the times of its appearance may be. But, in the same fashion, this does not entail that the natural force itself is a cause in the strict sense.[323] For it pertains to the immediate

---

[322] *Ibid.*; *Ibid.*

[323] *Ibid.*, S.178-179. "Es ist...unverständig, nach einer Ursache der Schwere, der Elekricität zu fragen: dies sind ursprüngliche Kräfte, deren Aeußerungen zwar nach Ursache und Wirkung vor sich gehn, so daß jede einzelne Erscheinung derselben eine Ursache hat, die selbst wieder eben eine solche einzelne Bestimmung giebt, daß hier jene Kraft sich äußern, in Zeit und Raum hervortreten mußte; keineswegs aber ist die Kraft selbst Wirkung einer Ursache, noch auch Ursache einer Wirkung. - Daher ist es falsch zu sagen: »Die Schwere ist Ursache, daß der Stein fällt«; vielmehr ist die Nähe der Erde hier die Ursache, indem diese den Stein zieht. Nehmt die Erde weg, und der Stein wird nicht fallen, obgleich die Schwere geblieben ist. Die Kraft selbst liegt ganz außerhalb der Kette der Ursachen und Wirkungen, welche die Zeit voraussetzt, indem sie nur in Bezug auf diese Bedeutung hat; jene aber liegt auch außerhalb der Zeit. Die einzelne Veränderung hat immer wieder eine eben so einzelne Veränderung, nicht aber die Kraft, zur Ursache, deren Aeußerung sie ist. Denn Das eben, was einer Ursache, so unzählige Male sie eintreten mag, immer die Wirksamkeit verleiht, ist eine Naturkraft, ist als solche grundlos, d.h. liegt ganz außerhalb der Kette der Ursachen und überhaupt des Gebietes des Satzes vom Grunde, und wird philosophisch erkannt als unmittelbare Objektität des Willens, der das Ansich der gesammten Natur ist."; *Ibid.*, pp.130-131.

or adequate objectification of the will where discourse about cause and effect does not hold true.

Now, given our earlier discussion, in no way whatsoever, can time, space, plurality, and being-conditioned by causes be characteristic of the noumenal will and the Idea, which Schopenhauer regards as the immediate objectification of the will. In this sense, a given natural force, as a particular Idea, "must manifest itself as such in entirely the exact, same way in all its millions of phenomena and only the external circumstances can modify the phenomenon."[324] Hence, a natural force which manifests itself in the sphere of inorganic phenomena will always have a certain constancy. Given the same circumstances and conditions, it will always reveal itself in like fashion. Accordingly, if experience, for example, teaches that a given chemical reaction ensues when certain materials are brought together under definite conditions, the same phenomenon will once again take place given the same conditions. This unchangeable constancy whereby a natural force makes itself known on the phenomenal sphere constitutes a law of nature.[325]

In this low and feeble grade of the will's objectification, the will reveals itself as a dull and blind urge.[326] This notwithstanding, the intangible and mysterious realities that the natural forces are, enable

---

[324] *Ibid.*, S.181; *Ibid.*, p.133.

[325] *Ibid.* "Diese Einheit ihres Wesens in allen ihren Erscheinungen, diese unwandelbare Konstanz des Eintritts derselben, sobald, am Leitfaden der Kausalität, die Bedingungen dazu vorhanden sind, heißt ein *Naturgesetz.*"; *Ibid.*

[326] *Ibid.*, §27, S.201. "...auf der untersten Stufe, den Willen sich darstellen als einen blinden Drang, ein finsteres, dumpfes Treiben, fern von aller unmittelbaren Erkennbarkeit. Es ist die einfachste und schwächste Art seiner Objektivation.; *Ibid.*, §27, p.149.

them to occupy a required middle place between the noumenal will and inorganic phenomena. Schopenhauer states that the natural force "lies outside all time, is omnipresent (*allgegenwärtig*), and seems as it were, to constantly wait for the appearance of those circumstances under which it can come forward and seize for itself a definite matter (*Materie*), supplanting the forces that have hitherto governed it."[327] It falls to chemistry and physics not only to unveil the forces that slumber in matter, but also determine the laws which regulate their appearance in the phenomenal sphere.[328] A law so determined reveals how similar phenomena under similar conditions manifest a natural force. The law facilitates the expression of the Idea that the natural force is on the phenomenal sphere.

Keeping in mind a claim made by Schopenhauer above that the Idea, as such, may be described as an act of will outside the temporal sequence of phenomena, it is underscored with regard to inorganic phenomena that "the Idea which reveals itself in some universal force of nature always has only a simple expression, although it presents itself differently according to external relations."[329] Because the Idea is beyond will-oriented

---

[327] *Ibid.*, §26, S.185; *Ibid.*, §26, p.136.

[328] *Ibid.*, §27, S.201. "Als solcher blinder Drang und erkenntnißloses Streben erscheint er aber noch in der ganzen unorganischen Natur, in allen den ursprünglichen Kräften, welche aufzusuchen und ihre Gesetze kennen zu lernen, Physik und Chemie beschäftigt sind, und jede von welchen sich uns in Millionen ganz gleichartiger und gesetzmäßiger, keine Spur von individuellem Charakter ankündigender Erscheinungen darstellt, sondern bloß vervielfältigt durch Zeit und Raum, d.i. durch das *principium individuationis*, wie ein Bild durch die Facetten eines Glases vervielfältigt wird."; *Ibid.*, §27, p.149.

[329] *Vorstellung I*, §28, I, S.207. "Nun behält, auf den niedrigsten Stufen der Objektität, ein solcher Akt (oder eine Idee) auch in der Erscheinung seine Einheit bei; während er auf den höhern Stufen, um zu erscheinen, einer ganzen Reihe von Zuständen und Entwickelungen in der Zeit bedarf, welche allen zusammengenommen erst den Ausdruck seines Wesens vollenden. So z.B. hat die Idee, welche sich in irgend einer allgemeinen Naturkraft offenbart, immer nur

cognition and thereby transcends the domain of the principle of sufficient reason, it pertains to the intelligible realm. Accordingly, empirically-given phenomena (such as inorganic things, for example) are related to the intelligible realm of the Ideas inasmuch as the former are revelatory of the latter. It is for this reason that Schopenhauer juxtaposes a thing's "empirical character" with its "intelligible character." With regard to the issue at hand, he states: "If in inorganic nature, the Idea, which is considered everywhere as a single act of will, also reveals itself only in a particular and always similar manifestation, then one can say that the empirical character here directly partakes of the unity of the intelligible."[330] In a word, in any empirically-given phenomenon the intelligible character coincides with the Idea.

> That which is known as the empirical character, through the necessary development in time and the division into particular actions conditioned by time, is, with abstraction of this temporal form of the phenomenon, the *intelligible character*, according to Kant's expression. In the establishment of this distinction and in the description of the relation between freedom and necessity, that is to say, between the Will as thing-in-itself and its appearance in time, Kant especially and brilliantly manifests his immortal merit.[331]

---

eine einfache Aeußerung, wenn gleich diese nach Maaßgabe der äußeren Verhältnisse sich verschieden darstellt: sonst könnte auch ihre Identität gar nicht nachgewiesen werden, welches eben geschieht durch Absonderung der bloß aus den äußeren Verhältnissen entspringenden Verschiedenheit."; *Representation*, I, §28, p.155.

[330] *Ibid.*, S.209; *Ibid.*, pp.156-157.

[331] *Ibid.*, S.208; *Ibid.*, pp.155-156.

World as Idea   117

3. The status of matter

At this point in our inquiry, a question arises about the exact status of matter. Schopenhauer distinguishes between empirical matter and pure matter. Empirically-given matter, or material (*Stoff*), has already entered the framework of the forms and manifests itself through qualities and accidents.[332] Pure matter, as an object of thought alone, is never an object of perception. Rather, it is "mere *acting* (*Wirken*) *in abstracto*, hence *pure causality* itself."[333] This being the case, matter is causality through and through. Accordingly, it is not an object, but rather is one of the conditions of experience, the others being time and space.[334]

Since knowledge of the Ideas excludes the subordinate forms of the principle of sufficient reason (those being space, time and causality), pure matter as causality through and through, cannot be expressive of an Idea.[335] As was stated just above, pure matter can be

---

[332] *Vorstellung II*, Kap.4, III, S.58. "Hingegen ist jede *empirisch gegebene* Materie, also der Stoff...schon in die Hülle der *Formen* eingegangen und manifestirt sich allein durch deren Qualitäten und Accidenzien..."; *Representation*, II, ch.4, p.45.

[333] *Ibid.*; *Ibid.*

[334] *Ibid.* "...eben ist die reine Materie ein Gegenstand des *Denkens* allein, nicht der *Anschauung*; welches den *Plotinus* (*Enneas* II, lib.4, c.8 u.9) und den *Jordanus Brunus* (*Della causa, dial.* 4) zu dem paradoxen Ausspruch gebracht hat, daß die Materie keine Anschauung, als welche von der Form unzertrennlich sei, habe und daher *unkörperlich* sei; hatte doch schon *Aristoteles* gelehrt, daß sie kein Körper sei, wiewohl körperlich...(*Stob. Ecl., lib.* I, c.12, § 5). Wirklich denken wir unter *reiner Materie* das bloße *Wirken in abstracto*, ganz abgesehn von der Art dieses Wirkens, also die *reine Kausalität* selbst: und als solche ist sie nicht *Gegenstand*, sondern *Bedingung* der Erfahrung, eben wie Raum und Zeit."; *Ibid.*

[335] *Vorstellung I*, §43, I, S.272. "Die Materie als solche kann nicht Darstellung einer Idee seyn. Denn sie ist...durch und durch Kausalität: ihr Seyn ist lauter Wirken."; *Representation*, I, §43, p.213.

seen as one of the conditions that makes perception even possible, supporting as it does the forms and qualities that reveal the Ideas as well. It is in this light that Schopenhauer considers matter the "common substratum (*das gemeinsame Substrat*) of all individual phenomena of the Ideas, [and] consequently as the connecting link and the phenomenon or individual thing."[336]

4. Ideas and organic matter

As Schopenhauer begins to discuss the will's objectification in organic phenomena, he is at pains to underscore that organic phenomena cannot be seen as aggregates of physical, chemical or mechanical forces that have in some way or another come together fortuitously. Were such a reductionist view true, then, according to Schopenhauer, the organism of a plant, animal or human being for that matter, would not entail the exhibition of a new Idea. Rather, organisms would be revelatory of those Ideas that objectify the will in electricity, chemistry and mechanism. Here Schopenhauer is strongly reacting to views espoused by the "electrical, chemical, and mechanical physiologists who obstinately want to explain the whole of life and all the functions of the organism from the 'form and combination (*Mischung*)'of its components (*Bestandtheile*)."[337] Insisting that organic life entails that a new level of the will's objectification is involved, and therefore, that a new Idea has manifested itself, Schopenhauer explains why he does not consider Ideas in organic life as aggregates of lower Ideas:

---

[336] *Ibid.; Ibid.*

[337] *Vorstellung I*, §27, I, S.191; *Representation*, I, §27, p.142.

> If one considers the matter closely, then ultimately at the basis of these views is the presupposition that the organism is only an aggregate of physical, chemical, and mechanical forces that have come together in it by chance (*zufällig zusammengekommen*), and have brought about the organism as a freak of nature (*Naturspiel*) without further significance. Therefore, the organism of an animal or of a human being would be, philosophically considered, not the exhibition of its particular Idea, in other words, not itself the immediate objectivity of the will at a determined higher grade, but there would appear in it only those Ideas which objectify the will in electricity, chemistry, and mechanism.[338]

In a word, lest the point be belabored, Schopenhauer categorically insists that "it is indeed a mistake of natural science...to try to refer the higher grades of the objectification of the will to lower ones."[339] Accordingly, what is involved here with organic substances is a new level of the will's objectification, and hence, a new and distinct Idea. So the passage from inanimate matter to organic phenomena is not by any means to be taken lightly given the above. That having been said, we can proceed with the argumentation of this study.

It has already been stated above, that plant life is more specialized and individualized both as regards internal organization and in terms of stimuli. In the plant kingdom, the will still acts without knowledge as an obscure driving force (*finstere treibende Kraft*). This notwithstanding, the plant expresses its particular Idea through an unfolding of its growth processes in time. "The plant already... expresses the

---

[338] *Ibid.*; S.192; *Ibid.*

[339] *Ibid.*; *Ibid.*, p.143.

Idea of which it is the phenomenon not all at once (*nicht mit einem Male*) and through a simple manifestation, but rather, in a succession of developments of its organs in time."[340] In a word, the very process of the plant's life-cycle manifests the Idea of its species. Hence, unlike inorganic phenomena, the Idea here does not express itself in a simple manifestation, which is to say, that the empirical character does not coincide with that of the intelligible as is the case with inorganic phenomena.

It goes without saying that the plant kingdom shows little if any individuality. Each rose, for example, manifests the characteristics of its species. For this reason, Schopenhauer asserts that the lower one goes on the phenomenological ladder of being, the more the trace of individual character is lost and the general character of the species predominates.[341]

5. Ideas and the animal kingdom

It is altogether logical that with the appearance of animal life as such, even more individualization and specialization take place. It was underscored above that because knowledge enters as an expedient required for the preservation of the species, the world now shows its second side, that is, it is now representation of a perceiver. But to avoid repetition and to set what follows in proper context, once again, I presuppose the treatment of the will's objectification in animal life which was discussed above.

---

[340] *Ibid.*, §28, S.207; *Ibid.*, §28, p.155.

[341] *Ibid.* §26, S.179. "Je weiter abwärts, desto mehr verliert sich jede Spur von Individualcharakter in den all gemeinen der Species, deren Physiognomie auch allein übrig bleibt."; *Ibid.*, §26, p.131.

For our purposes, however, what needs to be emphasized here is that with animals new and distinct Ideas emerge. This, in effect, means that the Ideas of "doghood", "catness", "cowness" and so forth do not make their emergence in the lower strata of the will's objectification, but only do so here. The expression of the Idea in the animal is similar to that of a plant in that the animal expresses the Idea of its species via a succession of developments of its organs in time. However, the complete expression of the Idea in this case can only be completed through the animal's actions which together comprise the empirical character, but also presuppose the definite organism itself as a fundamental condition.[342]

6. Man as a unique Idea

Man's case is unique in that his actions on the phenomenal sphere attest to an empirical character that is peculiar to each person.[343] Before proceeding further, let it be underscored that for Schopenhauer the character is the individually constituted nature of the will of a given individual that makes it subject to motives in the temporal and spatial complex that reality,

---

[342] *Vorstellung I*, I, §28, S.207-208. "Das Thier entwickelt nicht nur auf gleiche Weise, in einer Succession oft sehr verschiedener Gestalten (Metamorphose), seinen Organismus; sondern diese Gestalt selbst, obwohl schon Objektität des Willens auf dieser Stufe, reicht doch nicht hin zur vollständigen Darstellung seiner Idee, vielmehr wird diese erst ergänzt durch die Handlungen des Thieres, in denen sein empirischer Charakter, welcher in der ganzen Species der selbe ist, sich ausspricht und erst die vollständige Offenbarung der Idee ist, wobei sie den bestimmten Organismus als Grundbedingung voraussetzt."; *Representation*, I, §28, p.155.

[343] *Ibid.*, S.208. "Beim Menschen ist schon in jedem Individuo der empirische Charakter ein eigenthümlicher (ja, wie wir im vierten Buche sehn werden, bis zur völligen Aufhebung des Charakters der Species, nämlich durch Selbstaufhebung des ganzen Wollens)."; *Ibid.*

as given in perception, is.³⁴⁴ Human individuals in their uniqueness constitute particular instances of the will's highest level of objectification and, as such, may be regarded as unique Ideas. Schopenhauer is clear with regard to this as the following indicates: "The character of each individual man can be regarded as a special Idea (*besondere Idee*) corresponding to a specific act of the objectification of the will, insofar as it is thoroughly individual and not completely included in that which is of the species."³⁴⁵

The act of the will's objectification, to which we have just alluded, would comprise a given individual's intelligible character whereas the empirical character would be its phenomenon (*Erscheinung*).³⁴⁶ From an empirical point of view, the simple act of will that is united in the noumenal sphere is in the case of man (as with other organic phenomena) likewise divided into a succession of states and developments in time.

There is, however, a correspondence between the intelligible and empirical characters. Schopenhauer notes that "the empirical character must in the course of a lifetime (*Lebenslauf*) furnish a copy of the intelligible [character], and cannot fail to turn out differently than that which the essence of the latter

---

³⁴⁴ *Freiheit*, III., VI, S.87. "Diese speciell und individuell bestimmte Beschaffenheit des Willens, vermöge deren seine Reaktion auf die selben Motive in jedem Menschen eine andere ist, macht Das aus, was man dessen *Charakter* nennt und zwar, weil er nicht a priori sondern nur durch Erfahrung bekannt wird, *empirischen Charakter*. Durch ihn ist zunächst die Wirkungsart der verschiedenartigen Motive auf den gegebenen Menschen bestimmt." *Freedom*, III., p.49.

³⁴⁵ *Vorstellung I*, §28, I, S.211; *Representation*, I, §28, p.158.

³⁴⁶ *Ibid*. "Dieser Akt selbst wäre dann sein intelligibler Charakter, sein empirischer aber die Erscheinung desselben."; *Ibid*.

demands.³⁴⁷ In other words, how each person acts on the phenomenal sphere constitutes his or her *empirical* character, which always corresponds to an *intelligible* character, that is groundless because it pertains to the will's immediate objectification.

The empirical character of each person on the phenomenal sphere, which manifests itself in actions and the like, is peculiar, therefore, to each individual because the intelligible character of each is distinct. Thus, Schopenhauer underscores that "the empirical character is entirely determined by the intelligible that is groundless, i.e., will as thing-in-itself, not subject to the principle of sufficient reason (the form of the phenomenon)."³⁴⁸

Schopenhauer's discussion above concerning the intelligible and empirical character in the case of man can be regarded as a nuancing of his description of the Ideas as the immediate objectification of the noumenal will. But he also uses the same insight in speaking about all other "existents" in that they too, as phenomena, are each manifestations of an intelligible character. The following speaks for itself: "...not only the empirical character of every human being, but also that of every animal species, indeed every plant species, and even every original force of inorganic nature, is to be regarded as an appearance of an intelligible character, in other words, of an extra-temporal, indivisible act of will (*außerzeitlichen untheilbaren Willensaktes*)."³⁴⁹

---

³⁴⁷ *Ibid.*; *Ibid.*

³⁴⁸ *Ibid.*; *Ibid.*

³⁴⁹ *Ibid.*, S.208; *Ibid.*, p.156.

D. Ideas and the relatedness of phenomena

What has been described above is, in general terms, the way the will objectifies itself in the totality of phenomena. Though man is the will's highest objectification and, as such, occupies a place of primacy on the ladder of being as given in perception, the Idea of man cannot stand isolated apart from the lower grades of the will's objectification. In fact, for a complete objectification of the will to take place, all the grades are necessary as the following indicates:

> The Idea of Man would need to manifest itself not alone and torn apart (*abgerissen*) in order to appear in its proper significance, but rather, must be accompanied by all the grades downwards through all the forms of animals, through the plant kingdom to the inorganic. They all supplement one another (*ergänzen sich*) for the complete objectification of the will.[350]

Juxtaposed to this inner necessity of the gradations of the will's phenomena is an outer necessity expressed by the whole of the phenomenal sphere itself. "By virtue of [such necessity], man needs the animals for his preservation, the animals by degrees (*stufenweise*) [need] one another, then also the plants, which again are in need of the soil, water, chemical elements and their combinations, of the planet, the sun, rotation, and motion around the sun, the obliquity of the ecliptic, and so on."[351] Schopenhauer attributes all this to the

---

[350] *Ibid.*, S.205; *Ibid.*, p.153.

[351] *Ibid.*, S.206; *Ibid.*, p.154.

hungry will which feeds on itself, objectifying itself in that totality that phenomenal being is.[352]

The inner and outer necessity linking the levels of the will's objectification is not to obscure the universal conflict that is present in all phenomena therefore. At every grade of the will's objectification there can be gleaned a fight for the matter, the space, and the time of another which is only indicative of a will which is at variance with itself. The whole of reality is essentially a battleground in which particulars strive to express their own respective Ideas.

> Persistent matter must constantly change the form, inasmuch as under the guideline of causality (*am Leitfaden der Kausalität*), mechanical, physical, chemical, and organic phenomena, eagerly striving to appear (*sich gierig zum Hervortreten drängend*), snatch the matter from each other, for each wants to reveal its own Idea. Through the whole of nature can this struggle be followed; indeed, precisely again only through it, does nature exist.[353]

Now, exactly how and why distinct and new Ideas emerge in phenomena is not given an altogether clear and satisfactory explanation by Schopenhauer other than his asserting that the noumenal will that objectifies itself in all Ideas strives for the highest possible objectification. From the conflict to which the immediately preceding passage alludes, the phenomenon of a higher Idea emerges. But a higher Idea, interestingly enough, never obliterates a lower one.

For example, in the animal organism, there continue to exist chemical processes and the like which

---

[352] *Ibid.* "Im Grunde entspringt dies daraus, daß der Wille an sich selber zehren muß, weil außer ihm nichts daist und er ein hungriger Wille ist. Daher die Jagd, die Angst und das Leiden."; *Ibid.*

[353] *Ibid.*, §27, S.197; *Ibid.*, §27, p.147.

are themselves indicative of the presence of distinct Ideas. But the animal's very identity depends on a new Idea having emerged which overshadows, or holds in check, lower ones. Higher Ideas subdue all the less perfect phenomena previously existing, but in such a way that they allow their essential nature to continue in a subordinate manner. This process is intelligible for Schopenhauer "only from the identity of the will which appears in all the Ideas, and from its striving for an ever higher objectification."[354]

The above notwithstanding, Schopenhauer continues his discussion by asserting that tension always characterizes reality. "Since the higher Ideas, or objectification of the will, can come forward only through the subjugation (*Überwältigung*) of lower Ideas, they undergo the opposition of these [lower Ideas] which, though presently brought into subjection (*Dienstbarkeit*), nevertheless always strive to attain an independent and complete expression of their being."[355] Though levels of the will's objectification are inter-related, all higher phenomena of the will are involved in a permanent struggle against the many chemical and physical forces that are expressions of lower Ideas. In the final analysis, however, subdued lower Ideas have the last word against the backdrop of a living organism's relentless struggle to maintain life as death's foreboding shadow

---

[354] *Ibid.*, S.195. "Wenn von den Erscheinungen des Willens, auf den niedrigeren Stufen seiner Objektivation, also im Unorganischen, mehrere unter einander in Konflikt gerathen, indem jede, am Leitfaden der Kausalität, sich der vorhandenen Materie bemächtigen will; so geht aus diesem Streit die Erscheinung einer höhern Idee hervor, welche die vorhin dagewesenen unvollkommeneren alle überwältigt, jedoch so, daß sie das Wesen derselben auf eine untergeordnete Weise bestehn läßt, indem sie ein Analogon davon in sich aufnimmt; welcher Vorgang eben nur aus der Identität des erscheinenden Willens in allen Ideen und aus seinem Streben zu immer höherer Objektivation begreiflich ist."; *Ibid.*, pp.144-145.

[355] *Ibid.*, S.196; *Ibid.*, p.146.

World as Idea

menacingly draws near. As Schopenhauer writes: "...at last, favored by circumstances, those subdued forces of nature (*unterjochten Naturkräfte*) win back from the organism, itself wearied by the constant conquest, the matter snatched from them, and attain to the unhindered exhibition of their being."[356]

E. The Ideas as Dispersed

Before moving into the question as to how exactly the Ideas can be known by the human subject, attention ought to be given to an issue of importance. How is it that the unity of the Idea assumes the form of diversity and plurality characteristic to the phenomenon? Schopenhauer explicitly states that the Ideas are dispersed in the phenomenal order governed by the principle of sufficient reason. "Through time and space the Idea reproduces itself (*vervielfältigt sich*) into innumerable phenomena, but the order according to which these enter into the forms of multiplicity (*Mannigfaltigkeit*) is definitely determined by the Law of Causality."[357]

In another section of *Die Welt als Wille und Vorstellung* Schopenhauer mentions that the inner and outer teleology visible in nature is really the "*phenomenon of the unity of the one will so far in agreement with itself*, which has been broken apart into space and time for our manner of knowing (*Erkenntnißweise*)."[358] What the law of causality does

---

[356] Ibid., S.197; Ibid., p.146.

[357] Ibid., §26, S.183; Ibid., §26, p.134.

[358] Ibid., §28, S.214; Ibid., §28, p.161.

is provide a rule for the order in which the Ideas are to appear given the fact that phenomena constantly fight for the matter in which to express their particular Ideas.[359]

One cannot help but notice that by introducing once again jargon that pertains to the manner by which the world of perception is given, Schopenhauer takes his readers back to sections in *Die Welt als Wille und Vorstellung* and *Über die vierfache Wurzel des Satzes vom zureichenden Grunde* where he intertwines the law of causality with the *a priori* forms of space and time, which together yield the world as given in perception. Since the Ideas constitute what is most objective in those given phenomena, Schopenhauer's essential point in effect is this: the Ideas are indeed unities, but ones that are broken up or dispersed by the structure of our perceptive faculties. "The *Idea* is the unity that has fallen apart (*zerfallene Einheit*) into plurality by virtue of the form of the temporal and spatial form of our intuitive apprehension (*intuitiven Apprehension*)."[360]

Since the Ideas are dispersed by our cognitive knowing patterns linked as they are with the will, that unity can only be restored by a faculty distinct from

---

[359] *Ibid.*, §26, S.183. "[Das Gesetz der Kausalität]... ist gleichsam die Norm der Gränzpunkte jener Erscheinungen verschiedener Ideen, nach welcher Raum, Zeit und Materie an sie vertheilt sind. Diese Norm bezieht sich daher nothwendig auf die Identität der gesammten vorhandenen Materie, welche das gemeinsame Substrat aller jener verschiedenen Erscheinungen ist...Nur also weil alle jene Erscheinungen der ewigen Ideen an eine und die selbe Materie gewiesen sind, mußte eine Regel ihres Ein-und Austritts seyn: sonst würde keine der andern Platz machen. Diesergestalt ist das Gesetz der Kausalität wesentlich verbunden mit dem der Beharrlichkeit der Substanz: beide erhalten bloß von einander wechselseitig Bedeutung: eben so aber auch wieder verhalten sich zu ihnen Raum und Zeit."; *Ibid.*, §26, pp.134-135.

[360] *Ibid.*, §49, S.297; *Ibid.*, §49, p.234. Cf. Frederick Copleston, *Arthur Schopenhauer: Philosopher of Pessimism* (Andover: Burns Oates & Washbourne, 1946), p.106.

World as Idea

that of the understanding (*Verstand*). For it is the understanding which plays a central role in the very act of perception which disperses the unity of given Ideas. Accordingly, reason (*Vernunft*) alone empowers man to restore the unity of the Ideas which are scattered about in phenomena as perceived.[361]

There exists a passage from an early fragment found in Schopenhauer's handwritten notes dating from the years 1809-1810 (several years before the publication of *Die Welt als Wille und Vorstellung*) which casts light upon what has just been mentioned above. Commenting on Book 6 of Plato's *Republic*, Schopenhauer notes that the original forms of Nature, which constitute the Ideas, are scattered about by the world of sensible bodies in an analogous fashion to what happens, when rays of light are scattered about by a concave glass. The task of reason is to function like a convex glass and unite once again the dispersed Ideas veiled in the sensible bodies we perceive.[362]

This all sounds similar to what Schopenhauer essentially states in his main work about the Ideas being the most objective aspect of the phenomenon, and how only reason can grasp what the Ideas are, as grades of the will's immediate objectification. What transpires via our intuitive apprehension of the world is essentially a breaking-up or scattering of the prototypes, which Schopenhauer identifies with the Platonic Ideas. In this

---

[361] *Vorstellung II*, Kap.29, IV, S.434. "Dann aber wird, durch die Reflexion der Vernunft, jene Einheit wieder hergestellt, jedoch nur *in abstracto*, als Begriff, *universale*, welcher zwar an *Umfang* der Idee gleichkommt, jedoch eine ganz andere *Form* angenommen, dadurch aber die Anschaulichkeit, und mit ihr die durchgängige Bestimmtheit, eingebüßt hat."; *Representation*, II, ch.29, p.366.

[362] *Nachlaß*, I, #15, S.11. "Die Körperwelt ist ein Konkavglas, das die von den Ideen ausgehenden Strahlen zerstreut; die menschliche Vernunft ein Konvexglas, das sie wieder sammelt und die ursprünglichen Bilder der Ideen wieder zeigt, wenn auch verundeutlicht durch den Umweg."; *Remains*, I, #15, p.11.

sense, it can be said that our intuitive or perceptual faculties do function like a concave glass that scatters rays of light. What reason does, in like fashion, is akin to what happens with a convex glass gathering together rays of light that have been dispersed. For its function is precisely to restore the unity of the Ideas dispersed by ordinary cognitive knowing.

F. The Ideas and Antecedent Rationality

Considering what has already been said in the preceding sections about the inter-relatedness of Ideas and phenomena, coupled with Schopenhauer's refusal to even consider explaining a given organism as an aggregate of lower Ideas, a streak of rationality and purpose appears to color not only the crust of the real world as it presents itself in perception, but also in the inter-connectedness of the Ideas themselves as *universalia ante rem*. Schopenhauer does not resolve the apparent contradiction involved in saying that the noumenal will is blind and aimless while at the same time asserting that it objectifies itself in archetypal Ideas that would seem thereby to imply a certain rationality.

In short, it appears that there is more to the noumenon than Schopenhauer would perhaps care to admit. For one is struck at the very outset by the fact that levels of the will's objectification form part of a harmonious whole. Schopenhauer even likens this inner and outer suitability to the way voices harmonize: "...the whole world with all its phenomena is the objectivity of the one and indivisible will, the Idea, which is related to all other Ideas as harmony to individual voices; for that reason, that unity of the will must also show itself in the agreement of all its phenomena with one another."³⁶³

This notwithstanding, the teleology to which Schopenhauer alludes is not to be blown out of proportion. Once again, Schopenhauer's own words suggest this: "the reciprocal adaptation and accommodation of the phenomena springing from this unity does not eradicate the inner antagonism...which appears in the universal struggle of nature, which is essential to the will."³⁶⁴ Paradoxically, the order that characterizes the immediate objectification of the will in its various grades is forced to have a strange bedfellow: the chaotic state of affairs that necessarily scars the world of particulars and individuals, given the will's alienated intrinsic nature.³⁶⁵

A tension is thus visible between two aspects of reality: the chaotic or disordered which can be gleaned in the world of particulars as governed by will-oriented knowing (that falls under the principle of sufficient reason); and the implicitly-ordered as represented by the Ideas, which constitute the will's adequate or immediate objectification. In fact, for

---

³⁶³ *Vorstellung I*, §28, I, S.211. "...ja die ganze Welt, mit allen ihren Erscheinungen, die Objektität des einen und untheilbaren Willens ist, die Idee, welche sich zu allen andern Ideen verhält, wie die Harmonie zu den einzelnen Stimmen, daher jene Einheit des Willens sich auch in der Uebereinstimmung aller Erscheinungen desselben zu einander zeigen muß."; *Representation*, I, §28, p.158.

³⁶⁴ *Ibid.*, S.214. "Inzwischen kann das aus dieser Einheit entspringende sich wechselseitige Anpassen und Sichbequemen der Erscheinungen dennoch nicht den oben dargestellten, im allgemeinen Kampf der Natur erscheinenden innern Widerstreit tilgen, der dem Willen wesentlich ist."; *Ibid.*, p.161.

³⁶⁵ *Ibid.*, S.215. "Wenn demnach, vermöge jener Harmonie und Akkommodation, die *Species* im Organischen und die *allgemeinen Naturkräfte* im Unorganischen neben einander bestehn, sogar sich wechselseitig unterstützen; so zeigt sich dagegen der innere Widerstreit des durch alle jene Ideen objektivirten Willens im unaufhörlichen Vertilgungskriege der *Individuen* jener Species und im beständigen Ringen der *Erscheinungen* jener Naturkräfte mit einander, wie oben ausgeführt worden." *Ibid.*

Schopenhauer it is this aspect of the will's objectification that explains in part why reality has not been rent asunder by destructive forces. "That harmony goes only so far that it makes possible the *duration* of the world and its beings, without which, therefore, it would have long since perished."[366]

The question that arises is whether this world view that Schopenhauer espouses does not in some way imply Mind. Or, if one prefers to look at the issue from a different angle, it would appear that the noumenal will, desirous as it is for a highest possible objectification, is thereby marked by a paradoxical rationality. Though the Ideas may be the most objective aspect of what is given one in perception, it is not altogether clear whether they can merely have a logical character given Schopenhauer's claim that they constitute an immediate and antecedent objectification of the will, inasmuch as they can be considered *universalia ante rem*.

There is at least one passage where Schopenhauer implies that Ideas exist in the mind of divinity, which is highly significant for the discussion at hand. The fragment that follows is taken from the same passage alluded to above in which Schopenhauer comments on Book 6 of the *Republic*. To place the passage in context, it must first be underscored that Schopenhauer is making a distinction between the general concept (*Generalbegriff*) and the Platonic Idea that the human mind is capable of having.

> ...the difference is this: that these Ideas, though unequally more perfect and only as part of a greater Idea, must have resided in Divinity with the creation of the form and in this manner Divinity communicated its Idea to man through the organ of nature, which can be

---
[366] *Ibid.*, S.214; *Ibid*.

> regarded as its language. Metaphorically it will be clear when one says: Ideas are realities existing in God...Those Ideas...which lie within us without any object in the world of the senses, God has, as it were, therefore, communicated to us...through the language of nature.[367]

The passage speaks for itself and is fascinating because of the implications it raises for the discussion now being considered. Its importance though cannot be exaggerated since it is an isolated and early fragment. One cannot exactly be sure whether Schopenhauer, even at this early stage of his intellectual development, was commenting about what Plato said and meant, or whether the above sentences actually represented his views at that particular time.

In any case, while it is alluded that the Ideas are exemplars or prototypes in *Die Welt als Wille und Vorstellung*, there is no mention of their being realities in a divine mind. He does, however, cite ancient commentators of Plato who considered the Ideas to be exemplars of naturally existing things and alludes to one commentator in particular who explicitly calls the Ideas exemplars existing in the mind of God.[368] But as far as his own particular adaptation of the Ideas, a consideration of them as prototypes is as far as he is willing to go.

This having been said, the serious difficulty to which this study has been alluding still remains. How can what is blind, aimless, and irrational objectify itself in what exudes an evident rationality? The presence of the Ideas in his *Weltanschauung* gives

---

[367] *Nachlaß*, I, #15, S.11; *Remains*, I, #15, p.11.

[368] *Vorstellung I*, §25, I, S.177-178, 270; *Representation*, I, §25, pp.130, 211-212.

Schopenhauer's philosophy a paradoxical and even dualistic character, in that there is a cleavage between an order that can be known by reason, and a disorder that can be existentially experienced. A satisfactory reply to the dilemma at hand is not given. In short, an answer to the above difficulties is beyond human rational capacities. Even the raising of the question is flawed. For Schopenhauer succinctly states: "Everywhere a ground can be given only of phenomena as such, only of individual things, never of the will itself, or of the Idea in which it adequately objectifies itself."[369] Ultimately, why order and disorder are intertwined is a mystery to be contemplated, for which words can never suffice to describe and unravel.

G. Knowing the Ideas

1. Knower as individual

It was stressed above that for Schopenhauer the Idea remains a representation insofar as it retains the universal form of the phenomenon, that of being an object for a subject. As such, an Idea constitutes a known in someone's mind. Since the subordinate forms of the principle of sufficient reason do not pertain to the Ideas in that the latter are beyond space, time, and causality, knowing an Idea differs from the awareness we have of particular phenomena. Accordingly, Schopenhauer makes a distinction between the knowledge we have as *individuals* and the knowledge that we can theoretically have as *pure subjects of knowing*.

---

[369] *Ibid.*, §29, S.216; *Ibid.*, §29, p.163.

At this juncture, it is important to recall what was said earlier about the centrality of the body in knowing the world as it presents itself in perception. Each of us knows objects as given in perception via our corporeality, which is the point of reference for our interaction with the world. We are not disembodied cherubs. Rather, our bodies remind us of our rootedness in this world and indeed serve as the anchor by which all other objects, as given in experience, are related to our will. This in short is what Schopenhauer means when he says that we all know as *individuals*.

> ...originally and according to its essence, knowledge is thoroughly subservient to the will, and, like the immediate object which, by the application of the law of causality, becomes the starting-point of [knowledge], is only objectified will. Thus, all knowledge which follows the principle of sufficient reason remains in a nearer or remoter relation to the will. For the individual finds his body as an object among objects, to which it has manifold relations and connections according to the principle of sufficient reason, the consideration of which, therefore, always leads back by a nearer or farther path, to his body, therefore, to his will.[370]

What the principle of sufficient reason does is place objects in relationship to that body whose inner states comprise an immediate object of consciousness for each person. It is exactly this capacity that all objects have, as far as their being related to the perceiver who wills, that confers upon them an element of attraction or interest.[371] This is however all dependent upon the

---

[370] *Vorstellung I*, §33, I, S.230; *Representation*, I, §33, pp.176-177.

[371] *Ibid*. "Da es der Satz vom Grunde ist, der die Objekte in diese Beziehung zum Leibe und dadurch zum Willen stellt; so wird die diesem dienende Erkenntniß auch einzig bestrebt seyn, von den Objekten eben die durch den Satz vom Grunde gesetzten Verhältnisse kennen zu lernen, also ihren mannigfaltigen Beziehungen in Raum, Zeit und Kausalität nachgehn. Denn nur durch diese ist das Objekt dem Individuo *interessant*, d.h. hat ein Verhältniß zum Willen."; *Ibid.*,

corporeality of the perceiver, which necessarily makes him or her a knower as *individual*.

2. Scientific knowing

Scientific knowledge for Schopenhauer forms a bridge between ordinary will-oriented knowing and purely objective knowledge of the Ideas. Because it concerns primarily the apprehension of the relations that things have to one another (and not so much with the relations of things insofar as they serve as motives for the will), scientific knowledge forms a transition to the purely objective knowledge of the Ideas.[372] "What the sciences consider in things is also essentially nothing more than...their relations, the connections of time and space, the causes of natural changes, the comparison of forms, the motives of events, and thus merely relations."[373]

Recall that via will-oriented cognition what is also considered is the relations of objects. With scientific knowledge, however, the orientation towards willing is not as pronounced or as strong. But what essentially distinguishes scientific knowing from

---

p.117.

[372] *Vorstellung II*, Kap.29, IV, S.431. "...erkennt der im Dienste des Willens, also in seiner natürlichen Funktion thätige Intellekt eigentlich bloße *Beziehungen* der Dinge: zunächst nämlich ihre Beziehungen auf den Willen, dem er angehört, selbst, wodurch sie zu Motiven desselben werden; dann aber auch, eben zum Behuf der Vollständigkeit dieser Erkenntniß, die Beziehungen der Dinge zu einander. Diese letztere Erkenntniß tritt in einiger Ausdehnung und Bedeutsamkeit erst beim menschlichen Intellekt ein; beim thierischen hingegen, selbst wo er schon beträchtlich entwickelt ist, nur innerhalb sehr enger Gränzen. Offenbar geschieht die Auffassung der Beziehungen, welche die Dinge *zu einander* haben, nur noch *mittelbar* im Dienste des Willens. Sie macht daher den Uebergang zu dem von diesem ganz unabhängigen, rein objektiven Erkennen: sie ist wissenschaftliche, dieses die künstlerische."; *Representation*, II, ch.29, p.363.

[373] *Vorstellung I*, §33, I, S.230; *Representation*, I, §33, p.177.

ordinary will-oriented cognition is the more noticeable systematic element whereby particular things are summarized by means of the subordination of concepts.[374]

In this regard, for Schopenhauer concepts constitute "the proper material (*eigentliche Materie*) of the sciences (*Wissenschaften*), whose objectives in the end, can be reduced to knowledge of the particular through the general, which is only possible by means of the *dictum de omni et nullo*, and this again only through the existence of concepts."[375] What this implies is that the sciences all fall under one or another form of the principle of sufficient reason, which deals with mere relations among objects.[376] Consequently, no science can ever advance beyond the phenomenal sphere regardless as to its objectivity. At best, scientific knowledge can take one to the very threshold of the Ideas. This is why Schopenhauer considers scientific knowing to be transitional, in between as it were, normal will-oriented cognition and knowledge of the Ideas.

3. The path to insight

Schopenhauer repeatedly notes that the normal tendency of our intellect is to be ensconced in willing. Schopenhauer even distinguishes types of intelligence so as to illustrate this truth. For example, he refers to

---

[374] *Ibid.* "Was sie von der gemeinen Erkenntniß unterscheidet, ist bloß ihre Form, das Systematische, die Erleichterung der Erkenntniß durch Zusammenfassung alles Einzelnen, mittelst Unterordnung der Begriffe, ins Allgemeine, und dadurch erlangte Vollständigkeit derselben.";*Ibid.*

[375] *Grunde*, §27, V, S.117-118; *Reason*, §27, p.151.

[376] *Ibid.*, §51, S.174; *Ibid.*, §51, pp.230-231: "*Jede Wissenschaft hat eine der Gestaltungen des Satzes vom Grunde vor den andern zum Leitfaden.*"

the "ordinary man" who can only see things as they relate to his own will.³⁷⁷ The very "stamp of commonness," asserts Schopenhauer, is written on the faces of the great majority in that with them knowing is in strict subordination to willing.³⁷⁸ The intelligent and rational man (*verständige und vernünftige Mann*) is also singled out, as are prudent, eminent and practically-able individuals. But his point is always the same: in such cases, the intellect is concerned with choosing the best ends and means, which certainly suggests that the will is implicated.³⁷⁹ Though will-oriented knowing is essential for survival in the day-to-day vicissitudes of life, it can never make one privy to what the Ideas are.

In order to know the Ideas, a change must occur in the subject of knowing. An intellectual conversion ensues whereby the knower transcends the corporeality that stubbornly attaches him or her to willing. It entails a tearing of oneself away from service to the will and becoming what Schopenhauer calls "a pure will-

---

[377] *Vorstellung I*, §36, I, S.242. "Der gewöhnliche Mensch, diese Fabrikwaare der Natur, wie sie solche täglich zu Tausenden hervorbringt, ist, wie gesagt, einer in jedem Sinn völlig uninteressirten Betrachtung, welches die eigentliche Beschaulichkeit ist, wenigstens durchaus nicht anhaltend fähig: er kann seine Aufmerksamkeit auf die Dinge nur insofern richten, als sie irgend eine, wenn auch nur sehr mittelbare Beziehung auf seinen Willen haben."; *Representation*, I, §36, p.187.

[378] *Vorstellung II*, Kap.31, IV, S.450-451. "Der Stämpel der Gewöhnlichkeit, der Ausdruck von Vulgarität, welcher den allermeisten Gesichtern aufgedrückt ist, besteht eigentlich darin, daß die strenge Unterordnung ihres Erkennens unter ihr Wollen, die feste Kette, welche Beide zusammenschließt, und die daraus folgende Unmöglichkeit, die Dinge anders als in Beziehung auf den Willen und seine Zwecke aufzufassen, darin sichtbar ist."; *Representatation*, II, ch.31, p.380.

[379] *Ibid.*, S.458; *Ibid.*, p.387.

less subject of knowledge" (*reines, willensloses Subjekt der Erkenntniß*)."[380]

Schopenhauer underscores that scaling the plateaus of insight into the Ideas is rare. In fact, in the previous citation, he calls it an "exception" (*Ausnahme*) that takes place quite suddenly. In light of this insight, one sees an object in a different way, and thereby no longer according to the subordinate forms of the principle of sufficient reason, oriented as it is to willing. Rather, what ensues is the contemplation of an object as it truly is. In a word, ordinary knowledge is momentarily left behind.

In this respect, only the *what* of a thing matters; the *wheres*, *whys*, *whens*, and *whithers* pale into insignificance before the pristine beauty of what now fills the consciousness.[381] The intellect, temporarily liberated from the will, soars above normal knowing and fuses itself with the contemplated object. "One *loses* oneself (*sich verliert*) entirely in this object, that is to say, one even forgets his individuality, his will, and continues to exist (*bestehend bleibt*) only as a clear mirror of the object, so that it is as though the object alone existed without anyone to perceive it."[382]

---

[380] *Vorstellung I*, §34, I, S.231. "Der,wie gesagt, mögliche, aber nur als Ausnahme zu betrachtende Uebergang von der gemeinen Erkenntniß einzelner Dinge zur Erkenntniß der Idee geschieht plötzlich, indem die Erkenntniß sich vom Dienste des Willens losreißt, eben dadurch das Subjekt aufhört ein bloß individuelles zu seyn und jetzt reines, willenloses Subjekt der Erkenntniß ist, welches nicht mehr, dem Satze vom Grunde gemäß, den Relationen nachgeht; sondern in fester Kontemplation des dargebotenen Objekts, außer seinem Zusammenhange mit irgend andern, ruht und darin aufgeht."; *Representation*, I, §34, p.178.

[381] *Ibid.*, S.231-232. "Wann man, durch die Kraft des Geistes gehoben, die gewöhnliche Betrachtungsart der Dinge fahren läßt, aufhört, nur ihren Relationen zu einander, deren letztes Ziel immer die Relation zum eigenen Willen ist, am Leitfaden der Gestaltungen des Satzes vom Grunde, nachzugehn, also nicht mehr das Wo, das Wann, das Warum und das Wozu an den Dingen betrachtet; sondern einzig und allein das *Was*." *Ibid.*

[382] *Ibid.*, S.232.; *Ibid.*

Schopenhauer goes on to say that a fusion between the perceiver (*Anschauenden*) and the perception (*Anschauung*) takes place because the whole consciousness is filled and occupied by the single image of the perception. When this transpires, the subject passes out of all relation to the will and the object itself passes from all relation to anything outside it. Thus, the individual object as such is not known, but rather the Idea or immediate objectification of the will at this particular grade.[383] A two-fold change, therefore occurs: one in the knower as *individual* who now becomes the "pure subject of knowing"; the other in the particular thing which is now elevated to "the Idea of its species."[384]

What is most important though, is that as soon as one scales the summits of will-less knowing and beholds the Idea, a pristine picture of the world as representation arises in that what is most objective about the phenomenon becomes almost tangible. Schopenhauer states that "the *world as representation* stands out whole and pure, and the complete objectification of the will happens, for only the Idea is

---

[383] *Ibid.* "...so, daß es ist, als ob der Gegenstand allein dawäre, ohne Jemanden, der ihn wahrnimmt, und man also nicht mehr den Anschauenden von der Anschauung trennen kann, sondern Beide Eines geworden sind, indem das ganze Bewußtseyn von einem einzigen anschaulichen Bilde gänzlich gefüllt und eingenommen ist; wenn also solchermaaßen das Objekt aus aller Relation zu etwas außer ihm, das Subjekt aus aller Relation zum Willen getreten ist: dann ist, was also erkannt wird, nicht mehr das einzelne Ding als solches; sondern die *Idee*, die ewige Form, die unmittelbare Objektität des Willens auf dieser Stufe: und eben dadurch ist zugleich der in dieser Anschauung Begriffene nicht mehr Individuum: denn das Individuum hat sich eben in solche Anschauung verloren: sondern er ist *reines*, willenloses, schmerzloses, zeitloses *Subjekt der Erkenntniß*."; *Ibid.*, pp.178-179.

[384] *Ibid.*, S.232-233. "In solcher Kontemplation nun wird mit Einem Schlage das einzelne Ding zur *Idee* seiner Gattung und das anschauende Individuum zum *reinen Subjekt des Erkennens*. Das Individuum als solches erkennt nur einzelne Dinge; das reine Subjekt des Erkennens nur Ideen."; *Ibid.*, p.179.

the adequate objectification of the will."³⁸⁵ Thus, in contemplation of the Idea, the "real world as representation" arises once the subject and object mutually fill and penetrate each other.³⁸⁶

Apprehension of the Ideas always involves a temporary diminishing of self-awareness in that it involves a momentary abandonment of willing. For this reason, Schopenhauer calls the apprehension of the Idea an "act of self denial" (*Akt der Selbst-verleugnung*).³⁸⁷ Because the will is the source of all misery and disquiet, apprehension of the Idea brings momentary deliverance and peace. "For the moment when, torn from the will (*vom Willen losgerissen*), we have given ourselves up to pure, will-less knowing, we have, as it were, stepped into another world where everything which moves our will, and in that way fiercely agitates us, no longer exists."³⁸⁸

In fact, Schopenhauer adds that "the state of pure objectivity of perception" makes one thoroughly

---

³⁸⁵ *Ibid.*, S.233; *Ibid.*

³⁸⁶ *Ibid.*, S.233-234. "Wie, indem die Idee hervortritt, in ihr Subjekt und Objekt nicht mehr zu unterscheiden sind, weil erst indem sie sich gegenseitig vollkommen erfüllen und durchdringen, die Idee, die adäquate Objektität des Willens, die eigentliche Welt als Vorstellung, ersteht; eben so sind auch das dabei erkennende und das erkannte Individuum, als Dinge an sich, nicht unterschieden. Denn sehn wir von jener eigentlichen *Welt als Vorstellung* gänzlich ab, so bleibt nichts übrig, denn die *Welt als Wille*."; *Ibid.*, p.180.

³⁸⁷ *Vorstellung II*, Kap.30, IV, S.435. "Zur Auffassung einer Idee, zum Eintritt derselben in unser Bewußtseyn, kommt es nur mittelst einer Veränderung in uns, die man auch als einen Akt der Selbstverleugnung betrachten könnte; sofern sie darin besteht, daß die Erkenntniß sich ein Mal vom eigenen Willen gänzlich abwendet, also das ihr anvertraute theure Pfand jetzt gänzlich aus den Augen läßt und die Dinge so betrachtet, als ob sie den Willen nie etwas angehn könnten."; *Representation*, II, ch.30, p.367.

³⁸⁸ *Vorstellung I*, §38, I, S.254; *Representation*, I, §38, p.197.

happy.[389] It is consciousness of our willing that alone inhibits perception of the Ideas, which as it were, are already there in the objects as given in perception. In this regard, scaling the high plateaus of will-less knowing leaves in its wake a key to appreciating an order in things. For this reason, "all things present themselves the more beautifully the more one is merely conscious of them, and the less one is conscious of oneself."[390]

Unfortunately, apprehending the Ideas is difficult and temporary at best. Given our corporeal individuality, we are all too prone to once again fall into the normal day-to-day pattern of will-oriented knowing. Accordingly, the consciousness hitherto purged by contemplation of the Idea, is refilled with the emotions, passions and wants so characteristic of willing.[391] Moreover, the very grasping of the Idea itself, in the final analysis, is almost a futile endeavor since even this type of insight is too quickly related to the will or person of the perceiver.[392]

---

[389] *Vorstellung II*, Kap.30, IV, S.436. "Denn nur dann faßt man die Welt rein objektiv auf, wann man nicht mehr weiß, daß man dazu gehört; und alle Dinge stellen sich um so schöner dar, je mehr man sich bloß ihrer und je weniger man sich seiner selbst bewußt ist. -Da nun alles Leiden aus dem Willen, der das eigentliche Selbst ausmacht, hervorgeht; so ist, mit dem Zurücktreten dieser Seite des Bewußtseyns, zugleich alle Möglichkeit des Leidens aufgehoben, wodurch der Zustand der reinen Objektivität der Anschauung ein durchaus beglückender wird."; *Representatation*, II, ch.30, p.368.

[390] *Ibid.*; *Ibid.*

[391] *Ibid.*, S.437. "Sobald...das Bewußtseyn des eigenen Selbst, also die Subjektivität, d.i. der Wille, wieder das Uebergewicht erhält, tritt auch ein demselben angemessener Grad von Unbehagen oder Unruhe ein: von Uhbehagen, sofern die Leiblichkeit (der Organismus, welcher an sich Wille ist) wieder fühlbar wird; von Unruhe, sofern der Wille, auf geistigem Wege, durch Wünsche, Affekte, Leidenschaften, Sorgen, das Bewußtseyn wieder erfüllt."; *Ibid.*

[392] *Vorstellung I*, §38, I, S.254. "Sobald irgend eine Beziehung eben jener also rein angeschauten Objekte zu unserm Willen, zu unserer Person, wieder ins Bewußtseyn tritt, hat der Zauber ein Ende: wir fallen zurück in die Erkenntniß, welche der Satz vom Grunde beherrscht, erkennen nun nicht mehr die Idee, sondern

H. Knowledge of the Ideas as Genius

1. Context of Schopenhauer's theory of genius

The meaning of *genius* was being debated in intellectual circles during the height of Rationalism and Romanticism in Western Philosophy:[393] Is genius a power of heightened understanding or reason? Is it a condition related to the soul and the emotions? Is it a faculty of the subconscious? Is it essentially different from talent? Is it something spiritual or divine? Is it mere originality? Does it pertain to the arts or sciences, or to both? These were some of the questions that were being raised and which set the context for Schopenhauer's interpretation of genius in his system.[394]

Hübscher writes that the period of Rationalism was inclined to consider genius as an "intensification of the powers of the understanding."[395] As a case in

---

das einzelne Ding, das Glied einer Kette, zu der auch wir gehören, und wir sind allem unserm Jammer wieder hingegeben." *Representation*, I, §38, p.198.

[393] Cf. Arthur Hübscher, *Denker gegen den Strom*, S.84-107; Rüdiger Safranski, *Schopenhauer und die wilden Jahren der Philosophie*, S.98-107; "Genie,: *Historisches Wörterbuch der Philosophie*, Band I. Herausgegeben von Joachim Ritter (Basel/Stuttgart: Schwabe & Co., 1971), S.280-308; Giorgio Tonelli, "Kant's Early Theory of Genius," *Journal of the History of Philosophy*, 4 (1966), 109-131, 209-224.

[394] Cf. Hübscher, S.85. "Verwandtes und Trennendes aber wird erst im Rückgang auf die tieferen Zusammenhänge der romantischen Kunstauffassung deutlich sichtbar, in denen der Geniebegriff etwas seltsam Schillerndes gewonnen hat. Man stand in den Jahren um die Jahrhundertwende vor einer Fülle auseinandergehender und widersprüchlicher Deutungen des Wesens der Genialität. Seit der Zeit der Renaissance hatte die Vorstellung des überragenden, ruhmeswürdigen Menschen und seiner Ausnahmestellung in der großen Menge Raum gewonnen. Man fühlte, daß diese Menschen nur sparsam über die Jahrhunderte verteilt sind, man sprach von ihrer angeborenen, über alle Nachahmung, alle erlernbaren Regeln erhabenen Begabung, die Frage aber, wie diese Begabung zu erkären sei, wurde noch zu Anfang des 18. Jahrhunderts kaum gestellt. Ist das Genie eine Kraft erhöhten Verstandes, erhöhter Vernunft, oder ist es etwas Seelisches, Gefühlsmäßiges, eine Fähigkeit des Unbewußten? Hat es an beiden Sphären teil, gleichmäßig, oder überwiegt vielleicht die eine die andere: Es war schwer, sich zurechtzufinden."

[395] *Ibid.*, S.85.

point, Hübscher notes that Gottsched's *Vernünftige Tadlerinnen* (1717) describes genius as a "combination (*Mischung*) of all the intellectual capacities of a 'sound reason'"[396] He continues by juxtaposing the views of Baumgarten and Helvétius. In regard to the former, genius entails a harmony of the psychic powers with each other; while for the latter, genius is not an intuitive capacity, but neither is it mysterious nor irrational. It is, rather, the talent for making connections.[397] With Kant the balance between the cognitive powers of sensibility, judgement, spirit and taste is what is constitutive of genius.[398] More specifically, in the *Critique of Judgement*, Kant states that genius is "the talent (natural endowment) that gives the rule to art...the innate mental predisposition (*ingenium*) through which nature gives the rule to art."[399] Genius is a *talent* for producing something for which no determinate rule can be given. As such, the *first* and foremost property of genius is *originality*.[400] It is *exemplary* in that its products serve as models (as a rule by which to judge).[401] Moreover, genius as inborn, "cannot describe or indicate scientifically how it brings about its products..."[402] Schopenhauer's theory of genius,

---

[396] *Ibid.*

[397] *Ibid.*, S.85-86.

[398] Cf. Giorgio Tonelli, "Kant's Early Theory of Genius (1770-1779): Part I," *History of Philosophy*, 4 (1966), p.114 and pp.122-123.

[399] Cf. Immanuel Kant, *Critique of Judgement*, trans. Werner S. Pluhar (Indianapolis: Hackett Publishing Company, 1987), §46, p.174.

[400] *Ibid.*, p.175.

[401] *Ibid.*

[402] *Ibid.*

however, goes beyond the Kantian notion as espoused in the *Critique of Judgement* and was more profoundly influenced by the Romantic writings of Thieck, Wackenroder and Jean Paul in the early years prior to the crystallization of his metaphysical picture of reality in *Die Welt als Wille und Vorstellung*. Their influence was of marked significance in the Schopenhauerian analysis of the nature and disposition of the genius, the differentiation between genius and talent, the juxtaposition and contrast between the genius and philistine-mentality of the majority, the objectivity of genius, music as the highest of the arts and so forth.[403] Diderot's highlighting of the imagination, as the focal point of the creative spirit, was also an influence together with J.S. Sulzer's *Allgemeine Theorie der Schöenen Künste* which linked genius to the feeling of the beautiful.[404] Goethe's adaption of the Promethean motif (that had already been used in the writings of Shaftesbury as an emblem for that which is creative and divine in the artist), was also influential in Schopenhauer. Moreover, its use by Goethe as a symbol

---

[403] Cf. Hübscher, S.84-85 and S.90-94.

[404] *Ibid.*, S.86. "Mag sein, daß Schopenhauer in J.S. Sulzers »Allgemeiner Theorie der schönen Künste«, die er bereits im Mai 1806 im Hamburg erwarb, neben den gewohnten Hinweisen auf die Kräfte des Verstandes und des sittlichen Gefühls zum ersten Male auch die Rede vom Gefühl des Schönen fand, das sorglich gepflegt werden müsse, und von der göttlichen Kraft des Genies, das berufen sei, es zu pflegen, -- eine zaghafte, noch kaum vernehmbare Rede, gewiß. Aber schon Diderot hatte die Einbildungskraft, die empfängliche, leidenschaftlich suchende Tätigkeit der Seele geltend gemacht, das Dämonische in ihr, ihre schöpferische Kraft. Und mit Nachdruck hatte er seither oft wiederholte Meinung ausgesprochen: Regeln nützen dem Talent, sie schaden dem Genie. Es war Diderot, den Schopenhauer später neben Jean Paul als Vorläufer seiner eigenen Lehre vom Genie erklärt hat, aber freilich: »beide sind an der Oberfläche geblieben«. Diderots Auffassung kehrt bei Rousseau wieder: Merkmale des Genies sind das Intuitive, die Schöpferkraft, die Übermächtigung durch eine höhere Gewalt. Und auch von der Unabhängigkeit des Genies von allen Äusserlichkeiten und von der Unmöglichkeit der Regeln ist die Rede, ähnlich wie den Hinweisen Merciers, des berühmten Dramatikers und Sittenschilderers, auf das Wilde, Dynamische, Prometheische des Genies, das ohne die Regel auskommt."

and motif of the isolation of the creative man, finds echoes in Schopenhauer's thinking as well.[405]

One cannot properly speak of a direct influence of post-Kantian Absolute Idealism (Fichte, Hegel, and Schelling) on Schopenhauer's aesthetic theories inasmuch as he rejected any attempt to consider art as a reconciliation of the contradictions in human nature into a balance of the human faculties.[406] Hübscher writes:

> As much as [Schopenhauer] perceived art, in proximity to Wackenroder and Tieck, Schlegel and Schelling, as a power which intensifies and frees that which is human, his concern was not balance and reconciliation on any level of evolution. Rising to the Beautiful is for him as much as it is for Plato a severing of the human being from the lower half of his nature. Our capabilities should not be brought into balance; one is to maintain predominance over all the others. This is the meaning of aspiring towards a better consciousness.[407]

Genius in Schopenhauer's philosophy is not associated with the vocation to the supernatural as it is with Fichte.[408] Nor is it akin to Schelling's conscious-unconscious activity of the Ego, which as Intelligence, effects nature.[409] In short, for Schopenhauer genius is not an incarnation of the Absolute. Rather, as will be seen, in the section to follow, it is the capacity to recognize the Platonic Ideas in the phenomenon.[410]

---

[405] *Ibid.*, S.88-89.

[406] *Ibid.*, S.89-90.

[407] *Ibid.*, S.90.

[408] Cf. "Genio," *Enciclopedia filosofica*, III (Roma: Edipem, 1979), p.887.

[409] Cf. Hübscher, S.89.

[410] Cf. "Genio," *Diccionario de filosofia*, ed. José Ferrata Mora, II (Madrid: Alianza Editorial, 1982), p.1340. "Schopenhauer especificò la noción del genio en relación con su propria metafisica; el genio es para este autor...el que es capaz de ver la Idea en el fenomeno."

2. Schopenhauer's theory of genius

For Schopenhauer knowing the Platonic Ideas presupposes a certain strength of intellect necessary to rise above everyday will-oriented knowledge. The capacity for this type of transcendence is called *genius* by Schopenhauer. He states that it "consists in the ability (*Fähigkeit*) to know independently of the principle of sufficient reason, instead of individual things which have their existence only in relation, the Ideas of the things, and in the face of these, to be the correlative of the Idea, and hence no longer the individual, but rather the pure subject of knowledge."[411] Genius in Schopenhauer's *Weltanschauung* has nothing to do with the principle of sufficient reason which, even at its best, considers merely the relations of things, as in the case of scientific knowledge. Accordingly, it would be erroneous to regard genius as brilliance for the sciences, for example, inasmuch as genius completely transcends any type of knowing governed by the principle of sufficient reason: "the method of consideration (*Betrachtungsart*) that follows the principle of sufficient reason is the rational (*vernünftige*) method, and it alone is valid and useful in practical life and in science."[412]

At this point, Schopenhauer's aesthetical theories could be outlined and examined. But since such a task is incidental to the argumentation of the remainder of this study, only a few significant points about genius and human nature as such need to be mentioned. Schopenhauer states that the "ability to know

---

[411] *Vorstellung I*, §37, I, S.250; *Representation*, I, §37, p.194.

[412] *Ibid.*, §36, S.239; *Ibid.*, §36, p.185.

independently of the principle of sufficient reason, in a lesser and differing degree, must...be inherent (*einwohnen*) in all men."[413] All people have a susceptibility (*Empfänglichkeit*) to the beautiful and the sublime. Schopenhauer, accordingly, draws the conclusion that "we must assume as existing in all men...the power (*Vermögen*) to recognize in things their Ideas, and precisely therefore to momentarily divest themselves (*sich entäussern*) of their personality."[414]

True, while not everyone is gifted with the capacity to produce works of art which is another way of describing genius, all human beings have a natural capacity to sense what the beautiful is. Accordingly, natural beauty, as it were, invites contemplation and presses itself on the beholder whose tormented spirit seems to be revived with but "a free glance into nature."[415] The "genius" *per se* differs from ordinary individuals in light of the greater capacity he has for knowledge of the Ideas, not to mention his ability to remain in this higher state of knowing for a longer period of time. This in turn enables the genius to retain what he contemplates and repeat what is known in an arbitrary work of art in which the grasped Idea is

---

[413] *Ibid.*, §37, S.250; *Ibid.*, §37, p.194.

[414] *Ibid.*; *Ibid.*

[415] *Ibid.*, §38, S.253-254. "So viel leistet ganz allein die innere Kraft eines künstlerischen Gemüthes; aber erleichtert und von außen befördert wird jene rein objektive Gemüthsstimmung durch entgegenkommende Objekte, durch die zu ihrem Anschauen einladende, ja sich aufdringende Fülle der schönen Natur. Ihr gelingt es, so sie mit einem Male unserm Blicke sich aufthut, fast immer, uns, wenn auch nur auf Augenblicke, der Subjektivität, dem Sklavendienste des Willens zu entreißen und in den Zustand des reinen Erkennens zu versetzen."; *Ibid.*, §38, p.197.

communicated to others.⁴¹⁶ All the arts (except for music), for Schopenhauer, in effect entail the repetition of the contemplated Ideas on the part of the genius.⁴¹⁷ As Chanksy writes: "By means...of architecture, sculpture, painting, poetry, and drama, artists present for knowledge copies of the Ideas, and by means of these Ideas we gain insight into the inner nature of the world."⁴¹⁸

3. Music and the Ideas

It is interesting to note that Schopenhauer maintains that music, unlike the other arts, does not repeat the Ideas of phenomena as given in perception. Rather, it mirrors the noumenal will in a direct fashion. Schopenhauer is very clear on this point: "music is in no way like the other arts, namely a copy (*Abbild*) of the Ideas, but a *copy of the will itself*, whose objectivity

---

⁴¹⁶ *Ibid.*, §37, S.250-251. "Der Genius hat vor ihnen nur den viel höhern Grad und die anhaltendere Dauer jener Erkenntnißweise voraus, welche ihn bei derselben die Besonnenheit behalten lassen, die erfordert ist, um das so Erkannte in einem willkürlichen Werk zu wiederholen, welche Wiederholung das Kunstwerk ist. Durch dasselbe theilt er die aufgefaßte Idee den Andern mit. Diese bleibt dabei unverändert und die selbe: daher ist das ästhetische Wohlgefallen wesentlich Eines und das selbe, es mag durch ein Werk der Kunst, oder unmittelbar durch die Anschauung der Natur und des Lebens hervorgerufen seyn."; *Ibid.*, §37, p.195.

⁴¹⁷ *Ibid.*, §36, S.239. " - Welche Erkenntnißart nun aber betrachtet jenes außer und unabhängig von aller Relation bestehende, allein eigentlich Wesentliche der Welt, den wahren Gehalt ihrer Erscheinungen, das keinem Wechsel Unterworfene und daher für alle Zeit mit gleicher Wahrheit Erkannte, mit Einem Wort, die *Ideen*, welche die unmittelbare und adäquate Objektität des Dinges an sich, des Willens, sind? - Es ist die *Kunst*, das Werk des Genius. Sie wiederholt die durch reine Kontemplation aufgefaßten ewigen Ideen, das Wesentliche und Bleibende aller Erscheinungen der Welt, und je nachdem der Stoff ist, in welchem sie wiederholt, ist sie bildende Kunst, Poesie oder Musik. Ihr einziger Ursprung ist die Erkenntniß der Ideen; ihr einziges Ziel Mittheilung dieser Erkenntniß."; *Ibid.*, §36, pp.184-185.

⁴¹⁸ Cf. Chanksy, "Schopenhauer and Platonic Ideas: A Groundwork for an Aesthetic Metaphysics," as found in *Schopenhauer: New Essays in Honor of His 200th Birthday*, p.77.

are the Ideas."[419]   It is precisely for this reason that its effect is so pronounced, expressing as it does the very quintessence of life and human emotions.[420]

Schopenhauer underscores that music "expresses in a very sublime universal language the inner being, the in-itself, of the world, which we think of under the concept of will, according to its most distinct manifestation..."[421] He even claims that there is a correspondence between the four voices of harmony (bass, tenor, alto, and soprano) and the four levels of existence (mineral, plant, animal, man).[422] This notwithstanding, music completely passes over the Ideas and is even independent of the phenomenal world. Thus, Schopenhauer adds that, to a certain extent, music could still exist were there no phenomenal world at all which is not true of the other arts.[423]

---

[419] *Ibid.*, §52, S.324; *Ibid.*, §52, p.257.

[420] *Ibid.*, S.328, 329. "Man darf...nie vergessen, daß die Musik...allein das innere Wesen, das Ansich aller Erscheinung, den Willen selbst, ausspricht...Denn überall drückt die Musik nur die Quintessenz des Lebens und seiner Vorgänge aus..."; *Ibid.*, p.261. Also cf. *Ibid.*, S.331. "Das unaussprechlich Innige aller Musik, vermöge dessen sie als ein so ganz vertrautes und doch ewig fernes Paradies an uns vorüberzieht, so ganz verständlich und doch so unerklärlich ist, beruht darauf, daß sie alle Regungen unsers innersten Wesens wiedergiebt, aber ganz ohne die Wirklichkeit und fern von ihrer Quaal."; *Ibid.*, p.264.

[421] *Ibid.*, S.332; *Ibid.*, p.264.

[422] *Vorstellung II*, Kap.39, IV, S.526. "Die vier Stimmen aller Harmonie, also Baß, Tenor, Alt und Sopran, oder Grundton, Terz, Quinte und Oktave, entsprechen den vier Abstufungen in der Reihe der Wesen, also dem Mineralreich, Pflanzenreich, Thierreich und dem Menschen."; *Representation*, II, ch.39, p.447.

[423] *Vorstellung I*, §52, I, S.323-324. "Die adäquate Objektivation des Willens sind die (Platonische) Ideen; die Erkenntniß dieser durch Darstellung einzelner Dinge (denn solche sind die Kunstwerke selbst doch immer) anzuregen (welches nur unter einer diesem entsprechenden Veränderung im erkennenden Subjekt möglich ist), ist der Zweck aller andern Künste. Sie alle objektiviren also den Willen nur mittelbar, nämlich mittelst der Ideen: und da unsere Welt nichts Anderes ist, als die Erscheinung der Ideen in der Vielheit, mittelst Eingang in das *principium individuationis* (die Form der dem Individuo als solchem möglichen Erkenntniß); so ist die Musik, da sie die Ideen übergeht, auch von der erscheinenden Welt ganz unabhängig, ignorirt sie schlechthin, könnte

World as Idea 151

This is significant because it implies that music itself, since it directly mirrors the noumenal will, mediates truth in a way that the other arts never can. This is the reason why music has a universally powerful effect. Schopenhauer underscores that the clarity of its "language" surpasses even that of the world of perception itself which enables it to strike, as it were, a responsive chord within the depths of human nature.[424] Thus, music is not impaired by the limitations of human language in describing what the real is. It stands in a class by itself.

I. The Ideas and the True Nature of Reality

While music mirrors the noumenal will, grasping the Ideas of particular things can never provide the key to the true essence of things as revelatory of the will. Ideas never usher one into the in-itselfness of things, but rather unveil their most objective character.[425] Schopenhauer continues by underscoring that the essence of the phenomenon that presents itself to consciousness

---

gewissermaaßen, auch wenn die Welt gar nicht wäre, doch bestehn: was von den andern Künsten sich nicht sagen läßt. Die Musik ist nämlich eine so *unmittelbare* Objektivation und Abbild des ganzen *Willens*, wie die Welt selbst es ist, ja wie die Ideen es sind, deren vervielfältigte Erscheinung die Welt der einzelnen Dinge ausmacht."; *Ibid.*, §52, p.257.

[424] *Ibid.*, S.322. "...dennoch ist sie [die Musik] eine so grosse und überaus herrliche Kunst, wirkt so mächtig auf das Innerste des Menschen, wird dort so ganz und so tief von ihm verstanden, als eine ganz allgemeine Sprache, deren Deutlichkeit sogar die der anschaulichen Welt selbst übertrifft."; *Ibid.*, p.256.

[425] *Vorstellung II*, Kap.29, IV, S.433. "...die Ideen offenbaren noch nicht das Wesen an sich, sondern nur den objektiven Charakter der Dinge, also immer nur noch die Erscheinung: und selbst diesen Charakter würden wir nicht verstehn, wenn uns nicht das innere Wesen der Dinge, wenigstens undeutlich und im Gefühl, anderweitig bekannt wäre."; *Representation*, II, ch.29, p.364.

"could not be understood from the Ideas, and in general, through any merely *objective* knowledge."[426]

Given this important nuancing, the ambivalent character of Schopenhauer's picture of reality is evident. On the one hand, he asserts that the noumenal will is blind. Yet on the other hand, the will in its adequate objectification certainly is not purposeless inasmuch as it strives for an ever perfect manifestation of itself, as Taylor correctly suggests.[427] Moreover, the Ideas are expressive of an order that delights the mind and revives the human spirit. But, at the same time, they are incapable of revealing the will's true nature as aimless and blind. The *true essence* of the world as *scarred*, which obviously fascinated Schopenhauer, is known via another route.

The rationality, purpose and beauty that revive the human spirit in aesthetic experience does not leave in its wake insight into what Schopenhauer deems most real, the will. He speaks paradoxically here. Suddenly, it is as if he wishes the reader to focus once again on corporeal individuality essential to will-oriented knowing. For he states that the inner essence of reality "would remain eternally a secret if we did not have access (*Zugang*) to it from an entirely different side."[428] The other side that Schopenhauer is referring to is linked to our rootedness in this world as 'existents' of flesh and bone. "Only insofar as every

---

[426] *Ibid.*; *Ibid.*

[427] Cf. Taylor, p.50: "...I would like to mention a question that arises from my interpretation of Schopenhauer: is Schopenhauer really a pessimist? True, the Will, *qua noumena*, is purposeless; but, in its phenomenal representation it is seeking ever higher manifestations. Doesn't this teleology imply a theodicy: our individual lives might be miserable, but by golly we're suffering for a higher good?"

[428] *Vorstellung II*, Kap.29, IV, S.433; *Representation*, II, ch.29, p.364.

knowing being is at the same time an individual and in that way, a part of nature, does the approach to the interior (*Innern*) of nature stand open to him in his own self-consciousness where it manifests itself most immediately...as *Will*."[429]

It is important to highlight this last point because it illustrates where Schopenhauer's true interest lay and what motivated his philosophizing. He is not so much interested in the rationality and purposefulness of the real. What intrigues him is the element of the chaotic; the disorder and frustration that can be gleaned in human willing in particular, but also the scarredness that streaks the whole of the phenomenon. As he is recorded to have said to the French philosopher Frédérick Morin who visited him in Frankfurt at the beginning of the March of 1858: "A philosophy, in which one does not hear in between the pages, the noise of the tears, the moans, and the gnashing of teeth, and the fearful din of reciprocal and universal murder, is no philosophy."[430] Accordingly, it is not far-fetched to surmise that it is precisely the mystery of evil in the world, as well as the frustration and darkness of the human will, which intrigued him.

True, Schopenhauer grants that the other aspect of reality (namely: order, beauty, and rationality) is also present. He even adds that the human spirit, freed from the shackles of the will's firm clasp, can not only intuitively perceive, but also rejoice in it. But, mysteriously and perhaps because of his own pessimistic

---

[429] *Ibid.*; *Ibid.*

[430] *Gespräche*, S.337: "Une philosophie où l'on n'entend pas bruire à travers les pages les pleurs, les gémissements, les grincements de dents et le cliquetis formidable du meurtre réciproque et universel, n'est pas une philosophie."

disposition, he chooses to focus on the dark side of reality and invites his readers to do likewise.

J. Summary

An overview has now been given of Schopenhauer's world picture. This analysis was necessary so as to ground and contextualize the next issue to be treated in this study: namely, the reality of egoism and possibility of compassion for the human being as a subject of willing. As the argumentation of the following chapters unfolds, the importance of the first three will become clear in that Schopenhauer's views on ethics, God, and religion are based on his metaphysics.

As the title of this study indicates, the underlying issue is the problem of the Sacred in Schopenhauer's thought. From this standpoint, each of the chapters above, which comprise part one, already implicitly touch upon this issue. For it would seem, in the first place, that Schopenhauer's notion of causality excludes the possibility for a philosophical proof for the existence of God since causality is reduced to an infinite series of changes in the state of objects. Secondly, from the standpoint of the noumenon, aseity is attributed only to the will and not to God. Thirdly, the Platonic Ideas in Schopenhauer's system are not realities existing in a Divine Mind.

The religious question, however, specifically pertains to the concluding chapter of this study; where it shall be proposed that a "back door" to the question of the Holy exists in Schopenhauer's *Weltanschauung* from the very fact that the will, in its pristine in-itselfness (i.e. as non-temporal), is the end result of

World as Idea

ascetical praxis. But before addressing this issue, attention needs to be focused on two key notions: the affirmation of the will-to-live; and its antithesis, the denial of the will. The next two chapters, therefore, are directed respectively to that aim.

PART TWO

THE METAPHYSICS OF THE HUMAN PERSON

Chapter 4

The Human Situation

A. Insecurity of Man

It was argued in Part One of this study that the phenomenal world as cognitively grasped is in fact a re-presentation of the noumenal will estranged within itself.[431] In the world of phenomena, the aimless and scarred will, so to speak, loses itself in a numberless multiplicity of particulars.[432] Indeed, it may be said that the phenomenal world incarnates the will. Each grade of the will's objectification fights to conserve the space and time which corresponds to its matter, so as to best express its particular Idea.[433] Seen from this

---

[431] *Vorstellung I*, §60, II, S.413. "Die Welt ist gerade eine solche, weil der Wille, dessen Erscheinung sie ist, ein solcher ist, weil er so will. Für die Leiden ist die Rechtfertigung die, daß der Wille auch auf diese Erscheinung sich selbst bejaht; und diese Bejahung ist gerechtfertigt und ausgeglichen dadurch, daß er die Leiden trägt."; *Representation*, I, §60, p.331.

[432] Raúl Fornet Betancourt, "En favor de Schopenhauer," *Logos* 11 (1983), p.63. "...el mundo es de hecho la voluntad errente ya en la selva de la multiplicidad y la diversidad; la voluntad caída en el espacio y en el tiempo, sometida a la férrea ley del principio de razón sufficiente y condenada a quererse en la unilateralidad de las individualidades en que se ha desintegrado."

[433] *Vorstellung 1*, 1, §27, S.197. "Jede Stufe der Objektivation des Willens macht der andern die Materie, den Raum, die Zeit streitig."; *Representation*, I, §27, pp.146-147; *Ibid.*, §28, S.204-205. "Wir haben die große Mannigfaltigkeit und Verschiedenheit der Erscheinungen betrachtet, in denen der Wille sich objektivirt; ja, wir haben ihren endlosen und unversöhnlichen Kampf gegen einander gesehn. Dennoch ist, unserer ganzen bisherigen Darstellung zufolge, der Wille selbst, als Ding an sich, keineswegs begriffen in jener Vielheit, jenem Wechsel. Die Verschiedenheit der (Platonischen) Ideen, d.i. Abstufungen der Objektivation, die Menge der Individuen, in welchen jede von diesen sich darstellt, der Kampf der Formen um die Materie: dies Alles trifft nicht ihn, sondern ist nur die Art und Weise seiner Objektivation, und hat nur durch diese eine mittelbare Relation zu ihm, vermöge welcher es zum Ausdruck seines Wesens

point of view, the world mirrors a noumenal will that devours itself in the different stages of its objectification. Schopenhauer's ontological scenario, therefore, is not only characterized by an inherent frustration; a never-ending conflict or inner warfare marks it as well.

Given what has already been established by the above discussion, a foundation now exists for an analysis of Schopenhauer's anthropology -- a topic he considered "most serious" and of interest to everyone.[434] The inherent contradictions of man's central place in reality must have interested Schopenhauer from an early age, as biographers and scholars attest.[435] One need only look with an observant eye at some of the comments Schopenhauer made as a fifteen year old teenager in the travel diary he kept when he traveled with his parents through the Netherlands, England and France during their European trip in the years 1803-1804. Particularly poignant is the April 8, 1804 entry in which he describes the impression which the six-thousand galley slaves at Toulon left on his mind:

> The fate of those unfortunates I hold to be far more frightful than the death sentence. The galleys, which I have seen from the outside, seem to be the dirtiest, the most disgusting sojourn which can be imagined. The galleys no longer go to sea; they are old condemned ships. The bed of the Forcats is the bench to which they are chained. Their

---

für die Vorstellung gehört."; *Ibid.*, §28, p.153.

[434] *Ibid.*, §53, II, S.344; *Ibid.*, §53, p.271

[435] Arthur Hübscher, *Arthur Schopenhauer: ein Lebensbild* (Wiesbaden: Eberhard Brockhaus Verlag, 1949), S.16-17; Arthur Hübscher, *Denker gegen den Strom*, S.11; Safranski, *Schopenhauer und die wilden Jahre der Philosophie*, S.66f.; Helen Zimmern, *Arthur Schopenhauer: His Life and His Philosophy* (London: Longmans, Green and Co., 1896), pp. 24-25; V.J. McGill, *Schopenhauer Pessimist and Pagan* (New York: Haskell House Publishers, 1971), pp.50-51, 65-67.

> food is only water and bread, and I do not understand how they, without a more substantive nourishment and consumed by grief, do not succumb sooner with the hard work. For during their slavery, they are treated altogether like beasts of burden: it is frightful to think that the life of these miserable galley-slaves...is totally joyless.[436]

Another entry from the "Cholerabuch" section of his manuscript notes in the *Nachlaß* (1832) is in keeping with the above. What is significant below, however, is Schopenhauer's claim that the misery of life was a central factor that led to his subsequent rejection of Judeo-Christian theism.

> In my 17th year, without any academic formation, I was as moved by the *wretchedness of life* as Buddha was in his youth, when he saw sickness, old age, pain, and death. The truth which the world spoke loudly and clearly, soon prevailed over the Jewish dogmas which had been impressed in me, and my conclusion was that this world could not be the work of an infinitely-good Being, but rather that of a devil who had brought creatures into existence in order to delight at the sight of their affliction.[437]

It was this propensity of his to brood about life, together with his taciturn moods and rudeness, that certainly contributed to the strained relationship he had with his mother. Judging from a December 13, 1807 letter that his mother Johanna Schopenhauer wrote to him, he must have been difficult to live with. The letter indicates that his mother simply could not tolerate his "unpleasant arguing" and his lamentations about "the stupid world and human misery," which served only to vex

---

[436] Arthur Schopenhauer, *Reise-Tagebücher* (Zürich: Haffmans Verlag, MCMLXXXVIII), S.144-145.

[437] *Nachlaß*, IV.1, S.96; *Remains*, IV, p.119.

her spirit and wreck her evenings with sleepless nights and bad dreams.[438]

This pessimistic bent of his personality certainly influenced his *Weltanschauung*. In the context of the metaphysical view of reality that Schopenhauer gives us, human beings as phenomena also constitute a reflection of the aimlessly striving will whose entire essence can be likened to an unquenchable thirst. In fact, Schopenhauer maintains that an analysis of human consciousness is what provides the clue as to what the core of the real is, such that he even describes the world as a "makanthropos" in that it too is representation and will.[439] For it is the route of introspection that ushers one, and makes one privy to, the inner content of at least one phenomenon: one's own self as embodied consciousness that is willing through and through. The inner knowledge we have of ourselves as willers acts as a springboard, and is transferred to the totality of phenomena such, that the noumenon thereby is called will.

---

[438] Cf. *Arthur Schopenhauer: Ein Lebensbild in Briefen*, Brief: Johanna Schopenhauer an Arthur Schopenhauer (Weimar d.13 Dec.1807), zusammengestellt und herausgegeben von Angelika Hübscher (Frankfurt am Main: Insel Verlag, 1987), S.49. The passage reads as follows:

> Alle Mittage um ein Uhr kommst Du und bleibst bis drey, dann sehe ich Dich den ganzen Tag nicht mehr, außer an meinen Gesellschaftstagen wozu Du kommen kannst wenn Du willst, auch an den beyden Tagen Abends bey mir essen kannst wenn Du Dich dabey des leidigen Disputierens etc das mich verdrüslich macht, wie auch allen Lamentierens über die dumme Welt und das menschliche Elend Dich enthalten willst, weil mir das immer eine schlechte Nacht und üble Träume macht, und ich gerne gut schlafe.

[439] *Vorstellung II*, Kap.50, IV, S.753. "- Ebenfalls hatte man, seit den ältesten Zeiten, den Menschen als Mikrokosmos angesprochen. Ich habe den Satz umgekehrt und die Welt als Makranthropos nachgewiesen; sofern Wille und Vorstellung ihr wie sein Wesen erschöpft. Offenbar aber ist es richtiger, die Welt aus dem Menschen verstehn zu lehren, als den Menschen aus der Welt: denn aus dem unmittelbar Gegebenen, also dem Selbstbeswußtseyn, hat man das mittelbar Gegebene, also das der äußern Anschauung, zu erklären; nicht umgekehrt."; *Representation*, II, ch.50, pp.642-643.

Once Schopenhauer shows that the will constitutes the kernel of each phenomenon, he focuses his attention specifically to anthropological concerns by outlining his philosophy of the human person. Since human beings are the highest manifestation of the noumenal will, they best reveal its scarred essence and inner estrangement.[440] Thus, what has been said in broad terms about the lower gradations of the will's objectification, receives a more pronounced slant in the case of man endowed with the faculty of reason (*Vernunft*), which opens for him the horizons of the future and yet binds him to the parameters of his past. Occupying the highest position on the ladder of proportionate being, however, does not leave in its wake greater satisfaction of willing:

> Man, as the most complete objectification of the will, is accordingly the most necessitous of all beings. He is concrete willing and needing through and through; he is a concretion of a thousand needs. With these he stands on the earth, left to his own devices in uncertainty about everything except his own need and misery.[441]

Schopenhauer continues by underscoring the obsession and anxiety that man has about the very preservation of his existence in face of the constant demands that life brings. Concern about the propagation of the species also weighs upon him. In short, omnipresent dangers give him no security or peace. Even civilized life does not

---

[440] *Vorstellung I*, §56, II, S.389. "Wir wollen dieserwegen im *menschlichen Daseyn* das innere und wesentliche Schicksal des Willens betrachten. Jeder wird leicht im Leben des Thieres das Nämliche, nur schwächer, in verschiedenen Graden ausgedrückt wiederfinden und zur Genüge auch an der leidenden Thierheit sich überzeugen können, wie wesentlich *alles Leben Leiden* ist."; *Representation*, I, §56, p.310.

[441] *Ibid.*, §57, S.390-391; *Ibid.*, §57, p.312.

remove this basic ontological insecurity.[442] Why so? Because the source of the unhappiness and suffering that fills human consciousness is found within oneself.[443] Schopenhauer states:

> For the most part we refuse to have anything to do with the knowledge, comparable to a bitter medicine, that suffering is essential to life, and therefore does not flow in upon us from outside, but that everyone carries around within himself its inexhaustible source.[444]

B. The Source of the Human Sickness

1. Nature of willing

It is interesting to note that Schopenhauer repeatedly says, in one way or another, that the source of the sickness and disorder in reality is in the human spirit itself, as the two immediately preceding citations underscore. The basic reason for the malady in the human spirit lies in the essential nature of willing itself as

---

[442] Ibid., S.390-391. "Der Mensch, als die vollkommenste Objektivation jenes Willens, ist demgemäß auch das bedürftigste unter allen Wesen: er ist konkretes Wollen und Bedürfen durch und durch, ist ein Konkrement von tausend Bedürfnissen. Mit diesen steht er auf der Erde, sich selber überlassen, über Alles in Ungewißheit, nur nicht über seine Bedürftigkeit und seine Noth: demgemäß füllt die Sorge für die Erhaltung jenes Daseyns, unter so schweren, sich jeden Tag von Neuem meldenden Forderungen, in der Regel, das ganze Menschenleben aus. An sie knüpft sich sodann unmittelbar die zweite Anforderung, die der Fortpflanzung des Geschlechts. Zugleich bedrohen ihn von allen Seiten die verschiedenartigsten Gefahren, denen es zu entgehen eines beständiger Wachsamkeit bedarf. Mit behutsamem Schritt und ängstlichem Umherspähen verfolgt er seinen Weg: denn tausend Zufälle und tausend Feinde lauern ihm auf. So gieng er in der Wildniß, und so geht er im civilisirten Leben; es giebt für ihn keine Sicherheit."; Ibid.

[443] Nachlaß, I, #242, S.146. "Ueberhaupt...sehn wir daß Alles was ist nur Erscheinung von *Willen* ist, verkörperter *Wille*. Wir wissen aber daß alle unsre Quaal nur aus dem Willen kommt...wir nur in ihm unseelig, dagegen im reinen Erkennen, als von ihm befreit, seelig sind. -- Der Wille also is der *Ursprung* des Bösen und auch des *Uebels* das nur für seine Erscheinung, den Leib, da ist: und der Wille ist auch der *Ursprung* der Welt."; *Remains*, I, #242, p.158.

[444] *Vorstellung I*, §57, II, S.398; *Representation*, I, §57, p.318.

flawed and lacking any ultimate finality. For the willing that one introspectively discovers, presupposes an antecedent condition of needing and lacking which is incapable of final satisfaction.

> All striving originates from want, from dissatisfaction with one's own state, and is therefore suffering so long as it is not satisfied. No satisfaction, however is lasting; on the contrary, it is always merely the starting-point of a fresh striving. We see striving everywhere impeded in many ways, everywhere struggling; and thus, always as suffering. There is no ultimate aim of striving and hence no measure or end of suffering.[445]

The very core of reality manifests this striving energy which is even more distinct in the animal or man. Because the basis of all willing is a prior state of needing and lacking which is synonymous with pain, willing by its very nature and origin is destined to pain.[446] It is this flawed aspect of the real that makes the pursuit of happiness an illusion. Man's existence is, as it were, clouded by the given-ness of a never-to-be-healed willing.[447] Thus, Schopenhauer observes that:

> Life ...with its deluded hopes...bears so clearly the stamp of something which ought to

---

[445] *Ibid.*, §56, S.388; *Ibid.*, §56, p.309.

[446] *Ibid.*, §57, S.390. "Sahen wir schon in der erkenntnißlosen Natur das innere Wesen derselben als ein beständiges Streben, ohne Ziel und ohne Rast; so tritt uns bei der Betrachtung des Thieres und des Menschen dieses noch viel deutlicher entgegen. Wollen und Streben ist sein ganzes Wesen, einem unlöschbaren Durst gänzlich zu vergleichen. Die Basis alles Wollens aber ist Bedürftigkeit, Mangel, also Schmerz, dem er folglich schon ursprünglich und durch sein Wesen anheimfällt."; *Ibid.*, §57, pp.311-312.

[447] *Vorstellung II*, Kap.46, IV, S.671. "Das Glück liegt demgemäß stets in der Zukunft, oder auch in der Vergangenheit, und die Gegenwart ist einer kleinen dunklen Wolke zu vergleichen, welche der Wind über die besonnte Fläche treibt: vor ihr und hinter ihr ist Alles hell, nur sie selbst wirft stets einen Schatten. Sie ist demnach allezeit ungenügend, die Zukunft aber ungewiß, die Vergangenheit unwiederbringlich."; *Representation*, II, ch.46, p.573.

disgust us, that it is difficult to grasp how one can misconstrue this and allow oneself to be persuaded that [life] is to be thankfully enjoyed, and that man exists in order to be happy.[448]

The above notwithstanding, human consciousness remains such that knowledge as a rule remains in constant relation to the striving will. This being the case, it is as if an inner dynamism propels one to steadfastly walk in accordance with the aims of one's willing. Reason (*Vernunft*), accordingly, serves to enable one to select the right means to attain the objects of one's willing.[449]

2. Boredom

An existence full of multiform desires characterizes the human condition. Accordingly, basic inquietude is ingrained in human beings, given the nature of willing which can never be satisfied. It would seem that achieving the objects of one's willing would give one a measure of tranquility; but such is not the case, for a fearful boredom thereby ensues.

> What occupies all living things, and keeps them in motion is the striving after existence. If existence, however, is guaranteed to them, they do not know what to do with it. Therefore, the second thing that sets them in motion is the effort to get rid of the burden of existence, to make it no

---

[448] *Ibid.; Ibid.*, p.574.

[449] *Vorstellung I*, §60, II, S.409. "Der Mensch findet, vom Eintritt seines Bewußtseyns an, sich also wollend, und in der Regel bleibt seine Erkenntniß in beständiger Beziehung zu seinem Willen. Er sucht erst die Objekte seines Wollens, dann die Mittel zu diesen, vollständig kennen zu lernen. Jetzt weiß er, was er zu thun hat, und nach anderm Wissen strebt er, in der Regel, nicht. Er handelt und treibt: das Bewußtseyn, immer nach dem Ziele seines Wollens hinzuarbeiten, hält ihn aufrecht und thätig: sein Denken betrifft die Wahl der Mittel."; *Representation*, I, §60, p.327.

longer felt, "to kill time," in other words, to escape from boredom (*Langeweile*).[450] Schopenhauer goes on to underscore that boredom is not to be taken lightly. For once human beings are secure from want and burdens, they become, as it were, "burdens to themselves" (*sich selbst zur Last*). In fact, it is the phenomenon of boredom that causes beings who love each other as little as human beings do, to seek one another. Paradoxically, it can be said, therefore, that boredom becomes a source of social life (*Quelle der Geselligkeit*).[451]

From what has already been said, it can be gleaned that life swings like a pendulum between willing that leaves in its wake *pain*, and satiety that results in *boredom*. In fact, for Schopenhauer pain and boredom are the ultimate constituents (*letzte Bestandtheile*) of human existence.[452] The human spirit remains in a state of agitation and restlessness given life's basic inadequacy to satisfy the yearnings of the will.[453] For this reason, it is inconceivable in his eyes that man can be happy. This notwithstanding, the flux of life rolls irresistibly on for most. Human life continues to flow

---

[450] *Ibid.*, §57, S.392; *Ibid.*, §57, p.313.

[451] *Ibid.* "Demgemäß sehn wir, daß fast alle vor Noth und Sorgen geborgene Menschen, nachdem sie nun endlich alle andern Lasten abgewälzt haben, jetzt sich selbst zur Last sind und nun jede durchgebrachte Stunde für Gewinn achten, also jeden Abzug von eben jenem Leben, zu dessen möglichst langer Erhaltung sie bis dahin alle Kräfte aufboten. Die Langeweile aber ist nichts weniger, als ein gering zu achtendes Uebel: sie malt zuletzt wahre Verzweiflung auf das Gesicht. Sie macht, daß Wesen, welche einander so wenig lieben, wie die Menschen, doch so sehr einander suchen, und wird dadurch die Quelle der Geselligkeit."; *Ibid.*

[452] *Ibid.*, S.390; *Ibid.*, p.312.

[453] *Ibid.*, §58, S.403. "So sehr nun aber auch große und kleine Plagen jedes Menschenleben füllen und in steter Unruhe und Bewegung erhalten, so vermögen sie doch nicht die Unzulänglichkeit des Lebens zur Erfüllung des Geistes, das Leere und Schaale des Daseyns zu verdecken, oder die Langeweile auszuschließen, die immer bereit ist jede Pause zu füllen, welche die Sorge läßt."; *Ibid.*, §58, p.322.

between willing and attainment. "This is the life of almost all men: they will, they know what they will and they strive accordingly with enough success to protect them from despair, and enough failure to preserve them from boredom and its consequences."[454]

The above scenario, as portrayed by Schopenhauer, brings into focus the sickness of the human spirit and highlights what the source of the malady is: the disordered will. A close look at man reveals the disease in his spirit and gives one a vantage point to interpret the contradictions that scar the face of reality. Schopenhauer sees little that can be done to ameliorate this basic condition as he interprets it.

Human existence is flawed, in short, as the following passage from Schopenhauer's *Nachlaß* indicates: "The enduring existence of the *human species* is merely an indication of its rankness."[455] Why this is so is explained in the notion of the affirmation of the will-to-live (*die Bejahung des Willens zum Leben*) which further elucidates the human predicament. It is to this that I now turn.

C. The Affirmation of the Will-to-Live

1. Clarification of the notion

Schopenhauer in describing the human predicament often alludes to the so-called "affirmation of the will" or the "affirmation of the will-to-live" which are, in effect, one and the same thing. "The *affirmation of the will* is the persistent willing itself,

---

[454] *Ibid.*, §60, S.409; *Ibid.*, §60, p.327.

[455] *Nachlaß*, IV.1, S.312; *Remains*, IV, p.349.

interrupted by no knowledge, as it fills the life of man in general."[456] This willing is also further specified as an affirmation of the will-to-live because in man it manifests itself as a stubborn attachment to life despite its many sufferings and trials:

> ...this powerful attachment to life is irrational and blind; it is only explicable from the fact that our whole being-in-itself is indeed the will-to-live (Wille zum Leben), to which life therefore must appear as the highest good, however embittered, short, and uncertain it may be; and that will is originally and in itself without knowledge and blind.[457]

2. Affirmation of the body

Schopenhauer notes that the simplest affirmation of the will-to-live is an affirmation of one's body: that is, a satisfaction of its elementary needs, so as to maintain health, etc.[458] Accordingly, affirmation of the will is interchangeable with the affirmation of one's body because the body is, after all, the objectivity of the will as it appears in a given individual. Schopenhauer casts further light on the above in the following two citations:

---

[456] *Vorstellung I*, §60, II, S.408; *Representation*, I, §60, p.326.

[457] *Vorstellung II*, Kap.41, IV, S.545-546; *Representation*, II, ch.41, pp.465-466.

[458] *Vorstellung I*, §60, II, S.408. "Da schon der Leib des Menschen die Objektität des Willens, wie er auf dieser Stufe und in diesem Individuo erscheint, ist; so ist sein in der Zeit sich entwickelndes Wollen gleichsam die Paraphrase des Leibes, die Erläuterung der Bedeutung des Ganzen und seiner Theile, ist eine andere Darstellungsweise des selben Dinges an sich, dessen Erscheinung auch schon der Leib ist. Daher können wir, statt Bejahung des Willens, auch Bejahung des Leibes sagen. Das Grundthema aller mannigfaltigen Willensakte ist die Befriedigung der Bedürfnisse, welche vom Daseyn des Leibes in seiner Gesundheit unzertrennlich sind, schon in ihm ihren Ausdruck haben und sich zurückführen lassen auf Erhaltung des Individuums und Fortpflanzung des Geschlechts."; *Representation*, I, §60, pp.326-327.

> Because the will-to-live objectifies itself,
> its most general and essential phenomenon in
> the higher potencies is a living body with the
> iron command to nourish it. What gives power
> to this command is just that this body is the
> will-to-live as object.[459]

But the constant striving, which constitutes the inner nature of every phenomenon of the will, obtains at the higher grades of objectification its first and most universal foundation (*Grundlage*) from the fact that the will here appears as a living body with the iron command to nourish it. What gives force to this command is just that this body is nothing but the objectified will-to-live itself (*objektivirte Wille zum Leben selbst*).[460]

3. Sexual impulse as affirmation of the will

The most decided and strongest affirmation of the will-to-live, however, is the sexual impulse whose satisfaction is described by Schopenhauer "life's final end and highest goal."[461] In fact, Schopenhauer considers maintenance of the body by its own powers "so small degree of the will's affirmation" that if the will's affirmation could be reduced to that alone, "with the death of the body, the will that appeared in it would also be extinguished."[462]

What Schopenhauer clearly suggests is that satisfaction of the sexual impulse carries with it an

---

[459] *Nachlaß*, I, #498, S.335. "Indem der Wille zum Leben sich objektivirt ist in den höhern Potenzen seine allgemeinste und wesentliche Erscheinung ein lebendiger Leib mit dem eisernen Gebot ihn zu nähren: was diesem Gebot die Macht giebt, ist eben daß dieser Leib der Wille zum Leben als Objekt ist."; *Remains*, I, #498, p.369.

[460] *Vorstellung I*, §57, II, S.390; *Representation*, I, p.312.

[461] *Ibid.*, §60, S.412; *Ibid.*, §60, p.329.

[462] *Ibid.*, S.410; *Ibid.*, p.328.

added dimension that an assuagement of the other bodily appetites cannot have. Whereas the maintenance of the body by nourishing and caring for it entails an affirmation of the will here and now, satisfying the sexual impulse is an affirmation of the will for an "indefinite time" as the following indicates:

> The satisfaction of the sexual impulse alone goes beyond the affirmation of one's own existence which fills so short a time; it affirms life for an indefinite time beyond the death of the individual. Nature, always true and consistent, here even naive, displays quite openly before us the inner significance of the act of procreation.[463]

Schopenhauer continues by outlining a type of phenomenology of shame involved in the procreative act. He states that the act of procreation that results in the begetting of a new life is a symptom of the decided affirmation of the will-to-live, that it is a disguised willing of a new individual, and hence a re-introduction of suffering and death in the phenomenal realm. The act of procreation affirms life anew and declares salvation for the moment to be fruitless. Herein lies the reason, says Schopenhauer, for the shame that is often connected with procreation.[464] The following passage from

---

[463] *Ibid.*; *Ibid.*

[464] *Ibid.* "Das eigene Bewußtseyn, die Heftigkeit des Triebes, lehrt uns, daß in diesem Akt sich die entschiedenste *Bejahung des Willens zum Leben*, rein und ohne weitern Zusatz (etwan von Verneinung fremder Individuen) ausspricht; und nun in der Zeit und Kausalreihe, d.h. in der Natur, erscheint als Folge des Akts ein neues Leben: vor den Erzeuger stellt sich der Erzeugte, in der Erscheinung von jenem verschieden, aber an sich, oder der Idee nach, mit ihm identisch. Daher ist es dieser Akt, durch den die Geschlechter der Lebenden sich jedes zu einem Ganzen verbinden und als solches perpetuiren [fortdauern]. Die Zeugung ist in Beziehung auf den Erzeuger nur der Ausdruck, das Symptom, seiner entschiedenen Bejahung des Willens zum Leben: in Beziehung auf den Erzeugten ist sie nicht etwan der Grund des Willens, der in ihm erscheint, da der Wille an sich weder Grund noch Folge kennt; sondern sie ist, wie alle Ursache, nur Gelegenheitsursache der Erscheinung dieses Willens zu dieser Zeit an diesem Ort. Als Ding an sich ist der Wille des Erzeugers und der des Erzeugten nicht verschieden; da nur die Erscheinung, nicht das Ding an sich, dem *principium individuationis* unterworfen ist. Mit jener Bejahung über den eigenen Leib

"Metaphysik der Geschlectsliebe", a supplementary essay in volume two of *Die Welt als Wille und Vorstellung*, highlights the shame and remorse that accompanies coitus, especially after the completion of the act for the first time:

> Now the act...by which the will affirms itself and man comes into existence is an action of which all in their hearts are ashamed (*im Innersten schämen*), and which they, therefore, carefully conceal. Indeed, if they are caught in the act, they are as ashamed as if they had been detected in a crime. It is an action of which, with cold reflection, one thinks of often with aversion, and in an exalted disposition with disgust...A peculiar sadness and remorse follows close on it (*folgt ihr auf dem Fuße*); yet it is most felt after the consummation of the act for the first time, but generally it is more distinct, the nobler the character.[465]

The same essay from which the immediately preceding passage is taken, in fact constitutes a comprehensive analysis of human sexuality as a whole, which even includes a treatment of homosexuality. But Schopenhauer's basic thesis remains the same: 1) any satisfaction of the sexual impulse in general is a decided affirmation of the will-to-live; 2) sexual impulse directed to a definite individual is described as in itself "the will-to-live as a precisely determined

---

hinaus, und bis zur Darstellung eines neuen, ist auch Leiden und Tod, als zur Erscheinung des Lebens gehörig, aufs Neue mitbejaht und die durch die vollkommenste Erkenntnißfähigkeit herbeigeführte Möglichkeit der Erlösung diesmal für fruchtlos erklärt. Hier liegt der tiefe Grund der Schaam über das Zeugungsgeschäft."; *Ibid*.

[465] *Vorstellung* II, Kap.45, IV, S.666-667; *Representation*, II, ch.45, p.569.

individual."[466] Schopenhauer interestingly even states:

> The growing attachment of two lovers is really already the will-to-live of the new individual, an individual they can and want to produce. Indeed, already in the meeting of their longing glances is a new life kindled, and it announces itself as a future individuality, harmonious and well-constituted.[467]

Because the sexual impulse best exemplifies the affirmation of the will-to-live, sexuality has a negative connotation in Schopenhauer's thought. As a case in point, he refers to sexual love as a "malevolent demon" (*feindsäliger Dämon*) that "strives to pervert, to confuse, and to overthrow everything."[468] He surmises that life would be "easy and cheerful" if it were the case that the will-to-live exhibited itself merely as an impulse for self-preservation.[469] But such is not the case.

The will-to-live as sexual impulse more than anything else is a symptom of the disorder within man. "This impulse puts to an end that unconcern, cheerfulness, and innocence that would accompany a merely individual existence, because it brings into consciousness unrest and melancholy, and into the course

---

[466] *Ibid.*, Kap.44, IV, S.626. "Was im individuellen Bewußtseyn sich kund giebt als Geschlechtstrieb überhaupt und ohne die Richtung auf ein bestimmtes Individuum des andern Geschlechts, das ist an sich selbst und außer der Erscheinung der Wille zur Leben schlecthin. Was aber im Bewußtseyn erscheint als auf ein bestimmtes Individuum gerichteter Geschlechtstrieb, das ist an sich selbst der Wille, als ein genau bestimmtes Individuum zu leben."; *Ibid*, ch.44, p.535.

[467] *Ibid.*, S.627; *Ibid.*, p.536.

[468] *Ibid.*, S.624; *Ibid.*, p.534.

[469] *Ibid.*, Kap.45, S.665; *Ibid.*, ch.45, p.568.

of life misfortunes, cares and misery."[470] As such, a disordered sexuality is a principal source of man's existential pain which fetters him to the will. Moreover, its disorderedness for Schopenhauer is in itself a reason for pessimism.[471] This is the reason why Schopenhauer later in speaking of the will's denial mentions the sexual impulse as the first hurdle to clear in the path of salvation.

The above notwithstanding, Schopenhauer's thought is often paradoxical in that a seemingly uncompromising pessimism is, on occasion, given a strange twist. In the case of sexuality the same holds true. As a case in point, generative actions open to the possibility of conception and pregnancy do not receive the same bleak sentence as do homosexual actions. With regard to the latter, Schopenhauer writes that "the true, ultimate, and profound metaphysical reason for the reprehensibility of pederasty is that whereas the will-to-live affirms itself in it, the effect of that affirmation, which holds open the path to salvation and thus the renewal of life, is completely cut off."[472] But with regard to the former there is an interesting juxtaposition between sexual intercourse (described as the quintessence of the affirmation of the will-to-live) and conception and pregnancy (considered as an offer of salvation):

> The act of generation is the world-knot because it states: "The will-to-live has

---

[470] *Ibid.*; *Ibid.*

[471] *Ibid.*, S.667. "Hätte nun der Optimismus Recht, wäre unser Dasayn das dankbar zu erkennende Geschenk höchster, von Weisheit geleiteter Güte, und demnach an sich selbst preiswürdig, rühmlich und erfreulich; da müßte doch wahrlich der Akt, welcher es perpetuirt, eine ganz andere Physiognomie tragen."; *Ibid.*, p.570.

[472] *Ibid.*, Kap.44, S.644; *Ibid.*, ch.44, pp.566-567.

affirmed itself anew." ...Conception and pregnancy, on the other hand, say: "To the will is allotted once again the light of knowledge"; whereby, of course, it can again find its way out; and so the possibility of salvation has once more appeared.[473]

D. Death and the Affirmation of the Will

1. Fear of death as an affirmation of will-to-live

In his reflection about the reality of death as a philosophical problem, Schopenhauer wishes to use as his point of departure "an entirely empirical point of view" and thereby describe what he sees.[474] He maintains that with regard to death "we have before us the undeniable fact that, according to natural consciousness, man not only fears death for his own person more than anything else, but also weeps violently over the death of his friends and relations."[475] Schopenhauer continues by observing that the grief which accompanies death is not motivated solely by egoistical concern over one's own loss, but by sympathy for the misfortune that has befallen another human being.[476] Death, in short, appears "as a great evil" which in the language of nature signifies the terrifying prospect of the extinction or annihilation of the individual.[477]

---

[473] *Parerga II*, §166, IX, S.344; *Parerga*, II, §166, pp.316-317.

[474] *Vorstellung II*, Kap.41, IV, S.544. "Ich will, bei diesen Betrachtungen, zuvörderst vom ganz empirischen Standpunkt ausgehn."; *Representation*, II, ch.41, p.464.

[475] *Ibid.; Ibid.*

[476] *Ibid.; Ibid.*

[477] *Ibid.; Ibid.*

The fear of death, moreover, is independent of the faculty of reason. Animal life in-itself suggests this. For though it certainly is the case that animals do not as such "know" death (bound as they are to the present), it is as if fear of death comprises part of their very make-up. Accordingly, Schopenhauer notes that the fear of death is innate "to any thing that is born", such that it may even be considered as *a priori* the reverse side of the will-to-live.[478] The same innate fear of death that animals have can be said of man:

> By nature man is just the same. The greatest of evils, the worst thing that can be threatened at all times is death; the greatest anxiety is the anxiety of death.[479]

The vicissitudes and sufferings of life, as well as the frustration that characterizes willing, make the objective value of life very uncertain to reflective reason. Life's tragic dimension influences one to ask whether existence is to be preferred to non-existence.[480] In a word, attachment to life is irrational -- a fact which aptly illustrates that the nature of the human being is the very same will that

---

[478] *Ibid.*, S.544-545. "In der That ist die Todesfurcht von aller Erkenntniß unabhängig: denn das Thier hat sie, obwohl es den Tod nicht kennt. Alles, was geboren wird, bringt sie schon mit auf die Welt. Diese Todesfurcht a *priori* ist aber eben nur die Kehrseite des Willes zum Leben, welcher wir Alle ja sind. Daher ist jedem Thiere, wie die Sorge für seine Erhaltung, so die Furcht vor seiner Zerstörung angeboren: diese also, und nicht das bloße Vermeiden des Schmerzes, ist es, was sich in der ängstlichen Behutsamkeit zeigt, mit der das Thier sich und noch mehr seine Brut vor Jedem, der gefährlich werden könnte, sicher zu stellen sucht. Warum flieht das Thier, zittert und sucht sich zu verbergen? Weil es lauter Wille zum Leben, also solcher aber dem Tode verfallen ist und Zeit gewinnen möchte."; *Ibid.*, p.465.

[479] *Ibid.*; *Ibid.*

[480] *Ibid.*; *Ibid.*

comprises the inner essence of the animal.[481] Schopenhauer states: "it is not really the *knowing* part of our *ego* that fears death, but the *fuga mortis* comes simply and solely from the blind *will*, with which everything is filled."[482]

2. The illusion of the fear of death

This fear, however, is based on an illusion that stems from the basic egoism of all living organisms, namely, that with the destruction of one's organic make-up, the will perishes. The reason for the misperception is connected with the nature of our cognitive patterns as related to the will. The only way the will obtains knowledge of itself is in the individual knowing phenomenon that each of us is. With the impending destruction of that very phenomenon that knows, the will which by nature craves life, revolts at the unhappy scenario that death is, seeing its fortunes linked with a fragile and finite phenomenon, impotent before forces beyond its control.[483] With the dissolution of the organism that we are and the resulting end of

---

[481] *Ibid.*, S.545-546. "Jene mächtige Anhänglichkeit an das Leben ist mithin eine unvernünftige und blinde: sie ist nur daraus erklärlich, daß unser ganzes Wesen an sich selbst schon Wille zum Leben ist, dem dieses daher als das höchste Gut gelten muß, so verbittert, kurz und ungewiß es auch immer seyn mag; und daß jener Wille, an sich und ursprünglich, erkenntnißlos und blind ist. Die Erkenntniß hingegen, weit entfernt der Ursprung jener Anhänglichkeit an das Leben zu seyn, wirkt ihr sogar entgegen, indem sie die Werthlosigkeit desselben aufdeckt und hiedurch die Todesfurcht bekämpft."; *Ibid.*, p.465-466.

[482] *Ibid.*, S.548; *Ibid.*, p.468.

[483] *Ibid.*, S.584. "Daß [der Wille] in uns dennoch den Tod fürchtet, kommt daher, daß hier die Erkenntniß ihm sein Wesen bloß in der individuellen Erscheinung vorhält, woraus ihm die Täuschung entsteht, daß er mit dieser untergehe, etwan wie mein Bild im Spiegel, wenn man diesen zerschlägt, mit vernichtet zu werden scheint: Dieses also, als seinem ursprünglichen Wesen, welches blinder Drang nach Daseyn ist, zuwider, erfüllt ihn mit Abscheu."; *Ibid.*, p.498.

consciousness, we shirk in horror at the abyss of nothingness whence we came. In other words, "what makes death so frightful for us is not so much the end of life...as the destruction of the organism, really because this organism is the will itself which presents itself as body."[484]

Schopenhauer's point, however, is that there is something within man that remains immortal and which is not touched by the destruction of the phenomenon. His inner nature is comprised of the noumenal will that stands outside the causal nexus of time and space. Moreover, each human being is described by Schopenhauer as a special Idea, which entails that at least something pertaining to one's personhood, stems from an act of will outside of time, and, hence, in the intelligible order. The innermost kernel that man is, somehow is not affected by the violent destruction of one's individual nature (death) -- an annihilation which carries with it -- the extinction of consciousness, as we know it at least. Schopenhauer is clear on this point:

> The terrors of death rest for the most part on the false illusion (*Schein*) that...the ego (*das Ich*) vanishes, and the world remains. But rather is the opposite true: the world vanishes. On the other hand, the innermost kernel of the ego endures, the bearer and the producer of that subject in whose representation alone the world had its existence. With the brain the intellect perishes, and with the intellect the objective world, the intellect's mere representation.[485]

In *Über den Willen in der Natur* Schopenhauer underscores that "knowledge and its substratum, the intellect, is a

---

[484] *Ibid.*, S.549. "...was uns den Tod so furchtbar macht, nicht sowohl das Ende des Lebens...als vielmehr die Zerstörung des Organismus: eigentlich, weil dieser der als Leib sich darstellende Wille selbst ist."; *Ibid.*, p.468.

[485] *Vorstellung II*, Kap.41, IV, S.586; *Representation*, II, ch.41, p.500.

merely secondary phenomenon (*Phänomen*), which is completely different from the will, only accompanying the higher levels of its objectification, and not essential to it."[486] Unlike the spatially and temporally conditioned intellect, the noumenal will is that which alone is eternal and immortal. Though knowledge (*Erkenntniß*) is traditionally associated with what is spiritual in man (*das Geistige im Menschen*), in reality it is a mere product, or rather, a phenomenon of what is truly a spiritual element, the will.[487] Schopenhauer also surprisingly mentions that if one insists on keeping the term *soul* to describe what is "spiritual" in the human being, such a word is nothing more than the union of the will with the intellect. But the intellect, as a phenomenon (a mere brain function), always has a secondary nature.[488] Only the will is metaphysical and beyond the causal nexus. In this respect it may be called "spiritual".

---

[486] *Natur*, "Einleitung", V, S.203; *Nature*, "Introduction," p.217.

[487] *Ibid*. "Physiologie und Pathologie," S.219-220. "Bei mir ist das Ewige und Unzerstörbare im Menschen, welches daher auch das Lebensprincip in ihm ausmacht, nicht die Seele, sondern, mir einen chemischen Ausdruch zu gestatten, das Radikal der Seele, und dieses ist der Wille. Die sogenannte Seele ist schon zusammengesetzt: sie ist die Verbindung des Willens mit dem νους, Intellekt. Dieser Intellekt ist das Secundäre, ist das *posterius* des Organismus und, als eine bloße Gehirnfunktion, durch diesen bedingt. Der Wille hingegen ist primär, ist das *prius* des Organismus und dieser durch ihn bedingt. Denn der Wille ist dasjenige Wesen an sich, welches erst in der Vorstellung (jener bloßen Gehirnfunktion) sich als ein solcher organischer Leib darstellt: nur vermöge der Formen der Erkenntniß (oder Gehirnfunktion), also nur in der Vorstellung, ist der Leib eines Jeden ihm als ein Ausgedehntes, Gegliedertes, Organisches gegeben, nicht außerdem, nicht unmittelbar im Selbstbewußtseyn...Die wahre Physiologie, auf ihrer Höhe, weist das Geistige im Menschen (die Erkenntniß) als Produkt seines Physischen nach...aber die wahre Metaphysik belehrt uns, daß dieses Physische selbst bloßes Produkt, oder vielmehr Erscheinung, eines Geistigen (des Willens) sei, ja, daß die Materie selbst durch die Vorstellung bedingt sei, in welcher allein sie existirt."; *Ibid.*, "Physiology and Pathology," pp.236-237.

[488] *Ibid.*, S.219; *Ibid.*, p.236.

3. The significance of death

Notwithstanding the fact that the innermost kernel of the ego emerges unscathed from the irremediable shipwreck that death is, Schopenhauer underscores that dying has a significance of its own when juxtaposed against the willing that governs human existence. "Dying is certainly to be considered as the real aim of life; at the moment of dying, everything is decided which through the whole course of life was only prepared and introduced."[489] Its radical significance lay in exposing the futility of affirmation of the will-to-live in its various manifestations. As such, Schopenhauer says that it removes the scales that blind one from recognizing the folly of an egocentric, will-filled existence.[490]

Death is even described as "the great reprimand" (*die große Zurechtweisung*) which the will-to-live, and more precisely the egoism essential to it, receive through the course of nature."[491] Thus, it is not too much of a surprise that Schopenhauer even refers to it as "punishment for our existence" (*Strafe für unser Daseyn*).[492] He continues by stating that death may also

---

[489] *Vorstellung II*, Kap.49, IV, S.746; *Representation*, II, ch.49, p.637.

[490] *Ibid.*, S.746-747. "Hat also schon das Leiden eine solche heiligende Kraft, so wird diese in noch höherm Grade dem mehr als alles Leiden gefürchteten Tode zukommen...Der Tod ist das Ergebniß, das Résumé des Lebens, oder die zusammengezogene Summe, welche die gesammte Belehrung, die das Leben vereinzelt und stückweise gab, mit Einem Male ausspricht, nämlich diese, daß das ganze Streben, dessen Erscheinung das Leben ist, ein vergebliches, eiteles, sich widersprechendes war, von welchem zurückgekommen zu seyn eine Erlösung ist."; *Ibid.*, pp.636-637.

[491] *Ibid.*, Kap.41, S.594; *Ibid.*, ch.41, p.507.

[492] *Ibid.*; *Ibid.*

The Human Situation

be regarded as "the painful untying of the knot that generation with sensual pleasure had tied."[493]

In short, the finality of death reveals the true significance of will-filled existence: that it simply makes no sense, that it is irrational, and that it should not be this way. In this respect, death's chill is but a harbinger of insight that exposes the fundamental error of human existence as we know it. Accordingly, Schopenhauer states simply: "At bottom, we are something that ought not to be, therefore we cease to be."[494]

Because of the threatening shadow that death's ever- approaching sickle casts, one cannot but conclude that birth and existence seem absurd. For by existence dissolution becomes our lot, the grave our end. It is understandable, therefore, why Schopenhauer contends that "the shortness of life, so often lamented may be the best thing about it."[495] Except for a fundamental change within the core of man's essence, happiness is not even conceivable.[496] In short, man the desiring and willing being is ontologically sick; he exists in pain and suffering given the essential nature of willing. What can be best hoped for is that a *modus vivendi* ensue so that a swath of meaning might be carved through the Slough of Despond that life seems to be.

---

[493] *Ibid.*; *Ibid.*

[494] *Ibid.* "Wir sind im Grunde etwas, das nicht seyn sollte: darum hören wir auf zu seyn."; *Ibid.*

[495] *Vorstellung I*, §59, II, S.406; *Representation*, I, §59, p.325.

[496] *Vorstellung II*, Kap.41, IV, S.576-577. "Zu einem glücksäligen Zustande des Menschen wäre also keineswegs hinreichend, daß man ihn in eine »bessere Welt« versetze, sondern auch noch erfordert, daß mit ihm selbst eine Grundveränderung vorgienge, also daß er nicht mehr wäre was er ist, und dagegen würde was er nicht ist."; *Representation*, II, ch.41, p.492.

E. The Egocentric Predicament of Man

1. Reason for egoism

In Chapter Two of Part One of this study, it was underscored that the will manifests itself in human beings (as it does with other forms of organic life) as a great attachment to life, care for the individual and the species, egoism and a general lack of consideration for others. Because of the vehemence of the will's desire in individual persons, the scene is set for an altogether not too harmonious relationship among those who comprise society. The inner antagonism characteristic of the will-to-live in itself, is manifested with greater clarity in the case of man. The will attains full consciousness of itself in human beings who are the highest level of its objectification.

> Man...is the most complete phenomenon of the will...and ...in order to exist, this phenomenon had to be illuminated by so high degree of knowledge that...a perfectly adequate repetition of the inner nature of the world under the form of the representation, became possible in it...Therefore, in man the will can reach full self-consciousness, distinct and exhaustive knowledge of its inner nature, as reflected in the whole world.[497]

Recall that for Schopenhauer the noumenon stands completely outside the causal nexus of space and time. Plurality does not pertain to it in anyway whatsoever. Accordingly, plurality cannot pertain to the will in its pristine noumenal state. What is homogeneous in the noumenal realm becomes a plurality only via the *principium individuationis* with the cognitional forms of space and time referred to as "the essential forms of

---

[497] *Vorstellung I*, §55, II, S.362; *Representation*, I, §55, pp.287-288.

natural knowledge."⁴⁹⁸ However, the plurality of particulars, as known by will-oriented cognition, is but a manifestation of a noumenal will that can only partially reveal itself to the human mind because what knowledge one can have of the will via the path of introspection, nevertheless retains the form of *time*.

The blind will gains full consciousness of itself in human beings. This notwithstanding, the will once conscious of itself misinterprets the essential oneness of reality because it is initially only capable of recognizing its inner nature in its own phenomenon as corporealized.⁴⁹⁹ It is as if blinders are placed on consciousness that incapacitate total vision of the homogeneity of the will in reality. A basic egocentrism thereby ensues. Thus, Schopenhauer observes that "everyone wants everything for oneself, wants to possess, or at least, control everything, and would like to annihilate that which opposes one."⁵⁰⁰

The essential structure of normal day-to-day cognitive patterns adds fuel to the burning fire of the basic egocentrism of the will which, in the case of man, has become conscious of itself. Given the direct awareness one has of oneself and the only the indirect awareness one has of anything else, the latter appears as

---

⁴⁹⁸ *Vorstellung I*, §61, II, S.414. "Wir haben Zeit und Raum, weil nur durch sie und in ihnen Vielheit des Gleichartigen möglich ist, das *principium individuationis* genannt. Sie sind die wesentlichen Formen der natürlichen, d.h. dem Willen entsprossenen Erkenntniß. Daher wird überall der Wille sich in der Vielheit von Individuen erscheinen."; *Representation*, I, §61, p.331.

⁴⁹⁹ *Vorstellung I*, II, §61, S.414. "...diese Vielheit trifft nicht ihn, den Willen als Ding an sich, sondern nur seine Erscheinungen: er ist in jeder von diesen ganz und ungetheilt vorhanden und erblickt um sich herum das zahllos wiederholte Bild seines eigenen Wesens. Dieses selbst aber, also das wirklich Reale, findet er unmittelbar nur in seinem Innern."; *Representation*, I, §61, pp.331-332.

⁵⁰⁰ *Ibid.*; *Ibid.*

a mere phenomenon. Though one's own body as given in perception is also a phenomenon, it nevertheless has a certain immediacy that differentiates it from other representations in consciousness. It is precisely for this reason that Schopenhauer maintains that:

> the individual is the bearer of the knowing subject and the bearer of the world; which is to say, that the whole of nature outside him, therefore also all remaining individuals, exist only in his representation. He himself is always conscious of them only as his representation, hence merely indirectly, and as something dependent on his own inner being and existence.[501]

The egocentric predicament is such that the individual as microcosm links the macrocosm that the world is with his or her individuality. Accordingly, the individual, who pales in insignificance before the immensity of the universe, nonetheless "makes himself the center of the whole world, and considers his own existence and wellbeing before everything else."[502] Schopenhauer's *Über die Grundlage der Moral* likewise comments on the subjectivity of human consciousness that makes everything seemingly revolve around oneself.

> ...everyone is given to himself *directly*, the others are given to him only *indirectly*, through the representation in his head...Of course, in consequence of the subjectivity essential to every consciousness, everyone is himself the whole world; for everything objective exits only indirectly, as mere representation of the subject, so that

---

[501] *Vorstellung I*, §61, II, S.414; *Representation*, I, §61, p.332.

[502] *Ibid.*, S.414-415. "Die immer und überall wahrhafte Natur selbst giebt ihm, schon ursprünglich und unabhängig von aller Reflexion, diese Erkenntni einfach und unmittelbar gewiß. Aus den angegebenen beiden nothwendige Bestimmungen nun erklärt es sich, daß jedes in der gränzenlosen Welt gänzlic verschwindende und zu Nichts verkleinerte Individuum dennoch sich zum Mittelpunk der Welt macht, seine eigene Existenz und Wohlseyn vor allem Ander berücksichtigt..."; *Ibid.*

everything always depends on self-consciousness.⁵⁰³
The individual, in short, has a direct awareness of himself or herself given the immediacy of bodily sensations. The empirical world of other people, living things, and inorganic matter always has a representational character. Try as one may, the barrier of another's skin bars unrestricted entry into the sanctuary of his or her consciousness. The same holds true with other existents in reality. We simply cannot peer into the core of their in-itselfness. Everything other than the perceiver appears *only* as a representation. Thus, Schopenhauer can state: "The only world everyone has cognizance of and knows, is carried about by him in his head (*trägt er in sich*) as his representation, and is, for that reason, the center of the world."⁵⁰⁴

Accordingly, human beings are naturally prone to achieve the objects of their own willing rather than those of another. Egoism is part and parcel of human nature, permeated as it is with the will. In this respect, knowledge of other things has as its reference point the will-filled Ego. Hence, the first thing one perceives is not the nature of things in their relation to each other, but rather their relation to one's particular will.⁵⁰⁵

---

⁵⁰³ Arthur Schopenhauer, *Über die Grundlage der Moral*, §14, *Zürcher Ausgabe Werke in zehn Bänden*, Band VI, (Zürich: Diogenes Verlag, 1977), S.237. Henceforth cited as *Grundlage*. English translation: Arthur Schopenhauer, *On the Basis of Morality*, §14, trans. E.F.J. Payne (Indianapolis: Bobbs-Merrill, 1965), p.132. Henceforth referred to as *Basis*.

⁵⁰⁴ *Ibid.; Ibid.*

⁵⁰⁵ *Nachlaß*, III, S.166. "Ein *Ich* und ein *Egoismus* sind Eins: ist letzterer weg, so ist ersteres eigentlich schon nicht mehr da. Folgendes ist die Erläuterung hievon. Vermöge unseres Egoismus und des Sklavendienstes der Erkenntniß gegen ihn, d.h. vermöge des ängstlichen Antheils, den wir an unserm

Given the nature of the disordered will and the physical make-up of human cognitive faculties, man's initial condition is clearly egocentric.

> The chief and fundamental incentive in man as in the animal is *egoism*, that is, the craving for existence and well-being (*der Drang zum Daseyn und Wohlseyn*). The German word *Selbstsucht* (passion for self) carries with it a false subordinate notion (*Nebenbegriff*) of sickness (*Krankheit*). The word *Eigennutz*, however, denotes egoism insofar as it stands under the guidance of reason which enables it by means of reflexion to pursue its ends methodically (*planmäßig*). For this reason, one can call animals egoistic, but not self-interested (*eigennützig*). I will, therefore, retain the word *egoism* for the general concept. This *egoism*, in the animal as in man, is most closely linked with their innermost kernel and essence. For this reason, as a rule, all man's actions spring from egoism; from this, to begin with, is the interpretation of a given action always to be attempted.[506]

In light of the selfishness that darkens the human heart, "*good*" is defined in reference to the desiring individual will. "The concept is essentially relative, and denotes the *suitableness of an object to any definite effort of the will.*"[507] The concepts of "*bad*" (*schlecht*) and "*evil*" (*böse*), on the other hand, denote that which is not agreeable to the striving of the will in each case.

---

eigenen Ich nehmen, ist das Erste was wir wahrnehmen, nicht die Beschaffenheit der Dinge durch ihr Verhältniß zu einander; sondern ihr Verhältniß zu unserm Willen: d.h. unsre Erkenntniß zieht nicht sowohl Linien von einem Dinge zum andern, und so fort, wodurch ein bloßer planimetrischer Abriß entstünde, als vielmehr Linien von allen Dingen zum eignen Willen, wodurch eine Kugel mit vielen Radien entsteht, deren Centrum der eigne Wille, der Eigenwille ist: er ist das Centrum, das nur durch und in dem Zusammentreffen dieser Linien besteht: oder eigentlich und ohne Bild, der ängstliche Antheil am eignen Ich ist das Vermittelnde aller unsrer Erkenntniß der Dinge."; *Remains*, III, pp.182-183.

[506] *Grundlage*, §14, VI, S.235-236; *Basis*, §14, p.131.

[507] *Vorstellung I*, §65, II, S.448. "Dieser Begriff ist wesentlich relativ und bezeichnet die *Angemessenheit eines Objekts zu irgend einer bestimmten Bestrebung des Willens.*"; *Representation*, I, §65, p.360.

The Human Situation

But Schopenhauer underscores that properly speaking, "bad" is applied to existents without knowledge; whereas "evil" is predicated of both animals and other human beings who impede our own particular willing.[508]

The above being the case, in general human intercourse or social interchange, selfish inclinations abound. When meeting another person, almost as if by instinct, the first inclination is to see the other as a means for an end. It goes without saying that a new acquaintance is first seen as someone who might be useful. In fact, Schopenhauer claims that to see the other as a possible means for an end "lies close to the very nature of the human glance."[509]

---

[508] *Ibid.*, S.448-449. "-Der Begriff des Gegentheils wird, so lange von nichterkennenden Wesen die Rede ist, durch das Wort *schlecht*, seltener und abstrakter durch *Uebel* ausgedrückt, welches also alles dem jedesmaligen Streben des Willens nicht Zusagende bezeichnet. Wie alle andern Wesen, die in Beziehung zum Willen treten können, hat man nun auch Menschen, die den gerade gewollten Zwecken günstig, förderlich, befreundet waren, *gut* gennant, in der selben Bedeutung und immer mit Beibehaltung des Relativen, welches sich z.B. in der Redensart zeigt: »Dieser ist mir gut, dir aber nicht.« Diejenigen auch, deren Charakter es mit sich brachte, überhaupt die fremden Willensbestrebungen als solche nicht zu hindern, vielmehr zu befördern, die also durchgängig hülfreich, wohlwollend, freundlich, wohlthätig waren, sind, wegen dieser Relation ihrer Handlungsweise zum Willen Anderer überhaupt, *gute* Menschen genannt worden. Den entgegengesetzten Begriff bezeichnet man im Deutschen und seit etwan hundert Jahren auch im Französischen, bei erkennenden Wesen (Thieren und Menschen) durch ein anderes Wort als bei erkenntnißlosen, nämlich durch *böse*, *méchant*, während in fast allen andern Sprachen dieser Unterschied nicht Statt findet und κακος, *malus*, *cattivo*, *bad* von Menschen wie von leblosen Dingen gebraucht werden, welche den Zwecken eines bestimmten individuellen Willens entgegen sind."; *Ibid.*, pp.360-361.

Cf.David Cartwright, "Seeing through the principium individuationis," as found in *Schopenhauers Aktualität*, Hrsg. von Wolfgang Schirmacher (Wien: Passagen Verl., 1988), S.42.

[509] *Grundlage*, §8, VI, S.203. "Dieser *Egoismus* nämlich, von dem wir alle strotzen, und welchen als unsere *partie honteuse* zu verstecken, wir die *Höflichkeit* erfunden haben, guckt aus allen ihm übergeworfenen Schleiern meistens dadurch hervor, daß wir in Jedem, der uns vorkommt, wie instinkmäßig, zunächst nur ein mögliches *Mittel* zu irgend einem unserer stets zahlreichen *Zwecken* suchen. Bei jeder neuen Bekanntschaft ist meistens unser erster Gedanke, ob der Mann uns nicht zu irgend etwas nützlich werden könnte: wenn er dies nun *nicht* kann; so ist er den Meisten, sobald sie sich hievon überzeugt haben, auch selbst *nichts*. In jedem Andern ein mögliches Mittel zu unsern Zwecken, also ein Werkzeug zu suchen, liegt beinahe schon in der Natur des menschlichen Blicks: ob nun aber etwan das Werkzeug beim Gebrauche mehr oder weniger zu *leiden* haben

Because man is in the center of a world stage torn apart by a fierce struggle given the estrangement of the will with itself, a profound insecurity plagues him. He is not "at home" with himself let alone others. Accordingly, Schopenhauer maintains that the individual "is ready to annihilate the world, in order to maintain somewhat longer his very self, that drop in the ocean."[510] Though the person can sometimes use physical force to attain individual ends, cunning and dissimulation are the preferable routes to choose. As Schopenhauer observes: "I, as the wrongdoer (*ich, als Unrecht ausübend*), compel the other individual to serve my will instead of his own, or to act according to my will instead of to his." [511]

Closely allied to the boundless egoism within human nature is a storehouse of "hatred, anger, envy, rancor and malice" which, in Schopenhauer's eyes, "can be found more or less in every human breast"; which, accumulates like the poison within the fangs of a serpent, and waits for an apt opportunity to release itself.[512] But once again, Schopenhauer attributes this egoism to the malaise within the will itself: "it is the will-to-live which, more and more embittered through the constant suffering of existence, seeks to lighten its

---

werde, ist ein Gedenke, der viel später und oft gar nicht nachkommt."; *Basis*, §8, pp.97-98.

[510] *Vorstellung I*, §61, II, S.415; *Representation*, I, §61, p.332.

[511] *Ibid.*, §62, S.420; *Ibid.*, §62, p.337.

[512] *Parerga II*, §114, IX, S.232. " - Zum gränzenlosen Egoismus unserer Natur gesellt sich aber noch ein, mehr oder weniger in jeder Menschenbrust vorhandener Vorrath von Haß, Zorn, Neid, Geifer und Bosheit, angesammelt, wie das Gift in der Blase des Schlangenzahns, und nur auf Gelegenheit wartend, sich Luft zu machen, um dann wie ein entfesselter Dämon zu toben und zu wüthen."; *Parerga*, II, §114, p.213.

torment by inflicting it on others."[513] The world then becomes a hell in which human beings are "the tormented souls on the one hand, and the devils on the other."[514]

It is clear, therefore, that egoism is the first and principal force with which any moral incentive would have to contend.[515] In light of the prevalence of this egoism, a maxim which would call for justice ("*Neminem laede, imo omnes quantum potes, juva*") has little meaning. For as Schopenhauer writes, "egoism cries with a loud voice, *Neminem iuva, imo omnes, si forte conducit, laede*; indeed, malice or wickedness gives us the variant, *Imo omnes, quantum potes, laede.*"[516]

2. Degrees of egoism

It was established above that affirmation of the will-to-live is first manifested in the satisfaction of basic bodily needs like eating and sleeping, for example. But it was also emphasized that satisfaction of the sexual impulse best expresses the affirmation of that same will which egoistically strives without purpose. This in itself suggests that there are degrees of egoism inasmuch as affirmation of the will-to-live goes hand in hand with it. The argumentation of this section,

---

[513] *Ibid.*, S.234; *Ibid.*, p.215.

[514] *Ibid.*, §156, S.326. "Die Welt ist eben die *Hölle*, und die Menschen sind einerseits die gequälten Seelen und andererseits die Teufel darin."; *Ibid.*, §156, p.300.

[515] *Grundlage*, §14, VI, S.238. " - Der *Egoismus* also ist die erste und hauptsächlichste, wiewohl nicht die einzige Macht, welche die *moralische Triebfeder* zu bekämpfen hat."; *Basis*, §14, p.134.

[516] *Ibid.*, §7, S.199. "...*Neminem laede, imo omnes, quantum potes, juva*...Dieser ist und bleibt der wahre reine Inhalt aller Moral...Denn von der andern Seite schreiet mit lauter Stimme der Egoismus: *Neminem juva, imo omnes, si forte conducit, laede*...ja, die Bosheit giebt die Variante: *Imo omnes, quantum potes, laede.*"; *Ibid.*, §7, p.92.

therefore, aims to highlight how and why there are degrees of egoism that correspond to the intensity of willing.

In *Über die Grundlage der Moral* Schopenhauer states that there are three basic incentives for human actions, the first two of which are basic egoism and malice, with the third being compassion.[517] A supplementary essay ("*Zur Lehre von der Verneinung des Willens zum Leben*") found in Chapter 48 of the second volume of *Die Welt als Wille und Vorstellung* alludes to the so-called "ultimate motives" (*letzte Triebfedern*) of human conduct and lists four: 1) one's own weal; 2) another's woe; 3) another's weal; 4) one's own woe.[518] For our purposes in this chapter we shall focus our attention on the first two since they pertain to the issue at hand. Compassion and ascetical mortification, which pertain to the latter two motives listed above, are to be discussed in Chapter Five of this study.

Schopenhauer states very clearly that all actions that arise from malice (*Bosheit*), which have as their motive another's harm, are morally reprehensible (*moralisch verwerflich*). But actions which are motivated by the mere desire for one's particular weal (*Egoismus*), are characterized as "morally indifferent" (*moralisch indifferente*).[519] This notwithstanding, Schopenhauer's analysis of asceticism illustrates that this relatively

---

[517] *Grundlage*, §16, VI, S.249. "Es giebt überhaupt nur *drei Grund-Triefedern* der menschlichen Handlungen: und allein durch Erregung derselben wirken alle irgend möglichen Motive. Sie sind: a) Egoismus; der das eigene Wohl will (ist gränzenlos); b) Bosheit; die das fremde Wehe will (geht bis zur äußerster Grausamkeit); c) Mitleid; welches das fremde Wohl will (geht bis zum Edelmuth und zur Großmuth).; *Basis*, §16, p.145.

[518] *Vorstellung II*, Kap.48, IV, S.710; *Representation*, II, ch.48, p.607.

[519] *Grundlage*, §16, VI, S.249; *Basis*, §16, p.145. Cf. David Cartwright, "Seeing Through the principium individuationis: Metaphysics and Morality," in *Schopenhauers Aktualität*, p.43.

neutral affirmation of the will-to-live is left behind when one truly embraces what the denial of the will-to-live implies.

So as to contextualize what is exactly meant by *badness* or *malice* the concept of *wrong* (*Unrecht*) is introduced. It entails the affirmation of one's will to the extent that it becomes the denial of the will appearing in another. In fact, Schopenhauer underscores how easy it is to affirm one's own particular will at the expense of another. The following is a case in point:

> Now since the will manifests that *self affirmation* (*Selbstbejahung*) of one's own body in countless individuals beside one another, in one individual, by virtue of the egoism peculiar to all, it very easily goes beyond this affirmation to the *denial* (*Verneinung*) of the same will appearing in another individual. The will of the first breaks through the boundary of another's affirmation of will, since the individual either destroys or injures the other body itself, or compels the powers of that other body to serve *his* will, instead of serving the will that appears in that other body. Thus, if from the will which appears as the body of another, the individual takes away the powers of this body and thereby increases the power serving *his* will beyond that of his own body, he consequently affirms his own will beyond his own body by means of the denial of the will that appears in the body of another. This trespass (*Einbruch*) into the boundary of the affirmation of the will of another has at all times been distinctly recognized, and its concept has been denoted by the word *wrong* (*Unrecht*).[520]

Schopenhauer goes on to mention that there is an inherent feeling (*Gefuhl*) that accompanies the trespass involved when affirmation of the will-to-live exceeds its bounds. In this respect, the one whose sphere of affirmation is

---

[520] *Vorstellung I*, §62, II, S.417; *Representation*, I, §62, p.334.

violated "feels immediate and mental pain".[521] The inflicter of the suffering, on the other hand, seems to have an "obscure feeling" (*dunkles Gefühl*) about the basic homogeneity of Being as will.[522] Schopenhauer refers to this feeling as a "remorse of conscience" (*Gewissensbiß*) or simply "the feeling of *wrong committed* (*Gefühl des ausgeübten Unrechts*)."[523]

At its very worst, the most universal expression of the concept of *wrong* is cannibalism which frightfully reveals a picture of the will at conflict with itself. Closely connected with cannibalism is murder -- which inflicts such a wound on the conscience that even a lifetime cannot heal.[524] But Schopenhauer maintains that the intentional mutilation (*absichtliche Verstümmelung*), injury, or blow to another are of a similar nature to the act of murder in that these acts involve an extreme violation of another's will.[525] The forced subjugation of another individual by enslavement of any kind, as well as the seizure of another's

---

[521] *Ibid*. "Denn beide Theile erkennen die Sache, zwar nicht wie wir hier in deutlicher Abstraktion, sondern als Gefühl, augenblicklich. Der Unrechtleidende fühlt den Einbruch in die Sphäre der Bejahung seines eigenen Leibes, durch Verneinung derselben von einem fremden Individuo, als einen unmittelbaren und geistigen Schmerz, der ganz getrennt und verschieden ist von dem daneben empfundenen physischen Leiden durch die That, oder Verdruß durch den Verlust."; *Ibid*., pp.334-335.

[522] *Ibid*. "Dem Unrecht-Ausübenden andererseits stellt sich die Erkenntniß, daß er an sich der selbe Wille ist, der auch in jenem Leibe erscheint, und der sich in der einen Erscheinung mit solcher Vehemenz bejaht, daß er, die Gränze des eigenen Leibes und dessen Kräfte überschreitend, zur Verneinung eben dieses Willens in der andern Erscheinung wird, folglich er, als Wille an sich betrachtet, eben durch seine Vehemenz gegen sich selbst streitet, sich selbst zerfleischt."; *Ibid*., p.335.

[523] *Ibid*., S.418; *Ibid*.

[524] *Ibid*.; *Ibid*.

[525] *Ibid*. "Als dem Wesen nach mit dem Morde gleichartig und nur im Grade von ihm verschieden, ist die absichtliche Verstümmelung, oder bloße Verletzung des fremden Leibes anzusehn, ja jeder Schlag."; *Ibid*.

property, are likewise listed as clear manifestations of *wrong*.[526] It is to perpetrators of such deeds that Schopenhauer applies the adjectives "bad" or "cruel". But as was stated above, actions that are motivated merely by a desire for one's own weal appear to have a neutral connotation. Thus, one is not called "bad" because of a weakness for ice cream, for example. But one may be called "bad" because of thievery or sexual immorality.

An individual is called *"bad"* (*böse*) by Schopenhauer, if he or she is *always* inclined to do *wrong*, once the inducement to do so is within easy access in lieu of the absence of a restraining power.[527] Succinctly stated, given the above explanation of the concept of *wrong*, the "bad" person essentially affirms his or her will-to-live so vehemently that such affirmation involves the denial of the will that appears in others.[528] Schopenhauer goes on to state that such a behavior pattern has as its ultimate source (*letzte Quelle*) a high degree of egoism.

This egoism casts into clear focus two qualities (*Eigenschaften*) that are the fundamental elements of the *bad* character. In the first place, Schopenhauer notes that the behavior patterns of bad people are always clear signs as to the vehemence of

---

[526] *Ibid.*; *Ibid.*

[527] *Ibid.*, §65, S.450. "Wenn ein Mensch, sobald Veranlassung daist und ihn keine äußere Macht abhält, stets geneigt ist *Unrecht* zu thun, nennen wir ihn *böse.*"; *Ibid.*, §65, p.362.

[528] *Ibid.*, S.450-451. "Nach unserer Erklärung des Unrechts heißt dieses, daß ein solcher nicht allein den Willen zum Leben, wie er in seinem Leibe erscheint, bejaht; sondern in dieser Bejahung so weit geht, daß er den in andern Individuen erscheinenden Willen verneint; was sich darin zeigt, daß er ihre Kräfte zum Dienste seines Willens verlangt und ihr Daseyn zu vertilgen sucht, wenn sie den Bestrebungen seines Willens entgegenstehn."; *Ibid.*

their willing.[529] People with bad characters are intense willers. Secondly, it is underscored that people with bad characters are slaves to will-oriented cognition as governed by the principle of sufficient reason and the law of individuation that is involved therewith; a cognition that highlights the apparent absolute difference between the perceiver and the perceived.[530]

It is interesting to note that Schopenhauer emphasizes that the vehement willing in very bad people carries with it intense inner suffering which is manifested by an unhappy face.[531] From the inner torment, which is absolutely and directly essential to them, there can even result the extreme of "wickedness proper" (*eigentliche Bosheit*) or even "*cruelty*" (*Graumsamkeit*), to which Schopenhauer refers as a "disinterested delight (*uneigennützige Freude*) at the sight of the suffering of another."[532] In cases such as these, the suffering of another becomes an end in itself. Unlike the "bad" person whose affirmation of the will is oriented to a given end (the satisfaction of willing), the truly wicked person, consumed from within by

---

[529] *Ibid.*, S.451. "Zweierlei ist hier sogleich offenbar: *erstlich*, daß in einem solchen Menschen ein überaus heftiger, weit über die Bejahung seines eigenen Lebens hinausgehender Wille zum Leben sich ausspricht; *Ibid.*, p.363.

[530] *Ibid.* "...*zweitens*, daß seine Erkenntniß, ganz dem Satz vom Grunde hingegeben und im *principio individuationis* befangen, bei dem durch dieses letztere gesetzten gänzlichen Unterschiede zwischen seiner eigenen Person und allen andern fest stehn bleibt; daher er allein sein eigenes Wohlseyn sucht, vollkommen gleichgültig gegen das aller Andern, deren Wesen ihm vielmehr völlig fremd ist, durch eine weite Kluft von dem seinigen geschieden, ja, die er eigentlich nur als Larven, ohne alle Realität, ansieht. -- Und diese zwei Eigenschaften sind die Grundelemente des bösen Charakters."; *Ibid.*

[531] *Ibid.*, S.451-452. "...weil vieles und heftiges Leiden von vielem und heftigem Wollen unzertrennlich ist, trägt schon der Gesichtsausdruck sehr böser Menschen das Gepräge des innern Leidens: selbst wenn sie alles äußerliche Glück erlangt haben, sehn sie stets unglücklich aus, sobald sie nicht im augenblicklichen Jubel begriffen sind, oder sich verstellen."; *Ibid.*

[532] *Ibid.*, S.452; *Ibid.*

The Human Situation   195

desolation and emptiness, strives to mitigate the inner restlessness of his spirit by the very sight of another's suffering.[533]

In *Über die Grundlage der Moral* Schopenhauer refers to egoism (*Egoismus*) and ill will (*Übelwollen*) or spitefulness (*Gehässigkeit*) as being respectively the opposites of justice (*Gerichtigkeit*) and philanthropy (*Menschenliebe*). Listing them under the antimoral tendencies (*antimoralische Triebfedern*), he states that egoism leads to "all kinds of crimes and misdeeds" among which are vices such as "greed, intemperance, lust, selfishness, avarice, covetousness, injustice, hardness of heart, pride, arrogance, and so on."[534] But he notes that in the case of behavioral patterns induced by egoism, the pain and injury caused to others are merely the means and not the end.[535]

But with malice (*Bosheit*) and cruelty (*Grausamkeit*), a greater degree of moral depravity is

---

[533] *Ibid.*, S.452-453. "Die Erinnerung an größere Leiden, als die unserigen sind, stillt ihren Schmerz: der Anblick fremder Leiden lindert die eigenen. Wenn nun ein Mensch von einem überaus heftigen Willensdrange erfüllt ist, mit brennender Gier Alles zusammenfassen möchte, um den Durst des Egoismus zu kühlen, und dabei, wie es nothwendig ist, erfahren muß, daß alle Befriedigung nur scheinbar ist, das Erlangte nie leistet, was das Begehrte versprach, nämlich endliche Stillung des grimmigen Willensdranges; sondern durch die Erfüllung der Wunsch nur seine Gestalt ändert und jetzt unter einer andern quält, ja endlich, wenn sie alle erschöpft sind, der Willensdrang selbst, auch ohne erkanntes Motiv, bleibt und sich als Gefühl der entsetzlichsten Oede und Leere, mit heilloser Quaal kund giebt: wenn aus diesem Allen, was bei den gewöhnlichen Graden des Wollens nur in geringerm Maaß empfunden, auch nur den gewöhnlichen Grad trüber Stimmung hervorbringt, bei Jenem, der die bis zur ausgezeichneten Bosheit gehende Erscheinung des Willens ist, nothwendig eine übermäßige innere Quaal, ewige Unruhe, unheilbarer Schmerz erwächst; so sucht er nun indirekt die Linderung, deren er direkt nicht fähig ist, sucht nämlich durch den Anblick des fremden Leidens, welches er zugleich als eine Aeußerung seiner Macht erkennt, das eigene zu mildern. Fremdes Leiden wird ihm jetzt Zweck an sich, ist ihm ein Anblick, an dem er sich weidet: und so entsteht die Erscheinung der eigentlichen Grausamkeit..."; *Ibid.*, p.364.

[534] *Grundlage*, §14, VI, S.240; *Basis*, §14, p.136.

[535] *Ibid.* "Der Egoismus kann zu Verbrechen und Unthaten aller Art führen: aber der dadurch verursachte Schaden und Schmerz Anderer ist ihm bloß Mittel, nicht Zweck, tritt also nur accidentell dabei ein."; *Ibid.*

involved because the desire to inflict suffering on another human being becomes an end in itself and a source of pleasure.[536] As in the case of *egoism*, Schopenhauer lists vices that stem from sheer spite (*Gehässigkeit*) among which are "envy, disaffection, ill will, malice, malicious joy at another's misfortune, prying curiosity, slander, insolence, petulance, hatred, anger, treachery, perfidy, thirst for revenge, and so forth."[537]

As one can see from the immediately preceding discussion, egoism has its degrees which correspond to the intensity of willing. Given the above, mere affirmation of one's basic bodily needs is morally neutral. It is only when the affirmation of willing infringes upon the willing of another that it becomes morally questionable. Such willing is translated into an immoral and harmful praxis that violates the dignity of another human being. So at its very worst, egoism can become spite or malice which, unfortunately, ushers one into the very threshold of the diabolical.[538]

3. Egoism and the role of the State

Given this negative appraisal of the conduct of human beings towards one another, a restraining force is needed to keep anti-moral tendencies in check, which in this case, is the State. It is clear that acts of injustice, unfairness, hardness and even cruelty attest to that scarredness or sickness in the human spirit.

---

[536] *Ibid.* "Der Bosheit und Grausamkeit hingegen sind die Leiden und Schmerzen Anderer Zweck an sich und dessen Erreichen Genuß. Dieserhalb machen jene eine höhere Potenz moralischer Schlechtigkeit aus."; *Ibid.*

[537] *Ibid.; Ibid.*

[538] *Ibid.* "Die erste Wurzel [Egoismus] ist mehr thierish, die zweite [Gehässigkeit] mehr teuflisch."; *Ibid.*

"The chief source of the most serious ills affecting man is man himself: *homo homini lupus*."[539] Accordingly, beneath the veneer of seemingly peaceful co-existence or tolerance that characterizes civilization, a more accurate picture of man can be gleaned. In typical descriptive fashion, Schopenhauer observes that "the thousands who throng before our eyes in peaceful intercourse, are to be regarded as just so many tigers and wolves whose teeth are secured by a strong muzzle."[540] In fact, one would recoil in horror at the expected scene were the State to lose its effectiveness to place in abeyance the anti-moral tendencies in man. The following is a case in point:

> Now egoism pursues its purposes without fail where neither external force (of which is to be included all fear whether of earthly or supernatural powers) nor genuine moral incentive opposes it. Therefore, in view of the infinite number of egoistic individuals, the *bellum omnium contra omnes* would be the order of the day to the undoing of all (*Untheil Aller*).[541]

It can be said, then, that the State for Schopenhauer exists precisely as a powerful brace, or counter-motive, against the injurious consequences that would certainly ensue were the anti-moral tendencies of the human spirit allowed a free rein. The State is established under the assumption that right conduct from purely moral grounds is totally unrealistic. Were the opposite true, that is, were it the case that human beings by nature never over-extend their affirmation of the will at the expense of

---

[539] *Vorstellung II*, Kap.46, IV, S.676; *Representation*, II, ch.46, p.577.

[540] *Grundlage*, §13, VI, S.234; *Basis*, §13, p.129.

[541] *Ibid.*, §14, S.238; *Ibid.*, §14, p.133.

others, the State would cease to exist.[542] But experience illustrates that egoism and selfishness is the order of the day. From the deep roots of the diseased will emerge both the potentiality and reality of unjust actions. Linked with that facticity is the rationale for the State which, in reality, is "nothing more than an *institution of protection*, (*eine Schutzanstalt*) which became necessary by the manifold attacks to which man is exposed, and which he alone is not able to ward off, but only in alliance with others."[543]

Though an egoism carried to its extremes would certainly lead to dire consequences, it might be noted that a grasping of that ominous possibility, indirectly serves to bring individuals together. For reflective consciousness grasps the scenario that would ensue, were the dark side of the human spirit to universally cast aside its inhibitions and manifest its ugly face in actions. Schopenhauer states: "We have...learned to recognize in the State the means by which Egoism, endowed with reason (*mit Vernunft ausgerüstet*), seeks to avoid its own evil consequences which turn against itself; and thus each promotes the weal of all because he sees his own included therein."[544]

---

[542] *Vorstellung I*, §62, II, S.430. "Der Staat ist... so wenig gegen den Egoismus überhaupt und als solchen gerichtet, daß er umgekehrt gerade aus dem sich wohlverstehenden, methodisch verfahrenden, vom einseitigen auf den allgemeinen Standpunkt tretenden und so durch Aufsummirung gemeinschaftlichen Egoismus Aller entsprungen und diesem zu dienen allein daist, errichtet unter der richtigen Voraussetzung, daß reine Moralität, d.h. Rechthandeln aus moralischen Gründen, nicht zu erwarten ist; außerdem er selbst ja überflüssig wäre. Keineswegs also gegen den Egoismus, sondern allein gegen die nachtheiligen Folgen des Egoismus, welche aus der Vielheit egoistischer Individuen ihnen allen wechselseitig hervorgehn und ihr Wohlseyn stören, ist, dieses Wohlseyn bezweckend, der Staat gerichtet."; *Representation*, I, §62, p.345.

[543] *Vorstellung II*, Kap.47, IV, S.696; *Representation*, II, ch.47, p.594.

[544] *Vorstellung I*, §62, II, S.435; *Representation*, I, §62, p.349.

What the above in effect implies is that the existence of the State facilitates social interchange. For the machinery of the State restrains the outward manifestation of anti-moral tendencies and thus blunts fears and suspicions that human beings would normally have of each other. Yet, Schopenhauer also seems to suggest that there exists in man a *need* for social intercourse from another angle, not strictly connected with the reality of the an over-affirmation of the will. For *ennui*, the other constituent of human existence, is what brings people together notwithstanding the many negative qualities that result from a diseased will.[545] The burden that people can become to themselves motivates them to seek the company of others. But it is still the State that guarantees a tolerable *modus vivendi* among human beings given the scarredness of human willing.

4. Epistemological basis for egoism

Notwithstanding the tendency human beings have to affirm their will at the expense of others, egoism from an empirical point of view appears to be justifiable given human cognitive patterns. For once again, each person has a direct knowledge of the self as opposed to an indirect awareness of others who appear as representations before consciousness. Accordingly,

---

[545] *Parerga II*, §396, X, S.708. "Eine Gesellschaft Stachelschweine drängte sich, an einem kalten Wintertage, recht nahe zusammen, um, durch die gegenseitige Wärme, sich vor dem Erfrieren zu schützen. Jedoch bald empfanden sie die gegenseitigen Stacheln; welches sie dann wieder von einander entfernte. Wann nun das Bedürfniß der Erwärmung sie wieder näher zusammen brachte, wiederholte sich jenes zweite Uebel; so daß sie zwischen beiden Leiden hin und hergeworfen wurden, bis sie eine mäßige Entfernung von einander herausgefunden hatten, in der sie es am besten aushalten konnten. - So treibt das Bedürfniß der Gesellschaft, aus der Leere und Monotonie des eigenen Innern entsprungen, die Menschen zu einander; aber ihre vielen widerwärtigen Eigenschaften und unerträglichen Fehler stoßen sie wieder von einander ab."; *Parerga*, II, §396, pp.651-652.

experience suggests that the difference between the perceiver and perceived is very real indeed. The difference in space that separates individually existing things from each other, entails that there likewise be a direct and first-hand distance between the weal and woe of the perceiver and that of the perceived. Schopenhauer elaborates on this in the following citation:

> This conception that underlies egoism is, *empirically* considered, strictly justified. According to experience (*erfahrungsmäßig*), the *difference* between my person and another's appears to be absolute. The difference in space that separates me from him, separates me from his weal and woe.[546]

The problem, however, is that the egoistic individual makes too much of the perceived difference between himself and others who appear as mere representations in consciousness. Bound to will-oriented cognitive patterns that fall under the principle of sufficient reason, a grasping of the homogeneity of reality becomes impossible:

> 'Individuation is real; the *principium individuationis* and the difference of individuals, which rests on this, is the order of things-in-themselves. Each individual is a being radically (*von Grund*) different from all others. In my own self alone I have my true being. Everything else, on the other hand, is non-ego (*Nicht-Ich*) and foreign to me.' This is the knowledge to whose truth flesh and bone bear witness, which lies at the root (*zum Grunde*) of all egoism and whose real expression is each loveless, unjust, and malicious action.[547]

What Schopenhauer describes above is the typical and ordinary way of "knowing" which gives rise to the behavior patterns as described in this chapter. The

---

[546] *Grundlage*, §22, VI, S.307; *Basis*, §22, p.205.

[547] *Ibid.*, S.311; *Ibid.*, p.210.

morally bad individual operates under the delusion of the *principium individuationis* and sees himself or herself as an island apart from others who are perceived with indifference or as less real. As a result, the morally bad person regards all others as non-ego, only concerned with his personhood to the exclusion of that of others. Quite naturally, then, the other is seen as a means or an obstacle to his ends. Schopenhauer states:

> The *bad* man everywhere feels (*empfindet*) a thick partition (*starke Scheidewande*) between himself and everything outside him. The world is to him an *absolute non-ego* and his relation to it is primarily hostile. For this reason, the keynote of his disposition becomes animosity, suspicion, envy, malicious pleasure.[548]

The above citation serves to highlight the particular praxis that *can* result from the egocentrism that characterizes all will-oriented knowing. As is very evident, actions based on perception that is rooted in egoism, have the potentiality to become destructive in tone. They nakedly expose the horizons to which blatant affirmation of the will at the expense of another can extend. In this respect, the destructive praxis that results an egoism, allied as it is with a disordered will, makes one at least open to consider what Schopenhauer asserts. True, we may not agree with Schopenhauer's explanation of the malady that grips the human spirit. But it is senseless to blind oneself to the sufferings and atrocities that human hubris leaves in its wake.

---

[548] *Ibid.*, S.312; *Ibid.*, p.211.

F. Summary

The purpose of this chapter was to describe the human condition as Schopenhauer sees it from the perspective of the reality of the affirmation of the will-to-live at the expense of others. It was first explained why a profound insecurity plagues man in light of the basic *woundedness* of the will that has lost itself in a multiplicity of particulars on the phenomenal realm. The source of the malady in the human spirit was attributed to the frustrated essence of willing and ennui, which for Schopenhauer are the basic constituents of human life.

A sizeable section of the chapter was devoted to an analysis of what Schopenhauer means by affirmation of the will-to-live. Satisfaction of the sexual impulse and fear of death were both discussed as two essential characteristics of will-filled consciousness. In conjunction with this, it was suggested that Schopenhauer's interpretation of conception and death do not receive an altogether negative evaluation insofar as both leave open the possibility for transcendence or denial of the will-to-live.

The most lengthy section of the chapter pertained to an analysis of the egocentric predicament of man. It was asserted that man's egoism arises principally because the hitherto-blind will, which becomes conscious of itself in a given individual, cannot recognize the same inner essence in other phenomena that appear merely as indirect representations in the mind. Given the direct awareness one has of oneself, as opposed to the indirect cognizance that one has of others, egoism is connected with the structure of our cognitive patterns that make what is homogeneous appear as a plurality. In this respect, will-oriented knowing is governed by the principle of sufficient reason and subject to the illusion of the *principium individuationis*.

Schopenhauer's explanation of why there are degrees of egoism was also outlined together with the behavioral patterns that result from each. The necessity of the State as a restraining influence or institution of protection against the harmful effects of human egoism was treated prior to concluding the chapter with a brief résumé of why egoism, and the praxis that ensues therefrom, has an epistemological foundation.

It cannot be denied that Schopenhauer presents his readers with a bleak picture of reality given the tinged nature of human willing. In this respect, affirmation of the will-to-live at the expense of others is the order of the day. This notwithstanding, Schopenhauer's philosophy also leaves open the possibility for the will's denial, which in turn gives way to a different praxis. Accordingly, it is not uncompromisingly bleak.

Chapter 5

Human Transcendence

A. Contradiction of the phenomenon with Itself

1. The co-existence of freedom and necessity

Before delving into what Schopenhauer means by denial of the will-to-live by insight or knowledge, it must be underscored that the noumenal will, as independent of the principle of sufficient reason with its four forms, is "free" -- and hence independent of the necessity that binds all phenomena together without exception.[549] Recall Schopenhauer's claim, that every phenomenon has as an intelligible character which may be described as an act of will outside of time. Though a

---

[549] *Vorstellung I*, §55, II, S.361. "Daß der Wille als solcher *frei* sei, folgt schon daraus, daß er, nach unserer Ansicht, der Gehalt aller Erscheinung ist. Diese hingegen kennen wir als durchweg dem Satz vom Grunde unterworfen, in seinen vier Gestaltungen: und da wir wissen, daß Nothwendigkeit durchaus identisch ist mit Folge aus gegebenem Grunde, und Beides Wechselbegriffe sind; so ist Alles was zur Erscheinung gehört, d.h. Objekt für das als Individuum erkennende Subjekt ist, einerseits Grund, andererseits Folge, und in dieser letztern Eigensatz durchweg nothwendig bestimmt, kann daher in keiner Beziehung anders seyn, als es ist. Der ganze Inhalt der Natur, ihre gesammten Erscheinungen, sind also durchaus nothwendig, und die Nothwendigkeit jedes Theils, jeder Erscheinung, jeder Begebenheit, läßt sich jedesmal nachweisen, indem der Grund zu finden seyn muß, von dem sie als Folge abhängt. Dies leidet keine Ausnahme: es folgt aus der unbeschränkten Gültigkeit des Satzes vom Grunde. Andererseits nun aber ist uns diese nämliche Welt, in allen ihren Erscheinungen, Objektität des Willens, welcher, da er nicht selbst Erscheinung, nicht Vorstellung oder Objekt, sondern Ding an sich ist, auch nicht dem Satz vom Grunde, der Form alles Objekts, unterworfen, also nicht also Folge durch einen Grund bestimmt ist, also keine Nothwendigkeit kennt, d.h. *frei* ist."; *Representation*, I, §55, pp.286-287.

phenomenon's empirical character is bound to necessity, its intelligible character as adequately revelatory of the noumenon, is "free" since it is not subject to any of the four forms of the principle of sufficient reason.

> Each thing as phenomenon (*Erscheinung*), as object, is absolutely necessary; the same thing *in itself* is will, and this is perfectly free for all eternity. The phenomenon, the object, is necessarily and unalterably determined in the concatenation of grounds and consequents which cannot have any discontinuity. But the existence of the object in general and the manner of its existence, that is, the Idea which reveals itself in it, or in other words its character, is directly a phenomenon of the will.[550]

Schopenhauer speculates that given the freedom of the will in its noumenality, the object in general (to which he alludes in the above citation), might not exist or perhaps be something originally and essentially completely different.[551] But were this in fact so, everything else that comprises the world would likewise be affected. For any given thing in experience is but a link in the chain of objects that together comprise the appearance of the same will. This notwithstanding, it is underscored that once an "object" (an *Idea*) has entered the series of grounds and consequents, it is strictly determined and therefore "cannot either become another thing, i.e. change itself, or withdraw from the series, i.e. vanish."[552]

---

[550] *Vorstellung* I, §55, II, S.361.; *Representation*, I, p.287.

[551] *Ibid.*, S.361-362. "In Gemäßheit der Freiheit dieses Willens, könnte es also überhaupt nicht daseyn, oder auch ursprünglich und wesentlich ein ganz Anderes seyn."; *Ibid.*

[552] *Ibid.*, S.362. "...wo dann aber auch die ganze Kette, von der es ein Glied ist, die aber selbst Erscheinung des selben Willens ist, eine ganz andere wäre: aber ein Mal da und vorhanden, ist es in die Reihe der Gründe und Folgen eingetreten, in ihr stets nothwendig bestimmt und kann demnach weder ein Anderes werden, d.h. sich ändern, noch auch aus der Reihe austreten, d.h. verschwinden.";

Now all human beings as phenomena are subject to a similar necessity that cannot characterize the noumenal will in its pristine state since it is outside space, time and causality. "Like every other part of nature, man is the objectivity of the will; therefore all that we have said holds good of him also."[553] Hence, human beings are subject to the law of causality that links phenomena together. Given one's character which makes one susceptible to some motives but not to others, necessity is a hallmark of human existence as well.

> Just as everything in nature has its forces and qualities that definitely react to a definite impression, and constitute its character, so man also has his *character*, from which the motives call forth his actions with necessity. In this way of acting his empirical character reveals itself, but in this again is revealed his intelligible character, the will in itself, whose determined phenomenon he is.[554]

The above notwithstanding, Schopenhauer immediately goes on to say that there is something truly special about man in that with him the will reaches full self-consciousness. He states that man "had to be illumined by so high degree of knowledge that in this phenomenon even a perfectly adequate representation of the inner nature of the world under the form of the representation...became possible."[555] That is to say, the potentiality to grasp the Ideas, which constitutes the will's adequate or immediate objectification, exists only with man. Accordingly, the arts and aesthetic

---

Ibid.

[553] *Ibid.; Ibid.*

[554] *Ibid.; Ibid.*

[555] *Ibid.; Ibid.*

experience as a whole attest to a knowledge that differs from normal will-oriented cognition.

For Schopenhauer, therefore, the reality of aesthetic experience and holiness of life indeed reveal the uniqueness of the will as it appears in man. In fact, given their occurrence, the claim is made that "freedom" (which pertains as such to the noumenon) makes its entrance into the human phenomenal sphere. The following passage alludes to this:

> ...an elimination (*Aufhebung*) and self-denial (*Selbstverneinung*) of the will in its most perfect phenomenon (*Erscheinung*) is possible, by the will's relating such knowledge to itself. Thus freedom which otherwise, as belonging only to the thing-in-itself, can never show itself in the phenomenon, in such a case appears (*hervortritt*) in the phenomenon; and by abolishing the nature which lies at the ground of the phenomenon, while the phenomenon still endures in time, it brings about a contradiction of the phenomenon with itself. Just in this way, it exhibits the phenomena (*Phänomene*) of holiness and self denial.[556]

This negation of the will-affirming nature that lies at the very core of the conscious phenomenon that each human being is, suggests that going beyond the egocentric predicament is *possible* in Schopenhauer's philosophy. In this respect, contemplation of the Platonic Ideas in aesthetic experience and the manifestation of holiness in the lives of some people is highly significant because it suggests that the mode of affirmation of the will-to-live in cognition and action *need not necessarily* be the case. But this other alternative or mode of being can be attained only if the will (as conscious of itself in man) obtains such a knowledge of its essential scarredness,

---

[556] *Vorstellung* I, §55, II, S.362; *Representation*, I, §55, p.288.

that it no longer wants to assuage its diseased thirst.[557]

Schopenhauer notes that *insight* into one's true, inner nature serves, and indeed acts, as a springboard by which one can grasp the inner reality of the thing-in-itself as manifested in the totality of phenomena. This knowledge in turn results in a "quieter " that serves to debilitate the motives which had hitherto been so effective in evoking will-oriented behavioral patterns tied to the *principium individuationis*.[558] The "quieter", in other words, is "the appearance of an insight into the true nature of life which brings about the end of the will whose objectivity is the world. It is interesting to note, moreover, that Schopenhauer at this point even uses religious language to describe this occurrence:

> ...that which the Christian mystics call the *effect of grace* and the *new birth*, is for us the only direct expression of the *freedom of the will*. It appears only when the will, having attained the knowledge of its essence in itself, obtains from this a *quieter*, and is precisely in that way removed from the effect of *motives* which lies in the province of

---

[557] *Nachlaß*, I, #673, S.468. "Wenn Alles was sonst den Willen zu Thaten bestimmt ein *Motiv* ist, so mag jener Eintritt der ächten Gesinnung ein *Quietiv* heißen. Es ist der Eintritt der Einsicht in das wahre Wesen das Lebens und der Welt, welche dem Willen dessen Objektität die Welt ist, ein Ende macht, und nicht den Karakter *ändert*, noch *allmählig Aenderungen* des Thuns hervorbringt, sondern eine plötzliche Aenderung des Wollens, und eine *Aufhebung* des Karakters herbeiführt."; *Remains*, I, #673, pp.518-519.

[558] *Vorstellung I*, §70, S.498. "So lange nämlich die Erkenntniß keine andere, als die im *principio individuationis* befangene, dem Satz vom Grunde schlechthin nachgehende ist, ist auch die Gewalt der Motive unwiderstehlich: wann aber das *principium individuationis* durchschaut, die Ideen, ja das Wesen der Dinge an sich, als der selbe Wille in Allem, unmittelbar erkannt wird, und aus dieser Erkenntniß ein allgemeines Quietiv des Wollens hervorgeht; dann werden die einzelnen Motive unwirksam, weil die ihnen entsprechende Erkenntnißweise, durch eine ganz andere verdunkelt, zurückgetreten ist."; *Representation*, I, §70, p.403.

another kind of knowledge, whose objects are only phenomena.[559]
As is the case in the grasping of the Ideas in aesthetic contemplation, the self-suppression of the will comes from *knowledge*. But such knowledge has an element of surprise in that it cannot be forcibly arrived at by intention or design. Rather, it seems to come out of nowhere and makes a sudden entrance.[560] For this reason, Schopenhauer struggles to find language adequate to describe this occurrence and resorts to theological expressions like "new birth" (*Wiedergeburt*) or the "effect of divine grace" (*Gnadenwirkung*) to highlight the change that transpires in the "natural" man who had hitherto willed so vehemently. The following is a case in point:

> In consequence of such an effect of grace, the entire essence of man is fundamentally (*von Grund*) changed and reversed, so that he no longer wills anything at all that he previously willed so intensely; thus a new man, so to speak, takes the place of the old. For this reason, the Church calls this consequence of the effect of grace *new birth*. For what she calls the *natural man*, to whom she denies all capacity for good, is that very will-to-live that must be denied if salvation is to be attained from an existence like ours.[561]

Schopenhauer contrasts the two modes of being theoretically possible to man (affirmation of the will and its denial) by referring to the former, with which we

---

[559] *Ibid.*, S.499; *Ibid.*, p.404.

[560] *Ibid.* "...jene *Selbstaufhebung des Willens* von der Erkenntniß ausgeht, alle Erkenntniß und Einsicht aber als solche von der Willkür unabhängig ist; so ist auch jene Verneinung des Wollens, jener Eintritt in die Freiheit, nicht durch Vorsatz zu erzwingen, sondern geht aus dem innersten Verhältniß des Erkennens zum Wollen im Menschen hervor, kommt daher plötzlich und wie von außen angeflogen."; *Ibid.*

[561] *Ibid.*, S.500; *Ibid.*, pp.404-405.

are most familiar, as the "kingdom of nature" and to the latter as "the kingdom of grace."[562] The same fragment alluded to in footnote 557 in Schopenhauer's *Nachlaß* (Dresden 1817), also emphasizes the transition that occurs from natural will-oriented existence to "graced" existence:

> The Christian mystics called that insight and the complete change of will associated with it *grace* (*Gnade*) and *new birth* (*Wiedergeburt*). The former, because (like all knowledge) it cannot be forced by resolution, but comes as though flying in from outside and starts from knowledge, all knowledge, however, being involuntary. The latter, not because the character changes, which it can never do, but because it is abolished (*aufgehoben*) and actually a new man, so to speak, steps into the place of the old.[563]

Schopenhauer's choice of religious language to juxtapose the two modes of human existence indeed catches the eye and is in itself indicative of Pietistic influences in his thought.[564] The first mode of human existence has already been described as affirmation of the will-to-live in which the will of a given individual is determined necessarily by motives. The second, which we are in the process of describing, entails a radical denial of that same will, once insight results in a "quieter" that stills the efficacy of motives to evoke egoistic actions.

This double-sided potentiality reveals the paradox of man who, as it were, has one foot in the world of necessity and the other in the world of freedom. In

---

[562] *Vorstellung I*, §70, II, S.499. "Nothwendigkeit ist das Reich der Natur; Freiheit ist das Reich der Gnade."; *Representation*, I, §70, p.404.

[563] *Nachlaß*, I, #673, S.468; *Remains*, #673, p.519.

[564] Cf. Arthur Hübscher, "Von Pietismus zur Mystik," *Schopenhauer-Jahrbuch* 50 (1969), S.1-32 and Arthur Hübscher, *Denker gegen den Strom*, S.11-13 and S.27-28.

this regard Schopenhauer accepts the Kantian notion of the co-existence of freedom and necessity.[565] In fact, he considers this not only to be the most significant legacy that Kant has left to ethics, but the only part of the Kantian ethic that he is willing to integrate within his own system.[566] Alluding to the will's capacity to relate inner knowledge of its own essence to itself in man, Schopenhauer observes:

> Provisionally by this, is only generally indicated how man is distinguished from all the other phenomena of the will by the fact that freedom, that is, independence of the principle of sufficient reason, which belongs only to the will as thing-in-itself and contradicts the phenomenon, nevertheless with him can possibly appear even in the phenomenon, where it is then, necessarily exhibited as a contradiction of the phenomenon with itself. In this sense, not only the will in itself, but even man can certainly be called free, and in that way be distinguished from other beings.[567]

The possibility of freedom in the ethical sphere is man's greatest prerogative and distinguishes him from the animal which is bound to the present moment.[568] Though entrance into the state of freedom is not something that

---

[565] Immanuel Kant, *Critique of Pure Reason*, A532-A558.

[566] *Grundlage*, §10, VI, S.214-215. "Nachdem ich, im Dienste der Wahrheit, auf die Kantische Ethik Angriffe gethan habe, welche nicht, wie die bisherigen, nur die Oberfläche treffen, sondern sie in ihrem tiefsten Grund unterwühlen, scheint mir die Gerechtigkeit zu fordern, daß ich nicht von ihr scheide, ohne *Kants* größtes und glänzendes Verdienst um die Ethik in Erinnerung gebracht zu haben. Dieses besteht in der Lehre vom Zusammenbestehn der Freiheit mit der Nothwendigkeit..."; *Basis*, §10, p.109.

[567] *Vorstellung I*, §55, II, S.362-363; *Representation*, I, §55, p.288.

[568] *Ibid.*, §70, S.499. "Die Möglichkeit der also sich äußernden Freiheit ist der größte Vorzug des Menschen, der dem Thiere ewig abgeht, weil die Besonnenheit der Vernunft, welche, unabhängig vom Eindruck der Gegenwart, das Ganze des Lebens übersehn läßt, Bedingung derselben ist. Das Thier ist ohne alle Möglichkeit der Freiheit, wie es sogar ohne Möglichkeit einer eigentlichen, also besonnenen Wahlentscheidung, nach vorhergegangenem vollkommenem Konflikt der Motive, die hiezu abstrakte Vorstellungen seyn müßten, ist."; *Ibid.*, §70, p.404.

can be induced by one's own efforts, were it not for the deliberation of the faculty of reason which enables the whole of life to be surveyed at a glance, the golden gates to the "kingdom of grace" would be irrevocably bolted shut. Accordingly, though Schopenhauer's ethics does not arise from "reason", man's faculty of reason once enlightened is what translates insight into action.

All the above notwithstanding, a close study of Schopenhauer's philosophy illustrates that in no way whatsoever are the actions of any particular and definite individual said to be groundless. Alluding to the given human being with his individual character, Schopenhauer succinctly states: "This person is never free, although he is the phenomenon of a free will, for he is the already determined phenomenon of the will's free willing."[569]

Nevertheless, an awareness of "freedom" seems to accompany human actions on the phenomenal realm. While it may be true that one's *whole existence* is an expression of freedom in that it constitutes an act of will outside time, freedom is generally predicated of individual actions. This is only explicable in light of the direct awareness of the will in self-consciousness to which the consciousness of freedom is linked.

> ...the real origin of the concept of freedom in no way is an inference either from the speculative Idea of an unconditioned cause, or from the fact that the categorical imperative presupposes it. On the contrary, it springs directly from consciousness in which everyone recognizes himself, at once, as the *will*, that is, as that which, as thing-in-itself, does not have the principle of sufficient reason for its form, and itself depends on nothing, but rather everything else depends on it. Not everyone, however, recognizes himself with

---

[569] *Ibid.*, §55, S.363; *Ibid.*, §55, p.288.

philosophical criticism and reflection, as a definite phenomenon of the will which has entered into time, one might say as an act of will which differs from that will-to-live itself. Therefore, instead of recognizing his whole existence as an act of his freedom, he seeks freedom rather in individual actions.[570]

Accordingly, though a given man's inner essence as will (the intelligible character) is indeed groundless and free, the very fact that he is a phenomenon of the will means that he is determined in his actions.[571] Schopenhauer states: "only ignorance and coarseness could continue to speak about a freedom of man's individual actions, about a *liberum arbitrium indifferentiate*."[572] Therefore, a strict determinism characterizes man's actions because the empirical character (as manifested on the phenomenal sphere) is always a copy of the intelligible character, which is an act of will outside of time. Hence it is asserted in *Parerga und Paralipomena*: "...the entire empirical course of a man's life in all its events great and small is necessarily predetermined (*nothwendig vorherbestimmt*) as are the moments of a clock."[573] Any given action rooted as it is in phenomenal being, always involves three factors: the action itself, the character of the

---

[570] "Kritik der Kantischen Philosophie," *Vorstellung I*, II, S.615-616; "Criticism of the Kantian Philosophy," *Representation*, I, p.504.

[571] *Parerga II*, §16, IX, S.247. "Nach meiner Preisschrift über die *moralische Freiheit* kann keinem denkenden Menschen zweifelhaft bleiben, daß diese nirgends in der Natur, sondern nur außerhalb der Natur zu suchen ist. Sie ist ein Metaphysisches, aber in der physischen Welt ein Unmögliches. Demnach sind unsere einzelnen Thaten keineswegs frei; hingegen ist der individuelle Charakter eines Jeden anzusehn als seine freie That."; *Parerga*, II, §16, pp.226-227.

[572] *Grundlage*, §10, VI, S.215; *Basis*, §10, pp.109-110.

[573] *Parerga II*, §116, IX, S.247; *Parerga*, II, p.227.

agent, and the motive which elicits the action. Writes Schopenhauer concerning their relationship:

> As every effect in inanimate nature is a necessary product of two factors, namely, of the general *natural force* which manifests itself here and of the particular *cause* which calls forth this manifestation, just so every action of a man is the necessary product of his *character* and of the *motive* which has made its appearance. If both of these are given, the effect follows inevitably.[574]

2. Schopenhauer's concept of character

Before proceeding further, it would be useful to clarify what exactly Schopenhauer means by the term *character*. A passage from *Über die Freiheit des menschlichen Willens* is cited above which states that the *character* can be described as the determined nature of the will of a given individual which makes him or her subject to motives on the temporal and spatial complex that comprises phenomenal reality.[575] Each person, therefore, has a propensity to act in a certain way given the appearance of a motive. However, the same motive may not necessarily affect two diverse individuals in a like manner given the make-up of their respective characters, which are distinct acts of will outside time and, therefore, unique or special Ideas in their own right.

Schopenhauer is careful to point out that the appearance of motives does not make the character of a person what it is. The character, as an act of will outside of time, is already presupposed before the motive

---

[574] *Freiheit*, II, VI, S.95; *Freedom*, II, p.58.

[575] Cf. *Ibid*, III., S.87. Refer also to the following article: John E. Atwell, "Schopenhauer's Account of Moral Responsibility," *Pacific Philosophical Quarterly* 61 (1980), p.399. Here the author correctly states that the character is "something like a susceptibility to certain motives but not to others."

makes its appearance and gives rise to an action on the phenomenal sphere.[576] Thus, neither natural forces nor the character as such, can be causes in the strict sense of the word because they stand outside the causal nexus. Accordingly, with regard to human actions, only motives can be the causes which give rise to the actions that in turn reveal what a given individual character is.[577] Schopenhauer clarifies this in the following passage from *Die Welt als Wille und Vorstellung*:

> Motives do not determine the character of man, but only the appearance of this character: that is, the deeds, the external form of his course of life, not its inner significance and content. These proceed from the character, which is the direct phenomenon of the will, and is therefore groundless. Why one man is wicked and another is good, depends not on motives and external influence such as teaching and preaching, and is in this sense, absolutely inexplicable.[578]

In light of the above discussion, no person enters this life without a character, or as a *tabula rasa*. This, according to Schopenhauer, signifies that each person's particular individuality has a noumenal basis. In *Parerga und Paralipomena* it is stated that "*individuality does not rest solely on the principium individuationis* and, for that reason, is not through and through mere

---

[576] Cf. Atwell, p.502.

[577] *Vorstellung I*, §26, I, S.187. "Allerdings hat Malebranche Recht: jede natürliche Ursache ist nur Gelegenheitsursache, giebt nur Gelegenheit, Anlaß zur Erscheinung jenes einen und untheilbaren Willens, der das Ansich aller Dinge ist und dessen stufenweise Objektivirung diese ganze sichtbare Welt. Nur das Hervortreten, das Sichtbarwerden an diesem Ort, zu dieser Zeit, wird durch die Ursache herbeigeführt und ist insofern von ihr abhängig, nicht aber das Ganze der Erscheinung, nicht ihr inneres Wesen: dieses ist der Wille selbst, auf den der Satz vom Grunde keine Anwendung findet, der mithin grundlos ist...Also alle Ursache ist Gelegenheitsursache. So haben wir es gefunden in der erkenntnißlosen Natur: gerade so aber ist es auch da, wo nicht mehr Ursachen und Reize, sondern Motive es sind, die den Eintrittspunkt der Erscheinungen bestimmen, also im Handeln der Thiere und Menschen.; *Representation*, I, §26, p.138.

[578] *Ibid.; Ibid.*

phenomenon, but that it is rooted in the thing-in-itself, the will of the individual; for his character itself is individual."[579] Notwithstanding man's privileged position in the cosmos, he does not enter this world "baggage free", or as a bare particular. What he does in life, is but a reflection of who and what he already is, as an act of will outside time (Idea). Schopenhauer repeatedly states this in his writings as the two following citations from *Über die Freiheit des menschlichen Willens* and *Über die Grundlage der Moral* respectively illustrate:

> Here one must be reminded that every *existence* presupposes an *essence*, that is, every thing which is (*jedes Seiende*) must be precisely *something*, must have a definite nature (*Wesen*). It cannot *exist* and thereby still be *nothing*, namely, it cannot be something like the *ens metaphysicum*, that is, a thing which simply *is* and no more than *is*, without any definitions and properties, and consequently, without a definite way of acting which flows from this.[580]

> *Operari sequitur esse* is a pregnant proposition of scholasticism; everything in the world acts in accordance with its unchangeable nature (*Beschaffenheit*) which constitutes its being (*Wesen*), its *essentia*. It is the same with man. As a man *is*, so will he, so must he, act, and the *arbitrium indifferentiae* is an invention from the childhood of philosophy that has long since been exploded...[581]

Each person, then, who comprises a special Platonic Idea, has a unique character that is already present when the noumenon enters into the phenomenal realm at the moment

---

[579] *Parerga II*, §116, IX, S.248; *Parerga*, II, p.227.

[580] *Freiheit*, III., VI, S.96; *Freedom*, III., p.59.

[581] *Grundlage*, §20, VI, S.293-294; *Basis*, §20, pp.191-192.

Human Transcendence   217

of conception.[582] As something original, character is unchangeable which, of course, has ramifications in ethics. Because the individuality of a person is rooted in the thing-in-itself, virtue is inborn and cannot be the result of sermons or other forms of moral exhortation.[583] The same holds for its opposite, wickedness.[584] In short, "everyone does only that which is already irrevocably fixed in his nature, that is, in his inborn disposition (*in seinem Angeborenen*)."[585]

3. Character as intelligible and empirical

Recall that an action involves the interplay of three factors: the action itself, the character of the agent, and the motive. Akin to a natural force which is

---

[582] Cf. Magee, p.209 who states: "All that we can say is that when we are conceived, the noumenal enters into the phenomenon that is us, and the phenomenon that is us ceases to exist when we die. This makes conception and death, which are the temporal poles of our phenomenal existence, the twin points of our emergence from and return to the purely noumenal. As such they cry out for the most searching philosophical consideration."

[583] *Grundlage*, §20, VI, S.292-293. "*Kant*, aber ist es, der zuerst diesen wichtigen Punkt vollkommen aufgeklärt hat, durch seine große Lehre, daß dem *empirischen Charakter*, der, als Erscheinung, sich in der Zeit und in einer Vielheit von Handlungen darstellt, der *intelligibele Charakter* zum Grunde liegt, welcher die Beschaffenheit des Dinges an sich jener Erscheinung und daher von Raum und Zeit, Vielheit und Veränderung, unabhängig ist. Hieraus allein wird die jedem Erfahrenen bekannte, so erstaunliche, starre Unveränderlichkeit der Charaktere erklärlich, welche die Wirklichkeit und Erfahrung den Versprechungen einer den Menschen moralisch bessern wollenden und von Fortschritten in der Tugend redenden Ethik allezeit siegreich entgegengehalten und dadurch bewiesen hat, daß die Tugend angeboren und nicht angepredigt wird."; *Basis*, §20, p.190.

[584] *Ibid.*, S.290. "Vermag vielleicht die Ethik, indem sie die moralische Triebfeder aufdeckt, auch sie in Thätigkeit zu versetzen? Kann sie den hartherzigen Menschen in einen mitleidigen und dadurch in einen gerechten und menschenfreundlichen umschaffen? – Gewiß nicht: der Unterschied der Charaktere ist angeboren und unvertilgbar. Dem Boshaften ist seine Bosheit so angeboren, wie der Schlange ihre Giftzähne und Giftblase; und so wenig wie sie kann er es ändern."; *Ibid.*, p.187.

[585] *Parerga II*, §116, IX, S.248; *Parerga*, II, §116, p.229.

a prior condition for causes and effects on the natural realm, the character cannot, as such, be called the cause of an action.[586] It may serve as the internal ground on which a motive can elicit an action, but it cannot cause an action itself. The motive, on the other hand, serves as the external ground of an action -- eliciting, as it were, the given action from the innate character which, like a natural force, is presupposed. In this respect, only the motive can be called the *cause* and it acts as a catalyst would in a chemical reaction. It occasions the action which in turn results in an unveiling of the noumenal character.[587]

An interplay, therefore, occurs between the motive and the action on the phenomenal sphere where the principle of sufficient reason applies. But this presupposes a prior condition, a noumenon, which in this case, is the character of the individual. Schopenhauer clarifies this by distinguishing between two aspects: character as **intelligible** and **empirical**. The interplay between the **motive** and **action** pertains to the *empirical character* whereas the special *Idea* that each person is, as **an act of will outside time**, is the *intelligible character* and transcendental condition for the above.

---

[586] *Vorstellung I*, §26, I, S.178. "Als die niedrigste Stufe der Objektivation des Willens stellen sich die allgemeinsten Kräfte der Natur dar...Sie sind an sich unmittelbare Erscheinungen des Willens, so gut wie das Thun des Menschen, sind als solche grundlos, wie der Charakter des Menschen, nur ihre einzelnen Erscheinungen sind dem Satz vom Grund unterworfen, wie die Handlungen des Menschen, sie selbst hingegen können niemals weder Wirkung noch Ursache heißen, sondern sind die vorhergegangenen und vorausgesetzten Bedingungen aller Ursachen und Wirkungen, durch welche ihr eigenes Wesen sich entfaltet und offenbart."; *Representation*, I, §26, p.130.

[587] Cf. Atwell, p.402. "Strictly speaking, the character of a person is not to be regarded as the cause, or even one of the causes, of his actions. Whether the character is thought of as a 'natural force' or as a will -- both of which are legitimate conceptions -- in neither case can it be called the cause of an action. The sole cause of an action is the motive, which, given a certain character, 'occasions' the action, which in turn 'manifests' the character."

Referring respectively to the intelligible and empirical aspect of the character, Schopenhauer states:

> ...the former is the will as thing-in-itself, insofar as it appears in a definite individual in a definite degree, while the latter is this phenomenon itself as it manifests itself in the mode of action according to time, and in physical structure (*Korporisation*) according to space. In order to make the relation between both clear...the intelligible character of every man is to be regarded as an extra-temporal, therefore indivisible and unalterable, act of will. The phenomenon of this act of will, developed and pulled apart in time, space and the forms of the principle of sufficient reason, is the empirical character as it exhibits itself experientially (*erfahrungsmäßig*) in the man's whole manner of action and course of life.[588]

Now, why the noumenal will objectifies itself in a determined individual in a certain way and degree, is ultimately a mystery. This notwithstanding, Schopenhauer underscores that the "*individuality of every man*" acts as a penetrating dye that accompanies all his thoughts and actions whatever their degree of significance in the course of his life.[589] The type of character one has says everything about the capacity or potency of motives to prompt actions on the phenomenal sphere. But paradoxically, only actions that transpire within space and time provide the key to interpret what the intelligible character in fact is.

While it is true that the individuality or character of each individual person is an act of will

---

[588] *Vorstellung I*, §55, II, S.364; *Representation*, I, §55, p.289.

[589] *Parerga II*, §118, IX, S.250. "Zu bewundern ist es, wie die Individualität jedes Menschen (d.h. dieser bestimmte Charakter mit diesem bestimmten Intellekt), gleich einem eindringenden Färbestoff, alle Handlungen und Gedanken desselben, bis auf die unbedeutendeste herab, genau bestimmt; in Folge wovon der ganze Lebenslauf, d.h. die äußere und innere Geschichte, des Einen so grundverschieden von der des Andern ausfällt."; *Parerga*, II, §118, p.230.

outside time, insight into that character is only possible *a posteriori* via the actions human beings do. As is succinctly stated in *Über die Freiheit des menschlichen Willens*: "through that which we do we only experience what we are."[590] Note well that Schopenhauer does not assert that observance of human actions leaves in its wake an awareness of what one is *becoming*. Rather the opposite is true. One's actions as known on the phenomenal sphere de-code an already written script on the intelligible realm. They are an "unfolding" or a revelation of the truth of one's being as noumenal. Referring to the relationship between the intelligible and empirical character in respect to a given individual, Schopenhauer maintains that the empirical course of one's life is determined by the intelligible.[591]

What this points to, in effect, is that both the intelligible and empirical character are like two sides of the same coin.[592] Clearly, the intelligible character of a person is an act of will outside time to which the various forms of the principle of sufficient reason cannot be applied. In this respect it is

---

[590] *Freiheit*, III., VI, S.99. "Unsere Thaten sind allerdings kein erster Anfang, daher in ihnen nichts wirklich Neues zum Daseyn gelangt: sondern *durch das was wir thun, erfahren wir bloß was wir sind.*"; *Freedom*, III., p.62.

[591] *Grundlage*, §10, VI, S.215-216. "Das Individuum, bei seinem unveränderlichen, angeborenen Charakter, in allen seinen Aeußerungen durch das Gesetz der Kausalität, die hier, als durch den Intellekt vermittelt, Motivation heißt, streng bestimmt, ist nur die *Erscheinung*. Das dieser zum Grunde liegende *Ding an sich* ist, als außer Raum und Zeit befindlich, frei von aller Succession und Vielheit der Akte, Eines und unveränderlich. Seine Beschaffenheit *an sich* ist der *intelligible Charakter*, welcher in allen Thaten des Individui gleichmäßig gegenwärtig und in ihnen allen, wie das Petschaft in tausend Siegeln, ausgeprägt, den in der Zeit und Succession der Akte sich darstellenden, *empirischen Charakter* dieser Erscheinung bestimmt, die daher in allen ihren Aeußerungen, welche von den Motiven hervorgerufen werden, die Konstanz eines Naturgesetzes zeigen muß."; *Basis*, §10, p.110.

[592] Cf. Atwell, p.403. "Although a person cannot be divided into two wills or two characters, the character of the individual person, Schopenhauer holds, can and should be distinguished into two aspects: empirical and intelligible."

Human Transcendence 221

transcendental, but present insofar the inner being of man-in-himself is an abstraction from all the forms of the phenomenon.[593] The intelligible character thereby pertains to the noumenal sphere whereby the will is individuated in this and not that individual, thus giving him or her a certain susceptibility to certain motives, but not to others. The empirical character, on the other hand, is simply that metaphysical act of the free will which enters into consciousness as an intuitive perception, and entails that the intelligible unity characteristic of the noumenon, is now broken into parts (actions) as mediated by the forms of human cognition.[594] But both go hand in hand. The intelligible character, to which "freedom" is predicated insofar as it is an act of will outside time and hence subject to no

---

[593] *Freiheit*, V., VI, S.137. "Der empirische Charakter nämlich ist, wie der ganze Mensch, als Gegenstand der Erfahrung eine bloße Erscheinung, daher an die Formen aller Erscheinung, Zeit, Raum und Kausalität gebunden und deren Gesetzen unterworfen: hingegen ist die als Ding an sich von diesen Formen unabhängige und deshalb keinem Zeitunterschied unterworfene, mithin beharrende und unveränderliche Bedingung und Grundlage dieser ganzen Erscheinung sein *intelligibler Charakter*, d.h. sein Wille als Ding an sich, welchem, in solcher Eigenschaft, allerdings auch absolute Freiheit, d.h. Unabhängigkeit vom Gesetze der Kausalität (als einer bloßen Form der Erscheinungen) zukommt. Diese Freiheit aber ist *transcendentale*, d.h. nicht in der Erscheinung hervortretende, sondern nur insofern vorhandene, als wir von der Erscheinung und allen ihren Formen abstrahiren, um zu dem zu gelangen, was, außer aller Zeit, als das inner Wesen des Menschen an sich selbst zu denken ist.; *Freedom*, V., p.97.

[594] *Parerga II*, §116, IX, S.247. "...der Wille selbst und an sich ist, auch sofern er in einem Individuo erscheint, also das Ur- und Grundwollen desselben ausmacht, von aller Erkenntniß unabhängig, weil ihr vorhergängig. Von ihr erhält er bloß die Motive, an denen er successive sein Wesen entwickelt und sich kenntlich macht, oder in Sichtbarkeit tritt: aber er selbst ist, als außer der Zeit liegend, unveränderlich, so lange er überhaupt ist. Daher kann Jeder, als ein Solcher, der er nun ein Mal ist, und unter den jedesmaligen Umständen, die aber ihrerseits nach strenger Notwendigkeit eintreten, schlechterdings nie etwas Anderes thun, als was er jedesmal gerade jetzt thut. Demnach ist der ganze empirische Verlauf des Lebens eines Menschen, in allen seinen Vorgängen, großen und kleinen, so nothwendig vorherbestimmt, wie der eines Uhrwerks. Dies entsteht im Grunde daraus, daß die Art, wie die besagte, metaphysische freie That ins erkennende Bewußtseyn fällt, eine Anschauung ist, welche Zeit und Raum zur Form hat, mittelst welcher nunmehr die Einheit und Untheilbarkeit jener That sich darstellt als auseinandergezogen in eine Reihe von Zuständen und Begebenheiten, die am Leitfaden des Satzes vom Grunde in seinen vier Gestalten, - und dies eben heißt *notwendig*, - eintreten."; *Parerga*, II, §116, p.227.

necessity, may be described as the internal ground of a given action. Accordingly, Schopenhauer states that by virtue of the freedom which pertains to the intelligible character, all acts of man are "his own work" no matter how necessarily they proceed from the empirical character once it encounters motives on the phenomenological plane.[595] But the empirical character reveals what the internal ground is in that knowledge of the intelligible character is not *a priori*, but *a posteriori*. Alluding to the ramifications of this, Schopenhauer continues by stating:

> This is so because the empirical character is merely the phenomenon of the intelligible character in our cognitive faculty bound to time, space and causality, that is, the mode and manner in which the essence-in-itself (*das Wesen an sich*) of our own self presents itself (*sich darstellt*) to this faculty. Accordingly, the *will* is indeed free, but only in-itself and outside the phenomenon. In the phenomenon, on the other hand, it presents itself with a definite character, to which all its deeds are in accordance and therefore, when more precisely determined by motives which have supervened, necessarily must turn out thus and not otherwise.[596]

Is there any hope in light of the above for an individual born with susceptibility to motives that are disordered and wrong? Schopenhauer clearly states that there is not unless somehow the entire nature of one's susceptibility to motives is radically altered.[597]

---

[595] *Freiheit*, V., VI, S.137. "Vermöge dieser Freiheit sind alle Thaten des Menschen sein eigenes Werk; so nothwendig sie auch aus dem empirischen Charakter, bei seinem Zusammentreffen mit dem Motiven, hervorgehn."; *Freedom*, V., p.97.

[596] *Ibid.*; *Ibid.*

[597] *Grundlage*, §20, VI, S.295. "Dieser unglaublich großen, angeborenen und ursprünglichen Verschiedenheit gemäß, werden Jeden nur *die* Motive vorwaltend anregen, für welche er überwiegende Empfänglichkeit hat; so wie der *eine* Körper nur auf Säuren, der andere nur auf Alkalien reagirt: und wie Dieses, so ist auch Jenes nicht zu ändern. Die menschenfreundlichen Motive, welche für den guten

Accordingly, real improvement in the character of the egoist presupposes necessarily that the inner sanctum, and very essence, of his being be transformed. But for Schopenhauer, a radical redirection of willing is even more impossible than changing lead into gold.[598]

What concerns Schopenhauer is the basic willing that is fundamental in the character of an individual and is stamped on each of his or her actions.[599] He does admit that actions or behavioral patterns might be altered. The threat of punishment or fear of the consequences, for example, in many instances can act as a deterrent. In like fashion, the promise of reward is effective in eliciting constructive behavioral praxis. But the character, the way a person wills, cannot change:

> *Legality* may be enforced through motives, but not *morality*; one can remodel *what we do* (*das Handeln*), but not really *what we will to do*, (*das Wollen*) to which alone moral worth pertains. One cannot change the goal to which the will aspires, but only the path it follows there. Instruction can alter the choice of means, but not that of the ultimate general aims; these, every will determines for itself, in accordance with its original nature.[600]

Charakter so mächtige Antriebe sind, vermögen als solche nichts über Den, der allein für egoistische Motive empfänglich ist."; *Basis*, §20, p.193.

[598] *Ibid*. "Zu wirklicher Besserung wäre erfordert, daß man die ganze Art seiner Empfänglichkeit für Motive umwandelte, also z.B. machte, daß dem Einen fremdes Leiden als solches nicht mehr gleichgültig, dem Andern die Verursachung desselben nicht mehr Genuß wäre, oder einem Dritten nicht jede, selbst die geringste Vermehrung des eigenen Wohlseyns alle Motive anderer Art weit überwöge und unwirksam machte. Dies aber ist viel gewisser unmöglich, als daß man Blei in Gold umwandeln könnte. Denn es würde erfordern, daß man dem Menschen gleichsam das Herz im Leibe umkehrte, sein tief Innerstes umschüfe."; *Ibid*.

[599] *Freiheit*, V., VI, S.138-139. "Mit Einem Wort: Der Mensch thut allezeit nur was er will, und thut es doch nothwendig. Das liegt aber daran, daß er schon *ist* was er will: denn aus dem, was er *ist*, folgt nothwendig Alles, was er jedesmal thut."; *Freedom*, V., pp.98-99.

[600] *Grundlage*, §20, VI, S.296; *Basis*, §20, p.194.

Since the basic orientation of the will as incarnated in every human being cannot be altered given the doctrine of the inalterability of the character, what is there left to do? Ethics, as Schopenhauer sees it, does not have the exigence to transform the human will. Its task is merely to describe what man does and to establish criteria for actions of moral worth. All that can be done is to foster a better understanding of oneself and the motives that elicit actions. As Schopenhauer states somewhat stoically: "all we can do is clear the *head*, correct the insight, bring man to a more correct comprehension of what objectively exists, of the true circumstances of life."[601]

4. Freedom and the feeling of responsibility

Central to the discussion thus far has been the notion of the inalterability of the character which appears at first glance to contradict Schopenhauer's claim that necessity and freedom can co-exist. But both notions are not mutually exclusive. What the doctrine of the inalterability of character underscores, is that the actual function of the notion of the co-existence of freedom and necessity in Schopenhauer's system, is precisely to highlight that each phenomenon is an expression of a noumenally free will. The importance of the notion of freedom in Schopenhauer's system, accordingly, does not primarily consist in the possibility that some individuals have to cast off the shackles of will-oriented existence. In his "Kritik des Kantischen Philosophie," as found in the appendix of the

---

[601] *Ibid.*, S.295-296; *Ibid.*, pp.193-194.

first volume of *Die Welt als Wille und Vorstellung*, Schopenhauer states:

> ...notwithstanding all transcendental freedom (that is, independence of the will-in-itself of the laws of the connection of its phenomenon), no man has the capacity of himself to begin a series of actions...Therefore, freedom also has no causality; for only the will, which lies outside of nature or the phenomenon, is free. The phenomenon is only its objectification, but it does not stand to the will in a relation of causality.[602]

In short, the good and wicked alike (not to mention every other existent) have two dimensions to their being: an intelligible character that is an act of a free will outside of time; an empirical character that is subject to the laws of the phenomenal realm. *Freedom*, therefore, can be predicated of the intelligible characters of all human beings in spite of the doctrine of inalterability, since each character is an act of will outside time, and as such, a unique Idea. In this respect, Schopenhauer's characterization of the denial of the will-to-live as an entrance of freedom into the phenomenal realm of human actions, appears to be incidental to the issue at hand.

Because each individual as a unique Idea is an act of will outside of time, Schopenhauer maintains that the intuition of freedom that we all have in the depths of our essence is connected to the feeling of responsibility for our own actions. *Über den Willen in der Natur* (published in 1835) describes freedom and responsibility as "the foundation-pillar of all ethics (*Grundpfeiler aller Ethik*)" underscoring that both notions go hand in hand, and that freedom in turn presupposes the concept of originality (that we are doers

---

[602] "Kritik des Kantischen Philosophie," *Vorstellung I*, II, S.618; "Criticism of the Kantian Philosophy," *Representation*, I, p.507.

of our own deeds).⁶⁰³ These notions are further developed in his two ethical treatises: *Über die Freiheit des menschlichen Willens* (published a few years later in 1839) and *Über die Grundlage der Moral* (published in 1840). As a case in point, it is stated in the former work:

> There is...still a fact of consciousness which I have until now left aside...This is the wholly clear and certain feeling (*Gefühl*) of the *responsibility* (*Verantwortlichkeit*) for that which we do, of the *accountability* (*Zurechnungsfähigkeit*) for our actions, which rests on the unshakable certainty that we ourselves are doers of our deeds.⁶⁰⁴

In the latter work Schopenhauer maintains that freedom, which as such pertains only to the *esse* of our being (the intelligible character), proclaims itself solely through the *responsibility* we feel for our actions. Hence, the reproach of conscience which ensues after the completion of some actions, concerns not so much what one does, but what one is.⁶⁰⁵ *Über die Freiheit des menschlichen*

---

⁶⁰³ *Natur*, "Hinweisung auf die Ethik," V, S.338. "Sodann ist hier noch in Erwägung zu ziehn, daß Freiheit und Verantwortlichkeit, diese Grundpfeiler aller Ethik, ohne die Voraussetzung der Aseität des Willens sich wohl mit Worten behaupten, aber schlechterdings nicht denken lassen. Wer dieses bestreiten will, hat zuvor das Axiom, welches schon die Scholastiker aufstellen, *operari sequitur esse* (d.h. aus der Beschaffenheit jedes Wesens folgt sein Wirken), umzustoßen, oder die Folgerung aus demselben, *unde esse inde operari*, als falsch nachzuweisen. Verantwortlichkeit hat Freiheit, diese aber Ursprünglichkeit zur Bedingung. Denn ich *will* je nachdem *ich bin*: daher muß ich *seyn* je nachdem ich *will*."; *Nature*, "Reference to Ethics," p.374.

⁶⁰⁴ *Freiheit*, V., VI, S.134; *Freedom*, V., pp.93-94.

⁶⁰⁵ *Grundlage*, §20, VI, S.297. "Aber schon lange höre ich den Leser die Frage aufwerfen: wo bleibt Schuld und Verdienst? - Zur Antwort hierauf verweise ich auf §10. Daselbst hat, was sonst *hier* vorzutragen wäre, schon seine Stelle gefunden, weil es in enger Verbindung mit Kants Lehre vom Zusammenbestehn der Freiheit mit der Nothwendigkeit steht. Das dort Gesagte also bitte ich hier nochmals zu lesen. In Gemäßheit desselben ist das *Operari*, beim Eintritt der Motive, durchweg nothwendig: daher kann die *Freiheit*, welche sich allein durch die *Verantwortlichkeit* ankündigt, nur im *Esse* liegen. Die Vorwürfe des Gewissens betreffen zwar zunächst und ostensibel Das, was wir *getan haben*, eigentlich und im Grund aber Das, was wir *sind*, als worüber unsere Taten allein vollgültiges Zeugniß ablegen, indem sie zu unserm Charakter sich verhalten wie die Symptome zur Krankheit. In diesem *Esse* also, in dem was wir *sind*, muß auch Schuld und

Willens asserts that the feeling of responsibility for what we do induces us not to shift culpability for actions away from ourselves to motives that induced action.[606] Why? Because one recognizes that there is a subjective factor (the intelligible character of the willer and doer) that makes an action one's own. Objectively speaking, another action would have been possible under the existing circumstances if the inner being of the agent had only been different.[607] "To him, because he is this man and not another, because he has such and such a character, no other action was, of course possible; but in itself, therefore objectively, it was possible."[608]

In *Über die Grundlage der Moral*, however, there is an important nuancing of the earlier position. Here Schopenhauer underscores that human actions are accompanied by a consciousness of arbitrariness and originality. In light of this, actions are considered to be one's "own work." One thereby feels morally responsible for them.[609] Schopenhauer goes on to

---

Verdienst liegen."; *Basis*, §20, p.195.

[606] *Freiheit*, V., VI, S.134. "Vermöge dieses Bewußtseyns kommt es Keinem, auch nicht, der von der im Bisherigen dargelegten Nothwendigkeit, mit welcher unsere Handlungen eintreten, völlig überzeugt ist, jemals in den Sinn, sich für ein Vergehn durch diese Nothwendigkeit zu entschuldigen und die Schuld von sich auf die Motive zu wälzen, da ja bei deren Eintritt die That unausbleiblich war."; *Freedom*, V., p.94.

[607] *Ibid*. "Denn er sieht sehr wohl ein, daß diese Nothwendigkeit eine *subjektive* Bedingung hat, und daß hier *objektive*, d.h. unter den vorhandenen Umständen, also unter der Einwirkung der Motive, die ihn bestimmt haben, doch eine ganz andere Handlung, ja, die der seinigen gerade entgegengesetzte, sehr wohl möglich war und hätte geschehn können, *wenn nur Er ein Anderer gewesen wäre*: hieran allein hat es gelegen.; *Ibid*.

[608] *Ibid.*; *Ibid*.

[609] *Grundlage*, §10, VI, S.215. "Dabei bleibt es jedoch wahr, daß unsere Handlungen von einem Bewußtseyn der Eigenmächtigkeit und Ursprünglichkeit begleitet sind, vermöge dessen wir sie als unser Werk erkennen und Jeder, mit untrüglicher Gewißheit, sich als den wirklichen Thäter seiner Thaten und für

emphasize that the notion of responsibility carries with it an important presupposition: namely, the possibility of having acted otherwise, and hence "in some way" (*auf irgend eine Weise*), freedom. Accordingly, consciousness of freedom can be indirectly found in the awareness of responsibility.[610]

The above passages indicate that the exact relationship between responsibility and freedom is difficult to fathom and pin down. It seems clear enough, however, that the cited passages in *Über die Freiheit des menschlichen Willens* concerning that relationship, are not adequate. For they do not satisfactorily explain exactly why the notion of responsibility brings with it, and indeed presupposes, the feeling of freedom that accompanies human actions. In this respect, the later exposition in *Über die Grundlage der Moral* is more acceptable and less cumbersome. It states simply that responsibility for one's actions is accompanied by the feeling that one could have acted differently -- which presupposes in some way or another, the consciousness of freedom. Noticeably absent in this treatise is the unfortunate attempt in *Über die Freiheit des menschlichen Willens* to reduce the concept of freedom to the possibility of having acted differently by the invoking of a hypothetical condition: namely, one could have objectively acted differently in the circumstances at hand, if one's character had been different. It can be said, therefore, that the former, by suspending the issue, more aptly describes what transpires in human actions than the latter.

---

dieselben moralisch *verantwortlich* fühlt."; *Basis*, §10, p.110.

[610] *Ibid*. "Da nun aber die Verantwortlichkeit eine Möglichkeit anders gehandelt zu haben, mithin Freiheit, auf irgend eine Weise, voraussetzt; so liegt im Bewußtseyn der Verantwortlichkeit mittelbar auch das der Freiheit."; *Ibid*.

The above discussion serves only to indicate the complexity of the issues that freedom and necessity, the inalterability of the character, and the responsibility that accompanies human actions, involves. As is clearly evident, this part of Schopenhauer's philosophy is riddled with paradoxes and difficulties that cannot be easily systematized or reconciled. But they are of importance for the discussion to follow which is an attempt to ground denial of the will-to-live and asceticism in Schopenhauer's metaphysics.

B. Compassion as an Empirical Fact

In Chapter Four, it was argued that the affirmation of the will-to-live is characterized by an inordinate desire for the objects of one's particular will at the expense of those of another human being. In light of the direct knowledge we have of ourselves and the indirect, merely representational knowledge we have of others, actions which involve the weal of another human being are difficult at the outset. Egocentric blinders, as it were, give an alien character to the other who appears as an empirical representation before consciousness.

Yet, Schopenhauer's analysis of the human person is not uncompromisingly bleak. Notwithstanding human misery, depravity, and stupidity characteristic of will-oriented existence, phenomena of honesty, kindness, and nobility occur such that in there exists a "redeeming principle" within the *samsara* of human existence.[611] In

---

[611] *Parerga II*, §114, IX, S.238. "Dies ist *Sansara*, und Jegliches darin kündigt es an; mehr als Alles jedoch die Menschenwelt, als welcher, moralisch, Schlechtigkeit und Niederträchtigkeit, intellektuell, Unfähigkeit und Dummheit in erschreckendem Maaße vorherrschen. Dennoch treten in ihr, wiewohl sehr sporadisch, aber doch stets von Neuem uns überraschend, Erscheinungen der

Über die Grundlage der Moral he sets out to investigate the *empirical question* as to the possibility of actions of *voluntary justice* (*Handlungen freiwilliger Gerichtigkeit*) and *altruistic love* (*uneigennützige Menschenliebe*).[612] Admitting that the question cannot be altogether resolved empirically speaking, since experience merely gives the deed (*That*) and never the incentives (*Antriebe*) that give rise to such motives, he nevertheless suggests that there are *good* people:

> I believe that there will be very few who question and do not have the conviction from their own experience, that one often acts justly, simply and solely in order that no injustice occur to another. Indeed, I believe that there are people whose principle (*Grundsatz*), as it were, of giving others their due, is *inborn*, who therefore do not intentionally hurt anyone's feelings (*Niemanden absictlich zu nahe treten*), who do not unconditionally seek their own advantage, but who in doing so, also consider the rights of others.[613]

According to Schopenhauer, these "*truly honorable people*" are the few just among the numberless host of the egoistic and selfish unjust. Many a man lives out his life prompted by no other intention than alleviating the distress of others.[614] These rare individuals appear to

---

Redlichkeit, der Güte, ja des Edelmuths, und eben so auch des großen Verstandes, des denkenden Geistes, ja, des Genies auf. Nun gehn diese ganz aus: sie schimmern uns, wie einzelne glänzende Punkte, aus der großen dunklen Masse entgegen. Wir müssen sie als ein Unterpfand nehmen, daß ein gutes und erlösendes Princip in diesem *Sansara* steckt, welches zum Durchbruch kommen und das Ganze erfüllen und befreien kann."; *Parerga*, II, §114, pp.218-219.

[612] *Grundlage*, §15, VI, S.242; *Basis*, §15, p.138.

[613] *Ibid.*, S.243; *Ibid.*, pp.138-139.

[614] *Ibid.* "Dies sind die *wahrhaft ehrlichen Leute*, die wenigen *Aequi* unter der Unzahl der *Iniqui*. Aber solche Leute giebt es. Imgleichen wird man mir, denke ich, zugestehn, daß Mancher hilft und giebt, leistet und entsagt, ohne in seinem Herzen eine weitere Absicht zu haben, als daß dem Andern, dessen Noth er sieht, geholfen werde."; *Ibid.*, p.139.

do actions not out of selfish motivation. No threat of punishment motivates their behavior. The promise of bliss in an after-life, or the threat of a punishment in hell, does not ground their praxis. Actions done for that reason alone are, in Schopenhauer's eyes, basically egoistic and hence without moral worth.[615] In fact, it is the absence of all egoistic motivation that grants to an action the character of being morally praiseworthy.[616]

How this can be possible is *the* question Schopenhauer proposes to answer given the reality of the tendency to over-affirm the will-to-live so characteristic to man. If egoism is rooted in the disorderedness of the will and will-oriented cognition which regards the other as merely a representation, an explanation as to why at least *some* people are able to go beyond the egoistic predicament of human existence is necessary. How is it that another's *weal* and *woe* can move my will as immediately as does my very own? Schopenhauer provides an initial explanation:

> Obviously only through that other person becoming the *ultimate object* (*der letzte Zweck*) of my will in the same way as I myself am, and hence through my directly desiring *his* weal (*Wohl*) and not *his* woe (*Wehe*) just as immediately (*so unmittelbar*) as I ordinarily do only *my* own. But this necessarily presupposes that, in the case of his *woe* as such, I suffer directly with him (*geradzu mitleide*), I feel *his* woe (*sein Wehe fühle*) just as I ordinarily feel my own; and, likewise, I directly desire his weal in the

---

[615] *Ibid.*, §19, S.275. "Ueberdies läßt sich gegen jede ganz allein aus religiösen Ueberzeugungen hervorgegangene gute Handlung noch einwenden, daß sie nicht uneigennützig gewesen, sondern aus Rücksicht auf Lohn und Strafe geschehn sei, folglich keinen rein moralischen Werth habe."; *Ibid.*, §19, p.172.

[616] *Ibid.*, §15, S.244. "Die Abwesenheit aller egoistischen Motivation ist also das *Kriterium einer Handlung von moralischem Werth.*"; *Ibid.*, §15, p.140.

same way I otherwise desire only my own. But this requires that I am in some way *identified with him* (*mit ihm identificirt*), that is, that this entire *difference* between me and everyone else upon which my egoism rests, is eliminated (*aufgehoben*), to a certain degree at least.⁶¹⁷

In order to desire another's weal, however, as immediately as my own, *insight* is required. What opens the horizons for genuine moral behavior is the knowledge that the difference between myself and others is not absolute -- that, in some way, reality is homogeneous or one. In other words, so as to ascend this plateau of heightened awareness, the type of knowing associated with affirmation of the will-to-live must be left behind. Accordingly, one is no longer slave to the *principium individuationis* which presents reality merely as a plurality of particulars. Pivotal to the whole process is the notion of *compassion* for the other. Writes Schopenhauer:

> Since I do not exist *inside the skin* of another (*Da ich nun aber doch nicht in der Haut des Andern stecke*), then only by means of the *knowledge* I have of him, that is of the representation of him in my head, can I identify myself with him in that my deed declares, as abolished, that difference...It is the everyday phenomenon (*Phänomen*) of *compassion* (*Mitleid*), that is, of the completely immediate *participation* (*Theilnahme*) in the suffering of another, independent of all ulterior considerations, and thus in the prevention or elimination of this suffering.⁶¹⁸

In light of the above discussion, the phenomenon of compassion may be described as secondary in two respects. In the first place, it logically implies that suffering already exists which is in keeping with Schopenhauer's

---

⁶¹⁷ *Ibid.*, §16, S.247-248; *Ibid.*, §16, pp.143-144.

⁶¹⁸ *Ibid.*, S.248; *Ibid.*, p.144.

basic ontology as outlined and discussed in the first four chapters of this study. For the inherent and incurable frustration that characterizes the ever-striving will entails that phenomenal reality, as a representation of the diseased will, likewise be in a state of suffering. Given this presupposition, it also follows that the suffering present in the animal and human spheres of Being, is directly a result of the universal egoism that imbues all conscious, will-filled existents. The following elucidates this:

> Originally, we are all inclined to injustice and violence because our need, desires, anger and hatred immediately enter consciousness, and thus have the *ius primi occupantis*. On the other hand, the sufferings of others that are caused by our injustice and violence, come into consciousness merely on the secondary path of the *representation* and through experience, and thus *indirectly*.[619]

Notwithstanding its secondary nature, Schopenhauer very significantly maintains that compassion is part and parcel of human nature itself, such that it is original and immediate to everyone.[620] He even goes on to say that anyone who appears to lack compassion is in reality *inhuman*. In a word, to be a human being and to be compassionate are synonymous.[621] In this regard, both egoism and compassion can even be called primordial phenomena in the case of man, even though this gives way

---

[619] *Ibid.*, §17, S.253; *Ibid.*, §17, p.149.

[620] *Ibid.*, §17, S.252. "Dieses Mitleid selbst aber ist eine unleugbare Thatsache des menschlichen Bewußtseyns, ist diesem wesentlich eigen, beruht nicht auf Voraussetzungen, Begriffen, Religionen, Dogmen, Mythen, Erziehung und Bildung; sondern ist ursprünglich und unmittelbar, liegt in der menschlichen Natur selbst, hält eben deshalb unter allen Verhältnissen Stich, und zeigt sich in allen Ländern und Zeiten."; *Ibid.*, §17, pp.148-149.

[621] *Ibid.*, S.253. "...nennt man Den, dem [Mitleid] es zu mangeln scheint, einen Unmenschen; wie auch »Menschlichkeit« oft als Synonym von Mitleid gebraucht wird."; *Ibid.*, p.149.

to difficulties as to explaining exactly how this is in fact so.[622]

In order to give what appears to be the case on the empirical sphere (that is, the occurrence of compassionate actions) a metaphysical grounding, Schopenhauer introduces another characteristic of the will in man: its ability in some instances to turn on itself and deny its very essence, called the *denial of the will-to-live* (*die Verneinung des Willens zum Leben*). Accordingly, the remaining sections of this chapter are an attempt to illustrate why and how compassionate actions are related to Schopenhauer's metaphysical presuppositions in general, and the denial of the will-to-live in particular.

C. Degrees of Denial of the Will-to-Live

1. Justice

To understand what Schopenhauer means by denial of the will-to-live, it is clear that the will's tendency to affirm itself must first be presupposed. This means that the consciousness that the will gains for itself in man, does not initially serve to halt its willing of life. Though the will's inner nature appears as representation, nevertheless, life continues to be willed with knowledge.[623] The denial of the will-to-live,

---

[622] Cf.Schaefer, *Probleme Schopenhauers*, S.98. "Das Verhältnis des Urphänomens des Egoismus des Mitleids, auf dem die reine Moral beruht, ist das des rezeproken Scheiterns."

[623] *Vorstellung I*, §54, II, S.359. "Der Wille bejaht sich selbst, besagt: indem in seiner Objektität, d.i. der Welt und dem Leben, sein eigenes Wesen ihm als Vorstellung vollständig und deutlich gegeben wird, hemmt diese Erkenntniß sein Wollen keineswegs; sondern eben dieses so erkannte Leben wird auch als solches von ihm gewollt, wie bis dahin ohne Erkenntniß, als blinder Drang, so jetzt mit Erkenntniß, bewußt und besonnen."; *Representation*, I, §54, p.285.

while diverse from the will's affirmation, still involves the same type of knowledge whereby other existents appear as representations. However, with the will's denial, the particular phenomena that acted as motives in will-oriented cognition, lose their evocativeness in light of a mysterious grasping of the inner nature of the will as objectified in the Ideas. This insight in turn becomes the *quieter* of the will and leads to the will denying itself.[624]

Part and parcel of this occurrence is seeing through the *principium individuationis* which presents reality merely as a plurality of particulars. Schopenhauer is categorical on this important point and states that "if seeing through (*Durchschauen*) the *principium individuationis*, this direct knowledge of the identity of the will in all its phenomena, is present in a high degree of distinctness, it will at once show an influence on the will..."[625] Seeing through the principle entails, first of all, that the *egoistic* distinction between the person of the perceiver and that of others is no longer made.

Schopenhauer states that there are stages to this insight and the praxis to which it gives rise. But before proceeding in the argumentation, an important nuance must be made so as to avoid confusion and misinterpretation. Strictly speaking, the first stage of the will's denial is aesthetic contemplation whereby one momentarily leaves behind will-oriented cognition.

---

[624] *Ibid.* "Das Gegentheil hievon, die *Verneinung des Willens zum Leben*, zeigt sich, wenn auf jene Erkenntniß das Wollen endet, indem sodann nicht mehr die erkannten einzelnen Erscheinungen als *Motive* des Wollens wirken, sondern die ganze, durch Auffassung der *Ideen* erwachsene Erkenntniß des Wesens der Welt, die den Willen spiegelt, zum *Quietiv* des Willens wird und so der Wille frei sich selbst aufhebt."; *Ibid.*

[625] *Ibid.*, §68, S.469; *Ibid.*, §68, p.378.

However, since the issue has already been sufficiently addressed, I refer the reader to the pertinent sections in this study which examine this.[626]

In the immediate matter at hand that properly concerns denial of the will-to-live on the ethical plane, Schopenhauer first speaks about individuals inclined to *justice*. Such persons maintain a proper balance between their affirmation of the will, and that of others in that they avoid any behavioral patterns that over-affirm their will at the expense of another human being.[627] Though they may pursue their own well-being, they shun the infliction of suffering on another human being. In this respect the just person differs from the wicked person for whom the *principium individuationis* is like a thick partition that separates himself or herself from others. Just people, by the way they live, reveal that they implicitly recognize their own inner nature in other human beings:

> ...a just man (*Gerechte*)...shows by his way of acting that he *again recognizes* his own inner being, namely the will-to-live as thing-in-itself, in the phenomenon of another given to him merely as representation. Thus, he finds himself again in that phenomenon up to a certain degree, namely that of doing no wrong, i.e., of not injuring. Now in precisely this degree does he see through the *principium individuationis*, the veil of Maya. To this

---

[626] Cf. Robert A. Gonzales, "Schopenhauer's Demythologization of Christian Asceticism," *Auslegung* 9 (1982), pp.13-14.

[627] *Vorstellung I*, §66, II, S.459. "Bevor wir nun, im Gegensatz des dargestellten *Bösen*, von der eigentlichen *Güte* reden, ist, als Zwischenstufe, die bloße Negation des Bösen zu berühren: dieses ist die *Gerechtigkeit*. Was Recht und Unrecht sei, ist oben hinlänglich auseinandergesetzt: daher wir hier mit Wenigem sagen können, daß Derjenige, welcher jene bloß moralische Gränze zwischen Unrecht und Recht freiwillig anerkennt und sie gelten läßt, auch wo kein Staat, oder sonstige Gewalt sie sichert, folglich, unserer Erklärung gemäß, nie in der Bejahung seines eigenen Willens bis zur Verneinung des in einem andern Individuo sich darstellenden geht, -- *gerecht* ist."; *Representation*, I, §66, p.370.

extent, he treats the being outside of himself like his own; he does not injure it.[628]

This identification between the perceiver and the perceived is determined first by the insight that the other partakes in the same suffering reality as oneself. In this respect, the movement from the egocentric predicament into what Schopenhauer calls *justice* is evoked by *compassion*.[629] It is precisely for this reason that Schopenhauer states that the first degree of the effect of compassion is indeed the *just life-style*. He goes on to claim that if one's disposition is susceptible to compassion in this first degree (justice), using the sufferings of another as a means for selfish ends is out of the question.

> ...the first degree of the effect of compassion is that it opposes and impedes the sufferings which are caused to others by myself in consequence of my indwelling anti-moral forces. It calls out to me 'stop' and it places itself as a bulwark (*Schutzwehr*) before the other which protects him from the injury to which my egoism or malice would otherwise urge me to do. In such a manner, there arises from this first degree of compassion the maxim, *neminem laede*, i.e. the fundamental principle of *justice*.[630]

This level of the piercing through of the *principium individuationis* in justice is translated into behavioral patterns respectful of the other's dignity as a human being. Hence, the using of another's sufferings as a means for selfish ends cannot characterize the *just person*. Inflicting suffering, whether it be mental or physical, is also out of the question. In contrast to

---

[628] *Ibid.*, S.459-460; *Ibid.*

[629] Cf.notes 617 and 618 in the text.

[630] *Grundlage*, §17, VI, S.253; *Basis*, §17, p.149.

the disordered sexuality so characteristic of human existence that vehemently affirms the will-to-live, compassion (as manifested in a just life-style), respects the sexuality of another.[631]

Central to the compassion that gives rise to the maxim "hurt no one", and to just actions that ensue therefrom, is "the knowledge of the suffering which each unjust action necessarily brings to others, and which is sharpened by the feeling of enduring wrong (*das Gefühl des Unrechterduldens*), that is, of a stranger's superior strength."[632] It is to be kept in mind, however, that the *knowledge* to which Schopenhauer alludes (as in the case of the *knowing* that leads to the destructive praxis characteristic of the over-affirmation of the will-to-live) is not of an abstract nature. Quite the contrary! It is a "living knowledge" which expresses itself in the concreteness of deeds.[633]

---

[631] *Ibid*., S.253-254. "Ist mein Gemüth bis zu jenem Grade für das Mitleid empfänglich; so wird dasselbe mich zurückhalten, wo und wann ich, um meine Zwecke zu erreichen, fremdes Leiden als Mittel gebrauchen möchte; gleichviel ob dieses Leiden ein augenblickliches, oder später eintretendes, ein direktes, oder indirektes, durch Zwischenglieder vermitteltes sei. Folglich werde ich dann so wenig das Eigenthum, als die Person des Andern angreifen, ihm so wenig geistige, als körperliche Leiden verursachen, also nicht nur mich jeder physischen Verletzung enthalten; sondern auch eben so wenig auf geistigem Wege ihm Schmerz bereiten, durch Kränkung, Aengstigung, Aerger, oder Verläumdung. Das selbe Mitleid wird mich abhalten, die Befriedigung meiner Lüste auf Kosten des Lebensglückes weiblicher Individuen zu suchen, oder das Weib eines Andern zu verführen, oder auch Jünglinge moralisch und physisch zu verderben, durch Verleitung zur Päderastie."; *Ibid*., pp.149-150.

[632] *Ibid*., S.254; *Ibid*., p.150.

[633] *Vorstellung I*, §54, II, S.359. "Denn Beide gehn zwar von der *Erkenntniß* aus, aber nicht von einer abstrakten, die sich in Worten, sondern von einer lebendigen, die sich durch die That und den Wandel allein ausdrückt und unabhängig bleibt von den Dogmen, welche dabei, als abstrakte Erkenntniß, die Vernunft beschäftigen."; *Representation*, I, §54, p.285.

2. Philanthropy

It has been underscored that voluntary justice entails a certain degree of seeing through the *principium individuationis* which empowers one to close the chasm that egoism opens between oneself and others. Piercing through the veil of Maya, however, can take one beyond the plateaus of justice to the very heights of altruistic actions. "This seeing through (*Durchschauung*) can take place not only in the degree necessary for justice, but also in the higher degree which urges one to positive benevolence (*Wohlwollen*) and well-doing (*Wohlthun*), to philanthropy (*Menschenliebe*)."[634]

Schopenhauer notes, once again, that knowledge is absolutely essential in the scaling of these heights. He states at the outset that it cannot be maintained that persons who do altruistic actions are weaker instances of the will's affirmation. Rather, the opposite is true. Benevolence and philanthropy can occur in cases where the affirmation of the will is strongest provided that insight first transpire. Once this knowledge is attained, it acts as a counterbalance to that same will.[635] In fact, it can be said that in the final analysis, only knowledge masters the will.

Individuals who have advanced to the stage of philanthropy or loving-kindness (*die Menschenliebe*) are less shackled to the principle of sufficient reason and thereby are less bound to the firm grasp of the

---

[634] *Ibid.*, §66, S.461; *Ibid.*, §66, p.371.

[635] *Ibid.* "Immer kann die Erkenntniß ihm (Wille) das Gleichgewicht halten, der Versuchung zum Unrecht widerstehn lehren und selbst jeden Grad von Güte, ja von Resignation hervorbringen. Also ist keineswegs der gute Mensch für eine ursprünglich schwächere Willenserscheinung als der böse zu halten; sondern es ist die Erkenntniß, welche in ihm den blinden Willensdrang bemeistert."; *Ibid.*

principium individuationis. Accordingly, the noble person (*der Edle*) makes less of a distinction between his or her ego and that of another in light of a more profound intuitive knowledge into the suffering that unites *all* living existents.[636] Here compassion not only restrains one from harming another living thing, but has a positive character in that it actually prompts one to help the other.[637] Accordingly, in such individuals the maxim *omnes quantum potes juva* enfleshes itself in concrete actions -- not in mere words. Thus, it is stated:

> I shall be induced by that purely moral motive to bring an offering for the need or distress of another, which may consist in the expenditure of my bodily and mental powers for him, in the loss of my property, health, freedom and even life itself![638]

Because persons with noble dispositions have seen through the veil of Maya that obscures the vision of the selfish, a radical openness towards Being ensues. Reality in its suffering state, as manifested in each and every existent, is interiorly embraced by the individual

---

[636] *Ibid.*, S.462. "...das *principium individuationis*, die Form der Erscheinung, befängt ihn nicht mehr so fest; sondern das Leiden, welches er an Andern sieht, geht ihn fast so nahe an, wie sein eigenes: er sucht daher das Gleichgewicht zwischen beiden herzustellen, versagt sich Genüsse, übernimmt Entbehrungen, um fremde Leiden zu mildern. Er wird inne, daß der Unterschied zwischen ihm und Andern, welcher dem Bösen eine so große Kluft ist, nur einer vergänglichen täuschenden Erscheinung angehört: er erkennt, unmittelbar und ohne Schlüsse, daß das Ansich seiner eigenen Erscheinung auch das der fremden ist, nämlich jener Wille zum Leben, welcher das Wesen jeglichen Dinges ausmacht und in Allem lebt; ja, daß dieses sich sogar auf die Thiere und die ganze Natur erstreckt: daher wird er auch kein Thier quälen."; *Ibid.*, p.372.

[637] *Grundlage*, §18, S.266. "Der zweite Grad, in welchem, mittelst des oben thatsächlich nachgewiesenen, wiewohl seinem Ursprung nach geheimnißvollen Vorgangs des *Mitleids*, das fremde Leiden an sich selbst und als solches unmittelbar mein Motiv wird, sondert sich von dem ersten deutlich ab, durch den *positiven Charakter* der daraus hervorgehenden Handlungen; indem alsdann das Mitleid nicht bloß mich abhält, den Andern zu verletzen, sondern sogar mich antreibt, ihm zu helfen."; *Basis*, §18, p.163.

[638] *Ibid.*, S.266-267; *Ibid.*, p.163.

endowed with insight. Thus, it is understandable why
Schopenhauer states that:

> If that veil of Maya, the *principium individuationis*, is lifted from the eyes of a man that he no longer makes the egoistical distinction between his person and that of others, but takes as much interest (*Anteil*) in the sufferings of other individuals as in his own,...then it follows automatically (*folgt von selbst*), that such a man, who recognizes in all beings his innermost and true self, must also consider the endless sufferings of all that lives as his own, and thus take upon himself (*sich zueignen muß*) the pain of the whole world.[639]

This openness towards the totality of Being that nevertheless appears merely as a representation, puts to a halting end hostility and indifference to the plight of others that characterizes the selfish life-style. The positive character of philanthropy is significant because (*in theory at least*) Schopenhauer's ethics at this stage of denial of the will-to-live has ramifications for the betterment of the lot of others. For example, Schopenhauer states that in light of the heightened awareness that this high level of insight leaves in its wake, allowing another to starve while one lives in luxury is simply out of the question.[640]

---

[639] *Vorstellung I*, §68, II, S.469; *Representation*, I, §68, pp.378-379.

[640] *Nachlaß*, I, #675, S.471. "*Jeder der ein reines Liebeswerk thut, d.h. seinem Egoismus Abbruch thut zu Gunsten des fremden, d.h. sein Wohlseyn mindert um fremdes Leiden zu mindern, -- kann dies (wenn nicht irgend ein verkapptes egoistisches Motiv, dergleichen auch Vergeltung im Himmel ist, ihn treibt, wo dann die ganze Handlung nur Schein ist) allein dadurch thun, daß er, von der Erkenntniß nach dem Satz vom Grund in Etwas frei geworden, das principium individuationis durchschaut und daher erkennt daß zwischen ihm und andern Menschen der Unterschied nur scheinbar ist, und der Wille zum Leben, der er selbst ist, das an Sich seiner eigenen, wie der fremden Erscheinung ausmacht und er ist der in Allen lebt, ja daß sich dies auf die Thiere und die ganze Natur erstreckt. Sobald aber diese Erkenntniß eintritt und solange sie lebendig bleibt, (der Egoismus kann sie gewaltsam ersticken) wird er so wenig im Stande seyn Andre darben zu lassen, während er selbst Ueberflüssiges und Entbehrliches genießt, als irgend Einer einen Tag darben wird um am andern mehr zu haben als er genießen kann oder im Ueberflüß zu schwelgen.*"; *Remains*, I, #675, pp.521-522.

What motivates loving actions, therefore, is not one's own weal, but that of another. In this respect, this type of praxis may be described as "disinterested" insofar as one's own particular weal appears to be left aside as a primary motive for action. But once again, it is the antecedent recognition of the suffering of another, as translated in loving actions, that is central for Schopenhauer. This, in Schopenhauer's eyes, allows one to prescind from an objective consideration of the worth and dignity of an individual as such. Therefore, the other who presents himself before consciousness as a more indirect representation than oneself, is primarily a sufferer who is deserving of compassion. In this respect, for Schopenhauer charity is essentially compassion and the "*agape* to which the gospel summons us."[641]

It is in compassion, as incarnated by definite and positive actions to alleviate the sufferings of others, that the barrier between individuals is abolished ("*die Schranke zwischen Ich und Nicht-Ich für den Augenblick aufgehoben sei*").[642] "This wholly direct and even instinctive participation (*instinktartige Theilnahme*) in another's suffering -- compassion -- is the sole source (*alleinige Quelle*) of such actions when they have *moral worth*, that is, are free from all egoistic motives, and for that very reason, they ought to awaken in us that inward contentment, which one calls the good, satisfied, approving conscience."[643] With the bridging of the chasm between ego and non-ego, people who

---

[641] *Parerga II*, §109, IX, S.220-221; *Parerga*, II, §109, p.202.

[642] *Grundlage*, §18, VI, S.269; *Basis*, §18, p.166.

[643] *Ibid.*, S.267; *Ibid.*, pp.163-164.

love have peace of mind and heart. Unlike the malicious whose very faces express unhappiness, these individuals are friendly towards all.[644]

How and why the above phenomenon happens is a mystery, for which the faculty of reason can give no satisfactory account.[645] Yet, Schopenhauer states that it is a common occurrence which we all experience. Even the most hard-hearted and selfish are privy to it at times.[646] Compassion, therefore, is part of human nature, mysterious as it may seem. Schopenhauer even maintains that it has been planted in the human heart by nature itself as a counterbalance to the "burning egoism" that fills all beings and which, in man's case, can sometimes become malice.[647]

---

[644] Ibid., §22, S.312-313. "Der gute Charakter...lebt in einer seinem Wesen homogenen Außenwelt: die Andern sind ihm kein Nicht-Ich, sondern »Ich noch ein Mal«. Daher ist sein ursprüngliches Verhältniß zu Jedem ein befreundetes: er fühlt sich allen Wesen im Innern verwandt, nimmt unmittelbar Theil an ihrem Wohl und Wehe, und setzt mit Zuversicht die selbe Theilnahme bei ihnen voraus. Hieraus erwächst der tiefe Friede seines Innern und jene getroste, beruhigte, zufriedene Stimmung, vermöge welcher in seiner Nähe Jedem wohl wird...Der gute Charakter wird eben so vieler Zuversicht den Beistand Anderer anrufen, als er sich der Bereitwilligkeit bewußt ist, ihnen den seinigen zu leisten...Der Großmüthige, welcher dem Feinde verzeiht und das Böse mit Gutem erwidert, ist erhaben und erhält das höchste Lob; weil er sein selbsteigenes Wesen auch da noch erkannte, wo es sich entschieden verleugnete."; Ibid., §22, pp.211-212.

[645] Ibid., §16, S.248. "Allerdings ist dieser Vorgang erstaunenswürdig, ja, mysteriös. Er ist, in Wahrheit, das große Mysterium der Ethik, ihr Urphänomen und der Gränzstein, über welchen hinaus nur noch die metaphysische Spekulation einen Schritt wagen kann. Wir sehn, in jenem Vorgang, die Scheidewand, welche nach dem Lichte der Natur (wie alte Theologen die Vernunft nennen), Wesen von Wesen durchaus trennt, aufgehoben und das Nicht-Ich gewissermaßen zum Ich geworden."; Ibid., §16, p.144. See also Ibid., §18, S.269: "*Dieser Vorgang* ist, ich wiederhole es, *mysteriös*: denn es ist etwas, wovon die Vernunft keine unmittelbare Rechenschaft geben kann, und diesen Gründe auf dem Wege der Erfahrung nicht auszumitteln sind."; Ibid., §18, p.166.

[646] Ibid., §18, S.269; Ibid., §18, p.166.

[647] Ibid., §19, S.284-285. "Sehn wir ein Mal ganz ab von aller, vielleicht möglichen, metaphysischen Erforschung des letzten Grundes jenes Mitleids, aus welchem allein die nicht-egoistischen Handlungen hervorgehn können, und betrachten wir dasselbe vom empirischen Standpunkt aus, bloß als Naturanstalt; so wird Jedem einleuchten, daß zu möglichster Linderung der zahllosen und vielgestalteten Leiden, denen unser Leben ausgesetzt ist und welchen Keiner ganz entgeht, wie zugleich als Gegengewicht des brennenden Egoismus, der alle Wesen

Accordingly, as is true with aesthetic experience, all people are theoretically capable of compassion. But once again, the act of being compassionate is never attainable nor explainable by abstract reasoning. Rather, it involves an intuitive knowledge or perception. Schopenhauer states: "...for the awakening of compassion which has been established as the *sole source of disinterested actions and hence as the true basis of morality*, there is no need for abstract knowledge, but only for that of intuitive knowledge (*anschauenden Erkenntniß*), for the mere apprehension of the concrete case to which compassion appeals immediately without further mediation of thinking (*Gedankenvermittlung*)".[648]

In this sense, therefore, for Schopenhauer just and loving actions have an epistemological basis since they are based on a type of *knowing*.[649] Just as the egoistic individual acts in light of the particular manner by which he or she perceives reality, the same is true in the case of noble or good persons. The following description is a case in point:

> The man who perceives himself, his own essence in all others -- in fact, in everything which has life-- [is he] whose existence fuses with

---

erfüllt und oft in Bosheit übergeht, - die Natur nichts Wirksameres leisten konnte, als daß sie in das menschliche Herz jene wundersame Anlage pflanzte, vermöge welcher das Leiden des Einen vom Andern mitempfunden wird, und aus der die Stimme hervorgeht, welche, je nachdem der Anlaß ist, Diesem »Schon!« Jenem »Hilf!« stark und vernehmlich zuruft."; *Ibid.*, §19, p.182.

[648] *Ibid.*, S.285; *Ibid.*, p.183.

[649] *Vorstellung I*, §66, II, S.459. "Die ächte Güte der Gesinnung, die uneigennützige Tugend und der reine Edelmuth gehn also nicht von abstrakter Erkenntniß aus, aber doch von Erkenntniß: nämlich von einer unmittelbaren und intuitiven, die nicht wegzuräsonniren und nicht anzuräsonniren ist, von einer Erkenntniß, die eben weil sie nicht abstrakt ist, sich auch nicht mittheilen läßt, sondern Jedem selbst aufgehn muß, die daher ihren eigentlich adäquaten Ausdruck nicht in Worten findet, sondern ganz allein in Thaten, im Handeln, im Lebenslauf des Menschen."; *Representation*, I, §66, pp. 369-370.

the existence of everything which lives. Through death, he loses only a small part of his existence: for he continues to exist in all others in whom he always recognizes and loves his own essence and self. Thus, the illusion, which separated his consciousness from theirs, vanishes.[650]

Accordingly, in light of this mysterious insight that abstractive knowledge or intellectual acumen cannot grant, morally good individuals grasp that plurality is only apparent, pertaining to the phenomenon, and that reality is truly one. As a consequence of that knowledge, they are empowered to recognize themselves in others and attain to a wisdom of a high degree that is not a matter of books or erudition.[651]

3. Asceticism

As the preceding discussion indicates, justice and philanthropy are described in glowing terms by Schopenhauer. But properly speaking, it is asceticism that incarnates to the fullest the values of each. As is stated in a supplementary essay on the denial of the will-to-live in the second volume of *Die Welt als Wille und Vorstellung*: "Justice itself is the hairy shirt that causes its owner constant hardship, and philanthropy that gives away what is necessary provides us with endless fasting."[652]

---

[650] *Grundlage*, §22, VI, S.314; *Basis*, §22, p.213.

[651] *Ibid.*, S.311. "Indessen steht die moralische Trefflichkeit höher denn alle theoretische Weisheit, als welche immer nur Stückwerk ist und auf dem langsamen Wege der Schlüsse zu dem Ziele gelangt, welches jene mit Einem Schlage erreicht; und der moralisch Edle, wenn ihm auch noch so sehr die intellektuelle Trefflichkeit abgeht, legt durch sein Handeln die tiefste Erkenntniß, die höchste Weisheit an den Tag, und beschämt den Genialsten und Gelehrtesten, wenn dieser durch sein Thun verräth, daß jene große Wahrheit ihm doch im Herzen fremd geblieben ist."; *Ibid.*; p.210.

[652] *Vorstellung II*, Kap.48, IV, S.710; *Representation*, II, ch.48, p.607.

Accordingly, the highest plateau to be scaled in the quest for salvation constitutes the state of self-denying asceticism, which is the complete antithesis of the affirmation of the will-to-live[653] -- or what Schopenhauer in his early manuscripts refers to as the "empirical" or "temporal consciousness" which brings with it sinfulness, error, chance, wickedness, folly and death itself. There is a clear juxtaposition between two aspects of the human personality in Schopenhauer's early thought: an empirical consciousness which constitutes the human being's imperfect nature; and the so-called "better consciousness" which is associated with the eternal aspect of man's nature that is the source of virtue as such. The following passage from the *Nachlaß*, which dates from 1813, illustrates this dichotomy:

> An experience, in which the *double nature* (*Duplicität*) *of our consciousnes* becomes evident, is our different attitude at different times to death. There are moments when we think vividly (*lebhaft denken*) about death. It appears in so frightful a form that we do not grasp how anyone with such a prospect can have a peaceful moment and why everyone does not spend his life lamenting over the necessity of death. At other times we think of death with serene joy, indeed with longing. In both cases we are right. In the first mood we are completely imbued with the temporal consciousness (*vom zeitlichen Bewußtsein erfüllt*), and are nothing but a phenomenon in time. As such, death is to us annihilation (*Vernichtung*), and is rightly to be feared as the greatest evil. In the other mood, the better consciousness (*das bessre Bewußtsein*) is alive and rightly looks forward to the loosening of the mysterious bond by which it is combined with the empirical consciousness into the identity of *one I*. For with the empirical consciousness there is

---

[653] *Nachlaß*, I, #99, S.69. "Asketik ist Negation des zeitlichen Bewußtseins: und Hedonik seine Affirmation."; *Remains*, I, #99, p.74.

> necessarily assumed not only sinfulness, but
> also all the evils which follow from this
> kingdom of error, chance, wickedness and
> folly, and finally death...The temporal
> element (*Das Zeitliche*) in us belongs to time
> and must suffer and pass away in time...Only
> the eternal element (*das Ewige*) can save
> itself through self-affirmation (*durch
> Selbstbejahung*), i.e. virtue. If, on the one
> hand, we deny it, i.e, we are wicked.[654]

The aforementioned distinction between the "temporal consciousness" and the "better consciousness" later becomes the contrast between affirmation of the will-to-live and its denial in Schopenhauer's mature work. Accordingly, the first volume of *Die Welt als Wille und Vorstellung*, defines asceticism as the "*deliberate* breaking of the will through the refusal of the agreeable and looking for (*Aufsuchen*) the disagreeable, the penitential, voluntarily-chosen way of life and self-chastisement, for the constant mortification of the will."[655] This radical denial of the will-to-live makes of asceticism the most complete exercise of the moral virtues possible to man.[656]

In keeping with the lower stages of the will's denial, it goes without saying that asceticism involves a seeing through the *principium individuationis* characteristic to the denial of the will-to-live or

---

[654] *Ibid.*, S.68-69; *Ibid.*, p.194.

[655] *Vorstellung I*, §68, II, S.484-485; *Representation*, I, §68, p.392.

[656] *Vorstellung II*, Kap.48, IV, S.710. "...die Anhänglichkeit an das Leben und seine Genüsse muß jetzt bald weichen und einer allgemeinen Entsagung Platz machen: mithin wird die Verneinung des Willens eintreten. Weil nun diesem gemäß Armuth, Entbehrungen und eigenes Leiden vielfacher Art schon durch die vollkommenste Ausübung der moralischen Tugenden herbeigeführt werden, wird von Vielen, und vielleicht mit Recht, die *Askese* im allerengsten Sinne, also das Aufgeben jedes Eigenthums, das absichtliche Aufsuchen des Unangenehmen und Widerwärtigen, die Selbstpeinigung, das Fasten, das härene Hemd und die Kasteiung, als überflüssig verworfen."; *Representation*, II, ch.48, p.607.

"better consciousness".[657] But there is an important difference that appears specifically with asceticism. With the ascetic, the *quieter* to which Schopenhauer alludes in the phenomenon of the denial of the will-to-live, reaches such a degree of distinctness that the will shuns life and shudders at the pleasures in which it is affirmed.[658] Whereas earlier stages of insight indeed

---

[657] The "temporal" or "empirical consciousness" has its essential nature in thinking that appears as understanding and the faculty of reason (*Nachlaß*, I, #96, S.67; *Remains*, I, pp.72-73). As such, it pertains to the temporal, perceptual, comprehensible world where personality and causality are given (*Nachlaß*, I, #81, S.42; *Remains*, I, p.44) where sinfulness and vice are present (*Nachlaß*, I, #99, S.68-69; *Remains*, I, pp.73-74). The "better consciousness", on the other hand, may be described as the other aspect of the human personality that gives rise to a world in which neither personality and causality nor subject or object are given (*Nachlaß*, I, #81, S.42; *Remains*, I, p.44). Accordingly, is it is "beyond experience" and thereby lies beyond the competence of theoretical and practical reason (*Nachlaß*, I, #35, S.23; *Remains*, I, p.23). States Schopenhauer: "The better consciousness does not think and know since it lies beyond subject and object" (*Nachlaß*, I, #96, S.67; *Remains*, I, p.72).
This notwithstanding, in the individual there is a "mysterious connection" between the better consciousness and experience (as mediated by thinking patterns characteristic of the empirical consciousness), which has ramifications on both the theoretical and practical spheres. With the appearance of the better consciousness, reason (as theoretical) is displaced as *genius*; on the practical sphere, it is displaced by *virtue*. But it is important to note that the better consciousness is neither practical nor theoretical -- which are mere classifications of reason. For this reason, it transcends language (*Nachlaß*, I, #35, S.23; *Remains*, I, pp. 23-24).
Though reason distinguishes man from animals and is crucial in thinking and acting according to maxims, moral principles have their source in the better consciousness (*Nachlaß*, I, #87, S.50; *Remains*, I, pp.53-55). Accordingly, the better consciousness is the source of morality and loving kindness (*Nachlaß*, I,#215, S.122; *Remains*, I, p.132), in spite of the weakness of human understanding and reason. In this sense, Schopenhauer differs from Kant who would maintain that all moral value is grounded in reason (*Nachlaß*, I, #87, S.51-52; *Remains*, I, p.55). This being the case, the better consciousness as the source of all blessedness, entails that one free oneself from the shackles of the empirical world (*Nachlaß*, I, #128, S.79; *Remains*, I, p.86). Hence, "in order to become partakers of the peace of God (that is, entrance into the better consciousness)," a radical change must transpire in the man as governed by temporal consciousness: the illusion of the world of the senses must be left behind (*Nachlaß*, I, #189, S.104-105; *Remains*, I, pp.113-114).

Cf. Christopher Janaway, *Self and World in Schopenhauer's Philosophy* (Oxford: Clarendon Press, 1989), pp.27-28; Edoardo Mirri, "Un concetto perduto nella sistematica Schopenhaueriana: la «meliore coscienza»," as found in *Schopenhauer e il sacro*. Atti del seminario tenuto a Trento il 26-28 aprile 1984 a cura di Giorgio Penzo (Trento: Istituto Trentino di Cultura Pubblicazioni dell'Istituto di Scienze Religiose in Trento, 1987), pp.59-82.

[658] *Vorstellung* I, §68, II, S.470; *Representation*, I, §68, p.378-379.

grasp the basic unity of Being and result in virtuous praxis towards others, with asceticism there is an added dimension. The ascetic disengages himself from life. "His will turns about; it no longer affirms its own inner nature which mirrors itself in the phenomenon, but denies it."[659] Alluding to this phenomenon as the "transition from virtue to *asceticism*" (*der Uebergang von der Tugend zur Askesis*), Schopenhauer writes that "it is no longer enough for [the ascetic] to love others as himself, and to do as much for them as for himself, but there arises in him an aversion (*Abscheu*) to the nature, whose expression is his own phenomenon, to the will-to-live, the kernel and essence of that world recognized as full of misery."[660]

       The ascetic, therefore, begins to deny and mortify the very body that is a phenomenal expression of the will-to-live. Writes Schopenhauer: "Essentially nothing other than the phenomenon of the will, he ceases to will anything, guards against attaching his will to anything, seeks to establish in himself the greatest indifference to things."[661] Since sexual satisfaction as objectified in the genitals is the clearest expression of the affirmation of the will-to-live, voluntary and complete chastity is embraced. Though the body objectifies in the genitals the will to propagate, the propagation is not willed because of the intensity of insight into the will's nature, which acts as a "quieter"

---

[659] *Ibid.*; *Ibid.*, p.380.
[660] *Ibid.*; *Ibid.*
[661] *Ibid.*, S.471; *Ibid.*

in the person of the ascetic.⁶⁶² By renouncing sexual satisfaction in any form, strict chastity in effect states that the will, whose expression is his body, ceases with the life of the body at death.⁶⁶³

In this respect, renunciation of the sexual impulse has transcendental significance as does its satisfaction. An early manuscript dating from 1813 in the *Nachlaß* already conjectures that were chastity to become universal "the human race would die out, that is, there would no longer be the inexplicable co-existence of the temporal with the better consciousness."⁶⁶⁴ *Die Welt als Wille und Vorstellung* conjectures that since all phenomena are inter-linked, were the ascetical maxim to become universal, lower manifestations of the diseased will would likewise disappear.⁶⁶⁵ Accordingly, if one

---

⁶⁶² *Ibid.*, §62, S.416-417. "Es ist bereits auseinandergesetzt, daß die erste und einfache Bejahung des Willens zum Leben nur Bejahung des eigenen Leibes ist, d.h. Darstellung des Willens durch Akte in der Zeit, in so weit schon der Leib, in seiner Form und Zweckmäßigkeit, den selben Willen räumlich darstellt, und nicht weiter. Diese Bejahung zeigt sich als Erhaltung des Leibes, mittelst Anwendung der eigenen Kräfte desselben. An sie knüpft sich unmittelbar die Befriedigung des Geschlechtstriebes, ja gehört zu ihr, sofern die Genitalien zum Leibe gehören. Daher ist *freiwillige* und durch gar kein Motiv begründete Entsagung der Befriedigung jenes Triebes schon ein Grad von Verneinung des Willens zum Leben, ist eine, auf eingetretene, als *Quietiv* wirkende Erkenntniß, freiwillige Selbstaufhebung desselben; demgemäß stellt solche Verneinung des eigenen Leibes sich schon als ein Widerspruch des Willens gegen seine eigene Erscheinung dar. Denn obgleich auch hier der Leib in den Genitalien den Willen zur Fortpflanzung objektivirt, wird diese dennoch nicht gewollt."; *Ibid.*, §62, p.334.

⁶⁶³ *Ibid.*, §68, S.471. "Sein Leib, gesund und stark, spricht durch Genitalien den Geschlechtstrieb aus; aber er verneint den Willen und straft den Leib Lügen: er will keine Geschlechtsbefriedigung, unter keiner Bedingung. Freiwillige, vollkommene Keuschheit ist der erste Schritt in der Askese oder der Verneinung des Willens zum Leben. Sie verneint dadurch die über das individuelle Leben hinausgehende Bejahung des Willens und giebt damit die Anzeige, daß mit dem Leben dieses Leibes auch der Wille, dessen Erscheinung er ist, sich aufhebt."; *Ibid.*, §68, p.380.

⁶⁶⁴ *Nachlaß*, I, #99, S.69; *Remains*, I, #99, p.74.

⁶⁶⁵ *Vorstellung I*, §68, II, S.471. "Die Natur, immer wahr und naiv, sagt aus, daß, wenn diese Maxime allgemein würde, das Menschengeschlecht ausstürbe: und nach Dem, was im zweiten Buch über den Zusammenhang aller Willenserscheinungen gesagt ist, glaube ich annehmen zu können, daß mit der

can speak about a cosmic redemption in which the nature of the will (as manifested in phenomena other than man) is changed, any hope for such a happening somehow rests with man. Along these lines, Schopenhauer states that "the rest of nature has to expect its salvation from man who is at the same time priest and sacrifice."[666] He even surmises that the Pauline passage in Romans viii, 21-24, which alludes to the groaning of creation as it awaits the liberty of the children of God, is to be interpreted in this sense.[667]

Part and parcel of the ascetical state is voluntary and intentional poverty assimilated as ends in themselves, so as to further mortify the will and thus impede any further satisfaction of its stirring and yearning. "Asceticism shows itself further in voluntary and intentional poverty, which arises not only *per accidens*, since property is given away to alleviate the sufferings of others, but is here already an end in itself; it should serve as a constant mortification of the will, so that the satisfaction of desire, the sweets of life, may not again agitate the will, of which self-knowledge has conceived an object of aversion."[668] This is not to say, however, that the ascetic easily attains

---

höchsten Willenserscheinung auch der schwächere Wiederschein derselben, die Thierheit, wegfallen würde; wie mit dem vollen Lichte auch die Halbschatten verschwinden. Mit gänzlicher Aufhebung der Erkenntniß schwände dann auch von selbst die übrige Welt in Nichts; da ohne Subjekt kein Objekt."; *Representation*, I, §68, p.380.

[666] Ibid.; Ibid., p.381.

[667] Ibid.; Ibid. "...because the creation itself will be set free from its bondage to decay and obtain the glorious freedom of the children of God. We know that the whole creation has been groaning in travail together until now; and not only the creation, but we ourselves, who have the Spirit, groan inwardly as we wait for the redemption of our bodies. For in this hope we were saved. Now hope that is seen is not hope. For who hopes for what he sees?" *Romans*, viii, 21-24 (Revised Standard Version).

[668] Ibid., S.472; Ibid., pp.381-382.

to self-denying practices. Quite the contrary! The natural tendency to every kind of willing remains.

> ...we must not imagine that, after the denial of the will-to-live has once entered through knowledge which has become the quieter, such a denial no longer wavers, and that one can rest on it, as on a property that has been inherited. On the contrary, it must be always achieved afresh (*immer aufs Neue errungen werden*) by constant struggle.[669]

In short, the will-to-live and the illusions connected therewith, exist potentially so long as a glimmer of life remains in the body. Accordingly, asceticism requires vigilance by the deliberate and continuous suppression of any will-affirming tendencies. The illusion of this life to which all human beings are subject in their temporal consciousness, is radically curable *only* with death, described here as "sanctification".

> In order to take part in the *peace of God* (that is, for the appearance (*Hervortreten*) of the *better consciousness*), it is necessary that man, this frail, finite, and transitory being, be something altogether different, that he become aware of himself no longer as a human being, but as something entirely different. For insofar as he lives -- inasmuch as he is a human being, he is doomed not merely to *sin* and *death*, but also to *illusion*, and this *illusion* is as real as life, as real as the world of the senses itself, indeed it is one with these (Maya of the Indians). On it are grounded all our desires and cravings, which are again only the expression of life, just as life is only the expression of illusion. To the extent that we live, will to live, and are human beings, the illusion is truth. Only in reference to the better consciousness is it illusion. If peace, bliss, and tranquility are to be found, then the illusion must be abandoned, and if this is to be abandoned, then life must be given up. This is the difficult step, the

---

[669] *Ibid.*, S.484; *Ibid.*, p.391.

problem which is insoluble in life and is to be solved only with the help of death, which in itself dissolves not the illusion but only the appearance (*Ersheinung*) thereof, the body. This is sanctification (*Heiligung*).[670]

Sufferings of any form that come from the outside either by chance or the wickedness of others, are indeed welcomed by the ascetically-inclined.[671] In fact, Schopenhauer states that the ascetic "gladly accepts them as the opportunity to give himself the certainty that he no longer affirms the will, but gladly sides with every enemy of the will's phenomenon that is his own person."[672] For this reason, true ascetics undergo fasts and other forms of self-castigation for the purpose of annihilating that inner nature which is the source not only of their own suffering, but that others as well.

It is also important to underscore that the ascetic, illumined as he is by insight, regards the imminent prospect of death with "serene joy and indeed with longing".[673] With him or her, "the better consciousness is alive, and for good reason looks forward (*es freut mit Recht*), to the loosening of the mysterious bond by which it is combined with the empirical consciousness into the identity of the one *Ego* (*in die*

---

[670] *Nachlaß*, I, #189, S.104-105; *Remains*, I, #189, pp.113-114.

[671] *Vorstellung I*, §68, II, S.472-473. "Der zu diesem Punkt Gelangte spürt als belebter Leib, als konkrete Willenserscheinung, noch immer die Anlage zum Wollen jeder Art: aber er unterdrückt sie absichtlich, indem er sich zwingt, nichts zu thun von allem was er wohl möchte, hingegen alles zu thun was er nicht möchte, selbst wenn es keinen weitern Zweck hat, als eben den, zur Mortifikation des Willens zu dienen. Da er den in seiner Person erscheinenden Willen selbst verneint, wird er nicht widerstreben, wann ein Anderer das Selbe thut, d.h. ihm Unrecht zufügt: darum ist ihm jedes von außen, durch Zufall oder fremde Bosheit, auf ihn kommende Leid willkommen, jeder Schaden, jede Schmach, jede Beleidigung."; *Representation*, I, §68, p.382.

[672] *Ibid.*, S.473; *Ibid.*

[673] *Nachlaß*, I, #99, S.68; *Remains*, I, #99, pp.73-74.

Identität Eines Ichs verknüpft ist)."[674] Gone is the frightful fear that characterizes "temporal consciousness" or will-affirming existence. For the ascetic has long since taken that "difficult step" involved in exposing the illusion of that existence, which temporal and empirical consciousness deems as so real.[675] This being the case, when death "as the longed-for deliverance" (*ersehnte Erlösung*) finally comes, the will shall have already been crushed.[676]

It goes without saying that the severity involved in this type of life-style, serves only to highlight the radical nature of a decision to leave behind the existence characteristic of "temporal consciousness", in favor of that which pertains to the "better consciousness". It involves, in short, a choice between two alternatives. As is succinctly stated in a fragment from Schopenhauer's *Nachlaß*: "...as we set foot in the one sphere, we have at the same time abandoned and disowned the other."[677] This notwithstanding, Schopenhauer is convinced that it is *only* the "better consciousness", as incarnated in the life of the ascetic, that leaves in its wake true happiness and peace. For this reason, the ascetic with his "inner cheerfulness" and "true heavenly peace" is the

---

[674] *Ibid.*; *Ibid.*

[675] *Ibid.*, #189, S.104-105; *Remains*, #189, pp.113-114.

[676] *Vorstellung I*, §68, II, S.473. "Kommt endlich der Tod, der diese Erscheinung jenes Willens auflöst, dessen Wesen hier, durch freie Verneinung seiner selbst, schon längst, bis auf den schwachen Rest, der als Belebung dieses Leibes erschien, abgestorben war; so ist er, als ersehnte Erlösung, hoch willkommen und wird freudig empfangen. Mit ihm endigt hier nicht, wie bei Andern, bloß die Erscheinung; sondern das Wesen selbst ist aufgehoben, welches hier nur noch in der Erscheinung und durch sie ein schwaches Daseyn hatte; welches letzte mürbe Band nun auch zerreißt. Für Den, welcher so endet, hat zugleich die Welt geendet."; *Representation*, I, §68, p.382.

[677] *Nachlaß*, I, #204, S.111; *Remains*, I, #204, p.120.

complete antithesis of the wicked person, whose unhappy face is a sure indication of a troubled spirit.[678] It is not surprising that the great pessimist, who was certainly no saint, wonders about what this mode of being might be like:

> ...how blessed must the life of a man whose will is silenced not for a few moments, as in the enjoyment of the beautiful, but for ever, indeed completely extinguished, except for that last glimmering spark which maintains the body and is extinguished with it. Such a man, who after many bitter struggles with his own nature, has at last completely conquered, is then left only as a pure knowing being, as the undimmed mirror of the world.[679]

Accordingly, for the ascetic or saint, the world with all its multiplied phenomena -- with its galaxies and milky ways -- is ultimately 'nothing'(*Nichts*).[680] However, this is not to say that the word 'nothing' is to be taken absolutely or literally.[681] Given the above discussion about the better consciousness as that which is beyond the relation of subject and object, causality and personality, such a *caveat* seems to be in order. For the experience Schopenhauer strives to describe, transcends the conceptual and representational realm of philosophy,

---

[678] *Vorstellung I*, §68, II, S.482. "Wie wir oben den Bösen, durch die Heftigkeit seines Wollens, beständige, verzehrende, innere Quaal leiden und den grimmigen Durst des Eigenwillens zuletzt, wenn alle Objekte des Wollens erschöpft sind, am Anblick fremder Pein kühlen sahen; so ist dagegen Der, in welchem die Verneinung des Willens zum Leben aufgegangen ist, so arm, freudelos und voll Entbehrungen sein Zustand, von außen gesehn, auch ist, voll innerer Freudigkeit und wahrer Himmelsruhe.; *Representation*, I, §68, pp.389-380.

[679] *Ibid.*, S.483; *Ibid.*, p.390.

[680] *Ibid.*, §71, S.508. "Wir bekennen es vielmehr frei: was nach gänzlicher Aufhebung des Willens übrig bleibt, ist für alle Die, welche noch des Willens voll sind, allerdings Nichts. Aber auch umgekehrt ist Denen, in welchen der Wille sich gewendet und verneint hat, diese unsere so sehr reale Welt mit allen ihren Sonnen und Milchstraßen -- Nichts."; *Ibid.*, §71, pp.411-412.

[681] Bernard Bykhovksy, *Schopenhauer and the Ground of Existence,* trans. by Philip Moran (Amsterdam: B.R. Grüner Publishing Co., 1984), pp.172-174.

in the strict sense of the term. Accordingly, asceticism and other forms of "holy" behavior, may be described as a "transition into *nothing*" when understood in this sense.

> The saint is the phenomenon of *not*-willing-to-live (*Nicht-Lebens-Willens*), of a will that is not concerned with life. Indeed his body as such is a phenomenon of life-willing (*Lebenswollens*), but through death this body comes to an end. However, his character, that is to say, the common element (*das Gemeinsame*) in the whole series of his actions, is a phenomenon of the will which is not concerned with life, in other words, which has turned (*sich gewendet hat*), so that it is not the will whose phenomenon is the body as such. Now as this holy will is free from life and its horrors, it is a delightful phenomenon (*eine erfreuliche Erscheinung*) to the knowing subject (that is to say, to all men and women including the person of the saint). Here, of course, we can *express ourselves only negatively*, precisely because the material in which philosophy works, namely concepts, are representations and are therefore conditioned by life and belong to it. Accordingly, for our point of view, the turning of the will, holiness, salvation, everlasting bliss, are a transition into *nothing* (*ein Uebergang ins Nichts*)."[682]

Convinced that a life of holiness and asceticism constitutes the only path to deliverance from the fierce grasp of the will, Schopenhauer believes that his explanation as outlined above demythologizes the significance of such self-denying praxis. The following passage speaks for itself:

> Perhaps it is...here that for the first time, the inner nature of holiness, of self-renunciation, of mortification of one's will, of asceticism, is expressed abstractly and free from everything mythical, as *denial of the will-to-live* which appears after the

---

[682] *Nachlaß*, I, #389, S.245; *Remains*, I, #389, pp.269-270.

complete knowledge of its own inner being has become for it the quieter of all willing.[683]

He goes on to state that the denial of the will-to-live as propelled by an intuitive insight into the inner nature of the world, is the *same* as that of the Indian, Christian, and Lamaist saint.[684] But this indeed striking because authentic forms of asceticism have as their goal a definite transcendent end (i.e. God, re-absorption into the Absolute,etc.).[685] Schopenhauer certainly was aware of this since the springboard for much of his reflection on the phenomenon of holiness and asceticism are precisely the lives of saints in various religious traditions.[686] But there is one relatively late fragment from the *Nachlaß* dating from 1832 in which Schopenhauer still dabbled with the possibility of using the concept *God* (as devoid of all positive attributes) as an apt description for the ultimate goal of denial of the will-to-live.

> If, out of attachment to an old expression (which I, however, do not approve of), we wished to call what we know only as *will to live*, in the opposite state to this, where it denies the will-to-live and has turned away

---

[683] *Vorstellung I*, §68, II, S.474; *Representation*, I, §68, p.383.

[684] *Ibid*. "Hingegen unmittelbar erkannt und durch die That ausgesprochen haben es alle jene Heiligen und Asketen, die, bei gleicher innerer Erkenntniß, eine sehr verschiedene Sprache führten, gemäß den Dogmen, die sie ein Mal in ihre Vernunft aufgenommen hatten und welchen zufolge ein Indischer Heiliger, ein Christlicher, ein Lamaischer, von seinem eigenen Thun, jeder sehr verschiedene Rechenschaft geben muß, was aber für die Sache ganz gleichgültig ist. Ein Heiliger kann voll des absurdesten Aberglaubens seyn, oder er kann umgekehrt ein Philosoph seyn: Beides gilt gleich. Sein Thun allein beurkundet ihn als Heiligen: denn es geht, in moralischer Hinsicht, nicht aus der abstrakten, sondern aus der intuitiv aufgefaßten, unmittelbaren Erkenntniß der Welt und ihres Wesens hervor, und wird von ihm nur zur Befriedigung seiner Vernunft durch irgend ein Dogma ausgelegt."; *Ibid*.

[685] Cf. Höffding, *A History of Modern Philosophy*, vol.2, p.235; Copleston, *The Philosopher of Pessimism*, p.188.

[686] *Vorstellung I*, §68, II, S.475-476; *Representation*, I, §68, p.384.

(*nirvana*), and is yet totally unknown to us (insofar as knowledge accompanies it only as far as this turning away [*nur bis zu dieser Wendung begleitet*]); if, I say, we wished to call this completely unknown something God instead of X or Y; in short, if we wished to say: "God is what we are when we are not the world," then we should have preserved the word, but not its original meaning. We should then have a God who is utterly different from the world insofar as He would be its antithesis, -- the very denial of the world.[687]

The above notwithstanding, were the concept of God salvageable even in this sense, the goal of denial of the will-to-live would be a far cry from the religious experience to which authentic asceticism strives. Besides, manuscripts dating from the summer of 1812 (several years before the publication of *Die Welt als Wille und Vorstellung*) illustrate that Schopenhauer had by then, abandoned any semblance of belief in a Creator-God; generally using the concept of God usually only in a disparaging sense.[688] Accordingly, the asceticism demythologized by Schopenhauer, does not have God as its term -- even though the "nothing" that results from denial of the will-to-live, appears indeed to be a "something".

D. Summary

The purpose of this chapter was to describe the human condition from the perspective of the denial of the will-to-live. It seems that in light of the doctrine of the inalterability of the character, denial of the will by insight is experienced by few. Thus, Schopenhauer's

---

[687] *Nachlaß*, IV.1, #52, S.102-103; *Remains*, IV, p.125.

[688] Cf. Hübscher, *Denker gegen den Strom*, S.17-18.

Human Transcendence

claim that affirmation of the will and its antithesis constitute realistic alternatives for any given human being, is open to question.

A lengthy section of the chapter examined the thorny issue of the relationship between freedom and necessity and its ramifications for the claim that the will can be denied in at least some human beings. While admitting that the phenomenon of aesthetic contemplation and holiness suggest that in the case of man a "contradiction of the phenomenon with itself" occurs, Schopenhauer still maintains that human acts are determined given the interplay between the intelligible character and the motives which are respectively the internal and external ground of human acts. This notwithstanding, he connects freedom with the notion of responsibility, which is closely linked with the "feeling" that we are originators of our own deeds.

Justice and philanthropy as stages in the denial of the will-to-live were examined next and grounded in Schopenhauer's metaphysical picture of reality. It was emphasized that compassion is the source of all virtue and that the very occurrence of virtuous acts constitutes a mystery which transcends philosophical categories. This is in keeping with the claim made by Schopenhauer in the *Nachlaß* that the "better consciousness" is the source of all moral virtue. But it is also consistent with claims made in Schopenhauer's other works that reason is not the source of morality as such.

The chapter concluded with Schopenhauer's demythologization of asceticism. Of noteworthy significance here was the notion of "nothing" or "nothingness", that is not only the end result of ascetical praxis, but linked to the moral virtues of justice and philanthropy. It was underscored, however, that this troublesome and elusive concept is not by any means to be understood in an absolute sense. Accordingly, the "nothingness" or "nothing" that Schopenhauer alludes to in the closing lines of *Die Welt als Wille und Vorstellung* appears to be a "something" that goes beyond the exigence of philosophical categories. If one takes into consideration Schopenhauer's analysis of "the better consciousness" as that which is beyond subject and object, causality and personality, this interpretation appears to be tenable.

It goes without saying, that these aforementioned ambiguities have ramifications for the issue of religion and the question as to whether Schopenhauer's philosophy leaves ajar a "back door" to the Holy. The concluding chapter that follows, therefore, pursues these questions in light of Schopenhauer's apparent tolerance for religion, which he regards as another manifestation of the "better consciousness" -- or as a system of metaphysics that uses myth and allegory as a medium of truth that gives meaning in life to "non-philosophers".

Chapter 6

Religion and God

A. The Role of Religion

1. Introductory remarks

Having outlined Schopenhauer's metaphysical view of reality and alluded to the objective possibility that exists for going beyond the egocentric predicament, the central issue of this study can now be addressed: namely, religion and the question of God. The first three chapters already indicate that Schopenhauer's view of reality, as comprised of representation and will, seems to exclude the possibility for the existence of God. For in the first place, from the standpoint of the representation, Schopenhauer's reduction of the law of causality to an endless series of changes in states of matter leaves no room for an "un-moved" First Cause. Secondly, from the standpoint of the noumenon experienced as will, aseity is ascribed not to God, but to the will. Thirdly, notwithstanding the rationality that seems to characterize the inter-relationship among the Platonic Ideas which comprise the will's adequate objectification, Schopenhauer avoids asserting that the Ideas are realities existing in a Divine Mind. Hence, the tentative conclusion that there is no God in the philosophical system espoused and outlined in *Die Welt als Wille und Vorstellung* indeed seems viable.[689]

In short, as noted above, reality, as comprised of will and representation, cannot be considered the product of a divine creative act.[690] At first glance, Schopenhauer's system is totally immanent and self-contained leaving no room for the question of a Transcendent Being, as a scholar like Icilio Vecchiotti contends.[691] Alluding to the Schopenhauerian doctrine of "the total compenetration of mind and being in the Will," Cornelio Fabro likewise asserts that "the conscious and professed destination of this radical immanentism is *atheism*."[692] This certainly is in keeping with what Schopenhauer wrote to an overly eager follower of his (Frauenstädt) in an August 21, 1852 letter, about transfiguring his doctrine of will so as to make it attractive to theologians:

> My dear friend, I must remind myself of all your many and great merits for the sake of the proclamation of my philosophy in order not to lose my patience and composure...In vain, for example, have I written to you not to seek the

---

[689] Cf. R.J. Hollingdale, *Arthur Schopenhauer: Essays and Aphorisms* (Harmondsworth: Penguin Books, 1970), p.34; V.J. McGill, *Schopenhauer Pessimist and Pagan* (New York: Haskell House Publishers, 1971, pp.251-252.

[690] Cf. Schmidt, *Die Wahrheit im Gewande der Lüge*, S.33. "Hat kein Intellekt die Natur hervorgebracht, sondern diese im Stufengang ihrer Objektivationen den Intellekt, ist das Wesen der Natur »ein blinder Drang, ein völlig grundloser, unmotivirter Trieb«, so folgt hieraus eine radicale Absage an den Schöpfungsgedanken des christlichen Theismus. Schopenhauer hat denn auch redlicherweise auf den atheistischen Grundzug seiner Philosophie hingewiesen."

[691] Cf. Icilio Vecchiotti, "Osservazioni preliminari sulla possibilità di una nozione di «sacro» in Schopenhauer," in Penzo, *Schopenhauer e il sacro*, p.145: "Comminciamo col dire che è gia per definizione fuori causa e fuori tema il sacro delle religioni positive, il sacro delle religioni della trascendenza, ossia dell'ebraismo e dell'islamismo, esplicitamente e duramente avversati dallo Schopenhauer. Il filosofo ha detto chiaramente che la sua visione del mondo è immanente, non trascendente."

[692] Cornelio Fabro, *God in Exile: Modern Atheism*, trans. Arthur Gibbon (Westminster: Newman Press, 1968), p.873.

Religion and God

> thing-in-itself in cloud cuckoo land (*Wolkenkukuksheim*) [that is, there where the God of the Jews resides], but in the things of this world -- thus in the table on which you write, in the chair under your arse...My philosophy never concerns itself with cloud cuckoo land, but with **this** world; which is to say, that it is *immanent*, not transcendent.[693]

Along these lines, one will not find in the Schopenhauerian corpus of thought a philosophy of religion that assimilates belief in the personal Creator God of Judeo-Christian tradition. As will be illustrated below, according to Schopenhauer, philosophy and religion cannot be wedded together.[694] Accordingly, one would be looking in vain for a philosophy of religion in Schopenhauer's thought that would entail adjusting of one's philosophical presuppositions to the premises of one's faith.[695] Perhaps it is for this reason that Nietzsche states: "As a philosopher, Schopenhauer was the first admitted and inexorable athiest among us

---

[693] "An Julius Frauenstädt," Frankfurt a.M., den 21. August 1852, Brief 280, *Arthur Schopenhauer Gesammelte Briefe*, S.290-291.

[694] Cf. Heinrich Hasse, *Schopenhauer* (München: Verlag Ernst Reinhardt, 1926), S.371. "Dem äußeren Anschein nach steht Schopenhauer einer Religionsphilosophie als selbstständiger Disziplin völlig ablehnend gegenüber. Hat er doch eine Lehre, welche diesen Namen führt, als »Zwitter« und »Kentauren« nachdrücklich verworfen und dieser Verwerfung triftige Gründe beigesellt. Religionsphilosophie gilt ihm als unsachliche Verschmelzung wesensfremder Bestrebungen, deren Ergebnis nichts anderes als eine geistige Mißgeburt darstellen kann. Denn die Ziele der *Philosophie* fallen mit denen der *Religion* keineswegs zusammen."

[695] Cf. Schmidt, S.23. "Schopenhauer versteht unter Religionsphilosophie -- sich kritisch schon von dem Begriff distanzierend -- jedes philosophische System, dessen Urheber darauf bedacht ist, seine Resultate in Einklang zu bringen mit der Glaubenslehre einer positiven Religion. Wenn im folgenden dargetan werden soll, daß religionsphilosophische Erwägungen einen wichtigen (obgleich kaum gebührend beachteten) Aspekt des Denkgebäudes von Schopenhauer bilden, so kann damit, folgen wir seinem Selbstverständnis, keine eilfertige Adaptation des Philosophierens an vorgegebene Dogmen gemeint sein. Jede Vermengung, gar Fusion, des unabhängigen, begründenden Denkens mit Autorität und übernatürlicher Offenbarung ist Schopenhauer verhaßt."

Germans."[696] This notwithstanding, he did reflect intensely about the nature of religion and Christianity in particular.[697]

Even though Schopenhauer evidently rejected belief in a personal God once he directed his efforts to a serious study of philosophy, Hübscher contends that up until his twenty-fourth year "he stood under the confines of his Church."[698]. It goes without saying that one ought not forget that his early educational formation (1799-1803) was in the private school of Johann Christian Runge whose enlightened Pietism left a positive and life-long impression on Schopenhauer.[699] In this respect, notwithstanding his metaphysical presuppositions which exclude the possibility for a "front door" approach to the question of God, Schopenhauer was not categorically opposed to religion as Bridgewater contends, but rather to the bigotry and excesses often associated with it.[700] Certainly the following poem entitled "*Auf die Sistinische Madonna*," written in Dresden during the year 1815, is but one indication (among many) of his fascination with religious themes:

---

[696] Friedrich Nietzsche, *The Gay Science*, trans. by Walter Kaufmann (New York: Random House, 1974), Book V (No.357), p.307.

[697] Cf. Jörg Salaquarda, "Schopenhauer und die Religion," *Schopenhauer-Jahrbuch*, 69 (1989), S.321; also cf. Bernard Bykhovsky, *Schopenhauer and the Ground of Existence*, trans. by Philip Moran (Amsterdam: B.R. Grüner Publishing Co., 1984), pp.155-175.

[698] Hübscher, *Denker gegen den Strom*, S.13.

[699] Ibid., S.10-13.

[700] Patrick Bridgewater, *Arthur Schopenhauer's English Schooling* (London: Routledge, 1988), p.306. Alluding to Schopenhauer's unpleasant experience, as a boy of fifteen, at a British boarding school in which religion was crammed down his throat, Bridgewater writes: "Schopenhauer was not opposed to religion as such, or even to Christianity as such, for he is one of the most religious of all philosophers, and 'religion' is one of the key words in his work; but he was passionately opposed to the canting humbug, philistinism and prudishness by which he found himself faced."

> She bears him to the world, and startled
> He beholds the chaos of its abominations.
> The frenzy and fury of its turmoil,
> The never-cured folly of its striving,
> The never-stilled pain of its distress, --
> Startled: yet calm and confident hope and
> Triumphant glory radiate from his eye, already
> Heralding the abiding certainty of salvation.[701]

The essays "*Über das metaphysische Bedürfniß des Menschen*" in Chapter 17 of the second volume of *Die Welt als Wille und Vorstellung*, and "*Über Religion*" in Chapter 15 of the second volume of *Parerga und Paralipomena*, are further indications of the aforementioned fact -- not to mention passages that can be found in his other works. Accordingly, it is not incorrect to say with Hasse that much of Schopenhauer's philosophy is a "philosophical consideration whose object is religion."[702] Along these lines, it is even held by Horkheimer that Schopenhauer's system, emphasizing as it does the relationship between denial of the will-to-live and the ethical tendency of Christian asceticism, comprises "the last great philosophical attempt to preserve the kernel of Christianity."[703]

---

[701] "Auf die Sistinische Madonna," *Parerga II*, "Einige Verse," X, S.713; "To the Sistine Madonna," *Parerga*, II, "Some Verses", p.655. The translation is that of E.F.J. Payne. The original German reads as follows:

Sie trägt zur Welt ihn: und er schaut entsetzt
In ihrer Gräu'l chaotische Verwirrung,
In ihres Tobens wilde Raserei,
In ihres Treibens nie geheilte Thorheit,
In ihrer Quaalen nie gestillten Schmerz, -
Entsetzt: doch strahlet Ruh' und Zuversicht
Und Siegesglanz sein Aug', verkündigend
Schon der Erlösung ewige Gewißheit.

[702] Hasse, S.370.

[703] Max Horkheimer, "Religion und Philosophie," *Schopenhauer-Jahrbuch*, 48 (1967), S.5.

2. Suffering as "the second way"

Before analyzing Schopenhauer's claims about religion, his rejection of traditional proofs for God's existence, and proposing that a "back door" to the question of God nevertheless remains open in his system, the issue of *human suffering* as a second way to attain to the denial of the will-to-live must first be addressed. This is distinct from the path of *insight* or *knowledge* discussed in Chapter Five. Raising the issue of the human being's response to suffering and death serves to contextualize Schopenhauer's claim that philosophical and religious systems arise to make sense out of suffering and death as personally experienced by the human being. It is only against this backdrop that the positive and negative aspects of religion as a "system of metaphysics" in its own right can be evaluated.

The path that leads to compassionate behavioral patterns and ultimately to ascetical praxis, has as its point of departure, a mysterious grasping of the inner nature of reality that in turn acts as a quieter which halts willing. But Schopenhauer underscores that it would be erroneous to conjecture that once one attains the heights of denial of the will-to-live by knowledge, that struggle is no longer necessary. Rather the opposite is true. Stated succinctly, "as long as the body lives, the whole will-to-live exists in its potentiality, and always strives to reach actuality and to burn afresh with all its intensity."[704] Accordingly, the path of virtue and asceticism which is trekked by the few, requires constant struggle and vigilance.

---

[704] *Vorstellung I*, §68, II, S.484; *Representation*, I, §68, p.391.

> We...see the histories of the inner lives of
> the saints full of spiritual struggles,
> temptations, and dessertion from grace, in
> other words, from that kind of knowledge
> (*Erkenntnißweise*) which by making all motives
> ineffectual, as a universal quieter silences
> all willing, gives the deepest peace and opens
> the gate to freedom. Therefore we see also
> those who have once attained to denial of the
> will, keep to this path with all their effort
> through self-imposed renunciations of every
> kind, by a penitential, hard way of life, and
> by looking for what is disagreeable to them;
> all in order to suppress the will that is
> constantly springing up afresh.[705]

The deliberate breaking of the will by ascetical praxis is loathsome to the selfish and pleasure-seeking will, which seeks to shun suffering at all cost. But it is precisely the suffering that is not merely known, but *personally experienced*, which in the final analysis breaks the will. For this reason Schopenhauer calls it "the second way" of attaining the denial of the will-to-live. In this respect, given the universality of suffering and death, a Sabbath rest from the intensity of willing is open to all -- not merely to the few whose knowledge is sufficient enough to induce the will's denial.[706]

Schopenhauer, even as early as 1814, in the *Nachlaß* underscores how "pain, suffering and hard toil

---

[705] *Ibid.*; *Ibid.*, pp.391-392.

[706] *Ibid.*, S.485. "Wenn wir nun diese von den schon zur Verneinung des Willens Gelangten ausüben sehn, um sich dabei zu erhalten; so ist auch das Leiden überhaupt, wie es vom Schicksal verhängt wird, ein zweiter Weg (δεύτερος πλοῦς) um zu jener Verneinung zu gelangen: ja, wir können annehmen, daß die Meisten nur auf diesem dahin kommen, und daß es das selbst empfundene, nicht das bloß erkannte Leiden ist, was am häufigsten die völlige Resignation herbeiführt, oft erst bei der Nähe des Todes. Denn nur bei Wenigen reicht die bloße Erkenntniß hin, welche, das *principium individuationis* durchschauend, erstlich die vollkommenste Güte der Gesinnung und allgemeine Menschenliebe hervorbringt, und endlich alle Leiden der Welt sie als ihre eigenen erkennen läßt, um die Verneinung des Willens herbeizuführen...Meistens muß daher, durch das größte eigene Leiden, der Wille gebrochen seyn, ehe dessen Selbstverneinung eintritt."; *Ibid.*, p.392.

kill the will-to-live, whose appearance is this empty, unsatisfactory and dismal world."[707] Yet another fragment states: "*Suffering* is as necessary to our *moral* character as the pressure of the atmosphere is to our body. Without this the body would burst, and without suffering our character would become engulfed into sensual pleasures and passions of every kind (*diffluimus voluptate*)."[708] He states, moreover, that the experience of suffering serves to orient the thinking of "temporal" man towards the realm of the "eternal", or "better consciousness".[709] These early passages are in keeping with Schopenhauer's subsequent reflection as found in *Die Welt als Wille und Vorstellung* and *Parerga und Paralipomena*, for example. But in these two respective works the notion of the "better consciousness", which is repeatedly mentioned in the first volume of the *Nachlaß*, disappears and is substituted for by that of denial of the will-to-live.[710]

This notwithstanding, the essential idea remains the same, that is, that *suffering breaks the will*. As a case in point, a supplementary essay ("*Die Heilsordnung*") in the second volume of *Die Welt als Wille und Vorstellung* underscores that "suffering is in reality the process of purification (*Läuterungsprocess*) by which

---

[707] *Nachlaß*, I, #246, S.148; *Manuscript Remains*, I, #246, pp.160-161.

[708] *Ibid.*, #166, S.93; *Ibid.*, #166, p.101.

[709] *Ibid.*, #147, S.87. "Damit der Mensch eine erhabene Gesinnung in sich erhalte, seine Gedanken vom Zeitlichen auf das Ewige richte, mit einem Wort damit das *bessre Bewußtseyn* in ihm rege sey; ist ihm Schmerz, Leiden und Mißlingen so nothwendig wie dem Schiffe der es beschwerende Ballast, ohne welchen es keine Tiefe ermißt, ein Spiel der Wogen und Winde keinen bestimmten Weg gehet und leicht umschlägt."; *Ibid.*, #147, p.95.

[710] Cf. Edoardo Mirri "Un concetto perduto nella sistematica schopenhaueriana: la 'migliore coscienza'" in *Schopenhauer e il sacro*, pp.62-63.

man in most cases is sanctified, that is, led back from the path of error of the will-to-live."[711] In similar fashion, a passage from *Parerga und Paralipomena* notes that suffering in its various forms can be considered to be "metaphysically a blessing and at bottom a benefit," inasmuch as it hastens the silencing of the will's rage and brings one to the very threshold of salvation.[712]

In this respect, life with its trials, sufferings and tribulations, is nothing more than a long process of purification that frees one from the delusion that we exist in order to be happy in our present existence. The unpleasant vicissitudes of life, which come in the shape of various sufferings, serve to act as a purifying lye that can even make dross of previous immorality and wickedness.[713] Though the embracing of suffering meets with resistance given a consciousness so prone to willing, in the final analysis, even the very wicked (on occasion) can be purified by the deepest grief and sorrow.[714] Accordingly, denial of the will-to-live

---

[711] *Vorstellung II*, Kap.49, IV, S.745; *Representation*, II, ch.49, p.636.

[712] *Parerga II*, §171, IX, S.348; *Parerga*, II, §171, p.321.

[713] *Vorstellung II*, Kap.49, IV, S.750. "Das Leben stellt sich alsdann dar als ein Läuterungsproceß, dessen reinigende Lauge der Schmerz ist. Ist der Proceß vollbracht, so läßt er die ihm vorhergegangene Immoralität und Schlechtigkeit als Schlacke zurück..."; *Representation*, II, ch.49, 639.

[714] *Vorstellung I*, §68, II, S.485-486. "Meistens muß daher, durch das größte eigene Leiden, der Wille gebrochen seyn, ehe dessen Selbstverneinung eintritt. Dann sehn wir den Menschen, nachdem er durch alle Stufen der wachsenden Bedrängniß, unter dem heftigsten Widerstreben, zum Rande der Verzweiflung gebracht ist, plötzlich in sich gehn, sich und die Welt erkennen, sein ganzes Wesen ändern, sich über sich selbst und alles Leiden erheben und, wie durch dasselbe gereinigt und geheiligt, in unanfechtbarer Ruhe, Säligkeit und Erhabenheit willig Allem entsagen, was er vorhin mit der größten Heftigkeit wollte, und den Tod freudig empfangen. Es ist der aus der läuternden Flamme des Leidens plötzlich hervortretende Silberblick der Verneinung des Willens zum Leben, d.h. der Erlösung. Selbst Die, welche sehr böse waren, sehn wir bisweilen durch die tiefsten Schmerzen bis zu diesem Grade geläutert: sie sind Andere geworden und völlig umgewandelt. Die früheren Missethaten ängstigen daher auch ihr Gewissen jetzt nicht mehr; doch büßen sie solche gern mit dem Tode, und sehn willig die Erscheinung jenes Willens enden, der ihnen jetzt fremd und zum Abscheu

via the "second way" of suffering, to a certain extent, constitutes a substitute for virtue and holiness in that it likewise serves to break the will-to-live. In fact, Schopenhauer states that our hope for salvation and deliverance from the will's firm grasp, depends much more upon what we suffer than upon what we do.[715]

Given the sanctifying power that suffering has, Schopenhauer continues by emphasizing that this is even more true with the approach of death.[716] For he states that "in the natural course, the decay of the body in old age coincides with that of the will."[717] The enfeebling of the body as Death nears expresses ever so clearly how vain, fruitless and self-contradictory the striving of the will is.[718] Death is the reprimand that tumbles down the walls that will-filled egoism in the course of a lifetime builds. More than anything else, it is a catharsis for human hubris in that its violent

---

ist."; *Representation*, I, §68, p.393.

[715] *Vorstellung II*, Kap.49, IV, S.745-746. "Unter der Bezeichnung des δευτερος πλους habe ich das Leiden gewissermaßen als ein Surrogat der Tugend und Heiligkeit dargestellt: hier muß ich das kühne Wort aussprechen, daß wir, Alles wohl erwogen, für unser Heil und Erlösung mehr zu hoffen haben von Dem, was wir leiden, als Dem, was wir thun."; *Representation*, II, ch.49, p.636.

[716] *Ibid.*, S.746. "Hat also schon das Leiden eine solche heiligende Kraft, so wird diese in noch höherm Grade dem mehr als alles Leiden gefürchteten Tode zukommen."; *Ibid.*

[717] *Ibid.*, S.747; *Ibid.*, p.637.

[718] *Ibid.*, S.746-747. "Das Sterben ist allerdings als der eigentliche Zweck des Lebens anzusehn: im Augenblick desselben wird alles Das entschieden, was durch den ganzen Verlauf des Lebens nur vorbereitet und eingeleitet war. Der Tod ist das Ergebniß, das Résumé des Lebens, oder die zusammengezogene Summe, welche die gesammte Belehrung, die das Leben vereinzelt und stückweise gab, mit Einem Male ausspricht, nämlich diese, daß das ganze Streben, dessen Erscheinung das Leben ist, ein vergebliches, eiteles, sich widersprechendes war, von welchem zurückgekommen zu seyn eine Erlösung ist."; *Ibid.*

destruction of our phenomenon, exposes the fundamental error of will-filled existence.[719]

3. Philosophy and Religion as "Systems of Metaphysics"

The above notwithstanding, suffering and death for will-filled consciousness represent a cross to be shunned rather than embraced. As a rule, man struggles against trekking this path. He strives with all the powers at his disposal to secure a pleasant existence for himself whereby his will is fettered to life.[720] Accordingly, he shirks from the ominous shadow that the cross of suffering and death casts. In fact, man revolts against the seemingly cruel destiny and fate that entrance into the world bequeaths. The nothingness from which he comes haunts him. The need to find answers for the deep existential questions of life increases in its urgency, as sickness and old age become traveling companions in the steadfast march to the abyss of non-existence whence he came. His heart ripped apart by the decree of the Fates, man cannot unloosen the noose of the death to which he is sentenced by the mere fact that he was born through no will of his own. When all is said and done, the rocks of death loom in the horizon with a

---

[719] *Ibid.*, Kap.41, S.594. "Der Tod ist die große Zurechtweisung, welche der Wille zum Leben, und näher der diesem wesentliche Egoismus, durch den Lauf der Natur erhält; und er kann aufgefaßt werden als eine Strafe für unser Daseyn. Er ist die schmerzliche Lösung des Knotens, den die Zeugung mit Wollust geschürzt hatte, und die von außen eindringende, gewaltsame Zerstörung des Grundirrthums unsers Wesens: die große Enttäuschung."; *Ibid.*, ch.41, p.507.

[720] *Ibid.*, Kap.49, S.748. "Inzwischen sträuben wir uns, denselben zu betreten, und streben vielmehr, mit allen Kräften, uns ein sicheres und angenehmes Daseyn zu bereiten, wodurch wir unsern Willen immer fester an das Leben ketten."; *Ibid.*, ch.49, p.638.

foreboding certainty, and destroy the meager phenomenon whose expression he is.[721]

Yet, Schopenhauer clearly asserts in "*Über das metaphysische Bedürfniß des Menschen*," a supplementary essay found in Chapter 17 of the second volume of *Die Welt als Wille und Vorstellung*, that it is the death and chaos all about man that leads him to search for meaning, and thereby opens wide the doors for philosophical reflection. The tragic element of life, coupled with the existence of so much evil and wickedness in the world, moves man to philosophize and indeed to cry out.[722] It is his existential pain vis-à-vis his yearning for order that drives him to ask "Why?" -- the question at the basis of all philosophizing:

> ...without a doubt, it is the knowledge of death, and in addition to this, the consideration of the suffering and misery of life, that give the strongest impulse to philosophical reflection and metaphysical explanations of the world. If our life were endless and painless, it would perhaps not occur to anyone to ask why the world exists, and why precisely it has this nature, but everything quite certainly would be taken as a matter of course.[723]

Insofar as man is gifted with the faculty of reason (*Vernunft*), he is able to "feel surprised" at his own existence and wonder about his place in a vast universe

---

[721] *Ibid.*, S.748-749; *Ibid.*, pp.638-639.

[722] *Ibid.*, Kap.17, S.200-201. "Das philosophische Erstaunen ist demnach im Grunde ein bestürztes und betrübtes...Die soeben ausgesprochene nähere Beschaffenheit des Erstaunens, welches zum Philosophiren treibt, entspringt offenbar aus dem Anblick *des Uebels und des Bösen* in der Welt, welche, selbst wenn sie im gerechtesten Verhältniß zu einander ständen, ja, auch noch vom Guten weit überwogen würden, dennoch Etwas sind, was ganz und gar und überhaupt nicht seyn sollte. Weil nun aber nichts aus Nichts entstehn kann; so müssen auch jene ihren Keim im Ursprunge, oder im Kern der Welt selbst haben."; *Ibid.*, ch.17, pp.171-172.

[723] *Ibid.*, S.187-188; *Ibid.*, p.161.

that makes him pale in insignificance like a mere drop in the ocean.[724] Because he asks the fundamental question "Why?" -- especially when confronted with life's tragic element -- he towers above the rest of nature. The question "Why?" in its simplicity is in reality profound, inasmuch as it is an expression of a yearning and indeed a rage for order in the cosmos. For this reason, Schopenhauer states that "with this reflection and astonishment arises the *need for metaphysics* that is peculiar to man alone; accordingly, he is *an animal metaphysicum.*"[725]

It is important to keep in mind that Schopenhauer in this important essay (*"Über das metaphysisches Bedürfniß des Menschen"*) is using the term "metaphysical need" in a broad sense under which systems of religious belief can also be subsumed. He states: "Temples and churches, pagodas and mosques, in all lands and ages, testify to the metaphysical need of man which is strong and ineradicable, which follows close on the physical."[726] In *"Über Religion"*, the other important essay dealing with the phenomenon of religion found in the second volume of *Parerga und Paralipomena*, it is stated that "people need a system of metaphysics, i.e. an account of the world and its existence because such is

---

[724] *Ibid.*, S.186-187. "Erst nachdem das innere Wesen der Natur (der Wille zum Leben in seiner Objektivation) sich durch die beiden Reiche der bewußtlosen Wesen und dann durch die lange und breite Reihe der bewußtlosen Wesen und dann durch die lange und breite Reihe der Thiere, rüstig und wohlgemuth, gesteigert hat, gelangt es endlich, beim Eintritt der Vernunft, also im Menschen, zum ersten Male zur Besinnung: dann wundert es sich über seine eigenen Werke und frägt sich, was es selbst sei. Seine Verwunderung ist aber um so ernstlicher, als er hier zum ersten Male mit Bewußtseyn *dem Tode* gegenübersteht, und neben der Endlichkeit alles Daseyns auch die Vergeblickeit alles Strebens sich ihm mehr oder minder aufdringt."; *Ibid.*, p.160.

[725] *Ibid.*, S.186; *Ibid.*

[726] *Ibid.*, S.188; *Ibid.*, p.162.

one of the most natural needs of man."⁷²⁷ Also of noteworthy significance is the relationship that exists between "metaphysical need" and reason. This will prove to be highly significant in the ensuing paragraphs insofar as religion, understood as an expression of "metaphysical need", is a distinctly human phenomenon.⁷²⁸

Before proceeding further, what Schopenhauer means exactly by "metaphysics" in this context needs to be clarified. Two definitions are given which are useful for this inquiry. Since the present discussion revolves around the essay "*Über das metaphysisches Bedürfniß des Menschen*", it is best to begin with the definition furnished here:

> By metaphysics I understand all alleged knowledge which goes beyond the possibility of experience, and so beyond nature or the given appearance of things, in order to give information about that by which, in some sense or other, this experience is conditioned, or in popular language, about that which lies hidden behind nature, and makes nature possible.⁷²⁹

In his ethical treatise *Über die Grundlage der Moral* Schopenhauer approaches this issue with a slight nuance in that he emphasizes the importance and necessity for ethical acts to have a metaphysical grounding. The following illustrates this:

> Indeed, with ethics, the need for a metaphysical basis is all the more urgent, since philosophical as well as religious

---

⁷²⁷ *Parerga II*, Kap.15, §174, X, S.374; *Parerga*, II, ch.15, §174, p.338.

⁷²⁸ Cf. Salaquarda, S.322. "Religion ist für Schopenhauer etwas spezifisch Menschliches. Thiere haben keine Religion, wie er in Übereinstimmung mit Feuerbach eine damals diskutierte These abwehrend betont. Das dem Menschen Eigentümliche, ihn vom Tier Unterscheidende ist auch nach Schopenhauers Meinung die Vernunft. Also muß Religion etwas mit der Vernunft zu tun haben."

⁷²⁹ *Vorstellung II*, Kap.17, III, S.191; *Representation*, II, ch.17, p.164.

systems are in agreement that the ethical significance of actions must at the same time be metaphysical, i.e., this significance goes beyond the mere appearance of things, and consequently, must be in very close relation with the entire existence of the world and with the destiny of man; for the ultimate point at which the meaning of existence generally arrives is certainly ethical.[730]

In each of the two definitions, there is a common denominator: namely, that metaphysical knowledge goes beyond the mere surface of phenomena, and has for its aim, an explanation of experience and a grounding of nature. A crucial point to underscore, to which an allusion was already made above, is that for Schopenhauer the satisfaction of the metaphysical need for meaning is intrinsic to human nature. Accordingly, philosophical and religious systems of belief are attempts by man to answer the profound questions that arise from the existence of suffering, wickedness and death. As such, they can be regarded as two independent and different systems of metaphysics which, in the final analysis, arise not only because of differences in the faculty of understanding from person to person, but also because circumstances often inhibit its cultivation.[731]

Schopenhauer notes that in "civilized nations" the two systems of metaphysics can generally be found because the ideal conditions for philosophical reflection exist for at least some who have that capacity. Philosophy, which is thereby geared for the few, comprises the first "system." Its verification and

---

[730] *Grundlage*, §21, VI, S.302; *Basis*, §21, p.200.

[731] *Vorstellung II*, Kap.17, III, S.191. "Nun aber setzt die große ursprüngliche Verschiedenheit der Verstandeskräfte, wozu noch die der viele Muße erfordernden Ausbildung derselben kommt, einen so großen Unterschied zwischen Menschen, daß, sobald ein Volk sich aus dem Zustande der Rohheit herausgearbeitet hat, nicht wohl *eine* Metaphysik für Alle ausreichen kann."; *Representation*, II, ch.17, p.164.

credentials do not depend on any external authority, but arise from "within itself", which is to say that this system is grounded on reason.[732] Religious systems of belief, on the other hand, are subsumed under the epithet "metaphysics of the people" (*Volksmetaphysik*). This system of metaphysics is geared for the many, requires a grounding "outside of itself", and appeals to external authority, that is, revelation as authenticated by signs and miracles. Whereas philosophy uses arguments based on reasons, religion or the "metaphysics of the people" uses the threat of eternal and temporal punishment to convince.[733] It is evident that what ensues with the above distinction is that there are two radically different ways of looking at reality. But what is important to keep in mind is that there is no possibility of a rapprochement between knowledge and faith in Schopenhauer's *Weltanschauung*. Schopenhauer states this succinctly in *Parerga und Paralipomena*: "Faith and knowledge in the same mind do not go well together; they are like wolf and sheep in one cage, and of course, knowledge (*das Wissen*) is the wolf that threatens to

---

[732] *Ibid.* "...daher wir bei den civilisirten Völkern durchgängig zwei verschiedene Arten derselben antreffen, welche sich dadurch unterscheiden, daß die eine ihre Beglaubigung *in sich*, die andere sie *außer sich* hat. Da die metaphysischen Systeme der ersten Art, zur Rekognition ihrer Beglaubigung, Nachdenken, Bildung, Muße und Urtheil erfordern; so können sie nur bei einer äußerst geringen Anzahl von Menschen zugänglich seyn, auch nur bei bedeutender Civilisation entstehn und sich erhalten."; *Ibid.*

[733] *Ibid.*, S.191-192. Für die große Anzahl der Menschen hingegen, als welche nicht zu denken, sondern zu glauben befähigt und nicht für Gründe, sondern nur für Auktorität empfänglich ist, sind ausschließlich die Systeme der zweiten Art: diese können deshalb als Volksmetaphysik bezeichnet werden, nach Analogie der Volkspoesie, auch der Volksweisheit, worunter man die Sprichwörter versteht. Jene Systeme sind indessen unter dem Namen der Religionen bekannt und finden sich bei allen Völkern, mit Ausnahme der allerrohesten. Ihre Beglaubigung ist, wie gesagt, äußerlich und heißt als solche Offenbarung, welche dokumentirt wird Zeichen und Wunder. Ihre Argumente sind hauptsächlich Drohungen mit ewigen, auch wohl mit zeitlichen Uebeln, gerichtet gegen die Ungläubigen, ja schon gegen die bloßen Zweifler."; *Ibid.*, pp.164-165.

devour its neighbor."[734] Yet another passage from the above-mentioned work categorically states that unlike faith, philosophy has absolutely nothing to do with what should or may be believed, but merely with what can be known.[735] Because knowledge is intellectually more tenable than faith, the latter gives way when the two come into collision.[736]

Philosophy, as the first system of metaphysics, is concerned with the imparting of truth, in the proper sense of the term, without a recourse to myth or allegory. In his essay "*Über das metaphysische Bedürfniß des Menschen*", Schopenhauer states: "A system of the first kind, therefore a philosophy, makes the claim, and so has the obligation to be true *sensu stricto et proprio* in everything that it says; for it has recourse to thought and persuasion."[737] Accordingly, it may be said that philosophy, as it were, beholds truth without external props or supports. In this respect, it has its support from within.

Religion, on the other hand, cannot convey truth in its more pristine form, but must "water it down" by having recourse to allegory and mystery. Accordingly, Schopenhauer notes that the only obligation which religion as such has, is "to be true *sensu allegorico*" for the multitude that cannot grasp the most sublime

---

[734] *Parerga II*, §181, X, S.432; *Parerga*, II, §181, p.392.

[735] *Ibid.*, §175, S.398. "Die Philosophie hat, als eine Wissenschaft, es durchaus nicht damit zu thun, was *geglaubt* werden soll, oder darf; sondern bloß damit, was man *wissen* kann."; *Ibid.*, §175, p.360.

[736] *Ibid.* "...weil nämlich das Wissen aus einem härteren Stoff ist, als der Glaube, so daß, wenn sie gegen einander stoßen, dieser bricht."; *Ibid.*

[737] *Vorstellung II*, Kap.17, III, S.193-194; *Representation*, II, ch.17, p.166.

truths *sensu proprio*.[738] But he emphasizes that the inconsistencies, contradictions, and absurdities proper to religion, nonetheless remain inasmuch as they are part and parcel of its allegorical nature. This notwithstanding, these are the only suitable way by which the ordinary and uncultured mind can "feel" what would otherwise be incomprehensible to it: namely, that religion also deals with a noumenal order of things.[739]

To summarize before moving into the next section of this part of the chapter (which deals explicitly with the nature of religion), it has been established that any religious system of belief constitutes a "system of metaphysics" in its own right. As such, like any given philosophical system, its rationale for existence depends upon its capacity to answer the profound existential questions that the philosophically unlettered have when confronted with wickedness, suffering and death which scar the human condition. But it was stated that religion is only capable of expressing truth in *sensu allegorico* whereas philosophy does so in *sensu proprio*.

In the section immediately to follow, what comprises the positive and negative aspects of religion

---

[738] *Ibid.*, S.194. "Eine Religion hingegen, für die Unzähligen bestimmt, welche, der Prüfung und des Denkens unfähig, die tiefsten und schwierigsten Wahrheiten *sensu proprio* nimmermehr fassen würden, hat auch nur die Verpflichtung *sensu allegorico* wahr zu seyn. Nackt kann die Wahrheit vor dem Volke nicht erscheinen. Ein Symptom dieser *allegorischen* Natur der Religionen sind die vielleicht in jeder anzutreffenden *Mysterien*, nämlich gewisse Dogmen, die sich nicht ein Mal deutlich denken lassen, geschweige wörtlich wahr seyn können."; *Ibid.*

[739] *Ibid.* "Ja, vielleicht ließe sich behaupten, daß einige völlige Widersinnigkeiten, einige wirkliche Absurditäten, ein wesentliches Ingredienz einer vollkommenen Religion seien: denn diese sind eben der Stämpel ihrer *allegorischen* Natur und die allein passende Art, dem gemeinen Sinn und rohen Verstande *fühlbar* zu machen, was ihm unbegreiflich wäre, nämlich daß die Religion im Grunde von einer ganz andern, von einer Ordnung der *Dinge an sich* handelt..."; *Ibid.*

Religion and God   279

in Schopenhauer's thought will be delineated. Central for the discussion that follows is the dialogue between Demopheles and Philalethes which comprises the bulk of Chapter 15 (§174) in the second volume of *Parerga und Paralipomena*, entitled simply "*Über Religion*".[740] Through Demopheles, Schopenhauer addresses the positive elements of religion as a "system of metaphysics" in its own right. Philalethes, on the other hand, serves as Schopenhauer's spokesman for truth as *sensu proprio*. Insofar as Philalethes argues that religion has always impeded the progress of reason, he plays the role of the devil's advocate in the dialogue. In reality, Schopenhauer's actual position with regard to religion is a dialectic between the two positions as represented by Demopheles and Philalethes.[741] The discussion that ensues illustrates this claim.

4. Religion: its positive and negative aspects

Turning now to the dialogue in *Parerga und Paralipomena*, let us first focus on what Schopenhauer (personified as Demopheles and Philalethes) says about religion. The discourse begins with Demopheles' claim that religion is the only means by which "the high significance of life" can be made clear to the "crude intellect" of the masses, who are immersed in base

---

[740] Schopenhauer's remarks here are reminiscent of the dialogue format espoused in David Hume's *Dialogues Concerning Natural Religion* (1779), a work he greatly admired (cf. *Vorstellung II*, IV, Kap.46, S.681; *Representation*, II, ch.46, pp.581-582). But the more pertinent source is Ernst Platner's Dialogue, "Ueber den Atheismus," (1783) which has two central protagonists: Philalethes who is the friend of truth, and Theophil, the friend of God. Cf. Hübscher, *Denker gegen den Strom*, S.21.

[741] Cf. Hübscher, *Denker gegen den Strom*, S.21-22. Bykhovsky, *Schopenhauer and the Ground of Existence*, pp.169-170; Schmidt, *Die Wahrheit im Gewande der Lüge*, S.49-50; Hasse, *Schopenhauer*, S.371-372.

pursuits and material work.⁷⁴² Underscoring that as a rule man originally has no interest for anything else except the satisfaction of physical needs and desires, Demopheles states that founders of religions and philosophers "come into the world to shake man out of his lethargy and point out to him the lofty meaning of existence; philosophers for the few who are exempt, founders of religion for the majority, for mankind at large."⁷⁴³ Because this is so, argues Demopheles, religion as "the metaphysics of the people" is a value which ought to be respected and not taken away insofar "people absolutely need an *interpretation of life* which must be suitable to their power of comprehension."⁷⁴⁴

Next it is asserted that religion is "always an allegorical wording of the truth (*eine allegorische Einkleidung der Wahrheit*)... [which] as a guiding principle (*Richtschnur*) for conduct, and as a comfort and consolation in suffering and death, achieves perhaps just as much as could truth itself, if we were to possess it."⁷⁴⁵ Differences in religions are explicable simply by the different schemes wherein people grasp and "picture" the truth, which in itself, is incomprehensible to them. In fact, for any given system of religion, the

---

⁷⁴² *Parerga II*, Kap.15, §174, X, S.360. "Die Religion ist das einzige Mittel, dem rohen Sinn und ungelenken Verstande der in niedriges Treiben und materielle Arbeit tief eingesenkten Menge die hohe Bedeutung des Lebens anzukündigen und fühlbar zu machen."; *Parerga*, II, ch.15, §174, p.324.

⁷⁴³ *Ibid.*; *Ibid.*, pp.324-325.

⁷⁴⁴ *Ibid.*; *Ibid.*, p.325.

⁷⁴⁵ *Ibid.*; *Ibid.*

"pictured" truth becomes inseparable from the system itself.[746]

With Philalethes' first intervention, Schopenhauer underscores the negative dimension associated with religion. Here it is asserted that the "conventional metaphysics" that religion is, with its dogmas and precepts, is by nature opposed to genuine philosophical effort and the sincere investigation of truth. Moreover, because the teachings of religions are inculcated at an early age, they remain "indelibly impressed" with the result that the faculty of reason at the outset is "confused and deranged", and its capacity for original thought and unbiased judgement severely limited.[747] Typical of the counter-argument that Philalethes presents, is the claim that religions appeal to faith and revelation -- and not to conviction and argument -- seeking thereby to influence especially the minds of the very young.[748] Philalethes, in short, is obsessed with "the progress of the knowledge of the truth in the human race" and would rather that the "nightmare" of theism with its fundamental notions not block intellectual and philosophical efforts.[749]

Demopheles does not appear to deny that the ideal would be to grasp the truth by philosophical

---

[746] *Ibid*. "Die verschiedenen Religionen sind eben nur verschiedene Schemata, in welchen das Volk die ihm an sich selbst unfaßbare Wahrheit ergreift und sich vergegenwärtigt, mit welchen sie ihm jedoch unzertrennlich verwächst."; *Ibid*.

[747] *Ibid*., S.361; *Ibid*., p.326.

[748] *Ibid*. "Allein die Religionen wenden sich ja eigeständlich nicht an die Ueberzeugung, mit Gründen, sondern an den Glauben, mit Offenbarungen. Zu diesem letzteren ist nun aber die Fähigkeit am stärksten in der Kindheit: daher ist man, vor Allem, darauf bedacht, sich dieses zarten Alters zu bemächtigen. Hiedurch, viel mehr noch, als durch Drohungen und Berichte von Wundern, schlagen die Glaubenslehren Wurzel."; *Ibid*.

[749] *Ibid*., S.364-366; *Ibid*., p.329-330.

reflection alone, but advances the argument that religion serves as a powerful brace that refrains the anti-moral tendencies in man. Once again it is asserted that an allegorical coloring (*allegorische Einkleidung*) of the truth by parables and myth serves to make the truth comprehensible to the masses.[750] Philalethes, however, rejects the above conjecture that religion is indispensable to law and order in society given the different nature of religion in ancient culture, especially that of the Greeks -- which suggests for him that law and order are not necessarily intertwined with religion.[751]

Demopheles appears to grant the last argument advanced by Philalethes if silence is indicative of acquiescence. But he returns to the central issue which concerns whether or not religion has anything to do with truth. The dialogue comes to a climax here in that Demopheles and Philalethes both make claims that serve to trumpet Schopenhauer's views with clarity. The exchange begins with Demopheles insisting that "religion does not stand in contradiction to truth; for it itself teaches the truth."[752] He continues by repeating what has already been said above about the necessity of religion to water down the truth and symbolically express it via

---

[750] *Ibid.*, S.366; *Ibid.*, pp.330-331;

[751] *Ibid.*, S.367-368. "Es ist *falsch*, daß Statt, Recht und Gesetz nicht ohne Beihülfe der Religion und ihrer Glaubensartikel aufrecht erhalten werden können, und daß Justiz und Polizei, um die gesetzliche Ordnung durchzusetzen, der Religion, als ihres nothwendigen Komplementes bedürfen...Also, *Religion*, in unserm Sinne des Wortes, hatten die Alten wirklich nicht. Hat nun aber deswegen bei ihnen Anarchie und Gesetzlosigkeit geherrscht? ist nicht vielmehr Gesetz und bürgerliche Ordnung so sehr ihr Werk, daß es noch die Grundlage der unserigen ausmacht? war nicht das Eigenthum, obwohl es sogar großen Theils aus Sklaven bestand, vollkommen gesichert? Und hat dieser Zustand nicht weit über ein Jahrtausend gedauert?-"; *Ibid.*, pp.331-332.

[752] *Ibid.*, S.368; *Ibid.*, p.333.

a "mythical vehicle", so as to conform to the needs and powers of the public at large.[753]

But then a highly significant claim is advanced about the impossibility of grasping truth in its pure and pristine form even for the philosopher. This is in keeping with claims made by Schopenhauer in the final essay in the second volume of *Die Welt als Wille und Vorstellung*, which underscore that the human mind simply is not privy to all that can be known about the noumenon.[754] The passage from the dialogue, in which Demopheles is responding to Philalethes, speaks for itself:

> You can also, in this regard, compare truth to certain chemical substances which in themselves are gaseous, but which for medicinal use as well as for preservation or dispatch one must bind to a firm, palpable base, since they would otherwise volatilize. For example, chlorine, is applied to all such purposes only in the form of chlorides. However, in case the truth, pure, abstract,

---

[753] *Ibid.*, S.368-369. *Ibid.*

[754] *Vorstellung II*, Kap.50, IV, S.750. "Man kann z.B., nach allen meinen Auseinandersetzungen, noch fragen, woraus denn dieser Wille, welcher frei ist sich zu bejahen, wovon die Erscheinung die Welt, oder zu verneinen, wovon wir die Erscheinung nicht kennen, entsprungen sei? welches die jenseit aller Erfahrung liegende Fatalität sei, welche ihn in die höchst mißiche Alternative, als eine Welt, in der Leiden und Tod herrscht, zu erscheinen, oder aber sein eigenstes Wesen zu verneinen, versetzt habe? oder auch, was ihn vermocht haben möge, die unendlich vorzuziehende Ruhe des säligen Nichts zu verlassen? Ein individueller Wille, mag man hinzufügen, kann zu seinem eigenen Verderben allein durch Irrthum bei der Wahl, also durch Schuld der Erkenntniß, sich hinlenken: aber der Wille an sich, vor aller Erscheinung, folglich noch ohne Erkenntniß, wie konnte er irre gehn und in das Verderben seines jetzigen Zustandes gerathen? woher überhaupt der große Mißton, der diese Welt durchdringt? Ferner kann man fragen, wie tief, im Wesen an sich der Welt, die Wurzeln der Individualität gehn? worauf sich allenfalls noch antworten ließe: sie gehn so tief, wie die Bejahung des Willens zum Leben; wo die Verneinung eintritt, hören sie auf: denn mit der Bejahung sind sie entsprungen. Aber man könnte wohl gar die Frage aufwerfen: »Was wäre ich, wenn ich nicht Wille zum Leben wäre?« und mehr dergleichen. - Auf alle solche Fragen wäre zunächst zu antworten, daß der Ausdruck der allgemeinsten und durchgängigsten Form unsers Intellekts der *Satz vom Grunde* ist, daß aber dieser eben deshalb nur auf die Erscheinung, nicht auf das Wesen an sich der Dinge Anwendung findet: auf ihm allein aber beruht alles Woher und Warum."; *Representation*, II, ch.50, pp.640-641.

and free from everything mythical, should remain ever unattainable to us all, even to the philosophers, it could be compared to fluorine which by itself alone is not exhibitable, but only can appear bound to other substances. Or, to speak less learnedly, the truth which is in general not expressible, except mythically and allegorically, is like water which without a container is not transportable; but philosophers who insist on possessing it, pure and unalloyed, are like the man who breaks the vessel in order to have the water simply by itself. Perhaps this is actually the case.[755]

Philalethes responds to the above by saying: "I certainly understand; the whole thing amounts to truth appearing in the guise of falsehood. However, in so doing, it enters into an alliance that is harmful to it."[756] He continues by stating that the inauthenticity or double-maskedness of religion consists precisely in the fact that it maintains and asserts that it is true *sensu proprio*, while at best it can only be true *sensu allegorico*.[757] Accordingly, later in the dialogue he refers to religion as a "pious fraud" in that "as long as

---

[755] *Parerga II*, Kap.15, §174, X, S.369; *Representation*, II, ch.15, §174, p.333.

[756] *Ibid.*; *Ibid.*, pp.333-334.

[757] *Ibid.*, S.369-370. "*Philalethes*. Verstehe schon: die Sache läuft hinaus auf die Wahrheit im Gewande der Lüge. Aber damit tritt sie in eine ihr verderbliche Allianz. Denn was für eine gefährliche Waffe wird nicht Denen in die Hände gegeben, welche die Befugniß erhalten, sich der Unwahrheit als Vehikels der Wahrheit zu bedienen! Wenn es so steht, fürchte ich, daß das Unwahre an der Sache mehr Schaden stiften wird, als das Wahre je Nutzen. Ja, wenn die Allegorie sich eigeständlich als eine solche geben dürfte, da gienge es schon an: allein das würde ihr allen Respekt und damit alle Wirksamkeit benehmen. Sie muß daher als *sensu proprio* wahr sich geltend machen und behaupten; während sid höchstens *sensu allegorico* wahr ist. Hier liegt der unheilbare Schaden, der bleibende Uebelstand, welcher Ursache ist, daß die Religion mit dem unbefangenen, edlen Streben nach reiner Wahrheit stets in Konflikt gerathen ist und es immer von Neum wird."; *Ibid*.

religion lives, it has two faces, one of truth and one of deception."[758]

The above represents the gist of the dialectic in Schopenhauer's thought in this particular essay about the nature of religion. A further reading of the dialogue between Demopheles and Philalethes repeats the same notions already advanced. But another important claim that is brought to light in the dialogue is that religion acknowledges its allegorical nature in its *mysteries*, which for Schopenhauer are "absurd" dogmas which conceal within themselves sublime truths.[759] In fact, it is stated that everything in religion is reducible to mystery.[760] But, once again, what is interesting to note is that Schopenhauer via Demopheles admits that the notion of "mystery" is also summoned in philosophical discourse from time to time.[761] In fact, it was already seen above how Schopenhauer contends that the occurrence of compassion is at bottom a "mystery".

In what sense, however, do the mysteries of religion, and Christianity in particular, contain sublime truths that philosophers can behold without colored lenses? Underscoring once again that religion from the moral point of view is an excellent means for

---

[758] *Ibid.*, S.372; *Ibid.*, pp.336-337.

[759] *Ibid.*, S.370. "Sogar ist »Mysterium« im Grunde nur der theologische *terminus technicus* für religiöse Allegorie. Auch haben alle Religionen ihre Mysterien. Eigentlich ist ein Mysterium ein offenbar absurdes Dogma, welches jedoch eine hohe, an sich selbst dem gemeinen Verstande der rohen Menge völlig unfaßliche Wahrheit in sich verbirgt..."; *Ibid.*, p.334.

[760] *Ibid.* "Man könnte weiter gehn und behaupten, an den Religionen sei eigentlich Alles Mysterium."; *Ibid.*

[761] *Ibid.* "Zur Erläuterung kann ich hinzusetzen, daß sogar in der Philosophie der Gebrauch des Mysteriums versucht worden ist, z.B. wenn *Pascal*, welcher Pietist, Mathematiker und Philosoph zugleich war, in dieser dreifachen Eigenschaft sagt: Gott is Centrüm überall und nirgends Peripherie. Auch *Melebranche* hat ganz richtig bemerkt: *la liberté est un mystère.*" *Ibid.*

training "the perverse, obtuse, and malicious race of bipeds" that man is,[762] Schopenhauer repeats via Demopheles that it is not only true, but is "the most important of all truths."[763] But in which sense?

He provides that answer in yet another passage from the dialogue insofar as a standard is given by which the truth of a given religion's mysteries can be determined and measured. Reacting to Philalethes, who takes pleasure in prophesying the gradual weakening of religion's hold with the continued increase of knowledge,[764] Demopheles states that one must not forget that the value of Christianity as a system of metaphysics consists in its having imparted to Europe knowledge of the fundamental truth "that life cannot be an end in itself, but that the true purpose of our existence lies beyond it."[765] Inasmuch as Christianity teaches contempt for the world, rigorous self-denial, and the sanctifying value of suffering, it may be said to have value and impart truth.[766]

In fact, Schopenhauer underscores in *Die Welt als Wille und Vorstellung* that the "fundamental ascetic character" of Christianity and eastern religions, is akin

---

[762] *Ibid.*, S.378; *Ibid.*, p.342.

[763] *Ibid.*; *Ibid.*

[764] *Ibid.*, S.382-383; *Ibid.*, pp.346-347.

[765] *Ibid.*, S.383-384; *Ibid.*, p.347.

[766] *Ibid.*, S.384-385. "Von diesem platten und rohen Aufgehen in einem ephemeren, ungewissen und schaalen Daseyn befreite das Christenthum die Europäische Menschheit...Demgemäß predigte das Christenthum nicht bloß Gerechtigkeit, sondern Menschenliebe, Mitleid, Wohlthätigkeit, Versöhnlichkeit, Feindesliebe, Geduld, Demuth, Entsagung, Glaube und Hoffnung. Ja, es gieng weiter: es lehrte, daß die Welt vom Uebel sei, und daß wir der Erlösung bedürfen: demnach predigte es Weltverachtung, Selbstverleugnung, Keuschheit, Aufgeben es eigenen Willens, d.h. Abwendung vom Leben und dessen trügerischen Genüssen; ja, es lehrte die heiligende Kraft des Leidens erkennen und ein Marterinstrument ist das Symbol des Christenthums."; *Ibid.*, p.348.

Religion and God 287

to his doctrine of the denial of the will-to-live.⁷⁶⁷ It is evident, therefore, that the standard of any given religion's "truth" is the philosophy of salvation Schopenhauer outlines in his notion of denial of the will-to-live. In this respect, he rejects any given religion whose teachings seem to compromise or openly contradict his position. For this reason, a Christianity that adheres to an Augustinian notion of Original Sin and espouses a rigorous self-denial so as to attain salvation, is given a favorable nod.⁷⁶⁸ On the other hand, the "shallow" systems of religious belief as represented by Greek paganism, Judaism, and Islam are rejected by Schopenhauer because of their "pernicious optimism".⁷⁶⁹ He states that "in all religions, as well as in philosophy, optimism is a fundamental error which obstructs the way to all truth."⁷⁷⁰

Specifically with regard to Christianity, Schopenhauer criticizes the tendency of Protestant Christianity in general to eliminate asceticism and the

---

⁷⁶⁷ *Vorstellung II*, Kap.48, IV. S.720. "Denn nicht allein die Religionen des Orients, sondern auch das wahre Christenthum hat durchaus jenen asketischen Grundcharakter, den meine Philosophie als Verneinung des Willens zum Leben verdeutlicht."; *Representation*, II, ch.48, p.615.

⁷⁶⁸ *Parerga II*, Kap.15, §180, X, S.426: "Der *Augustinismus*, mit seinem Dogma von der Erbsünde und was sich daran knüpft, ist...das eigentliche und wohlverstandene Christenthum."; *Parerga*, II, ch.15, §180, pp.386-387.

⁷⁶⁹ *Vorstellung II*, Kap.48, IV. S.730-731. "In Wahrheit ist nicht das Judenthum, mit seinem πάντα καλά λίαν, sondern Brahmanismus und Buddhaismus sind, dem Geiste und der ethischen Tendenz nach, dem Christenthum verwandt. Der Geist und die ethische Tendenz sind aber das Wesentliche einer Religion, nicht die Mythen, in welche sie solche kleidet. Ich gebe daher den Glauben nicht auf, daß die Lehren des Christenthums irgendwie aus jenen Urreligionen abzuleiten sind...Vermöge dieses Ursprungs (oder wenigstens dieser Uebereinstimmung) gehört das Christenthum dem alten, wahren und erhabenen Glauben der Menschheit an, welcher im Gegensatz steht zu dem falschen, platten und verderblichen *Optimismus*, der sich im Griechischen Heidenthum, im Judenthum und im Islam darstellt."; *Representation*, II, ch.48, p.623.

⁷⁷⁰ *Ibid.*, S.733; *Ibid.*, p.626.

meritorious nature of celibacy.[771] Particularly loathsome to him, however, is the gradual transition of Protestantism into "shallow rationalism" or "modern day Pelagianism". For Schopenhauer this is a degenerate, arm-chair Christianity fit for married Protestant clergy.[772] Its anti-thesis, accordingly, would be Christianity in the true sense of the word. For its doctrine of the so-called "deep guilt of mankind" is expressive of the human heart's longing for deliverance from the vale of tears that this world is and teaches that salvation can only be had by self-denial and a complete reform of human nature.[773]

By citing Christianity with its doctrine of Original Sin, therefore, Schopenhauer illustrates how at least one religion with its ethical teaching is "true" insofar as its ethical teachings correspond "in a roundabout way" to what is taught *sensu proprio* in the doctrine of denial of the will-to-live. But the same may

---

[771] *Parerga II*, Kap.15, §179, X, S.427. "...der Protestantismus ist dadurch, daß er das Cölibat und überhaupt die eigentliche Askese, wie auch deren Repräsentanten, die Heiligen, verwarf, zu einem abgestumpften, oder vielmehr abgebrochenen Christenthum geworden, als welchem die Spitze fehlt: es läuft in nichts aus."; *Parerga*, II, ch.15, §179, p.387.

[772] *Vorstellung II*, Kap.48, IV, S.732-733. "Der Protestantismus hat, indem er die Askese und deren Centralpunkt, die Verdienstlichkeit des Cölibats, eliminirte, eigentlich schon den innersten Kern des Christenthums aufgegeben und ist insofern als ein Abfall von demselben anzusehn. Dies hat sich in unsern Tagen herausgestellt in dem allmäligen Uebergang desselben in den platten Rationalismus, diesen modernen Pelagianismus, der am Ende hinausläuft auf eine Lehre von einem liebenden Vater, der die Welt gemacht hat, damit es hübsch vergnügt darauf zugehe (was ihm dann freilich mißrathen seyn müßte), und der, wenn man nur in gewissen Stücken sich seinem Willen anbequemt, auch nachher für eine noch viel hübschere Welt sorgen wird (bei der nur zu beklagen ist, daß sie eine so fatale Entree hat). Das mag eine gute Religion für komfortable, verheirathete und aufgeklärte protestantische Pastoren seyn: aber das ist kein Christenthum."; *Representation*, II, ch.48, p.625.

[773] *Ibid.*, S.733. "Das Christenthum ist die Lehre von der tiefen Verschuldung des Menschengeschlechts durch sein Daseyn selbst und dem Drange des Herzens nach Erlösung daraus, welche jedoch nur durch die schwersten Opfer und durch die Verleugnung des eigenen Selbst, also durch eine gänzliche Umkehrung der menschlichen Natur erlangt werden kann."; *Ibid*.

be said of Brahmanism and Buddhism, which also espouse the need for salvation from an existence given up to suffering and death.[774] In this respect, Schopenhauer feels that he is justified in making the following claim: "Philosophy is related to religions as a straight line is to several curves running near it; for it expresses *sensu proprio*, and consequently reaches directly, that which religions show under disguise (*Verhüllung*), and reach in a roundabout way (*auf Umwegen erreichen*)."[775] In the dialogue between Demopheles and Philalethes the analogy Schopenhauer draws above is confirmed in that he maintains that while it cannot be said that there is one "true" religion, it can be stated that all religions have "degrees of truth".[776]

A serious drawback, however, in Schopenhauer's philosophical reflection about the phenomenon of religion, is his failure to go beyond the so-called metaphysical need for meaning and at least mention that religious experience involves an encounter with the Holy.[777] What is simply stated is that religion has a power to attract because it appeals to the metaphysical tendency that exists in man to make sense out of the enigma of existence. Furthermore, it also addresses a

---

[774] Ibid., S.737. "Jene große, im Christenthum, wie in Brahmanismus und Buddhaismus enthaltene Grundwahrheit also, nämlich das Bedürfniß der Erlösung aus einem Daseyn, welches dem Leiden und dem Tod anheimgefaliß ist, und die Erreichbarkeit derselben durch Verneinung des Willens, also durch ein entschiedenes der Natur Entgegentreten, ist ohne allen Vergleich die wichtigste, die es geben kann..."; Ibid., p.628.

[775] Ibid., S.737-738; Ibid., p.629.

[776] *Parerga II*, Kap.15, §174, X, S.372. "*Philalethes*...Eine wahre Philosophie kann es danach allenfalls geben; aber gar keine wahre Religion: ich meine wahr im wahren und eigentlichen Wortverstande und nicht bloß so durch die Blume, oder Allegorie...in welchem Sinne vielmehr jede wahr seyn wird, nur in verschiedenen Graden."; *Parerga*, II, ch.15, §174, pp.372-373.

[777] Cf. Salaquarda, S.324-325.

sense or feeling within the human consciousness that behind the physical aspect of the world, there must be something metaphysical.[778]

Schopenhauer thereby notes that religion at bottom appeals to the will, to the fear and hope of human beings who live burdened by constant sorrow and affliction -- to that will in man which creates gods and demons before whom the knee can bend in the hope of obtaining favor.[779] This claim made in *Parerga und Paralipomena*, Schopenhauer's last major published work in 1851, is even stronger in *Über den Willen in der Natur*, which was published several years beforehand (1835). In this passage it is contended that "demons and gods of every kind are always hypostases by means of which believers of every color and sect make comprehensible for themselves the *metaphysical*, that which lies *behind* nature, that which confers existence and permanence to her, and consequently rules over her."[780] But Schopenhauer's classical work, *Die Welt als Wille und Vorstellung* (1819), alludes to the folly of crying to a god hypostatized by human fears so as to alleviate the burden of existence given the will's omnipotence.[781] In

---

[778] *Parerga II*, Kap.15, §174, X, S.371-372. "Diese [Religion] nun, auf Auktorität gestützt, wendet sich zunächst an die eigentlich metaphysische Anlage des Menschen, also an das theoretische Bedürfniß, welches aus dem sich aufdringenden Räthsel unsers Daseyns und aus dem Bewußtseyn hervorgeht, daß hinter dem Physischen der Welt irgendwie ein Metaphysisches stecken müsse, ein Unwandelbares, welches dem beständigen Wandel zur Grundlage dient."; *Parerga*, II, ch.15, §174, p.336.

[779] *Ibid.* "...sodann aber an den Willen, an Furcht und Hoffnung der in steter Noth lebenden Sterblichen: sie schafft ihnen demnach Götter und Dämonen, die sie anrufen, die sie besänftigen, die sie gewinnen können."; *Ibid.*

[780] *Natur*, "Animalischer Magnetismus und Magie," V, S.309-310; *Nature*, "Animal Magnetism and Magic," p.344.

[781] *Vorstellung I*, §59, II, S.407. "Vergebens ruft dann der Gequälte seine Götter um Hülfe an: er bleibt seinem Schicksal ohne Gnade Preis gegeben. Die Rettungslosigkeit ist aber eben nur der Spiegel der Unbezwinglichkeit seines Willens, dessen Objektität seine Person ist. - So wenig eine äußere Macht diesen

fact, his essay "*Über das metaphysiche Bedürfniß des Menschen*" in the second volume of the aforementioned work (1844), states that belief in gods characteristic to systems of popular metaphysics, is not only linked to, but dependent upon, man's longing for immortality.[782]

It is clear, based on the above discussion, that Schopenhauer places no significance in religion as being an encounter with the Holy. For the Holy, as he sees it from a philosophical point of view, *does not* exist other than as a hypostatized projection of man's anxiety and fear. Individuals may indeed cry to Heaven (as they in fact do) in search for an answer to the enigma of life, only to be greeted by resounding silence.[783] The fate of man is such that "we exist

---

Willen ändern oder aufheben kann, so wenig auch kann irgend eine fremde Macht ihn von den Quaalen befreien, die aus dem Leben hervorgehn, welches die Erscheinung jenes Willens ist. Immer ist der Mensch auf sich selbst zurückgewiesen, wie in jeder, so in der Hauptsache. Vergebens macht er sich Götter, um von ihnen zu erbetteln und zu erschmeicheln was nur die eigene Willenskraft herbeizuführen vermag."; *Representation*, I, §59, pp.325-326.

[782] *Vorstellung II*, Kap.17, III, S.187-188. "Wenn unser Leben endlos und schmerzlos wäre, würde es vielleicht doch Keinem einfallen zu fragen, warum die Welt dasei und gerade diese Beschaffenheit habe; sondern eben auch sich Alles von selbst verstehn. Dem entsprechend finden wir, daß das Interesse, welches philosophische, oder auch religiöse Systeme einflößen, seinen allerstärksten Anhaltspunkt durchaus an dem Dogma irgend einer Fortdauer nach dem Tode hat: und wenn gleich die letzteren das Daseyn ihrer Götter zur Hauptsache zu machen und dieses am eifrigsten zu vertheidigen scheinen; so ist dies im Grunde doch nur, weil sie an dasselbe ihr Unsterblichkeitsdogma geknüpft haben und es für unzertrennlich von ihm halten: nur um dieses ist es ihnen eigentlich zu thun. Denn wenn man ihnen dasselbe anderweitig sicher stellen könnte; so würde der lebhafte Eifer für ihre Götter alsbald erkalten, und er würde fast gänzlicher Gleichgültigkeit Platz machen, wenn, umgekehrt, die völlige Unmöglichkeit einer Unsterblichkeit ihnen bewiesen wäre: denn das Interesse am Daseyn der Götter verschwände mit der Hoffnung einer nähern Bekanntschaft mit ihnen, bis auf den Rest, der sich an ihren möglichen Einfluß auf die Vorfälle des gegenwärtigen Lebens knüpfen möchte."; *Representation*, II, ch.17. p.161.

[783] *Parerga II*, Kap.15, §176, "Offenbarung," X, S.398. "Die ephemeren Geschlechter der Menschen entstehn und vergehn in rascher Succession, während die Individuen unter Angst, Noth und Schmerz dem Tode in die Arme tanzen. Dabei fragen es ermüdlich, was es mit ihnen sei, und was die ganze tragikomische Posse zu bedeuten habe, und rufen den Himmel an, um Antwort. Aber der Himmel bleibt stumm. Hingegen kommen Pfaffen mit Offenbarungen."; *Parerga*, II, ch.15, §176, "Revelation," p.361.

without knowing whence, whither, and to what purpose."[784] Nor is morality linked necessarily with theism or belief in the Holy. Though he praises the ethical aspects of Christianity and other religions to the extent that they correspond to his philosophy of the denial of the will-to-live, he underscores that "genuine morals and morality are not dependent upon any religion although every religion sanctions them and thereby gives them support."[785] Accordingly, for Schopenhauer, the moral consciousness exists in man independently of religion; and it is to this, that religion as a system of metaphysics, appeals.[786]

It is the ethical dimension of a given system of religious belief that makes it attractive for a philosopher. For Schopenhauer the fact that a given religion may be founded on a single event has little importance in comparison to its ethical teaching. In fact, he holds this to be senseless and having nothing to do with a religion's value.[787] Belief understood in that sense is more apropos for the childish mind which is incapable of realizing that revelation is nothing more than the thoughts of sages who, as human beings, are

---

[784] *Ibid.*; *Ibid*.

[785] *Ibid.*, §181, "Rationalismus," S.432; *Ibid.*, §181, "Rationalism," p.392.

[786] *Ibid.*, §174, S.372. "...endlich aber auch wendet sie sich an ihr unleugbar vorhandenes moralisches Bewußtseyn, dem sie Bestätigung und Anhalt von außen verleiht, eine Stütze, ohne welche dasselbe, im Kampfe mit so vielen Versuchungen, sich nicht leicht würde aufrecht erhalten können."; *Ibid.*, §174, p.336.

[787] *Ibid.*, §182, S.433. "Eine Religion, die zu ihrem Fundament eine *einzelne Begebenheit* hat, ja aus dieser, die sich da und da, dann und dann zugetragen, den Wendepunkt der Welt und alles Daseyns machen will, hat ein so schwaches Fundament, daß sie unmöglich bestehn kann, sobald einiges Nachdenken unter die Leute gekommen."; *Ibid.*, §182, p.393.

subject to error.[788] This notwithstanding, it is interesting to note that Schopenhauer contends that with the continued development of the sciences and knowledge, the influence of religion on mankind would continue to wane.[789] Yet, at the same time, a tension or dialectic exists in his thinking on this very point. One more glance at the dialogue between Philalethes and Demopheles will prove helpful to substantiate this claim of mine. Via Philalethes, the wish is expressed for the eventual disappearance of religion as a system of metaphysics, with the advance of knowledge and the capacity to assimilate it. But, on the other hand, Demopheles serves to trumpet the more realistic view that given man's metaphysical need and innate differences in the capacity to grasp truth, religions as a phenomenon of human experience will always exist.[790]

---

[788] Ibid., §176, S.399. "Der aber ist nur noch ein großes Kind, welcher im Ernst denken kann, daß jemals Wesen, die keine Menschen waren, unserm Geschlecht Aufschlüsse über sein und der Welt Daseyn und Zweck gegeben hätten. Es giebt keine andere Offenbarung, als die Gedanken der Weisen; wenn auch diese, dem Loose alles Menschlichen gemäß, dem Irrthum unterworfen, auch oft in wunderliche Allegorien und Mythen eingekleidet sind, wo sie dann Religionen heißen."; Ibid., §176, p.361.

[789] Ibid., §181, S.431-432. "So ist denn augenscheinlich, daß nachgerade die Völker schon damit umgehn, das Joch des Glaubens abzuschütteln: die Symptome davon zeigen sich überall, wiewohl in jedem Lande anders modificirt. Die Ursache ist das zu viele Wissen, welches unter sie gekommen ist. Die sich täglich vermehrenden und nach allen Richtungen sich immer weiter verbreitenden Kenntnisse jeder Art erweitern den Horizont eines Jeden, je nach seiner Sphäre, so sehr, daß er endlich eine Größe erlangen muß, gegen welche die Mythen, welche das Skelett des Christenthums ausmachen, dermaaßen einschrumpfen, daß der Glaube nicht mehr daran haften kann. Die Menschheit wächst die Religion aus, wie ein Kinderkleid; und da ist kein Halten: es platzt."; Ibid., §181, p.392.

[790] Ibid., §174, S.373-374; Ibid., §174, pp.337-338.

B. The Reality of God

1. The untenability of the proofs for God's existence

For Schopenhauer discourse about a personal, Creator God makes no philosophical sense in light of the Kantian critique which, in his eyes, discredits the ontological, cosmological and physico-theological proofs for God's existence.[791] A clear indication of what exactly is meant by the word *God* in Schopenhauer's *Weltanschauung* is given in *Über die vierfache Wurzel des Satzes vom zureichenden Grunde* (1813) where the following is stated: "The word *God*, honestly used, denotes such a cause of the world with the addition of personality."[792]

Another passage from the same work is even more specific in that the above notion is expanded. Here Schopenhauer contends that "the doctrine of God" entails that the Supreme Being be understood as "creator and ruler of the world, a personal and therefore an individual being endowed with understanding and will, who has brought it forth out of nothing and guides it with highest wisdom, power and goodness."[793] In *Parerga und*

---

[791] "Kritik des Kantischen Philosophie," *Vorstellung I*, II,S.623-624. "Was nun die Ausführung betrifft, so war zur Widerlegung des *ontologischen* Beweises des Daseyns Gottes gar noch keine Vernunftkritik von Nöthen, indem auch ohne Voraussetzung der Aesthetik und Analytik es sehr leicht ist deutlich zu machen, daß jeder ontologische Beweis nichts ist, als ein spitzfündiges Spiel mit Begriffen, ohne alle Ueberzeugungskraft...
Die Widerlegung des *kosmologischen* Beweises ist eine Anwendung der bis dahin vorgetragenen Lehre der Kritik auf einen gegebenen Fall, und nichts dagegen zu erinnern. - Der *physikotheologische* Beweis ist eine bloße Amplifikation des kosmologischen, den er voraussetzt, und findet auch seine ausführliche Widerlegung erst in der Kritik der Urtheilskraft."; "Criticism of the Kantian Philosophy," *Representation*, I, p.511.

[792] *Grunde*, §8, V, S.25; *Reason*, §8, p.18.

[793] *Ibid.*, §34, S.140; *Ibid.*, §34, p.182.

Paralipomena (1851) the same claims are once again clearly underscored.

> ...the assumption of some cause of the world different therefrom is still not theism. For this demands not only a world-cause that is different from the world, but one which is intelligent, that is, which knows and wills, thus is personal and consequently individual; it is only such a cause that is indicated by the word God. An impersonal God is no God at all, but merely a misused word, a misconception, a *contradictio in adjecto*, shibboleth for professors of philosophy...[794]

From a mere philosophical point of view that prescinds from the data of revelation, it is Schopenhauer's contention that the existence of a personal God with the above attributes cannot be proven from the data of experience. Thus, he is not in agreement with supporters of the *ontological proof for God's existence* who contend that the notion of existence is already contained in the concept of a supremely perfect Being.[795] This simply is not the case because existence does not follow from the mere definition of a thing.[796] Calling the proof a "delightful farce", Schopenhauer maintains that the attributes it ascribes to God are empirically groundless and that the ontological proof in effect is but a 'phantom' in one's brain. Besides, honesty demands that one admit that the attributes ascribed to God in this proof ultimately pertain to the order of the imagination

---

[794] *Parerga I*, §13, "Fragmente zur Geschichte der Philosophie," VII, S.131; *Parerga I*, §13, "Fragments for the History of Philosophy," p.115.

[795] Cf. *Grunde*, §7, V, S.22-24; *Reason*, §7, p.14-16 for a detailed critique of the ontological proof as outlined by Descartes, for example.

[796] *Ibid.*, S.23; *Ibid.*, p.16.

and, as such, are not valid from a philosophical point of view.[797]

With regard to the *cosmological* proof, Schopenhauer admits at the outset that if the exigence of reason could "attain to the concept of God, even without revelation, this obviously happens only under the guidance of causality."[798] But given his analysis of causality as pertaining only to an endless series of changes in states of matter, "a First Cause is as unthinkable as a beginning of time or a limit for space."[799] This means in effect, therefore, that there is but one correct formulation of the law of causality in Schopenhauer's *Weltanschauung*: "*every change has its cause in another change immediately preceding it.*"[800]

---

[797] *Ibid.*, S.23-24. "Uebrigens ist die einfache Antwort auf eine solche ontologische Demonstration: »Es kommt Alles darauf an, wo du deinen Begriff her hast: ist er aus der Erfahrung geschöpft; à *la bonne heure*, [recht so!], da existirt sein Gegenstand und bedarf keines weiteren Beweises: ist er hingegen in deinem eigenen *sinciput* [Halbkopf] ausgeheckt: da helfen ihm alle Prädikate nichts: er ist eben ein Hirnsgespinst."; *Ibid.*, p.15.

[798] *Vorstellung I*, "Kritik des Kantischen Philosophie," II, S.621; *Representation*, I, "Criticism of the Kantian Philosophy," p.509.

[799] *Freiheit*, III., VI, S.66. "Das Gesetz der Kausalität steht a *priori* fest, als die allgemeine Regel, welcher alle reale Objekte der Außenwelt ohne Ausnahme unterworfen sind. Diese Ausnahmslosigkeit verdankt es eben seiner Apriorität. Dasselbe bezieht sich wesentlich und ausschließlich auf *Veränderungen*, und besagt, daß wo und wann, in der objektiven, realen, materiellen Welt, irgend etwas, groß oder klein, viel oder wenig, sich *verändert*, nothwendig gleich *vorher* auch etwas Anderes sich *verändert* haben muß, und damit *dieses* sich *veränderte, vor ihm* wieder ein Anderes, und so ins Unendliche, ohne daß irgend ein Anfangspunkt dieser regressiven Reihe von Veränderungen, welche die Zeit erfüllt, wie die Materie den Raum, jemals abzusehn, oder auch nur als möglich zu denken, geschweige vorauszusetzen wäre. Denn die unermüdlich sich erneuernde Frage »was führte diese Veränderung herbei?« gestattet dem Verstande nimmermehr einen letzten Ruhepunkt; wie sehr er auch dabei ermüden mag: weshalb eine erste Ursache gerade so undenkbar ist, wie ein Anfang der Zeit oder eine Gränze des Raumes. - Nicht minder besagt das Gesetz der Kausalität, daß wenn die frühere Veränderung, - *die Ursache*, - eingetreten ist, die dadurch herbeigeführte spätere, - die *Wirkung*, - ganz unausbleiblich eintreten muß, mithin *nothwendig* erfolgt."; *Freedom*, III., p.28.

[800] *Vorstellung II*, Kap.4, III, S.54. "Der allein richtige Ausdruck für das Gesetz der Kausalität ist dieser: *jede Veränderung hat ihre Ursache in einer andern, ihr unmittelbar vorhergängigen*. Wenn etwas *geschieht*, d.h. ein neuer Zustand eintritt, d.h. etwas sich *verändert*; so muß gleich vorher etwas Anderes

Religion and God   297

For this reason, Schopenhauer states: "...show me an unmoved cause; it is simply impossible."[801] The law of causality, in short, is immanent to the world and has no transcendent application; which is to say, that it finds its application to all things in the world, but not to the world itself.[802] Quite obviously, therefore, discourse about a First Cause in this respect has no significance.

It is interesting to note that Schopenhauer in *Über die vierfache Wurzel des Satzes vom zureichenden Grunde* states that the *physico-theological* argument for God's existence "has much more plausibility (*viel mehr Scheinbarkeit*)."[803] Teleological factors in the cosmos seemingly suggest that the universe in some way or another is the product of a mind other than our own. A rationale for the appeal of this argument is given in *Über den Willen in der Natur*:

> The evident suitability of each animal to its manner of life and outward means of subsistence, even down to the smallest detail, and the exceeding perfection of its organization, is the richest material of teleological contemplation to which the human

---

sich *verändert* haben; vor diesem wieder etwas Anderes, und so aufwärts ins Unendliche: denn eine *erste* Ursache ist so unmöglich zu denken, wie ein Anfang der Zeit, oder eine Gränze des Raums. Mehr, als das Angegebene, besagt das Gesetz der Kausalität nicht: also treten seine Ansprüche erst bei *Veränderungen* ein."; *Representation*, II, ch.4, p.42.

[801] *Ibid.*; *Ibid.*

[802] *Ibid.*, S.56. "Ueberhaupt also findet das Gesetz der Kausalität auf alle Dinge in der Welt Anwendung, jedoch nicht auf die Welt selbst: denn es ist der Welt *immanent*, nicht transscendent: *mit ihr* ist es gesetzt und *mit ihr* aufgehoben. Dies liegt zuletzt daran, daß es zur bloßen Form unsers Verstandes gehört und, mit sammt der objektiven Welt, die deshalb bloße Erscheinung ist, durch ihn bedingt ist. Also auf alle Dinge der Welt, versteht sich ihrer Form nach, auf den Wechsel dieser Formen, also auf ihre Veränderungen, findet das Gesetz der Kausalität volle Anwendung und leidet keine Ausnahme: es gilt vom Thun des Menschen, wie vom Stoße des Steines; jedoch, wie gesagt, immer nur in Bezug auf Vorgänge, auf *Veränderungen*."; *Ibid.*, p.43.

[803] *Grunde*, §20, V, S.56; *Reason*, §20, p.62.

mind from time immemorial has readily applied itself...The universal fitness for their ends, the obvious intentionality in all parts of the animal organism clearly announce that here forces of nature are not working accidentally and without a plan, but rather that a will has been active.[804]

As the above indicates, the physico-theological proof for God's existence is grounded on the apparent finality in the cosmos as especially evidenced in animal organisms. This would imply that the world in some way or another is the product of an intellect or mind. Schopenhauer, however rejects this possibility at the very outset. Succinctly stated:

The world is not made with the help of knowledge and therefore not from without, but from within...The physico-theological thought that an intellect must have ordered and modeled nature, which is suitable to the unrefined mind, is superficial and nevertheless fundamentally wrong.[805]

Schopenhauer goes on to argue that the intellect, as secondary, can never have been the condition for the world's existence since it is a subordinate principle to the noumenal will, and consequently of a latter origin.[806] What teleological facticity there is in the cosmos, as particularly evidenced by the finality evident in each animal organism, is clearly ascribed to the noumenal will, which is the principle of being. The following passage makes this clear:

...the will, as that which fills everything and manifests itself immediately in each, thus characterizing everything as its phenomenon, appears everywhere as that which is primary.

---

[804] *Natur*, "Vergleichende Anatomie," V, S.235; *Nature*, "Comparative Anatomy," p.255.

[805] *Ibid.*, S.237; *Ibid.*, p.257-258.

[806] *Ibid.*, S.237-238; *Ibid.*, p.258.

> It is just for this reason, that all teleological facts are to be explained from the will of the being itself in which they are observed.[807]

This notwithstanding, it cannot be denied that one who contemplates the endless appropriateness in the structure of organic beings is seized with astonishment. Schopenhauer says that this in itself is natural, but rests on the false assumption that "the *agreement* of the parts with one another, with the whole of the organism, and with its aims in the external world, as we comprehend and judge it by means of *knowledge*....has also come into being in the same way; that as it exists *for* the intellect, it also was brought into existence *through* the intellect."[808] Besides, the physico-theological proof, as he sees it, is weakened by empirical observation itself inasmuch as the works of animal artistic instinct show themselves to be the work of a blind drive and not of a will that is led by knowledge.

> ...the physico-theological proof may already be refuted by the empirical observation that works produced by animal instinct, such as the spider's web, the bee's honeycomb, the termite's construction, and so forth, are throughout constituted as if they were the result of a concept of purpose, of a far-reaching providence, and of rational deliberation; whereas they are evidently the work of a blind impulse, i.e. of a will not guided by knowledge.[809]

Moreover, beneath the veneer of the teleological facticity of nature, there lies the will's diseased

---

[807] *Ibid.*, S.238; *Ibid.*.

[808] *Vorstellung II*, Kap.26, III, S.383; *Representation*, II, ch.26, p.327.

[809] *Natur*, "Vergleichende Anatomie," V, S.238; *Nature*, "Comparative Anatomy," p.258.

essence which alone explains reality's scarredness.[810] Schopenhauer, accordingly, is not swayed by the call to behold the world's external beauty given the reality of pain and suffering. He states categorically: "But is the world then a peep show (*Guckkasten*)? These things are beautiful to *behold*, but to *be* them is something altogether different."[811] In short, the suffering and pain that come to the foreground with the appearance of sensibility and intelligence in the animal and human sphere of phenomenal being, prohibit the honest person "to break out into hallelujahs."[812] It goes without saying, therefore, that the physico-theological argument is not acceptable for Schopenhauer.

2. Revelation and God

In light of the above, there is indeed no God in Schopenhauer's *Weltanschauung*, nor does reality serve as a bridge that might lead to Him. This notwithstanding, three passages from the corpus of his thought imply, at the very least, that God's existence does not hinge upon the aforementioned proofs. As a case in point, the claim is made in *Über die vierfache Wurzel des Satzes vom zureichenden Grunde* that the impossibility to prove the existence of God does not call into question that existence; inasmuch as it stands on the firmer

---

[810] *Vorstellung II*, Kap.46, IV, S.678. "...nur ein blinder, kein sehender Wille konnte sich selbst in die Lage versetzen, in der wir uns erblicken."; *Representation*, II, ch.46, p.579.

[811] *Ibid.*, S.680; *Ibid.*, p.581.

[812] *Ibid.*, S.681; *Ibid.*

ground of revelation.[813] So as to remove any doubt about what he means, Schopenhauer repeats himself later in the same section (§ 35) of the aforementioned work: "...the existence of God is a matter of revelation (*Sache der Offenbarung*) and is unshakably established thereby."[814] Given that God's existence in the Christian religion is an established fact according to Revelation, another passage from *Parerga und Paralipomena* highlights the futility of attempting to prove God's existence otherwise than from the scriptures.

> In the Christian religion the existence of God is an established fact and beyond all investigation. This is as it should be; for it belongs here and is itself established by revelation. I therefore regard it as a mistake of the rationalists, when they attempt in their dogmas to prove the existence of God otherwise than from the Scriptures.[815]

What Schopenhauer says in these three passages, however, is substantially weakened by his claim that revelation is nothing more than the thoughts of sages, who as human beings, are subject to error.[816] Given this unfortunate demythologization of revelation, it is difficult to see how Schopenhauer can still maintain that God's existence rests on unshakable ground. For theism and its claims

---

[813] *Grunde*, §34, V, S.141. "Denn durch jene Unbeweisbarkeit wird das Daseyn Gottes selbst nicht im Mindesten angefochten; da es auf viel sicherem Boden und unerschütterlich fest steht. Es ist ja Sache der Offenbarung, und zwar ist es Dies um so gewisser, als solche Offenbarung allein und ausschließlich demjenigen Volke, welches deshalb das auserwählte heißt, zu Theil geworden ist. Dies ist daraus ersichtlich, daß die Erkenntniß Gottes, als des persönlichen Regierers und Schöpfers der Welt, der Alles wohlgemacht, sich ganz allein in der Jüdischen und den beiden aus ihr hervorgegangenen Glaubenslehren, die man, im weitern Sinne, ihre Sekten nennen könnte, findet, nicht aber in der Religion irgend eines andern Volkes, alter oder neuer Zeit."; *Reason*, §34, p.183.

[814] *Ibid.*, S.145; *Ibid.*, p.188.

[815] *Parerga I*, §13, "Fragmente zur Geschichte der Philosophie," VII, S.121; *Parerga*, I, §13, "Fragments for the History of Philosophy," pp.105-106.

[816] Cf. footnote 787.

are said to spring solely from the agitated heart of man.[817] Instead of God's existence resting on the solid ground of a revelation whose origin is properly divine, it rests on the sandy soil of a hypostasis of human fear.[818] Accordingly for Schopenhauer, praying to a divine being is at bottom a form of *idolatry*, inasmuch as the God before whom the knee is bent in adoration, is as much a fabrication of human ingenuity as are idols of wood, stone or metal.

> Whether we make an idol out of wood, stone, or metal, or construct it from abstract concepts, it is all the same. It remains *idolatry*, as soon we have before us a personal being to whom we offer sacrifices and whom we invoke and thank. At bottom it is not so different whether we offer our sheep, or our inclinations. Each rite or prayer undeniably is evidence of *idolatry*.[819]

---

[817] *Parerga I*, §13, "Fragmente zur Geschichte der Philosophie," VII, S.133-134. "Der Theismus nämlich ist in der That kein Erzeugniß der *Erkenntniß*, sondern des *Willens*...Aus dem Willen aber entspringt er folgendermaßen. Die beständige Noth, welche das Herz (Willen) des Menschen bald schwer beängstigt, bald heftig bewegt und ihn fortwährend im Zustande des Fürchtens und Hoffens erhält, während die Dinge, von denen er hofft und fürchtet, nicht in seiner Gewalt stehn...dies stete Fürchten und Hoffen, bringt ihn dahin, daß er die Hypostase persönlicher Wesen macht, von denen Alles abhienge."; *Parerga*, I, §13, "Fragments for the History of Philosophy," p.117.

[818] *Ibid.*, S.134. "Das Wesentliche jedoch ist der Drang des geängsteten Menschen, sich niederzuwerfen und Hülfe anzuflehen, in seiner häufigen, kläglichen und großen Noth und auch hinsichtlich seiner ewigen Säligkeit. Der Mensch verläßt sich lieber auf fremde Gnade, als auf eigenes Verdienst: Dies ist eine Hauptstütze des Theismus. Damit also sein Herz (Wille) die Erleichterung des Betens und den Trost des Hoffens habe, muß sein Intellekt ihm einen Gott schaffen; nicht aber ungekehrt, weil sein Intellekt auf einen Gott logisch richtig geschlossen hat, betet er. Laßt ihn ohne Noth, Wünsche und Bedürfnisse seyn, etwan ein bloß intellektuelles, willenloses Wesen; so braucht er keinen Gott und macht auch keinen. Das Herz, d.i. der Wille, hat in seiner schweren Bedrängniß das Bedürfniß, allmächtigen, folglich übernatürlichen Beistand anzurufen: weil also gebetet werden soll, wird ein Gott hypostasirt; nicht umgekehrt."; *Ibid.*, pp.117-118.

[819] *Parerga II*, §178, X, S.416-417; *Parerga*, II, §178, pp.377-378.

3. Mystery of evil and God's existence

The basic stumbling block, however, for the reasonableness of belief in God, is the stubborn and continued existence of evil and wickedness, which Schopenhauer ascribes to the scarred will in man. As early as 1808-1809, the young Schopenhauer postulated that if there was a Good Will in reality, there then exists alongside of it an evil power that throws it offstride and compels it into detours, or one must ascribe that power to chance, which means that the Guiding Will is flawed.[820] Safranski in *Schopenhauer und die wilden Jahre der Philosophie* finds this passage particularly significant calling it a "dethronement of God by a dualistic construction."[821] Schopenhauer, of course, subsequently rejected this type of dualism and excluded God from his metaphysical picture of reality. Accordingly, the evil power in the aforementioned fragment from the *Nachlaß* becomes the streaked will-to-live which comprises the "true *ens realissimum*" with which we are most familiar.[822] Convinced of the glaring

---

[820] *Nachlaß*, I, #12 [vii], S.9; "Entweder ist alles vollkommen, das Größte wie das Kleinste, keins dem andern geopfert, es sind in allem zum besten Zweck die vollkommensten Mittel, die wie die einzige gerade Linie zu ihm führen, vorhanden: dann müßte jedes Leiden, jeder Irrtum, jede Angst nicht etwa notwendiges, durch andere Einrichtungen bedingtes und entschädigtes Uebel sein, sondern wirklich das unmittelbare, einzig rechte, beste Mittel, auch außer allem Zusammenhang mit dem übrigen; oder aber -- und wer könnte denn angesichts dieser Welt bei jener Annahme stehnbleiben? -- es sind nur zwei andere Fälle möglich: wir müssen -- wenn nicht alles zum bösen Zweck annehmen -- neben dem guten Willen einem bösen Willen Gewalt zugestehn, der jenen zu Umwegen zwingt, *oder* wir müssen diese Gewalt nur dem Zufall und also dem lenkenden Willen Unvollkommenheit in der Anordnung oder in der Macht zuschreiben." *Remains*, I, #12 [vii], p.9.

[821] Safranski, S.97.

[822] *Natur*, "Hinweisung auf die Ethik," V, S.340. "Wenn ich also sage »Wille, Wille zum Leben«; so ist das kein *ens rationis*, keine von mir selbst gemachte Hypostase, auch kein Wort von ungewisser, schwankender Bedeutung: sondern wer mir frägt, was es sei, den weise ich an sein eigenes Inneres, wo er es vollständig, ja, in kolossaler Größe vorfindet, als ein wahres *ens realissimum*."; *Nature*, "Reference to Ethics," p.376.

reality of diseased human willing, Schopenhauer in his mature work contends that no power exists which can straighten the crooked wood that man is.[823] But what continues to be problematic for him about the claim that the world is the product of a Creator-God, is precisely that the same Almighty Being seems so impotent before the reality of wickedness and evil in His creation -- the claim alluded to above in the early fragment from the *Nachlaß*.[824] Moreover, according to Schopenhauer, belief in a Creator-God leads to yet another problem: the thorny issue of moral responsibility for actions. For it would seem that responsibility for actions would ultimately boomerang to God who is Creator. As is stated in *Über die Freiheit des menschlichen Willens*: "If a bad act originates from nature, that is, the inborn constitution of man, then the guilt obviously lies with the creator of this nature."[825] Belief in a personal Creator-God is thereby unacceptable because it compromises the doctrine of moral responsibility for one's actions.[826] Here then is yet another reason for

---

[823] *Vorstellung I*, §59, II, S.407. "So wenig eine äußere Macht diesen Willen ändern oder aufheben kann, so wenig auch kann irgend eine fremde Macht ihn von den Quaalen befreien, die aus dem Leben hervorgehn, welches die Erscheinung jenes Willens ist."; *Representation*, I, §59, pp.325-326.

[824] *Vorstellung II*, Kap.17, III, S.200-201. "Die soeben Ausgesprochene nähere Beschaffenheit des Erstaunens, welches zum Philosophiren treibt, entspringt offenbar aus dem Anblick *des Uebels und des Bösen* in der Welt, welche, selbst wenn sie im gerechtesten Verhältniß zu einander ständen, ja, auch noch vom Guten weit überwogen würden, dennoch Etwas sind, was ganz und gar und überhaupt nicht seyn sollte. Weil nun aber nichts aus Nichts stehn kann; so müssen auch jene ihren Keim im Ursprunge, oder im Kern der Welt selbst haben. Dies anzunehmen wird uns schwer, wenn wir auf die Größe, Ordnung und Vollendung der physischen Welt sehn, indem wir meinen, daß was die Macht hatte, eine solche hervorzubringen, auch wohl hätte das Uebel und das Böse müssen vermeiden können."; *Representation*, II, ch.17, pp.171-172.

[825] *Freiheit*, IV., VI, S.113; *Freedom*, IV., p.74.

[826] *Parerga II*, §118, "Zur Ethik," IX, S.256. "Der Begriff einer *moralischen Freiheit* hingegen ist unzertrennlich von dem der *Ursprünglichkeit*. Denn daß ein Wesen das Werk eines Andern, dabei aber, seinem Wollen und Thun

rejecting traditional religion: "...theism and man's moral responsibility are irreconcilable because the responsibility quite certainly falls back upon the creator of the nature where it has its center of gravity."[827] In this respect, the doctrine of moral responsibility for actions is salvageable for Schopenhauer only to the extent that man is his "own work" -- and not that of another. The following passage from *Die Welt als Wille und Vorstellung* makes this clear:

> My philosophy...is the only one that grants to morality its complete and entire rights; for only if the essence of man is his own *will*, consequently only if he is in the strictest sense, his own work, are his deeds actually completely his and attributable to him. On the other hand, as soon as he has another origin, or is the work of a being different from himself, all his guilt falls back on to this origin or originator. For *operari sequitur esse*.[828]

It is clear that what comes to the foreground with this analysis of the phenomenon of religion and the question of God, is that Schopenhauer's thought is unmistakably atheistic in its main thrust. For he simply finds reverent belief in a Creator-God totally out of the question in light of his philosophical convictions.[829]

---

nach, *frei* sei, läßt sich mit Worten sagen, aber nicht mit Gedanken erreichen. Der nämlich, welcher ihn aus nichts ins Daseyn rief, hat eben damit auch sein Wesen, d.h. seine sämmtlichen Eigenschaften, mitgeschaffen und festgestellt. Denn nimmermehr kann man schaffen, ohne daß man ein Etwas schaffe, d.h. ein durchweg und allen seinen Eigenschaften nach genau bestimmtes Wesen."; *Parerga*, II, §118, "On Ethics," pp.235-236.

[827] *Ibid.*, S.257; *Ibid.*, p.236.

[828] *Vorstellung* II, Kap.47, IV, S.690-691; *Representation*, II, ch.47, pp.589-590.

[829] *Parerga II*, §178, X, S.416. "Wenn ich aber suche, mir vorstellig zu machen, daß ich vor einem individuellen Wesen stände, zu dem ich sagte: »mein Schöpfer! ich bin einst nichts gewesen: du aber hast mich hervorgebracht, so daß ich jetzt etwas und zwar ich bin;« - und dazu noch: »ich danke dir für diese Wohlthat;« - und am Ende gar: »wenn ich nichts getaugt habe, so ist das *meine*

But as was already implied above, the atheistic character of his philosophy first began to manifest itself in his teenage years. The following passage from the *Gespräche* is a case in point:

> As a young man I was always melancholic and on one occasion, I was perhaps eighteen years old then, I reflected, even at this early age: This world is supposed to have been made by God? No much rather by a devil![830]

Two more fragments from the *Nachlaß* are worth citing at this juncture so as to underscore the atheism of Schopenhauer's mature years. The biting sarcasm and tone which he employs clearly reveals his rejection of faith in God as a reasonable alternative for himself at least. The first passage is taken from the "Quartant" section of his manuscript notes written at Dresden in 1824. The second passage is taken from the collection of fragments entitled "Senilia" which dates from 1852 until his death in 1860, found in the last volume of the *Nachlaß*. They run as follows:

> *Prayer of a Skeptic*: God, -- if you exist, -- rescue my soul from the grave, -- if I have one.[831]
>
> *Conversation (Gespräch) from the year 33*: A. Have you heard the latest? / B. No, what's happening? / A. The world is redeemed! / B. What are you saying! / A. Yes, the loving God has assumed human form and allowed himself to be put to death in Jerusalem. For this reason, the world is now redeemed and the Devil beaten (*geprellt*). / B. Why, that's truly charming.[832]

Schuld;« - so muß ich gestehn, daß in Folge philosophischer und Indischer Studien mein Kopf unfähig geworden ist, einen solchen Gedanken auszuhalten."; *Parerga*, II, §178, p.377.

[830] *Gespräche*, S.131.

[831] *Nachlaß III*, S.190; *Manuscript Remains*, p.210.

[832] *Nachlaß*, IV.2, S.21; *Manuscript Remains*, IV, p.380.

What this chapter therefore illustrates up to this point is that the "front door" to God in Schopenhauer's *Weltanschauung* is irremediably bolted shut for these reasons: In the first place, his analysis of religion as the metaphysics of the people makes no mention whatsoever of an encounter with the Sacred or Holy. Secondly, he clearly rejects proofs for God's existence. Thirdly, while he does say that God's existence rests on the sure ground of revelation, his demythologization of the revealed scriptures as the mere thoughts of sages, makes of God a mere human fabrication. Fourthly, belief in God according to Schopenhauer cannot be reconciled with the existence of evil and moral responsibility for actions.

C. The "Back Door" to the Question of God

The immediately preceding section certainly suggests that Schopenhauer's system is completely closed to any possibility of the Sacred. But there are passages in his thought which clearly suggest that the very kernel of the real, which he has identified as the noumenal will, is nevertheless obscured by mystery. The principal reason for this ultimately consists in the fact that inward observation of ourselves as willers (which is the key to discovering what the noumenon is) comes only via successive states in time. Thus he states, for example, in a supplementary essay of *Die Welt als Wille und Vorstellung*:

> ...it is to be carefully taken into consideration, and I have always held fast to this, that even the inner perception (*Wahrnehmung*) which we have of our own will still does not by any means furnish an exhaustive and adequate knowledge of the thing-in-itself...there still remains the form of *time*, as well as that of being-known and knowing in general. Accordingly, in this

> inner knowledge the thing-in-itself has indeed cast off its veils, but still does not appear quite naked. In consequence of the form of time which still adheres to it, everyone knows his *will* only in its successive individual *acts*, but not as a whole, in and for itself.[833]

It is important to note that in every act of the will which emerges from the depths of our inner being into knowing consciousness, there ensues an immediate transition of the noumenon into the phenomenon.[834] In this respect, the act of the will, as known via the route of introspection, is the closest expression of the thing-in-itself in the phenomenal sphere. Accordingly, the Kantian doctrine of the unknowability of the noumenon is modified by Schopenhauer in that the thing-in-itself is merely *not absolutely and completely knowable*.[835]

The implications of this nuance are highly important because they serve to show that Schopenhauer's philosophical system is not completely closed. Given the ambiguity of the thing-in-itself, the end result of ascetical praxis with the complete denial of the will-to-live is not an absolute, but a relative nothingness, which is to say, that it involves a something. Moreover, it suggests that the will can have other modes of

---

[833] *Vorstellung II*, Kap.18, III, S.229-230; *Representation*, II, ch.18, pp.196-197.

[834] *Ibid.*, S.230. "Denn bei jedem Hervortreten eines Willensaktes aus der dunklen Tiefe unsers Innern in das erkennende Bewußtseyn geschieht ein unmittelbarer Uebergang des außer der Zeit liegenden Dinges an sich in die Erscheinung."; *Ibid.*, p.197.

[835] *Ibid.*, S.230-231. "Demnach ist zwar der Willensakt nur die nächste und deutlichste *Erscheinung* des Dinges an sich; doch folgt hieraus, daß wenn alle übrigen Erscheinungen eben so unmittelbar und innerlich von uns erkannt werden könnten, wir sie für eben Das ansprechen müßten, was der Wille in uns ist. In diesem Sinne also lehre ich, daß das innere Wesen eines jeden Dinges *Wille* ist, und nenne den Willen das Ding an sich. Hiedurch wird *Kants* Lehre von der Unerkennbarkeit des Dinges an sich dahin modificirt, daß dasselbe nur nicht schlechthin und von Grund aus erkennbar sei..."; *Ibid.*

existence that differ from its phenomenal expression as we know it. The following citation underscores this:

> ...the question may still be asked what that will, which manifests itself in the world and as the world, is ultimately and absolutely in itself; in other words, what is it apart from the fact that it manifests itself as *will*, or in general *appears*, that is to say, *is known* in general. This question can *never* be answered, because...being-known itself already contradicts being-in-itself, and everything that is known is, as such, only phenomenon (*Erscheinung*). But the possibility of this question shows that the thing-in-itself, which we know most immediately in the will, may have, entirely outside of all possible phenomenon, determinations, qualities, and modes of existence which for us are absolutely unknowable and incomprehensible, and which then remain as the essence of the thing-in-itself, when this...has freely abolished itself (*aufgehoben hat*) as *will*, therefore stepped out of the phenomenon altogether, and with regard to our knowledge, that is to say, as regards the world of phenomena, has passed over into empty nothingness. If the will were simply and absolutely the thing-in-itself, then this nothing would be *absolute*, instead of which it expressly appears to us there as a *relative* nothing.[836]

Even though the above references are taken from a supplementary essay found in the second volume of *Die Welt als Wille und Vorstellung* ("*Von der Erkennbarkeit des Dinges an sich*") first published in 1844,[837] the first volume of the aforementioned work (which first appeared in 1818) admits that the thing-in-itself (the Will) is a "known" insofar as the Ideas are only its "adequate" or "immediate" objectification; individual

---

[836] *Ibid.*, S.231; *Ibid.*, p.198.

[837] Cf. *Vorstellung I*, "Vorrede zur zweiten Auflage," I, S.18-20; *Representation*, I, "Preface to the second edition," pp.xxi-xxiii.

particular things being an "indirect" objectification.[838] In addition to this, while asserting that the will comprises the inner nature of the body which is the starting point for perception of the external world, Schopenhauer underscores that insight into oneself as a willer never comes as a whole, but via particular acts in time.[839] What this implies is that there is more to the will than what is experienced on the phenomenal plane via the route of introspection.

There are also early passages from the *Nachlaß* and the Berlin *Vorlesungen* dating from 1820 which highlight the difficulties involved in categorically stating that the will, as known on the phenomenal plane via the route of introspection, is absolutely the thing-in-itself.[840] As a case in point, the following passages[841] taken respectively from these works speak for themselves:

> The will, as we know it in ourselves, is not the *thing in itself*; for it appears only in individual and successive acts of will; these have *time* for a form and are already phenomenon (*Erscheinung*). However, this appearance is the clearest revelation of the thing-in-itself because it is altogether and *immediately* illumined by knowledge and has received no form other than that of time. With each emergence (*Hervortreten*) of an act of will from the depth of our inner self (*aus*

---

[838] *Vorstellung I*, §32, I, S.227-228; *Representation*, I, §32, pp.174-175.

[839] *Ibid.*, §18, S.145; *Ibid.*, §18, pp.101-102.

[840] Cf. Giuseppe Invernizzi, "Il problema della cosa in sé e la concezione della metafisica nella filosofia di Schopenhauer," *Acme*, 37 (1984), pp.96-97. "Fin dal 1820 dunque Schopenhauer ha individuato con chiarezza la difficoltà cui va incontro la sua dottrina della cosa in sé: per dirla con Kant, l'esperienza interna, in quanto esperienza, è sempre fenomenica."

[841] In this section I will cite some of the same passages from Schopenhauer's work used by Giuseppe Invernizzi in his article: "Il problema della cosa in sé e la concezione della metafisica nella filosofia di Schopenhauer," *Acme*, 37 (1984), 91-109.

der Tiefe unsers Innern) an altogether original and immediate passage of the thing-in-itself (that which lies outside of time) occurs in the phenomenon.[842]

The will, as we find and perceive it in ourselves, is not really the *thing-in-itself*. For this will appears in our consciousness merely in individual and successive acts of will; these therefore already have time for a form, and are for that reason, already phenomenon (*Erscheinung*). This phenomenon, however, is the *clearest revelation*, the clearest becoming-visible (*Sichtbarwerdung*) of the *thing-in-itself*, because it is altogether and immediately illumined by knowledge, object and subject here completely coincide, and here the essence itself which appears, has no other form except that of time.[843]

Though Schopenhauer had not yet made the attempt to identify, or at least relate, willing with the thing-in-itself in *Über die vierfache Wurzel des Satzes vom zureichenden Grunde*, for which he was awarded a Doctorate in philosophy by the University of Jena in 1813, it is important to note that this work already lists the knowledge one has of his willing as a special representation, and hence a phenomenon.[844] It was only with publication of *Die Welt als Wille und Vorstellung* in 1818 that the problem of the noumenal will's stubborn "phenomenality" via the inner experience of willing comes to a head, and serves as a point of departure for continued reflection in the *Nachlaß* and *Vorlesungen*, as

---

[842] *Nachlaß*, III, S.36; *Manuscript Remains*, III, pp.40.

[843] Arthur Schopenhauer, *Philosophische Vorlesungen aus dem handschriftlichen Nachlaß*, Band 2, *Metaphysik der Natur*, herausgegeben und eingeleitet von Volker Spierling (München: Piper, 1987), S.101-102.

[844] *Grunde*, §40, V, S.157. "Die letzte unserer Betrachtung noch übrige Klasse der Gegenstände des Vorstellungsvermögens ist eine gar eigene, aber sehr wichtige: sie begreift für Jeden nur *ein* Objekt, nämlich das unmittelbare Objekt des innern Sinnes, *das Subjekt des Wollens*, welches für das erkennende Subjekt Objekt ist und zwar nur dem innern Sinn gegeben, daher es allein in der Zeit, nicht im Raum, erscheint..."; *Reason*, §40, p.207.

well as in the supplements found in the second volume of *Die Welt als Wille und Vorstellung*. Another fragment from the *Nachlaß* dating from 1821 is significant:

> I have said: "we know our own willing only as a phenomenon (*Erscheinung*), not in-itself."-- I have said furthermore: "the will is the *thing-in-itself*." This is not contradictory. Everything which is *known*, is known only as phenomenon. For to-be-object (*das Objektseyn*), to-become-known (*das Erkanntwerden*), pertains already to the form of the phenomenon. For that reason, that something as thing-in-itself is known, is a contradiction. The thing-in-itself is never that which is known (*das Erkannte*); this is always already phenomenon. I say, "the *will* is the thing-in-itself; but knowledge of the will is already phenomenon." Precisely because it is *knowledge*. But the *cognitio intima* which each person has of his own will is the point where the thing-in-itself enters most clearly in the phenomenon, and must accordingly be the expounder (*der Ausleger*) of every other phenomenon.[845]

The above passages from the *Nachlaß* and the Berlin *Vorlesungen* clearly illustrate Schopenhauer's reluctance to make an *absolute* identification of the thing-in-itself with the will as perceived by the inner sense, as Hübscher indicates.[846] A fragment from the *Nachlaß*

---

[845] *Nachlaß*, III, S.103; *Manuscript Remains*, III, pp.113-114.

[846] Cf. Hübscher, *Denker gegen den Strom*, S.150. "Es ist beachtenswert, daß man bei Schopenhauers Verhältniß zu Kant und der Frage des Dinges an sich einsetzte, als man begann, sein Weltbild als in sich abgeschlossenes Gedankengebilde in Frage zu stellen und nach einem neuen grundsätzlichen Ansatz, nach Entwicklungen, Verschiebungen und Wandlungen in seiner Philosophie zu suchen. Man hat gesagt, Schopenhauer habe die ursprüngliche, im ersten Bande seines Hauptwerks vertretene Gleichsetzung von Wille und Ding an sich 25 Jahre später, im Ergänzungsbande, durch kritische Einschränkungen wieder abgeschwächt, um den Einwand abzuwehren, daß sie anderen Grundlehren seiner Philosophie widerstreite. Bei genauem Zusehen ergibt sich ein anderes Bild: Daß wir den Willen als Ding an sich nicht adäquat, sondern nur in seinen Akten, also zeitlich und erscheinungsmäßig zu erkennen vermögen, das war schon dem ersten Bande unmißverständlich zu entnehmen; auch die »kritischen Einschränkungen« sind da, sie finden sich im Werk ebenso wie in den frühen Manuskriptbüchern und in den Berliner Vorlesungen -- später gewonnener Einsichten bedurfte es nicht.";

(1824) succinctly re-confirms the one immediately above: "To know the *thing-in-itself* is a contradiction, because all knowledge is *representation* (*Vorstellung*); but the thing-in-itself signifies the thing insofar as it is not representation."[847] Accordingly, though the will differs from all other phenomena that appear to consciousness in that it does not have *space* for a form, the fact of the matter is that it remains a phenomenon because of its sole form of time.

> The will is for the intellect a phenomenon (*Phänomen*), an object of its perception, yet such an object differs from all others by the important fact that it does not have space as its form, but merely *time*. Therefore, the *thing-in-itself* has here cast off one of its forms of appearance and shows itself in the only other form; consequently, it appears much less veiled and clearer than anywhere else. For that reason, we describe it as *will* in accordance with this its most immediate appearance.[848]

What the above illustrates is that we have a dichotomy between the will that reveals itself on the phenomenal sphere as a constant striving which, as such, is the source of all discord and woe; and what the will **may be** in-itself independent of the forms of cognition. We have already seen above, the route to insight into the pristine nature of the will is bolted shut; which also serves to highlight the relative nature of the nothingness to which the ascetic, by denying the will-to-live, experiences. Once again, citing the *Nachlaß* and Berlin *Vorlesungen* casts light upon the issue at hand. For the following two passages indicate clearly enough

---

Cf. Invernizzi, pp.96-97 which alludes to the above passage as well in addition to others in footnote 27 in his article cited above.

[847] *Nachlaß*, III, S.178; *Manuscript Remains*, III, p.195.

[848] *Nachlaß*, IV.1, #136, S.134; *Manuscript Remains*, IV, p.159.

that Schopenhauer already by 1820 admitted that given the impossibility to know the will in the absolute sense, the nothingness to which the ascetic attains, is really a mode of existence of the will that transcends phenomenal experience.

> ...the question can still always be asked what, in the final analysis, is the will in-itself? That is to say, what is it apart from the fact that it presents itself as *will*, irrespective of the fact that it appears in general, and therefore is *known* in general. This question is obviously never to be answered, since as has already been said, to-be-known (*das Erkanntwerden*) contradicts the thing-in-itself; and each known thing (*jedes Erkannte*) is, as such, already a phenomenon. However, the existence of this question shows that even the thing-in-itself, which we can never clearly know, insofar as we know it as *will*, may have determinations, qualities and modes of existence, which are absolutely unknowable and incomprehensible to us; and which may even constitute the existence of the thing-in-itself after it has freely abolished itself... after this will has completely stepped out of the phenomenon and for our knowledge, that is, in contrast to the world of appearances, has gone over into empty nothingness. -- Were the will absolutely the thing-in-itself, this nothingness would be absolute nothingness instead of a nothingness which I have precisely presented as relative.[849]

> ...the question can always still be asked *what in the final analysis the will-in-itself may be*? That is to say, what it may be, apart from the fact that it presents itself as Will, that is to say, apart from the fact that it appears in general, hence is *known* in general and is *represented*. This question is obviously *never* to be answered. For to-be-known (*das Erkanntwerden*) contradicts the thing-in-itself; and everything which is represented, is already phenomenon (*Erscheinung*). - Solely from the possibility

---

[849] *Nachlaß*, III, S.36-37; *Manuscript Remains*, III, p.41.

> of this question, it arises that even the thing-in-itself...can have and may have, outside of all possible experience, determinations, qualities and modes of existence, which for us are absolutely ungraspable and unknowable. These qualities may now even constitute the existence of the thing-in-itself, which...presents itself as a passage into *nothingness*, after it has freely abolished itself as will, by means of which the entire world of phenomena is also abolished ...Were the will absolutely the thing-in-itself, then such a nothingness would be an absolute nothingness. But there we will find that it is only a relative nothingness.[850]

It is clear from the passages cited above that the will as purely noumenal *can* and *may* have qualities, determinations and modes of existence other than that which is experienced on the phenomenal realm. But it is aesthetic experience and the denial of the will-to-live as lived out by saints or ascetics, that reveals this. On the phenomenal realm the will *initially* manifests itself as a senseless striving, which is the source of man's depravity and suffering. But in-itself, the will has other potentialities that time to time make their appearance in creations of artistic genius as well as in lives of heroic virtue. It is precisely here where that other dimension of the will as truly noumenal and hence free, comes to light for consciousness. The following passage from the first volume of *Die Welt als Wille und Vorstellung* alludes to this:

> ...man is the most complete phenomenon of the will...Thus, in man the will can reach full self-consciousness, clear and exhaustive knowledge of its essence, as reflected in the whole world. As we saw...art results from the actual presence of this degree of knowledge. At the end of our whole consideration it will

---

[850] *Philosophische Vorlesungen*, II, S.102-103.

> also follow that, through the same knowledge, an elimination and self-denial of the will in its most perfect phenomenon is possible, by the will's relating such knowledge to itself. Thus, the freedom which otherwise, as belonging to the thing-in-itself, can never show itself in the phenomenon, in such a case, appears in the phenomenon; and by abolishing the essence which lies at the root of the phenomenon, while the phenomenon itself continues to exist in time, it brings about a contradiction of the phenomenon with itself. Directly through this, it exhibits the phenomena (*Phänomene*) of holiness and self-denial...By this it is only generally indicated how man is distinguished from all the other phenomena of the will by the fact that freedom, i.e. independence of the principle of sufficient reason, which only belongs to the will as thing-in-itself and contradicts the phenomenon, nevertheless with him can possibly appear even in the phenomenon, where it then presents itself, however, as a contradiction of the phenomenon with itself. In this sense not only the will in itself, but even man can certainly be called free, and in that way be distinguished from all other beings.[851]

It is important to recall that the noumenon reveals itself inasmuch as it emerges from the depth of our inner self in acts of willing. But if the arts and the very phenomenon of self-denial and holiness are indicative that the will as "free" has appeared on the phenomenal plane, their reality is connected with that aspect of the noumenon that is extra-temporal -- the relative nothingness which is also beyond linguistic grasp or explanation. The ramifications of this are important insofar as they serve to highlight the presence of mystery in Schopenhauer's thought, giving some indication as to why darkness and light are intertwined in his system.

---

[851] *Vorstellung I*, II, §55, S.362-363; *Representation*, I, §55, pp.287-288.

The religious question, accordingly, once again emerges inasmuch as by underscoring the relative nature of nothingness, there is a tacit admission that the pristine noumenon has an ulterior reality other than the one that appears in time.[852] Specifically with regard to the phenomenon of denial of the will-to-live, he states that "virtue and holiness do not proceed from reflexion, but from the depth of the will and its relation to knowledge."[853] As such, they are not explainable by a causality introduced by reason alone. Since pain, anguish and wickedness have their origin in the self-estrangement essential to the will in the phenomenon,[854] virtue and holiness are somehow rooted in the extra-temporal dimension of the will described as the "infinitely preferable peace of blessed nothingness."[855] The mind, however, is not satisfied with that explanation and wonders about what those qualities and modes of existence, characteristic to the noumenal will as independent of the temporal order, might in fact be; and why they are connected with, and in some way are, the source of virtue, for example.

Besides, given the presuppositions of Schopenhauer's *Weltanschauung*, the ascetical praxis of

---

[852] Cf. Invernizzi, p.103 "...viene tacitamente ammesso che [la volontà] abbia una realtà ulteriore a quella che appare nel fenomeno, una realtà che tuttavia si trova completamente al di fuori della portata della nostra facoltà conoscitiva."

[853] *Vorstellung* I, I, §12, S.95; *Representation*, I, §12, p.58.

[854] Cf. the following passage taken from an early fragment (1814) in the *Nachlaß*, I, S.146: "Ueberhaupt...sehn wir daß Alles was ist nur Erscheinung von *Willen* ist, verkörperter *Wille*. Wir wissen aber daß alle unsre Quaal nur aus dem Willen kommt...wir nur in ihm unseelig, dagegen im reinen Erkennen, als von ihm befreit, seelig sind. -- Der Wille also ist der *Ursprung des Bösen* und auch des *Uebels* das nur für seine Erscheinung, den Leib, da ist: und der Wille ist auch der *Ursprung* der Welt."; *Manuscript Remains*, I, p.158.

[855] *Vorstellung* II, IV, Kap.50, S.751; *Representation*, II, §50, p.640.

the authentic saint in effect represents the only knowledge we can have of the noumenon as "non temporal". The Thomistic scholar Leo C. Elders has this in mind when he contends that holiness of lifestyle in-itself testifies to a transcendent realm.[856] Martin Hielscher echoes these sentiments by noting that the artist, but most especially the saint, incarnate the very goal or purpose of Schopenhauer's philosophy as something that is no longer immanent to the system, but beyond it. In this respect, human self-transcendence as represented by the saint represents a "passing-over" (*Überschreitung*) into the realm of the noumenal which is beyond the capacity of human cognition to validly describe.[857] Because of this fact, Wolfgang Schirmacher contends that for Schopenhauer it is precisely "only through the phenomenon of the saint [that] we know about the Sacred."[858]

---

[856] Leo C. Elders, *The Philosophical Theology of St. Thomas Aquinas* (Leiden: E.J.Brill, 1990), p.139. The passage in question states:
> Not unlike truth and beauty goodness and love, encountered in our contact with our fellowmen, also refer to a transcendent goodness and love. Saintliness in particular witnesses to God's existence.

[857] Martin Hielscher, "Der Helige und die Überschreitung," in *Schopenhauers Aktualität*, hrsg. von Wolfgang Schirmacher (Wien: Passagen Verlag, 1988), S.207. The passage reads as follows:
> Schopenhauer ist einer der wenigen Philosophen, die ihrem eigenen System eine Grenze gesetzt haben, in dem Sinne, daß das Ziel ihrer Philosophie ihr nicht mehr immanent ist, ja quasi übergangslos ihr vor Augen steht. Diese Grenze wird vom Künstler, absolut aber vom Heligen verkörpert. Mit dieser Einschränkung seines philosophischen Systems makiert Schopenhauer zugleich den Übergang von der spekulativen zur empirischen Grundlegung der Philosophie, der seine philosophiegeschichtliche Stellung auszeichnet.

[858] Wolfgang Schirmacher, "Der Heilige als Lebensform Überlegungen zu Schopenhauers ungeschriebener Lehre," as found in *Schopenhauers Aktualität*, S.189. The passage reads as follows:
> Allerdings hält Otto das Heilige für die fundamentalere Ebene und ortet es in einem dem Menschen eigentümlichen sensus numinis. Wie wir das Heilige aufzufassen vermögen und unter anderem auch in der Person des Heiligen erkennen, ist für Otto ausschlaggebend. Damit verschiebt sich jedoch die Perspektive derart, daß aus dem Blick gerät, was der Realist Schopenhauer unbeirrt festhielt: nur durch die Erscheinung des Heiligen wissen wir vom Heiligen.

Philosophically speaking the door is barred when it comes to meaningfully describing what that "non temporal" element might in fact be. Nevertheless, the saint does not hesitate to identify that noumenal, non-temporal reality for the philosopher, for whom such a state, while indeed existing, does not pertain to "knowledge" since it transcends the phenomenal realm as known by will-guided cognition.[859] So notwithstanding Schopenhauer's philosophical presuppositions which appear to seal shut the "front" door to God, the saint and ascetic by their lifestyles point to the very potentiality which the "relative" nothingness of the noumenal will has, to effect the mysterious "*new birth*" (*Wiedergeburt*) and hasten the appearance of the "*kingdom of grace*" (*das Reich der Gnade*) as represented by Christ, who is the quintessential expression of the denial of the will-to-live. In juxtaposition to this, is the affirmation of the will, as characteristic of the "*natural man*" (*der natürliche Mensch*) whose will-oriented cognition is rooted in the temporality of the "*kingdom of nature*" (*das Reich der Natur*). Here Adam represents an archetypal Platonic Idea (that of affirming the will-to-live) which is extended to all human beings in time through the bond of generation.[860]

---

[859] *Vorstellung I*, II, §71, S.506. "Würde dennoch schlechterdings darauf bestanden, von Dem, was die Philosophie nur negativ, als Verneinung des Willens, ausdrücken kann, irgendwie eine positive Erkenntniß zu verweisen, den alle Die, welche zur vollkommenen Verneinung des Willens gelangt sind, erfahren haben, und den man mit den Namen Ekstasie, Entrückung, Erleuchtung, Vereinigung mit Gott u.s.w. bezeichnet hat; welcher Zustand aber nicht eigentlich Erkenntniß zu nennen ist, weil er nicht mehr die Form von Subjekt und Objekt hat, und auch übrigens nur der eigenen, nicht weiter mittheilbaren Erfahrung zugänglich ist."; *Representation*, I, §71, p.410.

[860] *Ibid.*, §70, S.499-501; *Ibid.*, §70, pp.404-406; *Vorstellung II*, IV, Kap.48, S.736; *Representation*, II, ch.48, p.628. Cf. also *Nachlaß*, I, S.85-86 and S.468; *Manuscript Remains*, I, pp.93-94 and pp.518-519.

In light of the above, the task falls to Schopenhauer's readers to determine whether the explanation of the non-temporal dimension of the noumenon considered as relative nothingness, is satisfactory enough not only to describe that reality which the ascetic deems so real, but to exhaust its significance. In like fashion, it is not so much the origin of evil (with which willing is linked) that is a problem, but rather the existence of its anti-thesis which is connected with genius and virtue. Schopenhauer clearly associates this denial with a "passing over into nothing" as the following passage from Parerga und Paralipomena indicates:

> ...I observe that the *denial of the will-to-live* does not in anyway assert the annihilation of a substance, but the mere act of not-willing. That which hitherto *willed* no longer *wills*. As we know the being, the essence, the *will* as thing-in-itself merely in and through the act of *willing*, we are incapable of saying or grasping what it still is or does after it has given up this act. Therefore, *for us* who are the phenomenon of willing, the denial is a passing over into nothing (*ein Uebergang in's Nichts*).[861]

As the above illustrates, Schopenhauer is struggling for adequate terminology to describe what non-willing entails given his metaphysical presuppositions. Moreover, with regard to virtue, holiness, and genius the so-called "temporal" or "empirical" human being does not seem to be "his own work" in the strict sense of the term, if it is the case that these phenomena have as their source the non-temporal *noumenon* which is antecedent even to the will's adequate objectification in the Ideas. Accordingly, the question of the Sacred remains an issue

---

[861] *Parerga II*, IX, Kap.14, §161, S.339. "; *Parerga*, II, ch.14, §161, p.312.

and serves as a springboard for further reflection in light of the "unanswerables" in his system of thought.

CONCLUSION

The objective of this study has now been fulfilled. I have systematically examined whether or not the question of the Sacred remains an open issue in Schopenhauer's analysis of the human condition. It is my contention (as the immediately preceding chapter indicates) that there indeed exists a "back door" to the question of God, via a careful analysis of Schopenhauer's anthropology and metaphysical presuppositions about the nature of reality. This is especially the case given certain "unanswerables" to which Schopenhauer himself alludes in his treatment of the denial of the will-to-live, as specifically manifested in aesthetical and ethical actions -- not to mention the exact place of the Platonic Ideas in his ontology. In the paragraphs to follow, I shall summarize my reasons for claiming the above.

In Chapter One, which pertains to the representational character of cognition, the question of God is closed. Why? In the first place, Schopenhauer contends that the only function of reason lies in the formation of concepts, and not in the demand for an "unconditioned". Human reason cannot advance beyond the phenomenal realm. Moreover, Schopenhauer would not agree with Kant's notion of the regulative use of reason with regard to the ideas of soul, *world*, and *God*.

As a specific case in point, is Schopenhauer's explanation of the law of causality, which is applicable only to the inter-connection of phenomena with one another. The law of causality pertains only to changes in perceptual and empirically-given representations which, for Schopenhauer, are what is meant by *real* objects. It is precisely here where the principle of sufficient reason of *becoming* concerns itself with the appearance and disappearance of states of objects as given in experience. It is thus invalid to ask what the cause of the "complete representation" (which constitutes the world as such) might in fact be.

Given this conception of causality, an appeal to a First Cause is impossible. For in the first place, no given object can strictly ever be regarded as a cause of another, since causes pertain not to the bringing of something else into existence, but to changes in the form of indestructible matter. Schopenhauer is insistent that since every cause is a change, we are necessarily bound to ask about the change that preceded it *ad infinitum*. Accordingly, given this univocal understanding of the law of causality, it is impossible to argue from the path of the representation to the existence of an object that is beyond perceptual and empirical experience.

Moreover, language about "God" has a certain hollowness given the essential poverty of the concept to capture what is perceptually given in experience. Schopenhauer repeatedly underscores that concepts derive their value and meaning only through their relation to perceptual representations. The more abstract the concept, the more empty and poor it becomes. Because the concept "God" has no perceptual representation to which it can be referred from the path of empirical and representational cognition, as such it is "empty".

Now, while it is true that God is not a sensibly given object in experience, a criticism can be raised against this claim of Schopenhauers. For though general concepts like "being", "essence", and the like, are highly abstract and empty of perceptual content, the concept "God" is not on the same plane. Notwithstanding its inability to be referred to a sensible object of experience, it has an inherent capacity to *evoke* much more within the human spirit than do the aforementioned notions. In this respect, Schopenhauer's theory of knowledge is superficial especially with regards to what exactly is meant by being an "object" of knowledge. Does to be "object" mean that one must sensibly see or touch it? What if the notion of "object" is expanded to that which is intended in human questioning, and better known as answers become more complete, as Bernard Lonergan suggests?[862] Discourse about God then becomes philosophically meaningful to the extent that one leaves behind a strictly etymological understanding of the term "object". Schopenhauer, however, does not explore this possibility. Representational knowledge under the principle of sufficient reason negates any possibility of a natural theology.

At first glance, Chapter Two (which deals with Schopenhauer's understanding of will) illustrates that the question of God is also closed inasmuch as aseity is ascribed not to God, but to the noumenal will. Though the will objectifies itself in every single phenomenon (such that every instance of the latter is a manifestation of the former), Schopenhauer clearly does not equate the scarred will with God. His system is not pantheistic. Why would one bend the knee to a reality that is impersonal, frustrated, and scarred -- certainly

---

[862] Bernard Lonergan, "Natural Knowledge of God," *Proceedings of the Twent third Annual Convention* Washington, D.C., 1968 [Yonkers, N.Y., 1969], pp.54-6

Conclusion 325

no *Summum Bonum*? Moreover, as was established in Chapter Six of this study, *God* for Schopenhauer denotes the cause of the world with the addition of personality. But this is not what he means by will. Thus, when he speaks about the aseity of the will as kernel of each and every phenomenon, a claim of natural theology is by no means being made.

This notwithstanding, he ascribes the teleology present in nature to the will that is devoid of knowledge, insisting that the world is not the product of mind or knowledge. A valid question, however, arises at this point. How is it possible for a blind, aimless, and universally striving will to objectify itself in a world of essents that are seemingly characterized by finality or purpose? In Chapter Six references are given which allude to the possibility that the thing-in-itself might indeed have other modes and qualities of existence, other than that of an aimless striving. Can it be that the order in the real is dependent upon them?

The difficulties that the above suggests in itself leaves the question open as to what really grounds the apparent intelligibility and finality of the real. But perhaps what is most interesting, is Schopenhauer's admission that the will in its pristine essence eludes human conceptual grasp. Though the path of introspection reveals one's nature as a willer, the content of this knowledge nevertheless remains bound to the form of time. Hence, only a partial glimpse of what the noumenon (or thing-in-itself) might in fact be, is granted to the beholder. For the thing-in-itself is veiled in mystery.

But this is problematic! For what then does Schopenhauer mean when he suggests that the in-itselfness of the real lies in the awareness that one has of oneself as a willer, given one's individuality or corporeality? Since the pristine in-itselfness of the noumenon cannot be known, the inner awareness that one has of oneself as a willer serves only to supply the clue for the sickness of the human spirit and the disorder of the real world as known in experience. But the point to be kept in mind is that notwithstanding the chaotic elements that streak the real, there is a backdrop of order that is over and above willing, which is always linked to the form of time. In this respect, the question of God, or at the very least, of mystery, appears to remain open for the student of Schopenhauer's thought.

In Chapter Three the aforementioned issues come to the foreground with Schopenhauer's doctrine of the Platonic Ideas and the exact role they play in his *Weltanschauung*. Given the above discussion, insight into the in-itselfness of scarred reality is obtained via the awareness that one has of oneself as a willer through and through. However, Schopenhauer also maintains that the will represents itself in various strata of being, which he calls the Platonic Ideas that constitute the will's immediate or *adequate* objectification. He clearly does not equate the Ideas with the thing-in-itself, notwithstanding the fact that both transcend space, time, and causality. This explains his rationale for maintaining that the Idea *is not* the thing-in-itself, but rather its *adequate* or *immediate* objectification. He goes on to state that the Idea is what is most objective in any given phenomenon; and that as such, it can be known provided that the human intellect can tear itself away from will-oriented cognition -- as does in fact happen in cases of genius.

The particular problem at hand arises because Schopenhauer also says that the world of particulars, which constitutes merely an *indirect* objectification of the thing-in-itself approximates the Ideas. In this respect, the latter may be considered prototypes or archetypes of the former, which as such, are beyond space, time and causality -- the medium of particular entities or individuals, as given in empirical perception. The Ideas seem to stand fixed in a world apart, subject to no change, referring to an intelligible realm in which the will *adequately* objectifies itself in a definite and fixed grade. In fact, Schopenhauer refers to the Ideas as specific grades of the will's objectification, which are simple acts of will in which its inner being is expressed "more or less".

Is this to say, therefore, that the realm of the Ideas constitutes a reality apart from that of the world as will and representation? Schopenhauer denies this insofar as he claims that reality consists precisely of will and representation. Accordingly, since he *does say* that the Idea is also that which is *most objective* in any given phenomenon, the Idea (inasmuch as it is object for a subject) constitutes a *known*. For this reason, the Idea is indeed a phenomenon albeit one that has cast aside its subordinate forms characteristic to empirically-given perceptions. Moreover, the Ideas are *universalia ante rem* insofar as they are unities that fall apart into pluralities given the nature of human cognitional faculties.

This notwithstanding, when Schopenhauer speaks about the will's objectification in the various strata of Being, a streak of rationality illumines his *Weltanschauung*. Phenomena are interconnected on the empirical and perceptual levels of experience, as they are in the realm of the intelligible, which pertains to the Ideas. Schopenhauer insists, for example, that the Idea of Man needs to manifest itself together with the Ideas of all the lower grades of the will's objectification so that its proper significance can be grasped. The inner relationship is further evidenced by the fact that higher Ideas, while subjugating lower ones, never obliterate them. In fact, he likens the relationship among the Ideas to the way voices harmonize.

This is not to say, of course, that Schopenhauer ignores the chaotic or disordered element that can be gleaned in the perceptual world of day-to-day will-guided cognition. But he does admit that the mysterious inner harmony among the Ideas explains why reality has not been rent asunder by chaotic forces. Accordingly, it cannot be denied that there exists in Schopenhauer's *Weltanschauung* a curious blending between the rational and irrational.

The problem that this suggests is to explain where the rationality or teleological elements come from, given Schopenhauer's principal claim that the will is blind and strives everywhere without aim. By underscoring that the will desires its highest possible objectification, does he not in some way or another ascribe awareness to the will? Moreover, if the will adequately objectifies itself in an intelligible sphere of Ideas whose inner relationship is far from chaotic, how can it be possible that the same will is blind and devoid of finality?

It is interesting to note that Schopenhauer insists at the very outset of the discussion that Idea and thing-in-itself are not to be equated because the

Conclusion

former still retains the universal form of the phenomenon, that of being object for subject. What this suggests is that knowing the Ideas (provided that one can muster the strength of intellect to do so) does not yield insight into the scarredness of the real. Quite the contrary! It is knowing what comprises the phenomenon in its most objective character that results in the grasping of the rationality of the real, offering in its wake a temporary respite from the thraldom of will-oriented cognition. Accordingly, it represents a crucial step to self-transcendence. But inasmuch as the will objectifies itself adequately in the Ideas (which constitute the most objective aspect of the phenomenon), it would seem to follow that knowledge of the Ideas involves a further insight into the noumenon -- but an understanding opposite to that of the will's inner estrangement and lack of aim.

   Accordingly, with regard to the central issue of this study (viz. the question of God), the problem is to find a sufficient explanation for the rationality that stubbornly clings to the real world we perceive. The ascribing of teleological factors to the will is not satisfactory given the will's blindness and lack of finality. There remains, in short, a serious cleavage between an order that can be known by reason, and a disorder that is existentially experienced. Unfortunately, Schopenhauer proposes no satisfactory answer to this dilemma. His contention that it is simply beyond rational analysis why the will should objectify itself in the realm of the Ideas, has a hollow ring and is evasive at best. This is yet another indication that the question of God remains an open issue for the student of Schopenhauer's thought.

Along the same lines, Schopenhauer is unable to explain in a sufficient manner the actual process of coming to know an Idea. He notes that while everyone has the capacity to tear oneself away from all will-oriented cognition, becoming a "pure will-less subject of knowledge" is indeed a rare phenomenon that takes place suddenly and inexplicably. Be that as it may, the result of insight into what comprises the most objective aspect of the phenomenon, leaves in its wake a consciousness that is temporarily filled with happiness and peace inasmuch as it has cast off the shackles of will-oriented cognition. What all this, of course, implies is that there appears to be more to the noumenal will than what introspective insight into the nature of willing suggests.

Whereas the key to grasp the irrational and disordered aspect of reality is supplied via the route of introspection given one's corporeality, trekking the path of the Ideas leads to a different conclusion: that the will adequately objectifies itself in a manifestly ordered world that not only delights the eye, but gives peace to the human spirit, as aesthetic experience attests. This is particularly true with regard to music, which mirrors the noumenal will in a direct fashion. Music is particularly effective, contends Schopenhauer, because it expresses in a sublime language the inner being of the world which is understood by the concept *will*. Music passes over the Ideas and touches upon the very mystery of the will -- which even the Ideas cannot fathom. But the question to be raised is this: can music be so absorbing if it merely mirrors the will as diseased and disordered? Does it not rather express something similar (yet beyond) that which the Ideas

Conclusion 331

convey? In short, music likewise seems to pertain to that aspect of the noumenon that is beyond self-estrangement. In this respect, Schopenhauer's theory of music only serves to highlight the essential ambiguity that characterizes the thing-in-itself, alluded to above.

Chapters Four and Five respectively may be approached as a unit inasmuch as they examine two central notions in Schopenhauer's anthropology: affirmation of the will-to-live and denial of the will-to-live. The question of God as such is not raised in a direct fashion in either of the chapters. However, the claims Schopenhauer makes with regard to the aforementioned alternatives in willing do implicitly involve the central issue of this study and accordingly have some relevance. It is to these that I now turn.

An analysis of Chapter Four highlights the impotence of God to change the disordered nature of human willing. It is very clear that Schopenhauer maintains that the malady in the human spirit is directly attributable to the ultimate lack of finality in willing. Given the nature of the will, life is not to be thankfully enjoyed. Human beings do not exist to be happy. Life is something that ought to disgust us. For it is characterized by a disordered sexuality, which best illustrates the nature of the will-to-live, and by an irrational fear of death. Ultimately, the grave unmasks the illusion of will-filled existence insofar as the true character of life, as something that ought to disgust us, is revealed. Given this scenario, happiness is not possible unless if can be imagined that a fundamental change transpire within the core of man's will-filled essence. But it is clear that for Schopenhauer man is ontologically sick. There is no one or anything that can heal his pain.

The essential self-estrangement that characterizes the will goes hand in hand with the nature of human cognition both of self and others. The human being has a direct awareness of himself or herself and only an indirect cognizance of others. This explains in part why the over-affirmation of the will-to-live at the expense of the other, who appears merely as a representation to consciousness, is often the order of the day -- resulting in a praxis that is characterized by unjust and sometimes even malicious actions. Given the nature of human egoism, it is only the State that keeps the anti-moral tendencies within the human breast in check. Though Schopenhauer suggests that the pangs of conscience (which accompany the doing of a wrong deed) attest to the basic homogeneousness of being, the fact of the matter is that human praxis is usually characterized by an over-affirmation of the will-to-live. All this suggests that there is little hope for the human condition. Hence, the question of God from the standpoint of the affirmation of the will-to-live has little significance in the existential realm.

Chapter Five highlights once again the paradoxical character of Schopenhauer's thought inasmuch as it qualifies the bleak analysis that characterizes human praxis grounded by affirmation of the will-to-live. In man's case, there appears a contradiction of the phenomenon with itself insofar as the propensity not only to appreciate the beautiful, but the capacity to create it in works of art, illustrates that human beings can transcend will-oriented cognition. Moreover, holiness of life as manifested in acts of justice, loving kindness

Conclusion 333

and asceticism indicate that freedom (which pertains as such only to the noumenal sphere) can make its appearance in the phenomenon with man.

Where the question of God once more comes to the foreground is precisely in the difficulty Schopenhauer encounters in explaining how and why the above transpires. He states that the denial of the will-to-live manifests itself in the moral sphere when the will (in some cases at least) obtains such a knowledge of its essential scarredness, that insight into suffering acts as a quieter that debilitates the motives that had hitherto been so effective in evoking will-oriented behavioral patterns. Accordingly, the phenomenon of compassion grounds the various degrees of the denial of the will-to-live: justice, loving-kindness, and asceticism.

What is problematic, however, is that Schopenhauer struggles to find appropriate language to describe the above. He likens the occurrence of the *quieter* in the denial of the will-to-live to the "effect of grace" and the "new birth" experienced by the Christian mystics. The transcendence characteristic to the denial of the will-to-live in actions of moral worth (as grounded in the occurrence of compassion) is likened to the entrance into the "kingdom of grace," or the deliverance from the "kingdom of nature" characteristic to will-oriented cognition. This all suggests that there simply exists no apt explanation as to why the above takes place. Schopenhauer underscores that such transcendence is not induced by one's efforts, nor grounded on reason. In short, the denial of the will-to-live on the ethical sphere is mysterious and beyond rational explanation.

This is not to say, however, that Schopenhauer would thereby appeal to God *ex machina* to explain why denial of the will-to-live does in fact take place in its various degrees. For it is clear that his demythologization of asceticism does not have a personal God as its motivating force or term. This notwithstanding, there is some indication that he at least toyed with the idea of using the concept "god" (when understood as devoid of all positive attributes) as an appropriate description for the end result of denial of the will-to-live. Yet even if the concept were salvageable in this sense, such an impoverished notion of God would be a far cry from the transcendent and personal reality experienced in authentic religious asceticism. Nevertheless, it is important to underscore that the end result of ascetical praxis, as demythologized by Schopenhauer, *is not* an "absolute nothingness". While it may be true that the ascetic succeeds in completely denying the phenomenon of scarred willing, the *nothing* that remains (once the will-to-live is denied), appears to be a *something* that merely eludes linguistic grasp.

This is certainly highlighted in section C of Chapter Six, which specifically deals with my reasons for maintaining that the question of God remains an open issue in Schopenhauer's thought. I make this claim notwithstanding factors in sections A and B that indicate that the "front door" to the aforementioned question is bolted shut. In the first place, his analysis of religion as being the "metaphysics of the people" includes no encounter with the Holy. Secondly, he maintains that the Kantian critique discredits the possibility of proving God's existence. In the third place, while admitting that God's existence rests solely

Conclusion

on the authority of the revealed scriptures, he demythologizes the latter as mere thoughts of sages and contends that God is a human fabrication or hypostasis of fear and anxiety. Fourth, he contends that belief in God cannot be reconciled with the existence of evil and moral responsibility for actions.

Notwithstanding these four factors, there are passages in Schopenhauer's thought which categorically state that the noumenal will is obscured by mystery. The reason for this simply consists in the fact that inward observation of ourselves as willers (which is key to discovering, in at least a partial way, what the noumenon is) comes via successive states in time. Accordingly, inner perception by no means yields an adequate and exhaustive knowledge of the thing-in-itself because the form of time remains, as well as that of "being-known" and "knowing-in-general". The thing-in-itself, so to speak, only partially "casts off its veil" via the act of willing. Schopenhauer underscores that in every act of willing there ensues an immediate transition of the extra-temporal thing-in-itself into the phenomenal sphere; such that acts of willing constitute the clearest expression of the thing-in-itself. Yet, given the discussion above, what acts of willing initially reveal is the aspect of the noumenon that is scarred and diseased -- what evidently most interested Schopenhauer. Knowledge of the Ideas, as representative of a crucial step in self-transcendence, however, does not yield insight into reality as scarred even though the Idea as such is described as an "immediate" objectification of the will.

Is there more to the will than what the act of willing initially suggests? Schopenhauer appears in fact to claim that the thing-in-itself can have determinations and modes of existence that are beyond the scope of philosophical grasp; and which remain as the very essence of the thing-in-itself, once the act of the complete denial of the will-to-live in ascetical praxis has taken place. What this implies is that the thing-in-itself cannot be categorically identified with scarred and diseased willing. For the "nothingness," which is the final goal of ascetical praxis, is by no means to be understood in an absolute sense. Rather, it is a "something" that eludes the philosopher's conceptual grasp.

It is clear that Schopenhauer in several key passages underscores that the will, as purely noumenal, can and *may* have qualities other than those experienced on the phenomenal realm via will-oriented cognition. But it is aesthetic experience and the denial of the will-to-live, as concretely lived by both the genius and saint, that aptly illustrate this. On the phenomenal realm, guided as it is by will-oriented cognition, the thing-in-itself initially reveals itself as a senseless striving. Yet, creations of artistic genius as well as the phenomenon of sanctity, illustrate that the thing-in-itself has another potentiality that makes its appearance from time to time in the phenomenal sphere. It is here where the other dimension of the will (as truly noumenal and free) manifests itself for consciousness. In light of this fact, it seems to follow that if the arts and sanctity in life are an indication that the will as free has stepped into the phenomenal sphere, their occurrence and reality are dynamically related to that aspect of the noumenon that is completely extra-temporal -- the relative nothingness which is also the end result of

Conclusion

ascesis and is beyond the exigence of philosophical speculation to describe.

The above, of course, has ramifications for the question of God. By underscoring the relative nature of nothingness, not to mention the essential ambiguity of the thing-in-itself, Schopenhauer tacitly admits that the pristine character of the thing-in-itself has an ulterior reality other than the one that appears in time and space via acts of willing. Moreover, aesthetic experience, virtue and holiness as degrees of denial of the will-to-live, themselves appear to be grounded in an extra-temporal dimension of the will that is beyond self-estrangement. For they neither arise nor proceed from diseased willing, nor have their ground in reason as such. Since philosophical speculation is rendered impotent before the mystery that all this suggests, it is reasonable to conclude that the question of God remains an open issue given the unaswerables in Schopenhauer's thought.

BIBLIOGRAPHY

Primary Sources:

Schopenhauer, Arthur. *Zürcher Ausgabe in zehn Bänden*. Der text folgt der historisch-kritisch Ausgabe von Arthur Hübscher (3. Auflage, Brockhaus, Wiesbaden 1972) Zürich: Diogenes, 1977.

Band I/II:
Die Welt als Wille und Vorstellung I
Band III/IV:
Die Welt als Wille und Vorstellung II
Band V:
Über die vierfache Wurzel des Satzes vom zureichenden Grunde
Über den Willen in der Natur
Band VI:
Die Beiden Grundprobleme der Ethik
I. *Über die Freiheit des menschlichen Willens*
II. *Über die Grundlage der Moral*
Band VII/VIII:
Parerga und Paralipomena I
Band IX/X:
Parerga und Paralipomena II

_____. *Über das Sehn und die Farben: eine Abhandlung*. In Schopenhauer, Arthur. *Sämmtliche Werke*. Herausgegeben von Grossherzog, Wilhelm. Leipzig: Inselverlag, 1905-1910.

_____. *Philosophische Vorlesungen*. Herausgegebenvon Volker Spierling. 4 Bände. München/Zürich: Serie Piper, 1986.
Band I:

Vorlesung: Theorie des Gesammten Vorstellens, Denkens und Erkennens

Band II:
Vorlesung: Metaphysik der Natur
Band III:
Vorlesung: Metaphysik des Schönen
Band IV:
Vorlesung: Metaphysik der Sitten

_____. *Der handschriftliche Nachlaß.* Herausgegeben von Arthur Hübscher. 5 Bände. München: Deutscher Taschenbuch Verlag, 1985.

Band I: *Frühe Manuskripte (1804-1818).*
Band II: *Kritische Auseinandersetzungen (1809-1818).*
Band III: *Berliner Manuskripte (1818-1830).*
Band IV.1: *Die Manuskriptbücher der Jahre 1830-1852.*
Band IV.2: *Letzte Manuskripte/Gracians Handorakel.*
Band V: *Randschriften zu Büchern.*

_____. *Die Reisetagbücher.* Herausgegeben von Ludger Lütkehaus. Zürich: Haffmans Verlag, MCMLXXXVIII.

_____. *Gesammelte Briefe.* Herausgegeben von Arthur Hübscher. Bonn: Bouvier Verlag Herbert Grundmann, 1987.

_____. *Gespräche.* Herausgegeben von Arthur Hübscher. Stuttgart: Friedrich Frommann Verlag, 1971.

English Translations:

Schopenhauer, Arthur. *Manuscript Remains.* Translated by E.F.J. Payne. Oxford: Berg, 1988-1990.

Volume One: *Early Manuscripts (1804-1818).*
Volume Two: *Critical Debates (1809-1818).*
Volume Three: *Berlin Manuscripts (1818-1830).*

Volume Four: *The Manuscript Books of 1830-1852 and Last Manuscripts*.

_____. *On the Basis of Morality*. Translated by E.F.J. Payne. Indianapolis: Bobbs-Merrill, 1965.

_____. *On the Fourfold Root of the Principle of Sufficient Reason*. Translated by E.F.J. Payne. La Salle: Open Court Publishing Co., 1974.

_____. *On the Freedom of the Will*. Translated by Konstantin Kolenda. Indianapolis: Bobbs-Merrill, 1960.

_____. *On the Will in Nature*. Published together with *On the Fourfold Root of Sufficient Reason* in *Two Essays of Arthur Schopenhauer*. Translated by Mme. K. Hillebrand. London: George Bell and Sons, 1889.

_____. *Parerga and Paralipomena*. 2 volumes. Translated by E.F.J. Payne. Oxford: Clarendon Press, 1974.

_____. *The World as Will and Representation*. 2 volumes. Translated by E.F.J. Payne. New York: Dover, 1966.

Secondary Sources:

A. Books

Anscombe, G.E.M. *An Introduction to Wittgenstein's Tractatus*. London: Hutchinson University Library, 1959.

Bäschlin, Daniel Lukas. *Schopenhauers Einwand gegen Kants Transzendentale Deduktion der Kategorien*. Meisenheim am Glan: Verlag Anton Hain, 1968.

Bergman, Ernst. *Erlösungslehre Schopenhauers*. München: Rosl & Cie, 1921.

Berkeley, George. *Principles, Dialogues, and Correspondence*. Indianapolis: Bobbs-Merrill, 1965.

Bibliography

Berry, Thomas. *Buddhism*. New York: Hawthorn Books, 1967.

_____. *Religions of India: Hinduism, Yoga, Buddhism*. New York: The Bruce Publishing Company, 1971.

Bridgwater, Patrick. *Arthur Schopenhauer's English Schooling*. London: Routledge, 1988.

Bykhovsky, Bernard. *Schopenhauer and the Ground of Existence*. Translated with an introductory essay by Philip Moran. Amsterdam: B.R. Grüner Publishing Co., 1984.

Ceppa, Leonardo. *Schopenhauer diseducatore*. Roma: Marietti, 1983.

Collins, Edward. *Interpreting Modern Philosophy*. Princeton: Princeton University Press, 1972.

Conze, Edward. *Buddhism: Its Essence and Development*. New York: Harper & Row, 1951.

Copelston, Frederick. *Arthur Schopenhauer: Philosopher of Pessimism*. Andover: Burns Oates and Washbourne, Ltd., 1946.

Cresson, André. *Schopenhauer sa vie, son oeuvre avec un exposé de sa philosophie*. Paris: Presses Universitaires de France, 1962.

Dauer, Dorothea W. *Schopenhauer as Transmitter of Buddhist Ideas*. Berne: Herbert Lang & Co., 1969.

Dewitt, Parker H. Editor. *Schopenhauer Selections*. New York: Charles Scribner Sons, 1928.

Elders, Leo J. *The Philosophical Theology of St. Thomas Aquinas*. Leiden: E.J. Brill, 1990.

Fabro, Cornelio. *God in Exile: Modern Atheism*. Westminster: Newman Press: 1968.

Fauconnet, André. *L'esthétique de Schopenhauer*. Paris: Librairie Félix Alcan, 1913.

Fox, Michael. ed. *Schopenhauer: His Philosophical Achievement*. Sussex: The Harvester Press, 1980.

Gardiner, Patrick. *Schopenhauer*. Harmondsworth: Penguin Books, 1963.

Gestering, Johann J. *German Pessimism & Indian Philosophy.* Jawahar Nagar, Delhi: Ajanta Publications, 1986.

Hamlyn, D.W. *Schopenhauer.* London: Routledge & Kegan Paul, 1980.

Hasse, Heinrich. *Schopenhauer.* München: Verlag Ernst Reinhardt, 1926.

Hobbes, Thomas. *Leviathan* as found in *The English Works of Thomas Hobbes of Malmesbury.* Edited by SirWilliam Molesworth. London: John Bohn, 1966.

Höffding, Harald. *A History of Modern Philosophy.* 2 volumes. Translated by B.E. Meyer. Toronto: over,1955.

Hollingdale, R.J. *Arthur Schopenhauer: Essays and Aphorisms.* Harmondsworth: Penguin Books, 1970.

Hübscher, Angelica. Herausgegeben von. *Arthur Schopenhauer. Ein Lebensbild in Briefen.* Frankfurt am Main: Insel Verlag, 1987.

Hübscher, Arthur. *Arthur Schopenhauer. Ein Lebensbild.* Weisbaden: Eberhard Brockhaus Verlag, 1949.

_____. *Arthur Schopenhauer. Mensch und Philosoph in seinen Briefen.* Weisbaden: F.A. Brockhaus, 1960.

_____. *Denker gegen den Strom.* Bonn: Bouvier Verlag, 4., durchgesehene Auflage, 1988.

_____. *Leben mit Schopenhauer.* Frankfurt am Main: Kramer, 1966.

_____. *Schopenhauer-Bibliography.* Stuttgart Bad Canstatt: Frommann-Holzboog, 1981.

_____. *Schopenhauer - Bildnisse. Eine Ikonographie.* Frankfurt: Kramer, 1968.

Hume, David. *Dialogues Concerning Natural Religion.* Indianapolis: Bobbs-Merrill, 1947.

_____. *A Treatise of Human Nature.* Harmondsworth: Penguin, 1969.

Janaway, Christopher. *Self and World in Schopenhauer's Philosophy* Oxford: Clarendon Press, 1989.

Kant, Immanuel. *Critique of Judgement*. Translated, with an Introduction, by Werner S. Pluhar. Indianapolis: Hackett Publishing Company,1987.

_____. *Critique of Practical Reason*. Translated by Lewis White Beck. Indianapolis: Bobbs-Merrill, 1975.

_____. *Critique of Pure Reason*. Translated by Norman Kemp Smith. London: Macmillan, 1987.

_____. *Foundations of the Metaphysics of Morals*. Translated by Lewis White Beck. Indianapolis: Bobbs-Merrill, 1959.

_____. *Prolegomena to Any Future Metaphysics*. A revision of the Carus translation with an introduction by Lewis White Beck. Indianapolis: Bobbs-Merrill, 1975.

_____. *Religion Within the Limits of Reason Alone*. Translated with an introduction and notes by Theodore M. Greene and Hoyt H. Hudson. New York: Harper Torchbooks, 1960.

Kimpel, Ben. *The Philosophy of Schopenhauer*. Boston: Student Outlines Company, 1964.

Kishan, B.V. *Schopenhauer's Conception of Salvation*. Waltair, Visakhapatnam: Andhra University Press, 1978.

Luft von der, Eric. Editor. *Schopenhauer: New Essays in Honor of His 200th Birthday*. Lewiston: The Edwin Mellen Press,1988.

Magee, Bryan. *The Philosophy of Schopenhauer*. Oxford: Clarendon Press, 1983.

Mandelbaum, Maurice. *History, Man and Reason*. Baltimore: John Hopkins Press, 1971.

Mayer von, Eduard. *Schopenhauers Aesthetik und ihr Verhältniß zu den aesthetischen Lehren Kants und Schellings*. Halle: Niemeyer, 1897.

McGill, V.J. *Schopenhauer Pessimist and Pagan*. New York: Haskell House Publishers Ltd., 1971.

Most, Otto J. *Zeit und Ewiges in der Philosophie Nietzches und Schopenhauers*. Herausgegeben von Hannes Böhringer. Frankfurt am Main: Vittorio Klostermann, 1977.

Naegelsbach, Hans. *Das Wesen der Vorstellung bei Schopenhauer.* Heidelberg: Carl Winter's Universitätsbuchhandlung, 1927.

Nietzsche, Friedrich. *Beyond Good and Evil.* Translated by R.J. Hollingdale. Harmondsworth: Penguin Books, 1984.

_____. *The Birth of Tragedy and The Genealogy of Morals.* Translated by Francis Golffing. Garden City, New York: Double Day Anchor Books, 1956.

_____. *The Gay Science.* Translated by Walter Kaufmann. New York: Random House, 1974.

_____. *Schopenhauer as Educator.* Translated by James W. Hillesheim and Malcolm R. Simpson. South Bend, Indiana: Gateway Editions, Ltd., 1965.

Passmore, John. *A Hundred Years of Philosophy.* Harmondsworth: Penguin Books, 1978.

Paton, H.J. *The Categorical Imperative.* London: Hutchinson's University Library, 1953.

Penzo, Giorgio. ed. *Schopenhauer e il sacro.* Atti del seminario tenuto a Trento il 26-28 aprile 1984. Trento: Istituto Trentino di Cultura Pubblicazioni dell'Istituto di Scienze Religiose in Trento, 1987.

Radha, Krishnan. *The Hindu View of Life.* New York: Macmillan Publishing Company, 1975.

Reardon, Bernard M.G. *Religious Thought in the Nineteenth Century.* Cambridge: Cambridge University Press, 1966.

Röhr, Reinhard. *Mitleid und Einsicht.* Frankfurt am Main: Peter Lang, 1985.

Russell, Bertrand. *A History of Western Philosophy.* New York: Simon and Schuster, 1945.

Safranski, Rüdiger. *Schopenhauer und die wilden Jahre der Philosophie/Eine Biographie.* München: Carl Hanser Verlag, 1987.

Schaefer, Alfred. *Probleme Schopenhauers.* Berlin: Berlin Verlag, 1984.

Schirmacher, Wolfgang. Herausgegeben von. *Schopenhauers Aktualität*. Wien: Passagen Verlag, 1988.

Schmidt, Alfred. *Idee und Weltwille*. München: Carl Hanser Verlag, 1988.

_____. *Die Wahrheit im Gewande der Lüge*. München: Serie Piper, 1986.

Simmel, Alfred. *Schopenhauer and Nietzsche*. Translated by Helmut Loiskandl, Deena Weinstein, and Michael Weinstein. Amherst: The University of Massachusetts Press, 1986.

Smith, Norman Kemp. *A Commentary to Kant's Critique of Pure Reason*. Second Edition. London: Macmillan, 1923.

Spierling, Volker. Kommentiert und eingeleitet von. *Materialen zu Schopenhauers »Die Welt als Wille und Vorstellung«*. Frankfurt am Main: uhrkamp, 1984.

_____. Herausgegeben von *Schopenhauer im Denken der Gegenwart*. München: Piper, 1987.

Strohm, Harald. *Die Aporien in Schopenhauers Erkenntnistheorie*. Tübingen: Sofort-Druck, 1984.

Taylor, Richard. *The Will to Live*. New York: Frederick Ungar Publishing Company, 1967.

Vecchiotti, Icilio. *Introduzione a Schopenhauer*. Roma-Bari: Editori Laterza, 1986.

Wagner, Gustav Friedrich. *Schopenhauer-Register*. Stuttgart-Bad Cannstadt: Frommann-Holzboog, 1960.

Whittaker, Thomas. *Schopenhauer*. New York: Dodge Publishing Company, 1909.

Young, Julian. *Willing and Unwilling: A Study in the Philosophy of Arthur Schopenhauer*. Dordrecht: Martinus Nijhoff Publishers, 1987.

Zimmern, Helen. *Arthur Schopenhauer: His Life and Philosophy*. London: Longmans, Green and Co., 1896.

B. *Articles*:

Alpherson, Philip. "Schopenhauer and Musical Revelation," *Journal of Aesthetics and Art Criticism* 40 (1981-1982): 155 - 166.

Ameriks, Karl. "Kant's Deduction of Freedom and Morality." *Journal of the History of Philosophy* 19 (1981): 53 - 79.

Atwell, John E. "Schopenhauer's Account of Moral Responsibility." *Pacific Philosophical Quarterly* 61 (1980): 396 - 410.

Ausmus, Harry J. "Schopenhauer and Christianity." *Illinois Quarterly* (April, 1974): 26 - 42.

Autrum, Hansjochen. "Der Wille in der Natur und die Biologie heute." *Schopenhauer-Jahrbuch* 50 (1969): 89 - 101.

Avila Crespo, Remedios. "Pessimismo y filosofia en A. Schopenhauer." *Pensamiento* 45 (1989): 57-75.

Basham, Arthur Llewellyn. "Hinduism." *Encyclopedia Britannica*. Volume II., 507 - 513.

Becker, Werner. "Das Paradoxon der Freiheit." *Schopenhauer-Jahrbuch* 62 (1981): 108 - 119.

Bergmann, David. "Spinoza's Spiders, Schopenhauer's Dogs." *Philosophical Studies* 29 (1982 - 1983): 202 - 209.

Betancourt, Raúl Fournet. "En favor de Schopenhauer." *Logos* 11 (1983): 57 - 81.

Birnbacher, Dieter. "Schopenhauer und das ethische Problem des Selbstmords." *Schopenhauer-Jahrbuch* 48 (1967): 108 - 118.

Boullart, Karel. "Schopenhauer et le problème de l'immanence ou l'impertinence du pessimisme intégral." *Revue Internationale de Philosophie* 64 (1988): 83 - 100.

Breidert, Wolfgang. "Schopenhauer und Berkeley." *Schopenhauer- Jahrbuch* 69 (1988): 373 - 385.

Brun, Jean. "Schopenhauer et le magnétisme." *Schopenhauer-Jahrbuch* 69 (1988): 155 -167.

Bucher, Ewald. "Schopenhauer und der Staat." *Schopenhauer-Jahrbuch* 48 (1967): 108 - 118.

Cartwright, David E. "Kant, Schopenhauer, and Nietzsche on the Morality of Pity." *Journal of the History of Ideas* 45 (1984): 83 - 98.

_____. "Scheler's Criticisms of Schopenhauer's Theory of 'Mitleid'." *Schopenhauer-Jahrbuch* 62 (1981): 144 -152.

_____. "Schopenhauerian Optimism and an Alternative to Resignation?" *Schopenhauer-Jahrbuch* 66 (1985): 153 - 164.

_____. "Schopenhauer's Axiological Analysis of Character." *Revue Internationale de Philosophie* 64 (1988): 18 - 36.

_____. "Schopenhauer's Compassion and Nietzsche's Pity." *Schopenhauer-Jahrbuch* 69 (1988): 557 - 567.

_____. "Seeing Through the principium individuationis: Metaphysics and Mora; lity." In *Schopenhauers Aktualität*. Herausgegeben von Wolfgang Schirmacher. Wien: Passagen Verlag, 1988. 41 - 48.

Churchill, John. "Wittgenstein's Adaption of Schopenhauer." *Southern Journal of Philosophy* 21 (1983): 489 - 501.

Ciolli, Simonetta. "Fenomeno." *L'Enciclopedia Garzanti di Filosofia*. Milano: Garzanti Editore, 1983. 297.

Clegg, Jerry S. "Jung's Quarrel with Freud." *Schopenhauer-Jahrbuch* 66 (1985): 165 - 176.

_____. "Logical Mysticism and the Cultural Setting of Wittgenstein's Tractatus." *Schopenhauer-Jahrbuch* 59 (1978): 29 - 47.

_____. "Nietzsche and the Ascent of Man in a Cyclical Cosmos." *The Journal of the History of Philosophy* 19 (1981): 81 - 93.

Delhomme, Jeanne. "Lire Schopenhauer. De la quadruple racine du principe de raison suffisante." *Les Études Philosophiques* 32 (1977): 441 - 450.

Diemer, Alwin. "Schopenhauer und die moderne Existenzphilosophie." *Schopenhauer-Jahrbuch* 43 (1962): 27 -41.

Elman, Benjamin A. "Nietzsche und Buddhism." *Journal of the History of Ideas* 44 (1983): 671 - 686.

Elósegui Itxaso, María. "La simpatia y la solidaridad: una confrontación entre Schopenhauer y Bergson." *Pensamiento* 45 (1989): 77-86.

Engel, S. Morris. "Schopenhauer's Impact on Wittgenstein." *Journal of the History of Philosophy* 28 (1969): 285 - 302.

Estrada, Juan A. "La prevalencia de Schopenhauer sobre Marx en la teoria critica de Horkheimer." *Pensamiento* 45 (1989): 43 - 55.

Friedman, R.Z. "The Importance and Function of Kant's Highest Good." *Journal of the History of Philosophy* 22 (1984): 325 - 342.

Gardiner, Patrick. "Schopenhauer, Arthur." *The Encyclopedia of Philosophy*. Volume 7. Edited by Paul Edwards. New York: The Macmillan Company, 1967. 325 - 332.

"Genie." *Historisches Wörterbuch der Philosophie*. Herausgegeben von Joachim Ritter. Band I. Basel/Stuttgart: Schwabe & Co., 1971. 280 - 308.

"Genio." *Diccionario de filosofia*. Ed. José Ferrater Mora. Volume 2. Madrid: Alianza Editorial, 1982. 1339-1340.

"Genio." *Enciclopedia filosofica*. Volume 3. Roma: Edipem, 1979. 886-887.

Gent, Werner. "Die Kategorien des Raumes und der Zeit bei Schopenhauer." *Schopenhauer-Jahrbuch* 44 (1963): 180 - 194.

Gilman, Sander L. "Hegel, Schopenhauer and Nietzsche See the Black." *Hegel-Studien* 16 (1981): 163 - 188.

Goodman, Russell B. "Schopenhauer and Wittgenstein on Ethics." *Journal of the History of Philosophy* 17 (1979): 437 - 447.

Gonzales, Robert A. "Schopenhauer's Demythologization of Christian Asceticism." *Auslegung* 9 (1982): 5 - 49.

Goyard-Fabre, Simone. "Droit naturel et loi civile dans la philosophie de Schopenhauer." *Les Études Philosophiques* 32 (1977): 451 - 474.

Granier, Jean. "Schopenhauer, éducateur integraliste." *Revue de Metaphysique et de Morale* 87 (1982): 1 - 13.

Hamburger, Käte. "Zum Problem der Mitleidsethik: Rousseau und Schopenhauer." *Philosophisches Jahrbuch* 92 (1985): 68 - 78.

Hamilton, Clarence Herbert. "Buddhism." *Encyclopedia Britannica*. Volume 4. 334 - 362.

Hamlyn, D.W. "Schopenhauer and Freud." *Revue Internationale de Philosophie* 64 (1988): 5 - 17.

_____. "Schopenhauer on the Will in Nature." *Midwest Studies in Philosophy* 8 (1983): 457 - 467.

Hein, Hilde. "Schopenhauer and Platonic Ideas." *Journal of the History of Philosophy* 4 (1966): 133 - 144.

Horkheimer, Max. "Religion und Philosophie." *Schopenhauer-Jahrbuch* 48 (1967): 3 - 9.

Hübscher, Arthur. "Schopenhauer und die Existenzphilosophie." *Schopenhauer-Jahrbuch* 43 (1962): 3 - 4.

_____. "Schopenhauer und die Religionen Asiens." *Schopenhauer-Jahrbuch* 60 (1979): 1 - 16.

_____. "Vom Pietismus zur Mystik," *Schopenhauer-Jahrbuch* 50 (1969): 1 - 32.

Humphrey, Ted. "Schopenhauer and the Cartesian Tradition." *Journal of the History of Philosophy* 19 (1981): 191 - 212.

"Idee." *Historisches Wörterbuch der Philosophie*. Herausgegeben von Joachim Ritter und Karlfried Gründer. Band 4. Basel/Stuttgart: Schwabe & Co. Verlag, 1976. 55 - 134.

Invernizzi, Giuseppe. "Il problema della cosa in sé e la concezione della metafisica nella filosofia di Schopenhauer." *Acme* 37 (1984): 91 - 109.

_____. "Schopenhauer attraverso il suo epistolario." *Rivista di storia della filosofia* n.2 (1986): 245 -264.

_____. "Schopenhauer e la filosofia di Schelling." *Acme* 37 (1984): 99 - 145.

Jouusain, André. "L'Essence et l'existence de l'individu chez Schopenhauer." *Archives de Philosophie* 27 (1964): 286 - 298.

Kishan, B.V. "Arthur Schopenhauer and Indian Philosophy." *Schopenhauer-Jahrbuch* 45 (1964): 23 - 25.

Kulenkampf, Arend. "Über einige begreifliche Voraussetzungen der Moralphilosophie Kants und Schopenhauers." *Archiv für Rechts-und Sozialphilosophie* LXVII (1981): 510 - 531.

Kraushaar, Otto F. "Kantianism." *Dictionary of Philosophy*. Edited by Dagobert D. Runes. Totowa, New Jersey: Littlefield, Adams and Company, 1971, 1971. 158 - 160.

Lamers, Robert W.Th. "Berkeley und Schopenhauer." *Schopenhauer-Jahrbuch* 62 (1981): 120 - 143.

Ledure, Yves. "L'Acte philosophique et la pensée de la mort dans la philosophie de Schopenhauer." *Revue des Sciences Philosophiques et Theologiques* 65 (1981): 373 - 386.

Lonergan, Bernard. "Natural Knowledge of God." *Proceedings of the Twenty-Third Annual Convention*, Washington, D.C., 1968 (Yonkers, N.Y., 1969), pp.54-69.

Lopez, Pilar. "Voluntad y nihilismo en A.Schopenhauer." *Pensamiento* 44 (1988): 257 - 278.

Maidan, Michael. "Schopenhauer on Altruism and Morality." *Schopenhauer-Jahrbuch* 69 (1989): 265 - 272.

Malter, Rudolf. "Schopenhauers Transzendentalismus." *Midwest Studies in Philosophy* 8 (1983): 433 - 455.

_____. "Schopenhauers Verständnis der Theologie Martin Luthers." *Schopenhauer-Jahrbuch* 63 (1982): 22 - 53.

Mensching, Gustav. "Das Christentum in der Kritik der anderen Weltreligionen." *Schopenhauer-Jahrbuch* 50 (1969): 56 - 62.

Mollowitz, Gerhard. "Die Assimilation der platonisch-augustinischen Ideenlehren durch Schopenhauer." *Schopenhauer-Jahrbuch* 66 (1985): 131 - 152.

Negrillo, Jesús. "Influencia de Schopenhauer en el Voluntarismo de Unamuno." *Pensamiento* 37 (1981): 171 - 190.

Negroni, Bruno. "L'essenziale ambiguità della volontà in Schopenhauer." *Schopenhauer-Jahrbuch* 69 (1988): 139 - 154.

Orts, Adela Cortina. "El lugar de Dios en el sistema trascendental kantiano." *Pensamiento* 37 (1981): 401 - 416.

Pandey, Kanti Chandra. "Svatantryavada of Kashmir and Voluntarism of Schopenhauer." *Schopenhauer-Jahrbuch* 48 (1967): 159 -169.

Perrot, Maryvonne. "Le rôle du corps propre dans la philosophie de Schopenhauer: Résonances biraniennes?" *Schopenhauer-Jahrbuch* 69 (1989): 417 -423.

Philonenko, Alexis. "Schopenhauer critique de Kant." *Revue Internationale de Philosophie* 64 (1988): 37 - 70.

Piclin, Michel. "Généalogie de Schopenhauer." *Les Études Philosophiques* 32 (1977): 421 - 439.

Pisa, Karl. "Schopenhauers Ethik." *Schopenhauer-Jahrbuch* 62 (1981): 67 - 77.

Raschke, Carl A. "Schopenhauer on the Delusion of Progress." *Schopenhauer-Jahrbuch* 58 (1077): 73 - 85.

Raulet, Gérard. "A quoi peut bien servir Schopenhauer?" *Dialogue* 20 (1981): 458 - 484.

_____. "What Good is Schopenhauer? Remarks on Horkheimer's Pessimism." Translated by David J. Parent. *Telos* 42 (1979): 98 - 106.

Reinhart, K.F. "Schopenhauer, Arthur." *New Catholic Encyclopedia*. Volume XII. New York: McGraw Book Company, 1967. 1176 - 1178.

Rotenstreich, Nathan. "The Thing in Itself and Will." *Schopenhauer-Jahrbuch* 69 (1988): 127 - 137.

Ruiz Pérez, Francisco. "Las »Ideas« en San Agustin." *Pensamiento* 43 (1987): 129 - 150.

Salaquarda, Jörg. "Schopenhauer und die Religion." *Schopenhauer-Jahrbuch* 69 (1988): 321 -332.

Schirmacher, Wolfgang. "Schopenhauer und die Postmoderne." *Revue Internationale de Philosophie* 64 (1988): 71 - 81.

Schmidt, Alfred. "Schopenhauer und der Materialismus." *Schopenhauer-Jahrbuch* 58 (1977): IX- XLVIII.

Siena, Robertomaria. "Considerazioni su Schopenhauer e Sartre." *Sapienza* 34 (1984): 27 -44.

Smith, Joseph Wayne. "Philosophy and the Meaning of Life." *Cogito* 2 (1984): 27 -44.

Stock, George. "Schopenhauer und die philosophische Theologie Englands." *Schopenhauer-Jahrbuch* 44 (1963): 134 - 179.

_____. "Schopenhauer und die philosophische Theologie Englands." (II. Teil: Mit dem Blick auf griechische und indische Weisheit). *Schopenhauer-Jahrbuch* 45 (1964): 55 - 121.

_____. "Schopenhauer und die philosophische Theologie Englands." (III. Teil: Soziales und politisches Leben). *Schopenhauer-Jahrbuch* 46 (1965): 109 - 129.

Tamelo, Ilmar. "Ungerechtigkeit als Grenzsituation." *Schopenhauer-Jahrbuch* 61 (1980): 30 - 50.

Taylor, Terri Graves. "Platonic Ideas, Aesthetic Experience, and the Resolution of Schopenhauer's 'Great Contradiction'." *International Studies in Philosophy* 19 (1987): 43 - 53.

Tonelli, Giorgio. "Kant's Early Theory of Genius." *Journal of the History of Philosophy* 4 (1966): 109 - 131, 209 -224.

Torres Queruga, Andrés. "El destino de la idea de Dios en el pensamiento moderno." *Pensamiento* 45 (1989): 3 - 25.

Ugazio, Ugo M. "La volontà nella metafisica: Heidegger e Schopenhauer." *Filosofia* 32 (1981): 13 - 32.

Vecchiotti, Icilio. "Sviluppo e senso delle annotazioni schopenhaueriane a Schelling (1. Teil)." *Schopenhauer-Jahrbuch* 69 (1988): 425 - 437.

Young, Julian. "Schopenhauer's Critique of Kantian Ethics." *Kantian-Studien* 75 (1984): 191 - 212.

DDS

INDEX

A posteriori 67, 68, 220, 222

A priori 8, 10, 12, 14, 22, 31, 41, 49, 67, 128, 176, 222

Absolute 257

Absolute Idealism 146

action
altruistic 230, 239-244
and body 57-61
and character 49
as determined 213, 220-222, 225
egoistic 186, 190, 201, 213, 231
and empirical/intelligible character 49, 116, 121, 123, 206, 212-222
and feeling of freedom/-responsibility 212-213, 225, 226-229, 304-305, 307, 335
moral 190, 224, 230, 234, 238, 244, 333
and law of motivation 12, 44-46, 49, 206, 210, 214-218, 224, 227
sexual 172-174
unjust 190, 198, 200, 238, 332
and will 36, 38, 56-59, 207, 210, 223

Adam 319

adequate objectification of will
as Idea 97-101, 109, 140-141, 261, 320, 326
and natural force 113-114
as purposeful 152

aesthetic contemplation 209, 235, 259

aesthetic experience
and denial of will 244, 315, 336
and Ideas xi, 206-207
and insight into will's other dimension 207, 315, 336-337
and purpose 152, 330

affirmation of the will
and Adam 319
as affirmation of the body's needs 169-170, 189
and attachment to life 169
clarification of notion 155, 168-169, 202-203
and fear of death 175-177, 202
and natural man 168
and over-extension of self 191-192, 197-199, 201, 203, 229, 332
and sexual impulse 170-175, 202, 249
transcendence of 207-210, 232f, 236-239, 246-247, 332-333
and unhappiness of man 194-195, 201-202, 331-332

after-life 231

agape 242

allegory 260, 277

animal
and affirmation of will 74-75
and character 49-50, 121-123
and egoism 186
and fear of death 176-177
and Idea 110, 118-121, 124-126
and intellect 2, 79-80, 82, 85
as limited 26-28, 87-88, 211
and law of motivation 10-11, 44-45, 87
as objectification of will 71, 124, 150
and perceptual representation 2-4, 25-28, 36, 45, 87-88
and stimulus 43-44
and suffering 89, 165, 233, 300
and teleology of will 88-89, 297-299
and understanding 19-21, 24
and will 77, 79-80, 86-87

animal metaphysicum 273

anti-moral tendencies
and religion 282
and the State 196-197-199, 332

arbitrium indifferentiae 216

Aristotle 99, 102

art
and genius 143-149, 315, 336
and the Idea 148-149, 206-207
and music 145, 148-151
and other dimension of will 315-316, 318, 332-333, 336

ascetical praxis
and denial of will 266-267, 334
end result of 154-155, 308, 335-336
and nothingness 259-260, 308, 334-336
and quieter 266
and thing-in-itself 317-319, 336

asceticism
and chastity 249-250
and Christianity 265, 287-288
and denial of will 190-191, 245-258, 265-266, 333
and God 257-258, 334
and salvation 256-257
and transition into nothing 256-258

atheism xiii, 262, 306

Atman 73-74

Atwell, John E. 214, 216, 218, 292

Baumgarten, Alexander Gottlieb 144

beauty 139, 148, 152-153, 300

being-in-itself 60, 69, 169, 309

Berkeley, George 6-7

Berry, Thomas 74

Betancourt, Raúl Fornet 159

better consciousness
and art 146
and co-existence with temporal consciousness 246-247, 250, 253-254
denial of will-to-live 246-248, 268
and eternal aspect of human being 246
and nothingness 259-260
and path of introspection 66-67
and religion xiii-xiv, 260
and sanctification 248, 252-254
and virtue 246-248, 259

Blessed Virgin 264-265

body
affirmation of 169-171, 191, 249-256, 266
centrality in perception 16-19, 22, 135, 310
as immediate object 16-18, 55, 183-184
as indirect object 17, 55, 57, 135
as representation 55, 183-184
and sensation 12-13, 17-18, 22-24
and the understanding 13-15, 17-18, 22-24
and will 57-62, 75-76, 88-89, 100, 135, 169-170, 178, 191, 249-255, 270, 310

boredom 166-168

Brahmanism 73-74, 289

Bridgewater, Patrick xiv, 264

Buddha 161

Buddhism 73, 289

Bykhovksy, Bernard 255, 279

cannibalism 192

Cartwright, David 187, 190

categorical imperative 212

Index

categories 19-20, 259

catharsis 270

cause
  and change 39, 41, 296
  as motive 44-46, 48-49,
    214-218
  narrow meaning of 42-43
  and natural forces 46-48,
    113-115, 214-215
  and necessity 39, 46, 115,
    296
  and origin of world 41, 323
  and sciences 136-137
  and sensation 14-15, 22
  as stimulus 43-44, 86
  and the understanding 14-
    15, 17, 22-23

Celibacy 288

chance 40, 119, 246, 247, 253,
  303

Chanksy, James D. 104, 149

chaos 84, 265, 272

character
  as act of will 214, 219-
    220, 225
  of animality 20, 49, 120-
    121
  as determined nature of
    will 49, 214-216
  as intelligible and empiri-
    cal 217-224
  as groundless 49, 212,
    215-216
  and the human being 49,
    121-122, 216-217, 225
  and Idea xi, 116, 132, 151,
    205, 216-217, 225
  as individual 120, 212
  in inorganic phenomena 86
  and necessity 206, 212-215
  as unchangeable 222-224,
    228-229, 258

Christ 319

Christianity 264-265, 285-288,
  292

Church iv, 209, 264

civilization 197

cognition
  and other dimension of will
    207, 313, 318-319, 326,
    330, 332-333, 336
  and plurality 182-183, 221,
    327, 332
  representational character
    of x, 231, 235, 322-323,
    332
  will-oriented xii, 108,
    115-116, 136-137, 183,
    194, 207, 231, 235, 319,
    326, 328-333

cognitive faculty
  as characteristic of animal
    life as such 20-21, 25
  as consciousness of other
    things 1, 51, 222
  and perceptual representa-
    tion 20-21, 23-25, 33,
    56
  and objective perception
    14, 222

coitus 172

compassion
  as basis for morality 242,
    244, 259
  as empirical fact 229-234,
    243-244
  and human nature 233, 243-
    244
  and insight into homogene-
    ity of being 232, 266,
    333
  and justice 234-239, 259,
    333
  and liberation from *princi-
    pium individuationis* 232
  as mysterious 243, 259,
    266, 285, 333
  as participation in suffer-
    ing 231-232, 242
  and philanthropy 239-245,
    259, 333
  possibility of 243-244
  as secondary 232-233

concept
  as abstract representation
    4, 24, 28-29, 78, 89,
    105-106, 109, 322
  as advantageous 26-27, 30,
    89
  of bad/evil 186-187
  of character 214-217
  of God 42, 257-258, 295-
    296, 323-324, 334
  of good 91
  and faculty of reason/
    thought 2, 4, 25-27, 32,

78, 322
of freedom 40, 83, 212-213, 225-226, 228
and Idea 105-108, 132-133
limitation of 5, 19, 24-25, 30, 41-42, 323
nature of 28-30
and Normal Intuitions 106-107
of Nothing(ness) 256, 258-260
and Principle of Sufficient Reason (of Knowing) 4, 9-10
relationship to perceptual representation 4-5, 25, 28-30, 41-42, 323
and scientific knowing 106, 136-137
as *universalia post rem* 29, 109-110
of will 35, 52, 62-63, 70, 73, 76, 150, 186, 330
of wrong/malice 191-193

conception and pregnancy 174-175

conscience 192, 226, 242, 332

consciousness
and animal 20-21, 44-45
and body 13, 19, 135, 178, 184
and the concept 29-30
of freedom 212-213, 226-228
and the Idea 110, 139-142, 151-152
in man 26-27, 44-45, 162, 175, 178, 182-183
and the motive 44-45
nature of 1-2, 25, 51
of other individuals/things 101, 135, 184-185, 199-200, 229, 233, 244-245, 332
and representation 4, 184-185, 199-200, 233, 242, 332
and subject of willing xii, 33, 51-52, 67, 81, 94, 202
and thing-in-itself (the Will) 62-63, 75-79, 81, 92, 101, 162-166, 173-174, 177-178, 182-183, 221, 234, 308, 311, 313, 315, 336

contemplation
and denial of will 235, 259

of the Ideas 108, 139, 141-142, 207, 209
and natural beauty 148, 297-298

Copleston, Friedrick 128, 257

corporeality
as individuality 55-56, 135-136
and introspection 56
and noumenon 68, 325-326, 330
and object 135-136
and willing 138-139, 325-326

cosmological proof 296-297

Creator-God ix, 258, 304-305

Dauer, Dorothea W. 73

death
and affirmation of will 72, 170-171, 175-178, 271, 331
and denial of will 72, 170, 253-254, 256
and empirical/temporal consciousness 246-247, 252
metaphysical significance of 180-181, 270-271
and organic phenomena 93, 126-127, 177-178
and philosophical reflection 161, 175, 246, 272-278
and religious system 266, 275-278, 280, 288-289
and the 'second way' 266-271
as sanctifying 252-254, 256, 270-271
and systems of metaphysics 266, 272-275
and tragedy of life 161, 272

demons and gods 290

denial of the will-to-live
and asceticism 190-191, 245-258, 259-260, 265, 286-287, 336-337
and better consciousness 246-255, 260, 268
and entrance into freedom

Index   359

225
and extra-temporal dimension of will 313-317, 336-337
and God 257-258, 334, 337
and justice 234-238, 259, 333
and nothingness 255-258, 260, 308-309, 320, 334, 336-337
and philanthropy 239-245, 259, 333
and possibility of transcendence 84, 234, 333
and quieter 248-249, 252, 257, 333
and 'second way' 266-271
and struggle 251-252, 266
and truth of religion 288-289, 292

Descartes, René 1, 295

destructive praxis 194, 230

determinism 213

Diderot, Denis 145

Diogenes Laertius 102

direct awareness (of self) 183, 185, 199, 202, 212, 332

disorder
as existentially experienced 134, 326, 329
and the human spirit 164-165, 173
and the noumenal will 96, 164-165, 173
and the phenomenal sphere 153, 326

Divine Mind 154, 261

dogma 161, 281, 285, 301

ego
and the ascetic 253-254
and the fuga mortis 177-178, 180
in the noble person 240, 242-243
in Schelling 146
as transcendental 3, 11, 34
as will-filled 177, 185

egocentric predicament
of man 182-199
and possibility of transcendence 207, 237

egoism
and animal 186, 233
degrees of 188, 189-196, 243
epistemological basis for, 182-189, 191, 199-201, 231
and the fear of death 177, 180, 270-271
in man 185-186, 188-189, 233-234
and moral incentive 189
reason for 188-189, 233
and the role of State 196-199, 332
and the will 80, 177, 180, 182, 189, 196, 198, 231, 233
transcendence of 231-232, 236-237, 239f, 243, 270-271

Elders, Leo C. 318

empirical character
and animal 121, 123
and intelligible character 116, 120, 122-123, 204-206, 213, 218-222, 225
and man 121-123, 206, 213, 218-222
and necessity 121-123, 205-206, 213, 220-222, 225
and phenomenal manifestation of the will 49, 121-123, 205-206, 213, 218-222

empirical consciousness 246f, 248, 254

ennui 199, 202

ens metaphysicum 216

ens realissimum 94, 303

error
and empirical/temporal consciousness 246-247
of human existence 181, 246-247
of optimism 287
of the will-to-live 269, 271
of religious systems 287,

292-293, 301

eternal element 247

ethics
and freedom/responsibility 225-226
and Kant's legacy 211
and the law of motivation 11
and metaphysical ground 274-275
as powerless to change willing 224
as stemming from will 74, 77, 81, 204, 211
and unchangeability of character 217

evil
concept of 186-187
as connected with will 93-94, 303, 320
and death 175-176, 246-247, 272-273
and God 303-307, 335
and philosophy 272-273
as positive reality 92, 94, 153, 272, 303-304

experience
aesthetic (cf. aesthetic experience)
and egoism 197-198, 200
and the law of causality 14, 37, 41-42, 112, 117
and the object 3, 17-18, 37, 41-42, 135, 200, 205, 323
and the principle of sufficient reason 3, 9-11, 200
and space and time 14, 30-32
and the understanding 14, 17-18, 22-24, 233, 323
and unveiling of will 49, 67-72, 100, 205

external ground (of motive) 218, 259

Fabro, Cornelio 262

faith xii, 263, 276-277, 281, 306

faith and knowledge 276

fear of death 175-178, 202, 331

Fichte, Johann Gottlieb iv, 146

finality
and God 298
and intelligibility of reality 325, 328
lack of in will 164-165, 181, 325, 328-329, 331
and the will 298-299, 328-329

First Cause x, 40f, 261, 296-297, 323

forma substantialis 99, 102, 108

Frauenstädt, Julius 93, 263

freedom
as absence of necessity 40, 83, 116, 221-222, 225
and co-existence with necessity 116, 204f, 211, 213, 224, 229, 259, 316
concept of 40, 212, 228
and concept of originality 225-226
and consciousness 212
entrance in the human phenomenon 207-208, 211-212, 225, 267, 316, 333
and ethical sphere 211, 225, 316
and feeling of responsibility 224-229, 259
inalterability of character 225, 229
intelligible character 221-222, 225-226
intuition of 225
of noumenal will 205, 207-208, 211, 221-222, 225, 316, 333
as related to determined action 213-214

Freud, Sigmund 71

front door (to question of God) ix, xiii, 264, 307, 334

Gardiner, Patrick 4, 14

Index

genitals 76, 249

genius
  context of theory of 143-146
  and the ideas 104, 146, 148-149
  Schopenhauer's theory of 147-149, 315, 320, 326, 336

God
  and aseity of will 83, 154, 261-263, 331
  and better consciousness 252-253
  back door to ix, 266, 307-321, 322, 326, 329, 337
  as beyond exigence of reason ix, xiii, 154, 261-263, 294-300, 307, 322-325
  concept of 257-258, 294-295
  cosmological proof x, 296-297
  and denial of will-to-live 251-253, 257-258, 333-334
  and evil 303-307, 331-332, 335
  front door to ix, xiii, 264, 307, 319, 322-325
  and the Ideas 132-133, 154, 261, 329
  and law of causality 40-42, 154, 261
  and mystery xii, 333, 337
  and nothingness 257-258
  ontological proof x, 295-296
  physico-theological proof x, 297-300
  and poverty of concept 41-42
  and religion xii, 261f
  and revelation 300-302, 307, 334-335
  Schopenhauer's rejection of iii-iv, 258, 262-264, 304-307, 334-335

Goethe, Johann Wolfgang von iv, 41, 145

Gonzales, Robert A. 236

Good Will 303

Gottsched, Johann Christoph 144

greek paganism 287

Guiding Will 303

Hamlyn, D.W. 4, 14, 102, 104, 107, 110

happiness 92, 165, 181, 254, 330, 331

Hasse, Heinrich xiii, 98, 263, 265, 279

heaven 231, 291

Hegel, Georg Wilhelm Friedrich v, 84, 146

Hein, Hilde 104

hell 189, 231

Helvétius, Claude-Adrien 144

Hielscher, Martin xiii, 318

Hobbes, Thomas 91

Höffding, Harald 69, 257

holiness
  and contradiction of the phenomenon with itself 259, 316, 332-333
  as deliverance from will 256
  as demythologized by denial of will-to-live 256-257, 269-270, 316-318, 332-333
  and extra-temporal dimension of will 316-318, 321, 337
  as transition into nothingness 256, 320
  and uniqueness of will in man 207, 315-318, 332-333

Holy Will 256

homo homini lupus 197

homosexuality 172

Horkheimer, Max 265

Hübscher, Angelika 162

Hübscher, Arthur 99, 103, 143, 145, 146, 160, 210, 258, 264, 279, 312

hubris 201, 270

human nature
and aesthetic theories 146-147
and compassion 233, 243
and egoism 185, 188
and metaphysical need for meaning 275
and music 151
and religion 288

Hume, David 29, 279

Idea
as acts of will 111, 115-116, 216-219, 225, 327
and adequate objectification of will xi, 97-101, 103-104, 110, 131-132, 134, 140-141, 206, 309-310, 320, 326, 335
and animal kingdom 115-116, 120-121
and antecedent rationality xi, 110, 130-134, 328-330
and Aristotelian substantial form 99, 102, 108
as beyond principle of sufficient reason 115-117, 127, 134
and denial of will-to-live 138-142, 207-209
as dispersed 127-130
and divine mind 132-133, 154, 261
as eternal form/prototype 99, 101-102, 111, 129, 133, 319, 327
and grades of the will's objectification 98-99, 103, 111-123, 129, 159, 327
in inorganic phenomena 112-116
and insight into noumenon 151-154, 329, 335
and intelligible character of 116, 120
knowledge of as genius 147-149, 206-207
and law of causality 127-128
man as unique 121-123, 178, 206-207, 214
and matter 125-128, 159
music and the 149-151, 330-331
and natural force 112-116
normal intuitions and 105-108
and noumenal will 100-101, 103-104, 111, 114, 130-131, 151-153, 205, 235, 326-329
ontological status of ix, 95, 99-104, 110-111, 115-116, 128-129, 322, 326-327
as opposed to concept 105-106, 109-110, 132-133
and organic matter 118-120
and pure matter 117-118
and rationality of will 152, 328-329
and reason 128-130
and the relatedness of phenomena 124-127, 130, 327-328
as representation 102-103, 108, 134, 140-141, 327
and scientific knowledge 136-137
and the true nature of reality xi, 151-154
as *universalia ante rem* xi, 109-111, 128, 130, 132, 327
as universal/objective form of phenomenon 108, 132, 326-327

idolatry 302

illusion
and animals 87
and asceticism 252, 254
and better consciousness 252-253
and the fear of death 177-179, 245
and happiness 165
and *principium individuationis* 203
and truth 252
and the will-to-live 252, 331

imagination 145, 295

immorality 291

indirect awareness 183, 199

individuality

and character 215, 219-220
as corporeal 142, 152
and egocentric predicament 184
and noumenal will 52, 56, 215-216, 219-220, 325-326
and the plant kingdom 120
and the *principium individuationis* 215
and sexuality 173
as transcended 139

injustice 195, 196, 230, 233,

inner knowledge 34, 68, 69, 162, 211, 308

inner sense
and body 59, 61
and introspection 70-71
and noumenon 64, 68-71, 312
as self-consciousness 33, 51-52
and sensations 18
and subject of willing 4-5, 10, 33-34, 36, 52, 61, 64, 70, 312
and time 13, 33, 52

insecurity
of man 159-164, 188, 202
as ontological 164
and will 202

insight
and the ascetic 253f, 257
and compassion 237
and denial of will-to-live 204, 210, 232, 235, 258
and the Idea 106, 139, 142, 149, 235, 329-330, 335
and homogeneity of reality 235-245, 248-249
and intelligible character 123, 220
metaphysical 11, 57, 149, 207
and possibility of justice 237-238
and possibility of philanthropy 239-241
and the quieter 208, 210, 235, 249-250, 333
and the will 152, 181, 208, 235, 249-250, 310, 313, 326, 330

intellect
and the animal 21, 44-45, 82

and the brain 21, 23, 77, 178
imperfection/impotence of 79-82
and law of causality 21, 44
and law of motivation 44-46
and knowledge of Ideas 108, 139, 147, 326, 329
and man 45-46, 80-82
and perceptual object 14, 45
as phenomenon 23, 77
purpose of 79-80, 178-179
and relation to will 80-82, 103, 108, 137-138, 178-179
secondary nature of 82, 178-179, 298-299

intelligible character
and act of will 122-123, 204, 213, 218-222, 225
and freedom 222, 225-227
as groundless 123, 205, 213
and the Idea 116, 123
and will in-itself 206, 221

internal ground 218, 222

introspection
and better consciousness 66-67
and noumenal will 62, 66-67, 70-71, 162, 183, 308, 310, 325
and subject of willing 4, 34, 52, 61-62, 67, 162

intuition 10, 14-15, 20, 30-32, 225

Invernizzi, Giuseppe 310, 313, 317

Islam 287

Ius primi occupantis 233

Janaway, Christopher 248

Jean Paul 145

Jewish dogmas 161

Judaism 287

Judeo-Christian tradition 255

justice xii, 189, 195, 230,

234-239, 245, 259-260, 332-333
Kant, Immanuel iv, 19, 26-28, 32, 51, 67, 73, 93, 99-100, 102, 116, 144-145, 211, 217, 248, 308, 310

kingdom of grace 210, 212, 319, 333

Kingdom of nature 210, 319, 333

knower 2, 3, 11, 40, 54, 56, 68, 134, 136, 138, 140

knowledge
as accidental 78, 80, 82
and animality 20-21, 44f, 82, 89, 110
and the concept 11, 137
and denial of will 207-209, 234-235, 252, 256-258, 266-267, 317, 333
and faith/religion 276-277, 281, 293
and homogeneity of reality 232, 235, 240, 244-245
and Idea 117, 136-139, 143f, 147-149, 152, 329-330, 335
as individual 56, 134, 177
and law of causality 21, 135
in man 87-90, 182, 206, 211, 315-316
and motive 44, 208-209
and perceptual representation 20, 44f, 54-56, 97, 110, 232 135, 229, 234
phenomenological 8, 12, 18, 20, 311
and philosophical reflection 272, 274-275
and the principle of sufficient reason 11, 28, 54, 117, 135
and the representation 12, 18, 50, 69, 87, 312-313, 324
as secondary 77, 82, 87, 90, 178-179, 298-299
scientific 136-137, 147, 293
and subject of willing 33f, 59, 69, 72
and virtuous acts 238-239, 240, 244-245, 317
and will 59, 66-67, 71-73, 75-80, 87-89, 119, 134, 162, 166, 168-169, 175,
177, 179, 182-183, 185, 239, 299, 307-315, 325, 335
from within (inner) 51-54, 59, 66, 68-69, 162, 164, 335

Lamark, Jean-Baptiste 104

law of causality
as a priori 41
and act of will 57
and action of body 57
and animal understanding 21
and efficient causality 37-38, 261, 296-297, 322-323
and human beings 206
and Ideas 127-128, 135
and natural forces 86
and necessity 38-40
and perceptual representation 9, 21, 37, 128, 135, 323
and understanding 12, 14, 20

Lonergan, Bernard 324

love 173, 230

macrocosm 184

Magee, Bryan 102, 104, 217

malice 188-191, 195-196, 237, 243

Malter, Rudolf 7

Mandelbaum, Maurice 6, 14

mathematics 106-107

matter:
and causality 41-42, 93, 117-118, 125, 261, 296, 323
as indestructible 93, 323
as inorganic 84-86, 93, 119, 185
and mundus sensibilis 82
and objectification of will 85, 90, 96, 125, 128, 159
as organic 85-86, 118-120
and original forces of

Index

nature 46-47, 112, 115, 127
  pure 117-118
  status of 117-118
  as substratum of phenomena 118
  and time and space 31-32, 90, 96, 125, 159

veil of maya 236, 239-241,

McGill, V.J. 262

metaphysical need 273-275, 289, 293

microcosm 184

Mirri, Edoardo xiv, 248, 268

Mora, José Ferrata 146

moral consciousness 292

moral responsibility 304-305, 307, 335

morality 78, 223, 244, 259, 292, 305

Morin, Frédérick 153

mortification 190, 247, 251, 256

mosques 273

music 145, 149-151, 330-331

mystery
  of evil xi, 94, 153, 303f
  of the noumenal will 69-70, 219, 307, 325, 330, 335
  of occurrence of compassion 243, 259, 285
  as open and possible 316, 326
  of order and disorder intertwined 134, 316
  and philosophical discourse 285
  and religion 277, 285,
  of suffering 94

mystics 208, 210, 333

myth 260, 277, 282

natural force
  and causality 47-48, 215, 218
  and character 215, 217-218
  as eternal 47
  as groundless/inexplicable 47-48, 113
  as idea 112, 114-115
  and inorganic phenomenon 47, 112-115, 214
  manifestations of 46-48
  and noumenal will 113-115
  as omnipresent 46, 115
  as outside of time 46, 115
  as unchangeable 114

natural man 209, 319

natural theology 324, 325

necessity
  as absence of determining ground 39, 83
  co-existence with freedom 204-214, 259
  and character 224, 229
  and law of causality 38-40, 42, 54
  and law of motivation 45-46
  logical 38
  mathematical 38
  moral 38-39, 45
  and the phenomenon 8, 39-40, 42, 65, 83, 116, 124-125, 204-206
  physical 38-39

neminem laede 189, 237

new birth 208-210, 319, 333

Newton, Issac 43

Nietzsche, Friedrich 264

normal intuitions 105-108

nothing
  as end result of ascesis 255-258, 259, 309, 320, 334
  as linked to virtue 256f, 259-260, 320-321
  as something 258, 260, 309, 334

nothingness
  and asceticism xii, 308f, 319-320, 334, 336
  and death 75, 178
  as linked to virtue 259-260, 316-317, 319-320
  as loathsome to will 75,

178
and man 271f
and noumenal will 314-317, 319
as relative xii, 308-309, 313-317, 319-320, 336-337
and the Sacred (Holy/God) xiii, 317, 319, 337
as something 260, 308-309, 319-320, 334, 336-337
and the thing-in-itself 308-309, 319

noumenon
and awareness 76, 84, 95, 130
as blind/irrational 84, 95
and character 216-218, 221
and corporeality 68
and form of time 69, 182, 307, 318, 335
and the Idea (cf. Idea)
and intelligible character 205, 216-217, 221
and mystery 69-70, 283, 307-308, 325f
as pristine 97, 182, 207, 317, 326, 336f
and rationality 130f, 316-317, 329, 331
and relative nothingness 320f
and subject of willing 33f, 64, 68-70, 162, 307-308, 316, 335

object
and body 16-18, 23-24, 60-61, 135
and Idea 102-103, 134, 139-142, 205, 327-329
and knowing subject 2-3, 7, 28, 312, 324, 327
and law of causality 37-39, 322-323
and perceptual representation 36-38, 60, 205, 312, 232-323
and principle of sufficient reason 3, 7-10, 18, 28, 37, 54, 135, 137
and pure matter 117
as representation 3-5, 8-10, 18, 36-37, 323
and space/time 31-32
and subject of willing 33-34, 36, 51-52, 54, 62, 71, 310

and the understanding 16-17, 22-24
and will 71-72, 104, 135, 312-313

objective perception 13-15

old age 161, 270-271

Omnes quantum potes juva 232

operari sequitur esse 216, 305

optimism 287

order
and Ideas 127-128, 131, 133f, 142, 152, 178
and noumenon 278, 317, 325-326
and phenomenon 40, 64, 84, 90, 95, 127, 317, 325
and reason 134, 272-273, 329
and religion 278, 282

original sin 287-288

Otto, Rudolf 318

Oxenford, John vi-vii

pagodas 273

pain
and animal 165, 300
and life 161, 165, 167f, 174, 265, 267-268, 300
and man 161, 165, 167f, 174, 181, 191-192, 195, 241, 272, 300, 332
and will 58, 91, 317

Passmore, John 6

peace 141, 163, 243, 252, 254, 267, 317, 330

Pelagianism 288

Penzo, Giorgio 248

perception
in animals 24, 87f
and centrality of body 16-19, 55-57, 60, 135, 184, 310
and compassion 244
and conceptualization 25f,

Index

29-30, 41
and Idea 108, 124, 128-132, 140-142, 149, 327
intellectual nature of 12-24
intuitive 15, 221
in man 24-25, 93, 124
and matter 117-118
objective 12-15
and plurality 95f
and sensation 14-18, 22, 31
and space and time 30-32, 128
and subject of willing 61-63, 67-68, 335
and understanding 12-15, 21, 23, 129
and the will 80-81, 84, 93, 97-98, 307-308, 310, 313, 335

perceptual representation
and animals 20-21, 36, 45
and the body 60f
and concepts 5, 29, 323
and the understanding 20-21
and willing 34, 36, 53-56, 60, 64, 70, 93

phenomenon
of compassion 323f, 242-243
contradiction of the 204f, 207, 211, 259, 308, 316, 332
as determined 205, 215
and freedom 207, 211, 213-214, 225, 316, 333
and Idea xi, 103, 108, 110, 114, 116, 118, 120-129, 134, 140, 151-152, 326-330
and the intellect (brain) 18, 23, 178-179
and intelligible character 116, 122-123, 204-206, 215-216, 219-221
and law of causality 9, 36-38, 112
man as 206-207, 211-212, 21-216, 225, 246-247, 315-316
and natural force 48, 114
and rationality 40, 85
as scarred 88-92, 153f, 317, 334
and will 52-59, 64-65, 69-77, 82-83, 92, 94-97, 111-112, 127, 163, 177-178, 183, 222, 298, 309-311, 317, 324-325
and willing 57, 69, 162, 311-315, 334

philanthropy xii, 195, 239, 241, 245, 259-260

philosophical reflection 272, 275, 281-282, 289

Pietism iii, 264

Platner, Ernst 279

Plato iv, 102, 107, 129, 132-133, 146

Platonic Ideas (cf. Idea)

plurality
and the concept 29, 105
and the Idea 99-100, 103, 105, 109, 111, 114, 127-128
and objectification of the will 85, 87, 97, 99, 103, 114, 182-182
and the *principium individuationis* 64-66, 85, 87, 96, 182f, 202f, 232, 235, 245
and the principle of sufficient reason 96-97, 127

praxis
and affirmation of the will-to-live xii, 196, 201
ascetical 155, 248f, 256f, 259f, 266-267, 308, 317f, 334, 336
constructive 203, 223, 230-231, 236-245, 266
and denial of the will-to-live 203, 235f, 238, 266, 308
as destructive 196, 201, 332
as epistemologically grounded 201
immoral 196, 201

principium individuationis
and individuality 200-201, 215f, 232
and morally bad person 200-201, 236
plurality 66, 96f, 182f, 235-236
seeing through 235-237, 239f, 241, 247f, 267
and space and time 64-66, 96f, 182f

and will-oriented knowledge 200, 203, 208, 232

principle of sufficient reason
and abstract representation 4, 9-10
and body 18, 59, 135f
and Idea 102-103, 112, 115-117, 127, 134, 139, 147
intuitive, complete, empirical representation 4, 9, 37, 322-323
and knowing subject 11, 23
and law of motivation 11, 218
meaning of 7-8
and natural forces 112-113
possibility of transcendence 147-148, 239-240, 315-316
and relation of objects (representations) 3, 11, 28, 54, 135, 147
as restricted to phenomenon 11, 18, 50, 54, 59, 96-97
and sciences 137, 147
and space and time 4, 10
and subject of willing 4, 10-11
and the will 59, 64-65, 83, 97, 101, 123, 135, 204-205, 219 211-212f, 220, 316
and will-oriented cognition 131, 135, 194, 200, 203

procreation 40, 171

Protestant Christianity 287-288

pure knowing being 255

pure knowing subject 55

pure matter 117-118

purification 268-269

quieter 208f, 210, 235, 248, 249f, 252, 257, 266-267, 333

rationality
and aesthetic experience 152

and the Ideas xi, 130-134, 261, 329
and the phenomenon 40, 85
of the real 153, 327-329
and the will 85, 95, 133f

Reason (Vernunft)
and concept 4, 25, 27, 32, 78, 105, 322
and egoism 182f, 186, 198
and ethics 77, 212, 259
as faculty of abstraction 25-26, 78, 105
as faculty of concepts 26, 105, 322
and fear of death 176
and the Idea 109-110, 129-13
Kantian conception of 27-28, 322
and knowing consciousness 2, 51
and metaphysical need 274
and philosophical systems 275-276
and possibility for transcendence 30, 89-90, 163, 243, 272-273, 333
reflective 26, 109, 176
role of 24-30
and source of morality 259
and uniqueness of man 20, 25-28, 30, 84, 88-90, 163, 166, 212, 272-274
and willing 166

redeeming principle 229

redemption 251

reflection
abstract 23
and abstract representation 26, 28
and act of will
and coitus 172
and the Idea 109, 216
and mystery 70, 321
philosophical 272-273, 275, 281-282
and reality of death 272
Schopenhauer's 73, 175, 257, 268, 289, 311f
and will 71-72, 162, 213

reflective consciousness 198

relative nothingness (cf. nothingness)

Index

religion
  and better consciousness
    xiii-xiv, 260
  as brace for anti-moral
    tendencies 282, 285-286
  and denial of will-to-live
    286-287, 292
  and faith/revelation 281
  as human phenomenon 274
  and moral consciousness 292
  and mystery 285-286
  and noumenal order of
    things 278
  and optimism 287
  philosophy of 263f, 265
  positive and negative aspects 266, 279-293
  and question of God (Holy/Sacred) xii, 42, 260,
    261, 289, 291, 301f,
    305, 307, 334
  and reason 274
  and relation to philosophy
    263, 289
  role of 261f
  Schopenhauer's attitude to
    260, 263-264, 266, 279f
  as system of metaphysics
    260, 271f, 274, 276,
    279-280, 292-293, 307,
    334
  and threat of punishment
    276
  and truth 277-278, 280f,
    282-289, 293
  and will 290

religious experience 258, 289

Representation (Vorstellung)
  and animality 20-21, 25,
    28, 44-45, 87-88
  and body 16-19, 55-57, 59-
    62, 184
  abstract (concept) 4, 9-10,
    24-26, 28-30, 41-42, 89,
    323
  as different from thing-in-
    itself 53-54
  and Idea 102-103, 107-108,
    110, 134
  intuitive, complete and
    empirical 4, 9, 16f, 18,
    20-21, 24-25, 28-33, 36-
    37, 42, 44, 53-55, 60,
    63, 70, 323
  and knowing subject 5-7,
    24, 40, 44, 55, 178
  meaning of 3-4
  object as 3-5, 28
  and principle of sufficient
    reason 7-11
  space and time 4, 10, 30-32
  subject of willing 4-5, 10-
    11, 33-36, 51-54, 61-64,
    68
  and Transcendental Idealism
    5-7
  and world 5-6, 19, 21, 38,
    46, 50, 53, 55, 70, 76,
    87, 103-104 102, 120,
    140-141, 162, 178, 182,
    185, 323

representational knowledge 50,
  97, 229, 324

responsibility (feeling of)
  and consciousness of freedom 228
  and culpability 227
  foundation of ethics 225
  and freedom 224-229
  and God 304-305, 307, 335
  man as being his own work
    226, 259, 305
  for our actions 225-226,
    228-229, 259, 304

revelation
  and fear 302
  of one's noumenality 220,
    311
  and personal God 295-296f,
    300-302, 307
  and religions 281
  and signs/miracles 276
  as thought of sages 292-
    293, 301, 307

Ritter, Joachim 143

Romanticism 143

Rousseau, Jean-Jacques 145

Runge, Johann Christian iii,
  264

Sacred i, ix, xii-xv, 42, 154,
  307, 318, 320f

Safranski, Rüdiger xiii, 66,
  71, 100, 143, 160, 303

saint 255-257, 267, 315, 318-
  319, 336

Salaquarda, Jörg 264, 274, 289

salvation
  and act of procreation 171

and asceticism 246
and Christianity 287-288
and conception/pregnancy
174-175
and denial of will-to-live
209, 287-289
and knowledge 89-90
and nature 251
and sexual impulse 174
and Sistine Madonna 265
and suffering 269-270
and transition into nothing
256

sanctification 253

sanctity xiii, 336

scarredness
clue to 94
and man 94, 196f, 199
and reality 92, 153, 300,
329
and will 207-208, 299-300,
333

Schaefer, Alfred 14, 23, 234

Schelling, Friedrich Wilhelm
146

Schirmacher, Wolfgang xiii,
318

Schlegel, Friedrich 146

Schleiermacher, Friedrich iv

Schmidt, Alfred xiii, 84, 85,
262, 263, 279

scholasticism 216

Schopenhauer, Heinrich Floris
iii, iv

Schopenhauer, Johanna Trosiener iii, iv, 161-162

scientific knowledge 136-137,
147

self-consciousness
and human consciousness 1,
88, 182, 184-185, 206,
212, 315f
and subject of willing 4,
10f, 33-34, 51-52, 54,
57, 62
and will 35-36, 49, 57, 62,
153, 212f, 315-316

self-denial 207, 286, 287,
288, 316

self-preservation 173

self-transcendence xi-xii,
318, 329, 335

selfishness 186, 195, 198

sensation (Empfindung) 12-18,
22-24, 35, 185

Sensibility (Sinnlichkeit) 2,
18, 25, 32, 51, 144

sensu allegorico 277, 278, 284

sensu proprio 277, 278, 279,
284, 288, 289

sexual impulse 170-174, 189,
202, 250

sexuality 172-174, 238, 331

shame 58, 171-172

soul 28, 143, 179, 189, 306,
322

space and time
and bodies 55f, 59-60
and empirical/perceptual
representation 30f, 39,
52-54, 82
as third class of representation 4-5, 10, 30-32
as non-applicable to will
59, 65, 70, 97, 182f
as *principium individuationis* 64f, 96-97, 111,
127-128, 182f

Spierling, Volker 71

spirit of nature 84-85

State
and anti-moral tendencies
196-197, 332
establishment of 197-198
as facilitator of social
interchange 199
as institution of protec-
tion 197-199, 203, 332
role of 197-98

subject of knowledge 56, 139,
147, 330

Index 371

subject of willing 1, 4-6, 33-36, 52-54, 154

substantial form 99, 102, 108

suffering
and animals 89, 233, 300
and the ascetic 251-253, 267
and bad people 194-196
and compassion 232-233, 237-243
as essential to life 94, 164-165, 169, 171, 176, 269, 272
human 89, 94, 163-165, 171, 176, 181, 194, 201, 233, 266f, 271f, 300, 315
and moral character 268-270
ontological xi, 90-94, 165
and philosophical/ religious systems 272-275, 278, 280
as the 'second way' 266-271
and will 35, 90-91, 188, 233, 268f, 315

Sulzer, Johann George 145

Summum Bonum 91, 325

tabula rasa 215

Taylor, Terri Graves 104, 152

teleology 40, 95, 127, 131, 325

temples 273

temporal consciousness 246-247, 252, 254

theism 161, 281, 292, 295, 301f, 305

Thieck, Ludwig 145

Thing-in-itself
ambiguity of xiii, 308-309, 331
and Idea 99-101, 103, 309, 326-329
as immanent to world 262-263
and individuality 215-217, 219-220
and inner nature of phenomenon 6
as irrational 100-101, 325
and Kant 5, 67, 73, 99-100, 116
as non-phenomenal 64-66, 77, 83, 85, 97, 99f, 103, 123, 207, 211-212
as ultimately unknowable 307-315, 320, 325, 335-337
as will x, 62-66, 73, 80, 93, 97, 100-101, 116, 307-310, 313, 320
and will-to-live 236
and world 100f

Tonelli, Giorgio 143, 144

Transcendental Idealism 5-7, 110

unconsciousness 78

understanding (Verstand)
and body 12-14, 17, 22
and brain 14, 17, 22
as characteristic of animal life 19-21, 24, 44
and consciousness 2, 25, 51
and law of causality 12, 14, 19-20, 22
as non-discursive 22
and perceptual objective world 12-16, 22-23, 32, 129
role of 13-16

unhappiness 164, 243

universal egoism 233

universalia ante rem 109-110, 130, 132, 327

universalia post rem 109-110

Vecchiotti, Icilio xiii, 262

veil of Maya 236, 239, 240, 241

vigilance 252, 266

violence 233

virtue
and asceticism 247-249, 259f, 266

and better consciousness 246-247, 248, 259
and compassion 259 (cf. justice and philanthropy under compassion)
as inborn 217
and second way of suffering 270f
and will 317f, 320f, 337

voluntary justice 230, 239

Wackenroder, Wilhelm Heinrich 145

wicked person 194f, 236, 255

Wieland, Christoph Martin 94

will
  act of 57f, 58f, 111, 115-116, 122-123, 178, 204, 212-214f, 216, 218-221f, 225, 310f, 320, 335
  adequate objectification of xi, 97-101, 113-114, 140-141, 152, 261, 320, 326
  in the animal 77, 79-80, 86-87 120, 176
  aseity of 83, 154, 261, 324-325
  awareness of 85, 130, 133f, 212f
  and being-in-itself 60, 69, 169, 309
  as blind 73, 75, 84-86, 114, 130, 133f, 152, 169, 177, 183, 299, 325, 328-329
  characteristics of 64-66
  concept of 35, 52, 62-63, 70, 73, 76, 150, 186, 330
  and corporeality (body) 57-62, 75-76, 88-89, 100, 135, 169-170, 178, 191, 249-255, 270, 310
  and consciousness 62-63, 75-79, 81, 92, 101, 162-166, 173-174, 177-178, 182-183, 221, 234, 308, 311,313, 315, 336
  as craving for life 74-75
  and egoism 80, 177, 180, 182, 189, 196, 198, 231, 233
  estranged x-xii, 95, 159
  and evil in reality xi, 93-94, 303, 320
  freedom of the 205, 207-208, 211, 221-222, 225, 316, 333
  gradations of 85-90, 98-99, 111-123, 124, 163
  groundlessness of 65, 83, 112, 123, 212-213, 215
  as irrational 73, 84, 95, 100, 133, 169, 176f, 181, 331f
  as kernel of phenomenon 70-76, 93, 94, 163, 178, 180, 249, 307, 325
  knowability of 66-70
  and knowledge (cf. will under knowledge)
  and music 149-151, 330
  as non-phenomenal (cf. noumenon)
  objectification of 81-86
  parts of body 75-76
  as principle of being 72-85, 298
  as pristine 68, 70, 154, 182, 206, 313, 317, 325-326, 337
  rationality of 85, 95, 130, 132-134, 152-153, 327-328
  as teleological x, 83-84, 90, 95, 127, 130-131, 297-299f, 325, 328-329
  as thing-in-itself x, 62-66, 73, 80, 93, 97, 100-101, 116, 307-310, 313, 320
  and virtue 317f, 320f, 337

Wolff, Christian 8

world of freedom 210f

world of necessity 210f

world-spirit 84

wretchedness of life 161

Zimmern, Helen 160